Praise for *Listen*

"An extraordinary and compelling 'journey into sound' which examines close and distant listening in all its myriad ramifications, mainly in the form of music both popular and otherwise—and it's particularly good at evaluating music's intrinsic worth from a commercial and aesthetic viewpoint... Michel Faber writes beautifully, non-condescendingly and provocatively about something as basic and fundamental to human existence as oxygen, and which like oxygen would be exceedingly hard to do without... I found this, Michel's first non-fiction book, brilliant and a joy to read—he's obviously listened and thought long and hard about the act and art of consuming sound/music—essentially, electrochemical reactions in the brain—in all its multitudinous splendor, and he raises many compelling points along the way... *Listen* is right up there with Richard Meltzer's *The Aesthetics of Rock* and Geoffrey O'Brien's *Sonata for Jukebox* at the top of my mental music shelf."

—Gary Lucas

LISTEN

On Music, Sound and Us

MICHEL FABER

HANOVER
SQUARE
PRESS

HANOVER
SQUARE
PRESS™

Recycling programs
for this product may
not exist in your area.

ISBN-13: 978-1-335-00062-0

Listen

First published in Great Britain in 2023 by Canongate Books. This edition published in 2023.

Hanover Square Press
22 Adelaide St. West, 41st Floor
Toronto, Ontario M5H 4E3, Canada
HanoverSqPress.com
BookClubbish.com

Printed in U.S.A.

For Louisa

Also by Michel Faber

LISTEN

CONTENTS

WHO THIS BOOK IS FOR

This is a book about music, and about the people who listen to it—your friends, your neighbors, me and you.

Reading this book will change the way you listen. I'm not here to change your mind about Dusty Springfield or Shostakovich or Tupac Shakur or synthpop. I'm here to change your mind about your mind.

o o o

Many thousands of books about music have been published, and more are coming out all the time, despite the quip that "writing about music is like dancing about architecture."* If writing about music is so pointless and absurd, why are there so many books about music? Because, as animals, we are intensely interested in ourselves and in our kinship group, and there's nothing more self-absorbed and tribal than music.

But hang on... Self-absorption and tribalism—aren't these

---

* The quip was made by a 1970s singer-songwriter called Martin Mull, who managed to remain obscure despite playing support sets for Frank Zappa, Bruce Springsteen, Billy Joel, Randy Newman and Sandy Denny. Mull later found modest fame as a television actor, but his main contribution to posterity is his witticism about music, which has been misattributed to Zappa, Laurie Anderson and Elvis Costello, among others.

   The notion of music's inherently undiscussable nature was not new. As far back as February 1918, "H.K.M." (possibly Helen Marot), a journalist for *The New Republic*, opined that "writing about music is as illogical as singing about economics." The next decade saw the debut of Brecht and Weill's *The Threepenny Opera*, a song cycle about economics.

opposite concepts? Not at all. Your tribe is just multiple reflections of the person you think you are. You bond with the music
that reminds you of you, and you seek out like-minded souls
who've ended up in the same habitat. Your dream refuge is a
harmonious community of your kind of person—the people
who know exactly what you mean when you allude to a song
lyric or a BWV number; your fellow folkies, metalheads, ravers, wrinklies, Deadheads, Beliebers or whatever. Your homies,
in the fullest sense of the word.

Art does not "hold a mirror up to nature." It holds a mirror
up to you.

o   o   o

Most music books pretend, to some degree or other, that music
exists outside of humans and has intrinsic qualities that have
nothing to do with the emotions and cultural programming of
the individual listener. Passionate idealists talk about their favorite classics—Bach's *Goldberg Variations*, The Beach Boys' *Pet
Sounds*, Marvin Gaye's *What's Going On*, Burial's *Untrue*—as
though music is some sort of wondrous natural phenomenon
or historical landmark—the Grand Canyon, the Pyramids—
that human pilgrims can only contemplate in worshipful awe.

I like that story. It's a lovely story. I can understand why people keep telling it.

But in mundane truth, in modern megacapitalist society,
music is something we use. We use it constantly, in industrial
quantities. We socialize to it, exercise to it, relax to it, screen out
traffic noise with it, shop to it, show it off to visitors, advertise
snack foods and mortgages with it, use it to hustle us out of bed
in the morning or lull us to sleep at night, artificially boost our
enthusiasm for sports or sex with it, add it to movies to under-
score plot twists and explosions, take the edge off uncomfort-
able silences with it. Stressed consumers who long for the Zen
tranquility of the ancients play CDs or digital streams with titles

like *Moments of Silence* or *Evening Stillness*—soft music to banish the wrong kind of quiet.

Music is a commodity. We get a lot of it for free, bundled in with other stuff we're consuming, embedded in our routine transactions. But we also buy a lot of it. We stock up. Reviewers, and the artists themselves, promise us that if we give music the attention it deserves, it will reveal great depths, but our attention is often divided and we postpone the depths till later.

At the end of the day, having served multifarious purposes, music decays in the air. When the vibrations stop, it vanishes into nothingness.

That's if it even got played at all. Much of the recorded music in our civilization is stored unheard as data on phones, or crammed into dusty bookcases, cupboards and crates in our spare rooms and garages. Millions of CDs are discarded every year, almost all of them destined for landfill sites.*

Yet still we declare how much we love music. Because, in the glow of the moment, when the need is upon us, our love is true.

This book will not do for you what other books about music will do for you. It will not help you bond more securely with the artists or genres you're already bonded with, making you feel part of a clique of the enlightened. It will not confirm your cleverness and good taste for liking Perfume Genius, or Prince, or Mozart, or Cabaret Voltaire (pre-1982 Cabs, that is, before Chris Watson left and they signed to Virgin). If you come on this journey with me, you'll learn a lot, but it won't be the sort of information you usually learn when you read music books.

Instead, you may get closer to understanding why you love what you love and despise what you despise.

---

* "Perfect sound forever" was the marketing catchphrase of the compact disc medium when it was invented in the 1980s.

   In listening terms, "forever" is a sad overstatement, as many CDs are bought for one or two songs that are played a few—or a few dozen—times during a brief portion of a person's life before being discarded.

   In environmental terms, "forever" is much more apt, since the discs may take as long as a million years to decompose.

o   o   o

In my home, there is a room wholly given over to music—thousands of CDs, vinyl LPs and singles, thousands of self-compiled cassettes and CD-Rs, and a computer crammed to capacity with mp3s. Yet, in the pages ahead, you won't learn much about my collection. My all-time-favorite albums will remain a mystery to you. There's no need for me to tell you, and no need for you to know.

Many books about music are a glorified display of the stuff the author owns, which he (it usually *is* a he) thinks you should own too.* It's not the aim of this book to make you own more stuff. The aim is to help you perceive your stuff differently.

o   o   o

Music writers often come across like evangelists on a mission, to convert you or strengthen your faith. They'll give you the message that "any serious music lover"—anyone with "taste"—must admire this or that artist. Failing to appreciate an important musical deity is a cause for shame. You may not "get" Charlie Parker yet (or Sufjan Stevens, or Schoenberg) but one day the light will go on inside you.

However, this evangelism does not simply alert you to things you might love. Explicitly or implicitly, it also steers you away from "bad" music—music made by the wrong tribes, sung in the wrong languages, played in the wrong styles at the wrong time in history, celebrating the wrong things.

In this book, we'll be looking at how that psychological pressure works.

---

*   Or wish to own. Many authors of music books relish telling you about rare albums they possess that you can't get hold of yourself. So, as well as feeling you should buy more of the stuff that's still available to buy, you regret the now-unavailable stuff you didn't buy when you had the chance.

o   o   o

More broadly, we'll explore what really happens when we hear, and what's really going on when we listen. There's a lot going on, and it has nothing to do with whether Van Morrison can still sing or whether Ludwig van Beethoven's oeuvre exemplified a pan-German nostalgia for vanished medieval Christendom, as postulated by Carl Schmitt.

It has to do with your biology—the brain that floats in your skull, contoured like a cauliflower but as squishy as marmalade, sensitive to every stimulus.

And it has to do with your biography—the way you were raised, the way you were pushed down, the voice you were given or denied, the people you've met or avoided, the way you were encouraged or discouraged to feel about your gender, skin color, nationality and social class. Life has put you in your place. You are a cultural artifact passing judgment on other cultural artifacts.

Our response to music feels so instinctive to us, so basic and unmediated, that we convince ourselves it really *is* an instinct. Surely the instant thrill we feel when we hear the first note of Billie Holiday or Umm Kulthum singing, or the opening guitar riff of Led Zeppelin's "Whole Lotta Love," or the fanfare of Richard Strauss's *Also sprach Zarathustra*, shows that we've had no time to cogitate about whether we approve or not—this music stirs our blood, gives us goose pimples, feels so utterly *right*. The sounds must be coming straight from some Platonic heaven, no?

No.

You were not born knowing that Baroque music should be played without vibrato, or that The Clash were more important than Siouxsie and the Banshees, or that Cliff Richard is cheesy, or that disco sucks, or that on a good night The Rolling Stones are still the greatest rock 'n' roll band in the world, unquestionably, or that, come off it, U2 took that crown ages ago, or that U2 have nothing to do with real rock 'n' roll and only the terminally uncool could possibly imagine otherwise, or that Alice Coltrane bastardized John Coltrane's music, sorry to put it so bluntly but it's the truth, or that Alice Coltrane's detractors are patriarchal misogynists, or that all those overhyped young divas coming up today can't compete with the queen of soul, Aretha, or that there will never be a decade as musically vibrant as the 1960s (or the 1970s or 1980s or 1990s or the noughties…).

When you were born, what did you know about music? The only sounds you instinctively loved were made by your mom.

○   ○   ○

Anyway, getting back to the title of this chapter: Who is this book for? It's for you. You who are holding it in your hands because you've bought it or been given it. So, who are you?

You are probably aged between twenty-five and sixty-five. (You may be younger or older, but statistically, younger people are likely to be streaming the latest chart fodder on their phones rather than reading a book, while the old folks don't need a book to tell them that they like the old tunes from long ago.)

You are a confident reader—confident enough to tackle a substantial book that's not a rehash of stuff you know already. This actually puts you in an elite minority. Most people find reading quite arduous, hence the simplified prose in top-selling publications like *The Daily Mail*, *What's on TV* or *Take a Break*. Up to a quarter of people in the UK have "very poor literacy skills."* The percentage who can manage the occasional undemanding thriller or celeb biography but who would steer well clear of a book like *Listen* must be much higher still. If you've made it this far, you're already exceptional.

But don't let that swell your head. Being exceptional is not

---

*   "Adult literacy statistics," National Literary Trust, 2017. The figures, which are from 2012, vary across the UK, with Scotland the worst on 26 percent. Statistics for the USA are very similar. Fifty-four percent of American adults get by with the reading skills of an eleven-year-old child, or less.

a badge of honor, it's just a divergence from the general standard. Intellectuals (or bookish types or deep thinkers or cultured souls or whatever label you choose) are a minority like any other. They find validation in their specialness while missing out on easy communion with the larger herd. They console each other, reassure each other that they're not weird or poncy even though, statistically speaking, they are.

Fortunately, the average nonintellectual person has better things to do than ponder the nature of Art. Everything that keeps you and me alive and comfortable and clean and supplied with the necessities of existence is provided by people who, in all likelihood, would never bother to read a book like this one. You have the luxury of meditating upon elegant sounds, edging closer to a definitive opinion on Mozart's *Requiem* or Joni Mitchell's *Mingus*, while garbagemen take away your rubbish and farmers grow your food and lorry drivers deliver your medicines to pharmacies and poorly paid shop assistants stock shelves with clothing made by industrious Bangladeshis. You twist the handle of your kitchen tap and water comes out.

Such things are more essential to you than the tootlings of a clarinet or a bass riff from 1969, but you may want to deny that. Stubbornly, you may feel that music surpasses and transcends everything.

That's fine. I feel the same way.

o   o   o

This doesn't mean we're coming from the same place, though. You bring with you certain preconceptions of what kinds of music are good and bad. *Listen* will challenge those preconceptions, so you'll need to be the sort of person who can be challenged and not get pissed off or defensive. You may regard yourself as very much that sort of person, but let's see how we get on. Our journey together is just beginning.

You may be from a culture that speaks a non-English language and has "foreign" traditions. If so, you may be quite stunned to find yourself reading a book about music that doesn't automatically assume that you are an Anglo person with Anglocentric reference points. If that makes you feel a bit dizzy, take a seat.

There's a chance you may have dark skin, but if so, you'll be defying the demographic odds. Most serious books about music are directed at people with pale skin. They may not be intended that way, but that's how it pans out. Even the books about forms of music predominantly composed and played by non-white people—blues, funk, soul and so on—are read largely by white people, and until quite recently they were written by white people too. Even today, you could collect a large stack of books with titles like *Harlem in Montmartre: A Paris Jazz Story Between the Great Wars (Music of the African Diaspora)*; *Theory of African Music, Volume II*; *The Original Blues: The Emergence of the Blues in African American Vaudeville*; and *Brick City Vanguard: Amiri Baraka, Black Music, Black Modernity (African American Intellectual History)* without encountering a black author. Why is this so? Maybe it's because for hundreds of years music scholarship was about classical music, and classical music was haughtily, complacently racist. I don't know what to do about that except say hi, come in, let's think about some things together.

I'm hoping you may just as likely be female as male. My novels attract an evenly mixed readership, gender-wise. The readers of books about music are more often males, but I think that's because music appreciation tends to be a very nerdy activity and women are less apt to get excited by an exhaustive discography of Phil Spector or the sexual exploits of a misogynist guitarist. To put it another way: females often relate to music in ways that male music critics find baffling or contemptible. If you have ever felt the chill of that contempt, I hope the atmosphere will be a bit warmer in here.

You may have reached a point in your life where you still want to think about and discuss music but are no longer satisfied with how it's thought about and discussed elsewhere. If so, this book could be the thing you've been waiting for.

But that doesn't mean you'll like it. Most of us are set in our ways, well-defended, snugly rooted in our tribes. We hanker for alternatives to our old habits and limitations, but those alternatives ask us to make changes that we're just not prepared to make. Maybe you will realize, minutes or hours from now, that you really don't want to go where I want to take you. If so, forgive me.

o   o   o

One last possible reason why you're holding this book is that you're not that interested in music at all, but you loved *The Crimson Petal and the White* or *Under the Skin* or *The Book of Strange New Things*, and, in the absence of any more novels by Michel Faber, you thought you'd give my nonfiction a try.

If so, you may find that the sensibility that suffuses my fiction—an outsider looking at insiders, alien but not aloof, unsentimental but compassionate—suffuses this book too.

o   o   o

On which note, I must come clean and admit that this book is for me. Music is my oldest love, and *Listen* is the book I've wanted to write all my life.

DO YOU HEAR WHAT I HEAR?

Whee! I have tinnitus.

It came on in 2017, as I started writing this book. That was decades after I attended the loudest concerts of my concertgoing life—like The Birthday Party in Melbourne's Seaview Ballroom in 1983, after which my ears rang for days, or The Young Gods in the Sarah Sands Hotel in 1992, which rattled the windows, warped the walls and damn near lifted the roof.

My tinnitus came on in my own quiet home, at a time when I couldn't even bear to play a CD, not even at the lowest volume.

People who know me well know that when I stop listening to music, something must be badly wrong with me. But none of my friends was in a position to notice the dust gathering on my audio gear. I was alone in the flat at the time. Just me and the tinnitus.

What caused it? Possibly the stress of the nervous breakdown I was having. Or maybe it was provoked by me sticking sharpish objects into my ear canals to scrape out maddeningly itchy wax. Whatever. One month I was a human whose head was silent when there was silence. The next month I was a human whose head has a sound in it that a person next to me can't hear.*

That sound is still there, six years later. You can sit by my side if you like, with your ear against my head. At that proximity, you may hear air being sucked softly into my nose by my lungs,

---

* I console myself that this is merely the physical manifestation of what's always been the case metaphorically.

if you're not distracted by the same pneumatic activity happening in your own body. But you won't be able to detect the metallic squeal—like the brakes of a train that's forever cutting its speed and never coming to a stop. That sound is mine alone.

I can make the ringing in my ears much louder by pushing my jaw forward. This fact reminds me that my ears are structures made of bone, flesh, hair and membrane, whose design is subtly altered when I alter the shape of my face.

We think of hearing as a sort of magical receptor into the brain. We think the sounds exist in the world, enter holes in the sides of our heads and travel into our minds.

But that's not really the way it is. The world is intrinsically silent. When trees fall or bombs explode or violinists pluck pizzicato, all that happens is that the surrounding air is disturbed in various ways. Atmosphere is displaced. This displaced atmosphere is what enters our ears, and we do the rest. Our ears and brains are musical instruments. To be precise: our eardrums are conceptually no different from the drums we see a drummer playing.

The world is playing us.

o o o

This has big implications for how we perceive music. Push your jaw out. Does it create a ringing sound in your brain? If not, your head is a different musical instrument from mine.

There are many different shapes of head in the human population, and many different designs of ear, and infinitely various brains floating in their bony globes of cerebrospinal fluid. Most probably, they all make slightly different noises when the world plays them. And you will never know, because you can't help assuming that you hear the same way the next person hears.

Of course, it could be argued that there is a basic design to which we all conform. We are a specific kind of hominid primate, after all, not insects or crustaceans or even apes.

But there's a limit to the standardization. Some of us came

from production lines in Asia, others in Africa, others in Scandinavia. We are all handmade and organic—no prefab components or artificial substances whatsoever. Imagine eight billion guitars, all handmade, manufactured in a hundred and ninety-five different countries using local materials. How many will work exactly the same?

Face it: you are a different guitar from the people around you.

Maybe a *very* different guitar.

o   o   o

My hearing used to be pretty good.

By that I don't necessarily mean I experienced music in a superior way to Brian Wilson, who only had one functioning ear to make "God Only Knows" with, or in a superior way to the eminent percussionist Evelyn Glennie, who has been profoundly deaf for her entire career.* I just mean that when I was manufactured, nothing went wrong and all the bits were present and correct.

As we grow older, we typically lose some "top end"—the ability to detect higher-pitched treble sounds. Since my fifties, I've been turning the treble knob on my music system's amplifier up full. The younger me would no doubt find it harsh. But the younger me no longer exists.†

I am, admittedly, quite old now, seven years older than Beethoven when he died. Beethoven only made it to fifty-six—the same dying age as Rick James, Ranking Roger, Warren

---

*   Glennie makes a distinction between "profound" and "total" deafness. Her meditation "Hearing Essay" is worth reading in its entirety, but suffice to say that as well as hearing via other parts of her body, Glennie can detect some sound via her ears too—it's just that the quality is so crap that she's better off listening with her fingers, feet, chest, neck, etc.

†   Every seven to ten years, your entire body—except for certain kinds of brain cells—has died and been replaced at least once. The cells in your stomach and intestines last only a few days; your skin sloughs off and grows anew every month or so. We are in constant cellular flux.

Zevon, Denise Johnson from Primal Scream, Grant Hart from Hüsker Dü, and David R. Edwards, main man of my favorite Welsh band, Datblygu. Less lucky were Tchaikovsky (fifty-three), Mahler (fifty), John Coltrane (forty), Chopin (thirty-nine), Mozart (thirty-five) and Robert Johnson (twenty-seven). None of them died of drug overdoses or murder. It's just that a good few of those billions of guitars coming off the assembly line aren't built to last.

On the bright side, none of these musicians, apart from Beethoven, would've lost much top end from their hearing.

Also: whee! No tinnitus.

o   o   o

Is tinnitus unbearable? Possibly, for some. The language that sufferers use when describing it can be pretty extreme. "Desperation," "distress," "disabling," "debilitating" and "suicide ideation" are fearsome words.

The link between tinnitus and suicide, however, is tenuous. The story of the man who was told by doctors there was nothing they could do to stop the ringing in his head and who immediately jumped off a tall building seems to be an urban myth. Mostly, people just learn to live with the humiliations that afflict their ears (and their eyes and their joints and their teeth and their genitals and their skin) as they grow older. They have to.

Even so, there are days when my yearning to switch my tinnitus off becomes uncomfortably acute. It's about consent, and lack thereof. Certain pieces that I might play for pleasure, by Pan Sonic or Einstürzende Neubauten, generate sounds very similar to my tinnitus. But I choose to play them at that moment. Whereas my tinnitus never asks if I'm OK with a high-pitched whine. It follows me into the toilet. It gets into bed with me.

o   o   o

What's interesting about the ailment is that it is relieved by noise. One popular treatment option is a "tinnitus masker"—an audio feed that patients describe as the sound of wind in trees or a waterfall. Me, I don't fancy hearing waterfall noises when I'm not actually standing next to a waterfall. My remedy for tinnitus is to play music.

Some music, such as the aforementioned Pan Sonic, occupies similar frequencies to the tinnitus. Other music—for example acoustic folk or solo piano—definitely doesn't. It makes little difference to me. What helps is not the specific noise the music makes, but the quality of my concentration. Maybe I'm laying new auditory pathways, or maybe I'm just not sophisticated enough to notice a high-pitched whine when I'm focusing hard on five other sounds.

I once met a man whose eyes were damaged in such a way that he perceived large dark cylinders floating right in the middle of his field of vision. In time, these obstructions faded away. The damage to his eyes had not been repaired and the cylinders must therefore still have been there. But he'd trained himself not to see them. This is what I'm trying to do with my tinnitus.

Some days are better than others.

o   o   o

My tinnitus has taught me to be more aware of my organic nature, rather than conceiving of myself as a self-contained consciousness—an operating system—installed in an android console. I am not a ghost in a machine. I am meat and gristle and osseous tissue. I am the same category of creature as the roadkill on the streets, the once-living contents of my spaghetti marinara, the hunks of fish I wrap in tinfoil and put in my oven. On the sole occasion I've cooked a pheasant, I was puzzled by all the weird little bones it had, so many more than you find inside a chicken. What were they all for?

The human body has so many odd little bits, and while some of them are for fairly basic purposes like making more humans or digesting food, others are for judging such conundrums as whether the 2017 Decca remaster of Georg Solti's 1962 rendition of Verdi's *Aida* brings out sufficient nuances to counterbalance Solti's tendency for Wagnerian bombast, or whether the mono mix of Aretha Franklin's "(You Make Me Feel Like) A Natural Woman" has the edge over the stereo one, or whether the spectral "unraveling" sounds in Björk's "Unravel" might be backward clavichord.

It beggars belief that we process something as exquisitely subtle as music using only the most absurdly low-tech tools—bits of bone, lymphy gunge, tiny bundles of hair.

It's like equipping a spaceship with an engine made of twigs, rubber bands and cheese.

But it flies.

WHO DOESN'T LIKE MUSIC?

In his memoir *Speak, Memory*, Vladimir Nabokov reflected: "Music, I regret to say, affects me merely as an arbitrary succession of more or less irritating sounds."[*]

The furor over *Lolita* may have died down, but this confession still has the power to shock. Did the man just say he *doesn't like music*? That's not a matter of preference, such as not caring for sports or pets; it's a pathological condition.

Accordingly, it's been given one of those Greek-derived diagnostic labels that allow us to imagine we've established a scientific truth rather than merely invented a term: "musical anhedonia."

And it gets worse: you might have "congenital amusia" (no laughing matter). That's when, "despite the universality of music," you find yourself in that "minority of individuals" who, according to *The Oxford Handbook of Music and the Brain*, "present with very specific musical deficits that cannot be attributed to a general auditory dysfunction, intellectual disability, or a lack of musical exposure."[†] In other words, there are people who don't get on with music even though they're not deaf, stupid or ignorant.

Musical anhedonics are thought to account for up to 5 percent of the world's population. (But how could neuroscientists possibly know that? And if it's true, that would be…erm…almost *four hundred million* people!)

---

[*]   Vladimir Nabokov, *Speak, Memory* (Gollancz, 1951).

[†]   "Musical Disorders" by Isabelle Royal, Sébastien Paquette and Pauline Tranchant, in *The Oxford Handbook of Music and the Brain*, edited by Michael H. Thaut and Donald A. Hodges (Oxford University Press, 2019).

The syndrome is often discussed in the same articles that ponder the mysteries of autism. The subtext is that normal people feel and react in certain ways (e.g. laughing at the "right" moments, getting chills when they hear "sublime" sounds), and that abnormal people—the autists, the anhedonics—don't.

As someone who is "on the spectrum," I do understand what it's like to have a brain that functions differently from other people's. Does this mean that something has "gone wrong" with me? Respect for neurodivergence is all very well, but not all differences are desirable. There is such a thing as a glitch on the human assembly line—glitches that result in serious problems like blindness, paralysis, missing limbs, intellectual impairment.

Yet I'm also mindful that notions of normalcy are used by dominant social groups to maintain control and to organize systems in ways that suit them. Historically, it's a scarily short time ago that homosexuality was classified a disease and feminism was seen as a disorder that might require surgery. How judgmentally normative is a "normal" relationship with music?

Strikingly, a "musical anhedonic" who offered himself for study at Boston's Northeastern University told one of the professors that admitting to not liking music was rather like coming out as gay. The "problem" was not his relationship with music per se, but his relationship with the normal people who couldn't tolerate him being different. The researchers didn't seem very interested in this social alarm bell. Instead, they used biomedical imaging to study the auditory regions of his cerebrum.*

Another thing the researchers do is measure what happens to the tiny hairs on an anhedonic's arm, noting when those dermal filaments fail to respond as they should. I can't help wondering what would happen if you were someone who hadn't yet discovered the music you could love. What if your soul was holding out for sub-Saharan Gnawa or ancient Tuscan dances, which you weren't destined to hear until years later, and instead

---

*   "What people who don't like music might tell us about social interaction," *Neuroscience News*, January 18, 2020.

the researchers played you Bach and The Beatles and U2 and Charlie Parker and Van Halen and finally Whitney Houston, and then pronounced you as malfunctioning because your arm hairs didn't budge during "I Will Always Love You"?

o   o   o

What intrigues me about musical anhedonia, and the 5 percent of the human population who supposedly suffer from it, is the possibility—indeed, the likelihood—that 5 percent is an underestimate. I strongly suspect there are a lot more than four hundred million people out there who would rather opt out.

The analogy with coming out as gay is useful here. We know there are lots of homosexuals around, because faking one's sexuality is so difficult to sustain. Gay people who try to live as straights keep colliding with their desires, over and over, and those collisions have consequences, whereas the absence of a love for music can be much more easily managed. The music lovers assume you're no different from them and, to keep the peace, you let them believe that. You learn to talk the talk of music-love.

In private, you're free to do without the stuff, and doing without it doesn't hurt. In public, you will often be assailed by those unwanted sounds, but, as one anhedonic put it (unconsciously echoing Nabokov), "music sits in an odd spot halfway between boring and distracting."* Being bored or distracted is hardly hellish torture. You could cope with it all your life and never shed a tear or cause a scene.

o   o   o

The real problem, then, is other people.

In our society it is considered shameful not to appreciate music. By "our society," I mean those who regard themselves as part of Culture, an amorphous elite anyone can join. In Shakespeare's

---

★   "Inside the Heads of People Who Don't Like Music" by Divya Abhat, *The Atlantic*, March 10, 2017.

The Merchant of Venice, noble Lorenzo mistrusts "the man that hath no music in himself," the man who is not "moved with concord of sweet sounds,"* while Friedrich Nietzsche declared that "without music, life would be a mistake."† Closer to our own age, Billy Joel described music as "an explosive expression of humanity. It's something we are all touched by. No matter what culture you're from, everyone loves music."‡

The trouble with these declarations of art's universal appeal is that they are made by artists, and they resonate with the people who already like art, or who trust Billy Joel to know an explosive expression of humanity when he sees one. The self-appointed elite speak for us all, and never hear the silence from those who don't share their values.

How many humans feel that without music, life would be a mistake? Not as many as Friedrich, Will and Billy would like to think. A *Melody Maker* journalist once declared that listening to Björk was "as essential as breathing,"§ but biological and historical evidence suggests that breathing is of unrivaled importance, followed by eating, drinking and sleeping.

o o o

I don't doubt that for some listeners, music delivers profound, transcendent experiences. It does it for me, and probably for you, too.

But music is also tremendously overhyped. Every day, heaps and heaps of superlatives are shoveled onto it by people who, in truth, did not feel what their words tell you they felt. They heard

---

* William Shakespeare, *The Merchant of Venice* (self-published, 1600).

† Friedrich Nietzsche, *Twilight of the Idols, or, How to Philosophize with a Hammer* (C. G. Naumann, 1889).

‡ "Billy Joel: The Rolling Stone Interview" by Anthony DeCurtis, *Rolling Stone*, November 6, 1986.

§ Ian Gittins, "Geezer Gushes Over Gushing Geyser" [review of Bjork concert], *Melody Maker*, August 28, 1993.

a record/went to a concert and had a pleasant time, whereupon they tell you that their mind exploded into a million iridescent fragments, propelled around the cosmos on waves of dervish ecstasy. Or they declare that they would rather gnaw off their own arm than have to listen to a certain song again. Really? Their own arm? Gnawed off? Music, even more than the visual arts or Literature, seems to give people a license to bullshit.

No journalist would dare to say that if you don't love model trains, T. S. Eliot, jogging or *Star Wars*, you must be clinically dead. They feel free to say it about your failure to adore their favorite sounds.

o o o

This book will not add more hype to the landfill. Let's look at the world as it really works. Music has its place, and for many people that place is small.

I'm not referring to the 5 percent, or whatever the number is, who are willing to let scientists study their arm hairs to establish the severity of their musical anhedonia.

No, this is about the ordinary folks who wish the restaurant wouldn't play music while they're eating, the person who hates the way her flatmate switches the radio on as soon as she wakes up, the person who nods with feigned approval when his pals enthuse about a forthcoming concert that he has not the faintest desire to attend, the tourists who return from an overseas adventure unable to recall anything they heard, the driver who has the car radio tuned to talk shows and the news, the rambler who explores the woods all day, feeling no need for any musical accompaniment to that activity.

It's about the unlucky souls who write in to online communities like Mumsnet and Quora, shyly confessing that music does little or nothing for them, only to be shamed and overwhelmed by their music-worshipping peers who rave like a chorus of Lorenzos.

o   o   o

A lifetime of listening to how people relate to music has taught me that the love of music *for its own sake* is comparable to the love of cooking, gardening, antique furniture, animals, poetry and so on. Some people have it; a lot don't.

And why should they? Our society's sonic saturation is quite a recent development and may prove to be an abortive detour in human evolution. Our species managed to thrive through millions of years without multinational entertainment corporations, YouTube and Spotify. In the distant past, there was simply a lot less music around. Music had its appointed role in rituals and ceremonies. It was an occasional treat, an occasional obligation, a banquet once in a while; it was not a constant feed. Some people no doubt sang as they worked. Others were content with the rhythm of their carpentry, or walked to the well in silence, hearing only the tread of their feet on the earth and the sloshing of their bucket. Unaccompanied silence was normal.

Capitalism has changed that landscape. What were once luxuries are now considered basics, what was once communal is now atomized, what was once functional is now a superfluous add-on, and what were once deliberate commitments are now barely noticed ephemera supplied through invisible pipelines from everywhere and nowhere. There's a glut of artistic product. We have the fruits of our civilization coming out of our ears. It's not even a matter of seeking them out anymore, of foraging for the good stuff. Art is in the air, plentiful as oxygen, and we are under pressure to inhale deeply.

o   o   o

Just because there's an excess of art, however, doesn't mean everyone is lovin' it.

A few people love music, yes.

Others quite enjoy it in certain moods.

Others can take or leave it.

Others would rather leave it.

Yet everybody wants to be accepted as a member of society. And our society has decided that not caring for music is unacceptable.

How to get around that?

o   o   o

"I read this scary statistic from America," Peter Gabriel told *Rolling Stone* in 1987, just after *So* had hit pay dirt, "that the average album is played 1.2 times. It's an impulse buy, or something to impress a girlfriend, part of the artillery with which you announce yourself to the world."[*]

For someone like Gabriel, an artist to the marrow, that statistic must indeed have been scary. But it is probably true. The majority of people have little use for music purely as an aesthetic proposition. But they do need to bond with their friends, colleagues, neighbors and anyone else who might require impressing.

Almost every product in the capitalist marketplace is advertised in the same way—by telling the purchaser that if they have this thing, they will appear to be a particular sort of person in the eyes of others (and thereby in their own eyes as well). Music is as much a part of this artillery as clothing, gadgets, decor, books, hairstyle and so on.

What happened to Peter Gabriel, when he finally hit the "big time" in America, was that his album *So* was selected by the then-dominant culture as an object that sophisticated, up-to-date people should own. So, *So* was bought by millions of people.

I'm confident that if I played each of those millions of people the first thirty seconds of the opening track, "Red Rain," the vast majority of them would be stumped as to what album it was

---

[*]   "Peter Gabriel Hits the Big Time" by Steve Pond, *Rolling Stone*, January 29, 1987.

from, or even if they'd ever heard it before. They would recognize "Sledgehammer" because it was programmed for "high
rotation" on the radio and is still played on oldies stations today.
This means that even if they haven't played their own copy for
years (which will almost certainly be the case), they will have
heard it more recently at the supermarket or in the car or while
having a pee in a restaurant loo.

o o o

There are certain CDs that you can buy for a pittance in just
about any charity shop: the discards from all the houses in your
street. The selection changes as the population ages, but as I write
this book, a typical lineup might include albums by The Streets,
Gabrielle, Moby, M People, David Gray, Madonna, Robbie Williams, Will Young, Westlife, Duffy, Susan Boyle, Blur and Oasis.

It's possible that the people who owned these albums and then
discarded them loved them passionately once. It's more likely
that they bought them because the other members of their social group were buying them. But when your peers no longer
bring up The Streets' *Original Pirate Material* in conversation,
and you've played it only 1.2 times, why on earth would you
keep it in the house?

o o o

There are albums people keep in the house and never discard,
because their social usefulness never devalues. Miles Davis's *Kind
Of Blue*, for example, is the bestselling jazz album ever. Year in,
year out, it shifts thousands of copies a week, and almost none
of them end up in Oxfam.

It would be nice to think that thousands of people every week
are falling under the spell of Jimmy Cobb's understated mastery
of the cymbals, or that they share Davis's excitement about the
greater improvisational possibilities when players employ modes

rather than chords. The reality is that most of these purchasers feel they should own at least one jazz album and *Kind Of Blue* is that album.

Class snobbery enters the equation too. A lower-class person might cheerfully declare that they can't be bothered with jazz; a lower-middle-class person might buy a budget compilation called *The Best Jazz Album Ever*; a middle-class person might be equally satisfied with that compilation but get the message that proper music appreciators buy proper albums like *Kind Of Blue*; an upper-middle-class person might show their dinner guests the expanded double-disc *Kind Of Blue* 50th Anniversary Collector's Edition; and an upper-class person might cheerfully declare that they can't be bothered with jazz.

o   o   o

During my half century of music-collecting, I've visited the homes of many people. I'm one of those visitors who squats down in front of your shelving and checks out what LPs or CDs you've got. The overwhelming majority of music collections I've perused were of modest scale, not so big as to crowd out the baby photos or the ornaments. A little dusty, perhaps; the spines faded by the same shaft of sunlight falling on them at the same angle for years on end.

The number of items was commonly less than a hundred, most of them "the usual suspects" bought when the person was a lot younger. Married couples would often have duplicate copies of the Dire Straits or Badly Drawn Boy or Nina Simone album that was ubiquitous before they met each other. Any exotic or obscure item that surprised me usually turned out to have been a Christmas/birthday/thank-you gift from someone peripheral to their lives.

In 2005—just two years before the iPhone changed the game and CD sales plummeted—Barclays Insurance, in an effort to nudge homeowners into insuring their audio valuables, published a survey proclaiming that music collections had "soared." By this they meant that men now owned an average of 178 albums each (women owned 135, apparently).* Their hobby had outgrown the IKEA shelving units or the stainless steel Art Deco–esque storage spiral holding "up to forty CDs." They were getting serious.

A few years later, that no-longer-valuable collection was dustier than ever, if it hadn't already been donated to the local charity shop. People's music collection migrated to their phones, where it took up no room and didn't need tidying, dusting or, indeed, noticing.

o   o   o

I'm not whipping up a polemic here. I'm just noting the way things are. Most people want to check out the cultural phenomena that their peers are checking out because they don't want to be left out of the tribe. The item itself—the TV show, the gadget, the nail polish, the fitness toy, the CD, the download— means little or nothing to them. It will be forgotten and discarded when the crowd moves on.

A survey published on World Book Day in 2014 found that the average British home contained 138 books, more than half of which had never been read.† Another report asserted that 15 percent of the DVDs people bought gathered dust with the shrink-wrap still intact.‡ In 2011, it was established that more

---

*   I haven't been able to locate the original Barclays survey. Its findings were quoted in a number of newspapers and websites in mid-2005. One such report can be found in "Music Collections Soar," a forum post by Quadophile, in *PC Review*, June 18, 2005.

     I have no idea how many albums I own. Counting them would take hours—time that I would rather spend listening.

†   Survey conducted by Shurgard, quoted in various newspaper articles including "Land of the Unread" by Alan Jones, *The Independent*, March 6, 2014.

‡   Unidentified "studio home entertainment president" interviewed by Ben Fritz in *The Big Picture: The Fight for the Future of Movies* (Houghton Mifflin Harcourt, 2018).

than three-quarters of the tracks people downloaded from iTunes into their music "libraries" had been played zero times.[*]

Sales of vinyl LPs have struggled up from total oblivion in the 1990s to a small millennial niche, thus provoking talk of vinyl's "resurgence." However, social research specialists ICM Unlimited recently found that 48 percent of the people who'd bought vinyl LPs in the last month had yet to get around to listening to them. Seven percent of those purchasers didn't even own a turntable. "I have vinyls in my room but it's more for decor. I don't actually play them," a student in Manchester told the BBC. "It gives me the old-school vibe."[†]

Two separate teams of researchers, ten years apart—one from Guildhall School of Music and Simon Fraser University, the other from Keele University and the University of Leeds—came up with essentially the same findings when they examined people's listening habits. The sort of engagement with music in which the person focuses on the music for its own sake, rather than "having it on" in the background during some other activity, accounts for just 2 percent of all listening.[‡] And that doesn't even include the nonlisteners—the ones who never partake of the stuff but merely "own" it as a social signifier.

Another way of phrasing this 2 percent statistic is that ninety-eight out of a hundred people who tell you they've been listening to music have actually been doing something else.

This is especially true of millennials, who often perceive

---

[*]   "Most of the average digital music collection goes unplayed," CMU, May 27, 2011.

[†]   "Music streaming boosts sales of vinyl" by Mark Savage, BBC website, April 14, 2016.

[‡]   "Functions of Music in Everyday Life: An Exploratory Study Using the Experience Sampling Method" by John A. Sloboda, Susan A. O'Neill and Antonia Ivaldi, *Musicae Scientiae*, Vol. 5 Issue 1, March 2001; and "Exploring Engagement with Music in Everyday Life Using Experience Sampling Methodology" by Alinka E. Greasley and Alexandra Lamont, *Musicae Scientiae*, Vol. 15 Issue 1, March 2011.

music as an ambient noise that emanates vaguely and ignorably from the environment. For these young people (according to a research team employed by the British Phonographic Industry and Entertainment Retailers Association to identify their target audience) "music is becoming increasingly like the torrent of continually updated and essentially transient content that fills their social feeds."*

o   o   o

Later chapters of this book will dwell on the multifarious uses to which music is put in our culture. Some of those applications signal respect (sincere or feigned) for the artistic value of the sounds. Others not so much.

When a government department or a hospital switchboard plays you a loop of Vivaldi's *Four Seasons* while you wait on the phone, you and the institution both understand that nobody respects this music. Its sole purpose is to let you know that the phone connection hasn't gone dead.

Similarly, when a musclebound Lycra-clad exercise enthusiast takes advantage of Samsung's offer to feed Spotify playlists directly into his Galaxy Active2 watch, it's understood that music is not what this transaction is about. The Spotify tunes on this dude's Galaxy watch, which others might revere as Art, serve the much more useful purpose of helping him shape his abs and deltoids.

"I've been playing a lot of AC/DC," he may say, to his music-loving friends. "Classic."

Arguably, there's nothing shameful or corrupt about this. In the past, music generally had an explicit purpose. Gods needed to be placated, illnesses needed to be healed, messages needed to be drummed across the river, babies needed to be soothed to

---

*   Report on "Gen Z: Meet the New Millennials" Insight Session by Mark Mulligan of MIDiA Research, held June 27, 2017, published on website of BPI/ERA.

sleep, armies needed to march. If a person from many centuries ago were transported to our time and allowed to survey the music on offer, I'm pretty sure they'd have no trouble understanding the validity of CDs and digital streams like *Relaxing Birth Music, Serenity Spa Relaxation Music, Sex Lounge, Work It Out!: The Ultimate R&B Fitness Album*, and *Now That's What I Call Running*—goal-oriented stuff that critics and connoisseurs despise. But our time traveler might struggle to see the point of Radiohead, John Coltrane or Max Richter. What on earth is a person supposed to *do* with these sounds?

o   o   o

If you don't particularly care for music, one of the best ways you can hide this—even from yourself—is by exploiting its endless potential as a talking point. Humans may not need to hear clarinets or clavinets, but they need to converse. They love to gossip—to express disapproval of strangers, to be indignant on behalf of allies they'll never meet, to comment on other people's poor relationship choices and moral misdeeds and manners of grooming.

It is entirely possible to "keep up" with "music" and have vehement, complex opinions on it while barely listening to the stuff at all.

Courtney Love: Was she Kurt Cobain's best friend or a vampire who caused his death? Cardi B shouldn't sing about her wet pussy, it's degrading. Dave Mustaine should get over being kicked out of Metallica, it was thirty years ago, dude, why keep bad-mouthing Lars? Adele was a better role model when she was overweight. Can drill still be drill if the lyrics aren't about drilling? Who honestly likes Yoko Ono, I mean, come on? Wagner—proto-Nazi, wasn't he? Well, let's have a long discussion about what "proto-Nazi" means. Sting is *such* a hypocrite—flying off to the Amazon in a private jet to protest about the environment. And all that tantric sex stuff! What a prat. Forget the sanctification of Jacqueline du Pré, she was a nasty piece of work. Paul Simon: underappreciated genius or arrogant exploiter of Africans?—new evidence from the disgruntled Los Lobos! Beyoncé a feminist? What planet are you on? Axl Rose's braids-and-bandanna combo—what *was* he thinking? Rumor has it that there's been some sort of night of the long knives behind the scenes at English National Opera. Lady Gaga shouldn't have said that thing she said. Was Michael Jackson's doctor murdered? Nothing against jazz, but Radio 3 is not the place for it. Never mind those bad-boy rappers and punks, Jerry Lee Lewis did it all sixty years ago. Janis Joplin was more gay than straight, which explains a lot. Roger Waters should stop banging on about Palestine. What a wonderfully naughty boy Keith Richards is—here's my favorite Keef anecdote…

The chat is inexhaustible, and the sounds made by the artists are irrelevant to it.

o o o

Whenever I've asked someone how long it's been since they actually sat down and listened to a piece of music on which they've just pronounced a fervent opinion, it's often apparent that it's been a while. A long while. Or let's be totally frank: a very, *very* long while. We thought we were discussing music, but what we were talking about was not music, nor even a feeling, but a memory of a feeling.

A piece of music made them happy long ago, or it was in the air when they were feeling happy for some other reason, on a day when they really needed to feel happy, and they've remembered that happy feeling ever since, and the memory does the business for them without the need to rummage through a bunch of CDs or LPs, which in any case may be locked in a self-storage unit in Romford.

Or they may see themselves as a person who regularly goes to a certain music festival or concert series, even though they didn't go last year, because of the bathroom renovation, and not the year before that either, because of COVID, or the year before *that*, because of work, and actually it's been quite a while, because the gang they used to go with is older now, and the traffic always was a nightmare, and besides there'll never be a lineup as good as 2009 or 1998 or 1976.

I'm not saying I've caught these people out in a lie. I'm only observing that life goes on, and the days and years pass, and people are busy, and what with one thing and another, music doesn't actually figure as much as they'd like to think.

o   o   o

You are still near the beginning of your journey in this book. You may be unsure where it's heading, and whether it's for you. I can't help you there. I don't know you.

But I can tell you this: I am not watching the hairs on your arm to see if you respond to my favorite music. This is not a test.

I love music, but loving music is not obligatory and it is not a measure of your worth as a human being. The fact that you're reading this book suggests that some sounds do interest you. That's enough for me.

o   o   o

A thousand years ago, the people who could take or leave music were, most of the time, free to leave it. Today, you and music are forced into a relationship—an arranged marriage of sorts. Nobody asked you if you wanted it or if you were ready. You were bonded to certain kinds of music (and subjected to aversion therapy for others) from your birth onward. Every day of your life since then, you've been reminded of the music that's embracing or harassing you. Vast societal forces have shaped your loves and hates.

Is there a "you" that exists independently of that shaping

process, with loves and hates that are yours alone? If there isn't, could you step back and create one?

I don't know.

Let's try and find out.

THE EARS OF A CHILD 1:
HIP UNHIP HOORAY

A winter's morning in a seaside town, a year before COVID.

I'm in an artsy café—all pale wood, panini and cappuccino steam—that is hosting the weekly get-together of the Miniature Music Makers. Tiny kids, in other words. Fifteen moms (several of them heavily pregnant) and two dads have brought their toddlers and preschoolers along to a session convened by Karen Blanch, a sprightly music therapist whose main qualifications are that "I love music and I love children."*

Karen runs another Miniature Music Makers eight miles further east, in Dover, a depressed port blighted by poverty and neglect. There, the sessions are geared toward parents struggling to give their children an advantage—*any* advantage—in a tough world. Here in Folkestone, a town that's on the up, Karen's clientele is a different demographic.

I get chatting to the dad of two-and-a-half-year-old Toby, because Toby walked straight up to me with a confident smile and said hello. Toby clearly thinks the world is a nice safe place full of nice safe people. Dad wears a hipster cardigan, cloth cap, braces, a neatly fashioned beard. He moved down from London a little while ago, attracted by the sea and the standard of living. I don't ask him what his job is. Whatever it is doesn't require his presence on a Tuesday.

The parents and their tots sit in a semicircle around Karen, who sings a welcome song for each and every child:

---

* Karen Blanch, interview with me, January 22, 2019.

"Rory is here today/We all clap our hands today/Hip hip hooray…"

"Willow is here today/We all clap our hands today/Hip hip hooray…"

"Sandra is here today…"

And so on. The kids are charmed and, apart from one worried-looking little girl who doesn't want to clap and doesn't respond well to tickling, they all get in the swing of things quite quickly.

The session has a winter theme, with plenty of fluffy fabric snowflakes thrown about and songs about mittens and cold feet. It's warm in the café and presumably warm in the houses where these families live, but the tots are just old enough to remember how chilly it is outside. A couple of them may even have seen snow, not here in their sea-breezy Kentish town but on holiday in the Alps or the Scottish Highlands.

But it doesn't matter if they're vague about what snow is. They're new to the world and vague about everything. Singing these little songs and clapping and shaking rattles gives them a sense that they've got the hang of *something*. They are Miniature Music Makers.

o   o   o

Their play-mom Karen is quite miniature herself, a dynamo of positive energy who, unbeknownst to the singing toddlers and their parents, needs to ration that energy carefully, because she has chronic fatigue syndrome. Tomorrow she will rest. Today, she's bouncing around in her specially monogrammed polo shirt, petite to me and very big to her ensemble.

One of the kids is slower than the others, mesmerized. She raises her hands and moves them through the air, almost clapping. She seems not to understand what rhythm is, but she figures it's got something to do with arms and she knows she's got arms. A few winters ago, she wasn't even an egg yet.

o o o

I don't ask, but it's conceivable that one or two of the parents here have been trying to interest their babies in music even before birth.

For decades now, there has been a persistent myth that playing fetuses music—specifically Mozart—boosts their intelligence.

Mozart is no longer around to hoover up the royalties from increased sales, but there are many modern composers who've moved into the prenatal market. Go to Amazon, and you will find a comprehensive range of albums with titles like *New Pregnancy Music for Baby in Womb for Brain Development* and *Prenatal Music for Baby in Womb: Relaxing Music Supporting the Proper Development of the Baby,* by artists with monikers like Hypnotherapy Birthing and Nature Music Pregnancy Academy. One company selling classical music to expectant mothers even calls itself Baby Genius.

o o o

What can unborn babies hear, and what do they think of it?

For the first few months of development, embryos are deaf. They start off resembling slugs or shellfish, then grow into eerie little humanoids with decorative but nonfunctioning ears. Then, at about eighteen weeks, the auditory system begins to react to stimulus.

However, the inside of the mother's body is not like the Queen Elizabeth Hall during that decorous hush when the conductor's raised hands signal that celestial loveliness is about to issue forth. It's bloody loud. Literally bloody. The veins and arteries are pumping like a factory. Recordings made inside the human body are like horror movie sound effects, or—if we must choose a music genre—the gray zone of avant-garde electronica called Industrial.*

---

*   If, by some magic of verbal precocity, a baby were to sit up in its crib and confide to me that she really, really missed the sounds of being inside her

Have you ever failed to hear a doorbell or someone calling to you from outside your home, because there was too much going on indoors? Fetuses have a lot going on indoors. We can't say for certain if they're *thinking*, but we know that they're in a sack of fluid and everything is literally and figuratively in their face, including that ceaseless *gurrrgle-whoosh-whump* of the mammalian interior.

What sorts of sounds from the outside world have a chance of penetrating the din? Punk and heavy metal might get through; Mozart possibly not.

A "study" performed by a fertility clinic in Barcelona, quoted without a shred of caution by the tabloid press and radio stations such as Classic FM, claimed that fetuses enjoy Mozart's *Eine kleine Nachtmusik*, don't much care for Adele's "Someone Like You," and actively dislike the Village People's "Y.M.C.A."[*]

I'm pretty sure the crucial factor here is not how the fetus felt about the Village People but how the mother felt. The mother, after all, was the one hearing these artists' music rather than a barrage of abstract biological noise. If I'm going to ponder speculative theories about the unborn, I'd be more inclined to believe a study that suggests that fetuses groove on their mothers being in a good mood.

o o o

The so-called "Mozart effect" has its origins in an IQ study conducted by psychologist Frances Rauscher in the early 1990s. Rauscher examined thirty-six college students who'd listened to either a Mozart sonata, a "relaxation track" or nothing at all before performing a range of spatial reasoning tasks. In one task,

---

mom, the best I could do for her would be to play her Throbbing Gristle's *After Cease To Exist*, or maybe *Pagan Muzak* by NON. Music that her parents would almost certainly find repulsive.

[*]   "Babies are stimulated by classical music in the womb, study finds" by Sian Moore, Classic FM, October 17, 2019.

involving bits of folded paper, the students who'd just heard Mozart seemed to do better than the ones who hadn't.

Leaving aside the inherent problems with IQ testing as a concept, the findings of this study were debatable and tentative. Rauscher was bemused to see her name popping up in newspaper and magazine articles all over the world, in a story that metamorphosed with astonishing speed. Her college students became children, then babies, then babies in the womb. A temporary (and possibly coincidental) improvement in paper-folding skills transmogrified into a lifelong upgrade in general intelligence.

Subsequent studies confirmed that the Mozart effect was nonexistent, and Rauscher herself said "there is no compelling evidence that children who listen to classical music are going to have any improvement in cognitive abilities. It's really a myth, in my humble opinion." Asked why she thought her experiment had been so grossly misrepresented and so virally disseminated, she mused: "I think parents are very desperate to give their own children every single enhancement that they can."*

o   o   o

In *The Mozart Effect® for Children: Awakening Your Child's Mind, Health, and Creativity with Music*, a bestselling book by former music critic and fantastically successful entrepreneur Don Campbell, there's a chapter called "Twinkle Twinkle, Little Neuron." Clearly, purchasers/parents are being invited to imagine their child's neurons lighting up with intellectual energy. But the selling point of Campbell's books and CDs is not solely a fad notion invented in the 1990s; his materials are cannier than that. One of the other bases they cover is a perennial desire in the parents of newborns, a longing that's as ancient as the old-

---

★   "Fact or Fiction?: Babies Exposed to Classical Music End Up Smarter: Is the so-called 'Mozart effect' a scientifically supported, developmental leg up or a media-fueled 'scientific legend'?" by Nikhil Swaminathan, *Scientific American*, September 13, 2007.

est lullaby: How—oh, please, God, how—can we get the little treasure to shut up and go to sleep?

The Mozart rondos, allegros and variations that Campbell collates for the first half of *Music for Newborns: A Bright Beginning* are meant to "awaken and stimulate the brain," and exhausted parents can console themselves that their well-awakened kid is getting smarter by the minute.* But these lively pieces are followed by "soothing serenades to gently carry the new infant (and new parent) to restful, rhythmic sleep…" And so it goes for the other CDs in his arsenal—lots of serenades, andantes, adagios and larghettos on albums with titles like *Music for Babies Vol. 1: From Playtime to Sleepytime* and *Music for Babies Vol. 2: Nighty Night.*

Here we glimpse an industry that dates back to the earliest days of recorded music, and then into classical repertoire like Chopin's "Berceuse" and Brahms's "Wiegenlied" and "Sandmännchen." The magic melodies that cause the clamor to stop, replaced by soft snuffling.

It has been hypothesized that the first music ever made by humans was the singing of mothers to their babies and that these lullabies may indeed be the origin of language itself. We cannot visit our Australopith ancestors to verify this, but it seems reasonable to make two generalizations: 1) humans have been keen to get their bawling newborns off to sleep since day one, and 2) music that's of some practical use has always trumped music that can only be admired as Art.

o o o

Back in the hipster café in Folkestone, I watch the Miniature Music Makers do their thing. No doubt the parents who've brought their infants here genuinely want them to grow up with an enhanced enthusiasm for music. There may also be an element of finding enough activities for them each day, fun exertions that will tire them out a bit and make it more likely

---

*   Don Campbell, *Music for Newborns: A Bright Beginning* (The Mozart Effect, 2000).

that they'll sleep through the night. Singing and hand-clapping could be as useful as a visit to the play equipment in the park.

Plus, there's good coffee and cake, and a chance to hang out with one's fellow thirtysomething middle-class parents.

While I watch, I reflect on tribal identity, class, fashion, and the demarcations between cool and uncool. For grown-ups, music is a battleground of identity and allegiance. As Peter Gabriel despondently remarked in the previous chapter, it is "part of the artillery with which you announce yourself to the world." Liking the right music wins you recognition and approval from your peer group; liking the wrong music provokes alienation and exclusion.

Each of the adults here is a veteran of this conditioning process. They've been working at it for many years. They've been rewarded, and they've had moments when they were given a poke with a prod, warning them that they were out of line, straying toward music that Other People Who Are Not Us identify with. To each tribe their own artillery.

The babies are not veterans yet. Granted, their musical diet, like their food diet, is determined by their kinship group, so there are certain sounds they'll be exposed to and others that are absent from their world. But they're open-minded, impressionable, malleable in ways that their parents no longer are.

In other words, they have no taste.

Soon, their parents and siblings and friends will remedy that.

o   o   o

There's an age when kids start fretting about their musical taste and measuring their cred against that of their cooler peers. As I sit in the hipster café watching the Miniature Music Makers, I surmise that eighteen months to thirty-six months is not that age.

Singing "twinkle, twinkle, little star" and "hip hip hooray" is A-OK, as far as these kids are concerned. The expressions on some of their moms' and dads' faces tip me off that singing

"twinkle, twinkle, little star" and "hip hip hooray" is a bit em-
barrassing for a thirty-five-year-old. But the embarrassment is
reduced if their fellow grown-ups submit to the same silliness.
(We've all come here to be infantile, haven't we?)

Indeed, I've often noticed that all sorts of social anxieties are
soothed or suppressed when there are little kids in the room.
People relax their poses and let go of their pretensions and allow
their defenses to be breached, because they know there's no point
trying to maintain the facade—it will only get punctured, because the infants don't know how to play the game.

Society's response to this dynamic has been to ensure that
children are kept out of as many serious meeting places as possible.

I would be very much in favor of taking the opposite approach. Allow young kids to be present at political debates,
academic lectures, literary awards, in TV newsrooms, business
conferences, fashion parades, war strategy headquarters—any
context where illusions must be rigorously maintained and nervous people are under pressure to deny or disguise their humanity. I have a hunch that many of those occasions would turn out
much better all around if a child was free to interject "That's my
daddy!" or "Are you ticklish?" or "I done poo!"

o   o   o

One of the greatest sources of needless suffering in human society is insecurity and shame about one's clothing and how it
compares to the clothing of others. It sets in quite early. But
maybe not as early as eighteen months.

All the Miniature Music Makers are wearing what their parents have dressed them in and don't seem to be bothered. There
are lots of cheerful mismatches of colors and styles, indicating a
compromise between what still fits, what's comfortable, what allows quick access to the diaper, what's clean, what is this week's
favorite thing, and what can be located in the scramble to get

ready for leaving the house. Quite a few of the kids have an ac-cidental eighties vibe. Stripy leg warmers with trainers and poly-ester smocks, frilly pink dresses with UGG boots, short-sleeved tops over long-sleeved ones, and so on. In the toddler ecosystem, hasty preparations for going out lead to honorary membership of Haysi Fantayzee or Bananarama.

One child wears a rather cool pink sweater with a sort of *Aladdin Sane* lightning bolt on it, but I can't ask him his opinion of David Bowie because he's sucking a pacifier and concentrating on standing upright.

The main function of this event, for him, is to be among other toddlers. In that sense, this is a musical gathering like any other, whether it be a classical concert at Wigmore Hall or the annual Metalfest in a booze-soaked field: an opportunity to hang out with your kind.

o   o   o

But never mind all that. What about the music? How good is the music?

The Miniature Music Makers sing in tune, pretty much. They sound like ducklings or kittens gamely joining in with another species, and I'm suitably impressed. Sure, there are no Pavarottis or Celine Dions here, because toddlers aren't physically capable of doing that stuff. Their tongues and larynxes are still devel-oping. They pronounce "love" as "wuv" and their problems with palatal fronting and consonant clusters would make it im-possible for them to describe wuv as a many-splendored thing.

Doh, way, me, and no F-sharp suspended fourths, thank you very much. The songs chosen by Karen Blanch have a very small number of notes, and the patterns in which they're arranged are simple. Have you ever wondered why, in our Anglo world, there's such a modest repertoire of familiar nursery rhymes and lullabies? The repertoire of pop songs for grown-ups changes all the time; old standards drop out and new ones come in to replace them. But the same old nursery rhymes stick around for centuries. London Bridge just keeps falling down and those three mice remain blind. Why?

It's because the familiar songs have survived a harsh Darwinian selection process, proving themselves fit for purpose. They just work, that's all. Infants are able to follow the melodic steps in a way that they aren't able to follow more sophisticated tunes, even ones written by talented composers who love children and who'd be ever so chuffed if something they wrote was a hit with the tots. The "dead simple/instantly memorable" combination turns out to be a big ask.

For a toddler, "Three Blind Mice" is quite challenging enough: almost as challenging as using a potty. When your brain is only a few months old, the obvious is not yet obvious and the facile is not yet easy. No baby ever sighed in disdain over a major scale stepping from C to F to G and back again. The need to have one's jaded palate pepped up with a diminished seventh is some way off yet.*

o o o

But it's not the babies who are paying money to be here, and Karen recognizes that grown-ups who've progressed to Radiohead, Rufus Wainwright or Rihanna may not relish a five-year stretch of "Baa Baa Black Sheep." So, Karen puts fresh words to overfamiliar tunes. "Frère Jacques" turns up several times in her session, revamped as "Eyes are watching, ears are listening..." and "Teeny tiny ball, made of snow..." "Baa Baa Black Sheep" appears as "Snowballs, snowballs." "This Old Man" appears as

---

*   There's a sweet interview on a Swedish TV show with the British singer Adele. Adele, known for her vocal acrobatics and celebrated as "the voice of a generation," is asked by Fredrik Skavlan if she sings lullabies to her infant son. "Yeah," Adele replies. "I don't do anything special, I just do, like, 'Twinkle Twinkle' and 'Row, Row Your Boat.' If I try to sing him anything that's *actually* amazing, he just tells me to shut up." ("The bigger your career gets, the smaller your life gets," uploaded to YouTube by SVT [Sveriges Television] on December 11, 2015).

"Little Owl." "Jingle Bells" appears as "Icy toes, chilly nose." And so on.

At one point, musical instruments are handed out. Glockenspiels, frame drums, maracas, shakers, bells. I brace myself for a cacophonous free-for-all, but the kids are surprisingly careful.

"Play and play and play and STOP," chants Karen, strumming her guitar. "Play and play and play and STOP."

It's a game. It's play, and playing is what children do. It's the same principle as underlies a skipping pattern, a hoedown, a headbang, The Temptations putting their left foot forward while clicking their fingers.

"A-B-C," as the Jackson 5 once sang. "Easy as one-two-three."

o   o   o

Are there any kids in this room who are destined to become proper musicians? I note that one tiny girl beats a bodhrán in perfect time, as if taking herself seriously as an accompanist. Karen and I discuss her afterward. Some infants, says Karen, have "inherent rhythm." She mentions that when her son was a babe in arms, he would pat her back in rhythm to the hymns at church.*

YouTube, that ever-expanding cabinet of curiosities, has made us confused about how talented little tots can be. We may be shown a two-year-old dancing and singing along to Cardi B with great panache. (Is she *really* two? She doesn't *look* two, but her parents, who uploaded the clip, should know… But then, the clip is making them a tidy fortune in advertising revenue.) How many families all over the world are deriving their income from millions of clicks on "private moments" caught on video? How many kids like this exist? Does a two-year-old think Cardi B's wet pussy is a cat, and, if not, what does she think it is?

_____

* I don't quiz Karen on her religious beliefs but I get the impression she's sustained by a benign form of Christianity. There are certainly no intrusive deities in the songs—only sleepy little bunnies, hedgehogs and incy wincy spiders.

These are questions bigger than Kierkegaard would be competent to tackle. Best to focus on Karen Blanch's bunch of tinies in my own seaside town on a winter Tuesday morning.

o   o   o

It's perhaps inevitable that this ensemble of singing instrumentalists, all of them under three, cannot quite manage a 100 percent smoothly running gig. A few kids have minor emotional crises or need to go to the toilet. One mom gratefully accepts some teething gel from another. And there are moments when individual tots become absorbed in their own agendas, dawdling to the fringes, losing connection with their appointed role as Miniature Music Makers.

This sort of behavior would not be tolerated at a rehearsal of the Berlin Philharmonic, or a recital by Frederica von Stade, but it's acceptable here.

Indeed, when you think about it, this sort of behavior is acceptable and normal at many grown-up venues—nightclubs and discos, for example, or the sites of open-air festivals. Ostensibly musical gatherings at which a significant proportion of the audience don't have their attention on the music at all, because they're wandering around looking for a loo, or they're shouting into each other's ears, or they're pursuing a quest to obtain beer or cannabis or a sexual partner, or they're too cold or hot or hungry or angry. At any gig in your town on any night of the week, quite a few of the attendees will be distracted by dramas that loom so large in their lives or their bloodstreams that no amount of melody or instrumental magnificence can compete.

Compared with *that* degree of self-absorption, the toddlers at the Miniature Music Makers session are admirably open to the communal joy music can bring. Karen and the parents and a couple of the taller toddlers hold aloft a large blanket, the underside of which is embroidered with stars. The rest of the kids lie on the floor, gazing up at the artificial night sky. "Twinkle, twinkle, little star…" everybody sings.

It might not equal the transcendence of being in the Royal Albert Hall when Beethoven's Choral Symphony is reaching its climax. But if you're two, it may be the nearest thing.*

---

*   If you took a baby to the Royal Albert Hall and exposed them to Beethoven, what would they make of it? We can't really determine that, because babies lack the vocabulary to articulate how they perceive art. We can tell by their gurgles and screams if they're happy or unhappy, but those feelings could have any number of causes. I've been at many cultural events where parents have taken along a babe in arms. Often, a moment comes when they have to hurry to the exit, loud baby noises trailing behind them like clouds of exhaust. Was it the C-sharp that set the baby off? Were they creeped out by the scrape of the violin? Is their diaper wet? Did a scary stranger look at them? Is milk turning acid in their intestines? Does the venue smell of wrongness? Who knows?

THE EARS OF A CHILD 2:
SOMETHING REALLY BAD,
LIKE CAT POO

A middle-aged man once shared with me the utter mortification he'd felt when he made the mistake, in 1976, of expressing his love of Slade to a bunch of his fellow schoolchildren, who sneeringly informed him that Slade were over and nobody had liked them for ages. Anyone who knew *anything* knew that. He was nine.

The children who inflicted this humiliation were not musicologists or even music lovers. They hadn't mulled upon the instrumentation of Slade's oeuvre and decided that ELO were more imaginative. They hadn't come to the conclusion that Noddy Holder's voice was unequal to the challenges of the band's more recent material. They'd simply decided that their gang *used* to like Slade but wouldn't like Slade anymore because Slade are stupid and only stupid kids like them.

o   o   o

Grown-ups are better defended, better prepared against such shocks. They've learned to read the cultural primers before opening their mouths. Journalists and other "influencers" tip them off that the mainstream perspective on Madonna or Taylor Swift is shifting (Madonna downgraded; Swift up a notch), and coach them in how to handle that.

But even well-coached grown-ups get it wrong sometimes. I've seen the looks on the faces of those who've misjudged which musicians are OK to like. The fake relaxed grin, the nervously raised pitch of their voice, the glimmer of fear in their eyes. Suddenly, they're the kid who turned up in the school playground wearing a *Flintstones* T-shirt when it had been decided, apparently overnight, that Marvel superheroes were the thing.

o   o   o

On a train recently, I saw a poster advertising an app called Treatwell that offers to help its customers make appointments at beauty salons and hairdressers. "Do you need a haircut?" asks the poster, depicting a flowchart of frustrating, time-wasting options that you can blissfully avoid if you sign up for the Treatwell app. One such annoyance is attempting to phone up a salon yourself and being forced to listen to a recorded message. "You're on hold," sighs the poster. "It's Enya. 17 minutes of Enya."*

There was a time, in the 1990s or even the early 2000s, when Enya's music was precisely what the women having their hair done would be expected to like. Enya was elegant and enigmatic and Celtic and a little bit strange, and she played synthesizers, which meant that the listener could feel as though she'd ventured out of a bourgeois comfort zone to explore progressive hinterlands.

At what point in history did Enya cease to mean all that, and suddenly mean irritating muzak on an answering machine, which any sensible person would pay to avoid?†

Or take U2. (*Please, take them,* I hear voices cry.) U2 were

---

*   Treatwell advert, London to Sandwich train, circa 2018.

†   My editor alerted me to the fact that a journalist called Luke Turner is on a one-man crusade to salvage Enya's critical rep. While acknowledging "the prevailing view of her as a dated, patchouli car-freshener relic of 80s MOR," he has praised her to the skies in several forums. See: "Space Celts & A Voyage Into the Avant-Garde" in *The Quietus*, 24 November 2015 (subtitled: "Thought Enya was naff? Think again") and "Enya's greatest songs—ranked!" in *The Guardian*, May 27, 2021. In that article, he enlists support from Nicki Minaj, Gazelle Twin and Throbbing Gristle's Chris Carter, as well as mentioning that "I have it on good authority that she's the choice for serious contemporary Wiccan rituals."

once a trendy band. Nowadays, they are not. Their management spends a fortune to convince you that they still are, but the hipsters (and large numbers of the masses who aspire to be hip) regard Bono as a boring old prat and The Edge as not even remotely edgy.

As recently as 2005, Paul Morley, a music journalist who started out as one of the *NME*'s self-styled "hip young gunslingers" and forged a career as the arrogantly authoritative voice of Cool, wrote a worshipful article about U2 for *The Observer*, insisting on the band's undiminished importance. "U2 alone take on the ideas and ideals of the late Seventies and early Eighties, a period that we can now see, sonically, philosophically and artistically, has more actual truth and meaning than most, and thrust them deep into the dissolving new century."*

2005 was only yesterday, but also an age ago. In the 2020s, beating the drum for U2 would be the kiss of death for any hipster's credibility. They're too unhip even to warrant insults. Anyone who's keeping up simply ignores them as if they've ceased to exist, even though they carry on and on, selling out stadiums wherever stadiums are to be found.

When did the switch occur? Difficult to say exactly. Many trend-surfers had already become disenchanted with U2 by the late nineties. Paul Morley must've been aware that singing the group's praises in 2005 was a risky exercise for a gunslinging pundit. But he was forty-eight years old, and seduced by U2's shtick of being battle-scarred men in their midforties who were still hungry and potent.

So, the *Observer* readers who wanted to be cool, and who accepted that Paul Morley was cooler than them, were persuaded that the band they'd come to think was no longer cool was in fact cooler than ever, because so many fickle, faux cool people

---

* "In a world of their own" by Paul Morley, in *The Observer Music Magazine*, December 18, 2005.

had moved on, thus leaving the field open for genuine, cool-to-the-bone people to show they knew better.

I'm not sure how best to describe what's going on there. A double bluff? A quadruple bluff? Whatever it is, it's sociologically exhausting.

Paul Morley was a baby once, reaching out his pink little fingers toward whatever sounds were aimed at his crib. So were all the *Observer* readers who, over the decades since their birth, have cravenly pretended that they were into Nick Drake long before the Volkswagen advertisement, have been embarrassed by their teenage infatuation with Ned's Atomic Dustbin, have felt aghast at the way they once remarked (in an era before traceable evidence, thank God) that disco was all very well for girls, gays and black people but what if you wanted something more intelligent?

o o o

At what age do kids start getting doctrinaire about music, and anxious about the social esteem and reproof that society attaches to various stylistic allegiances? At what age do kids start to be dishonest about what they like and envious of others' taste? At what age does the shame begin?

o o o

Influence begins on an animal level, with subtle patterns of reward and absence of reward. Which responses might earn the approval of those who provide the food and shelter? You want them to smile down at you.

Sophisticated middle-class parents who value particular kinds of culture will beam and crow over their young daughter if she waves her hands in a conductorly manner to Beethoven, or if their young son gyrates enthusiastically to Curtis Mayfield, whereas they may stiffen and exchange pained glances if those same children stomp gleefully to football anthems or the latest manufactured pop franchise. Conversely, children growing up in households where the adults enjoy precisely those things will feel themselves more embraced if they enjoy them too.

Psychology aside, parents and carers wield almost absolute control of input in the first few formative years. They buy the music, or choose not to buy it. They attend the musical events, or they stay away. They switch the radio on, or off, or change the channel.

They change the channels in their infants' brains. There are neural pathways in your head that were etched by Radio 1 or Kiss FM or silence or the piano in the big leafy-smelling room or the cassettes that blended with car engine noise on long drives.

o   o   o

Babies, and the toddlers we met in the previous chapter, make no aesthetic judgments. They may dislike the experience of being forced to listen to music when there are other things they want instead (a feed, a tickle, a sleep, a roll in the grass) but they have no opinion on the artistry of Astor Piazzolla or Paul Weller.

For an infant, Paul Weller at the wrong moment is like having your arms twisted around to fit into a jumper when you're already feeling too hot. Piazzolla at the wrong moment is a spoon loaded with mashed vegetables nudging at your closed mouth. Sure, rocking in Daddy's arms to the rhythm of his favorite sounds is marvelous while he's rocking and you're comfy, but once your diaper is wet, or Mommy (who's been watching and smiling) leaves the room, the sounds are suddenly all wrong.

A few years further on, the child will learn that Paul Weller is not something enigmatic that issues forth from nowhere, like the weather. Paul Weller is a bunch of specific tunes that Daddy fetches from where the tunes are kept, in much the same way that he fetches cereal from a cupboard or Mommy produces clean underpants from a basket.

A year or two later still, Paul Weller is no longer a game that Daddy plays, but a person who isn't Daddy, a person with funny hair who makes music that Daddy likes and that *you* can like too, thus making Daddy happy.

A year or two later, you will discover the thrill of other, un-PaulWellery music that's been composed and marketed especially for a child your age, poppy perky twerky fizzy music by musicians who look like colorful toys, music that other children your age squeal over.

By the time you're nine, you may have learned that Paul Weller is "dad rock," and that dad rock is not a cool thing.

○ ○ ○

Peer groups are more adept than parents at teaching which responses are correct and incorrect. Most children can take their parents' love for granted, whereas membership of a peer group is more conditional, more subject to the whims of the ringleaders. Next time you pass by a playground or a schoolyard where kids appear to be frolicking in a carefree manner, remind yourself: This is a complex social ecosystem of dominance and submission. The top dogs can train potentially deviant members of the pack with simple tools like a shrug, a blank stare, a roll of the eyes, laughter.

For a child to love The Pussycat Dolls when all of her pals don't love them anymore requires almost superhuman self-confidence—especially since self-confidence tends to arise from doing stuff that inspires the approval of others. By contrast, the social rewards for pledging allegiance to the latest thing that everyone likes are instant and plentiful.

Yet, even as young humans strive to conform, they also become aware of a contradictory imperative—to be special. Capitalism promotes standardized mass consumption while at the same time mocking those who are mere "sheep." What is true individualism? Society tells you you're unique and rebellious when you align yourself with this or that market demographic.

Where does that leave your own distinctive personality and innate character? Surely we have a self that exists separately from outside influences?

Perhaps the best definition of character is the ability to love The Pussycat Dolls when all your peers have decided The Pussycat Dolls are worthless.

o o o

By the time children are old enough to understand that expressing opinions can charm or bite, flatter or scandalize, they're ready to be music critics. They're ready to use songs and artists as talismans to assert their own position on a perch of rightness, and to knock other people down from their perches.

Society, like music, needs dynamics. You can only feel yourself to be up high if others are low. In order for nine-year-old arbiters of taste to derive satisfaction from no longer liking Slade, there have to be some clueless losers who still do.

o o o

Adults are experts in this arena. With the aid of record reviews, TV documentaries, magazine articles, social media and conversations with other adults who've consumed such data, they develop a codified language in order to justify their tastes and distastes. They can talk about how Depeche Mode are "past their sell-by date" or else that the latest Depeche Mode album is "a return to form." They may not know the names of different flowers, plants and trees, but they can name music genres, motivated by the contemptuous look somebody gave them in 2007 when they let slip that they'd never heard of dubstep. They can refer to a "wall of sound," call things "overproduced" or "stripped-back," they can throw the word "seminal" around, they know how to add the "-esque" suffix to various nouns, as in "Beatlesque" or even "Stockhausen-esque."

Children don't have any of this verbal armory but neverthe-less need to join the game. They sense that ignorance is a sign of weakness, a baring of the soft underbelly to potential preda-tors. So, the young animal must know everything, or pretend to.

They learn fast. I've heard kids of eight making fine distinctions between "rock" and "metal," and I've seen them rolling their eyes in scorn as they characterize a song as "emo," a genre that they sense has less cred than it did a while back (i.e. when they were wearing a bib and regurgitating mouthfuls of rusk).

o   o   o

My favorite music-appreciating kids are the ones between three and seven. Gloriously confused, but brashly certain, they get by on bluffery alone with barely any tools to bluff with. Within a few short years they will develop the skills to toe the line, but right now their toes are too clumsy.

God bless clumsiness, I say. Grown-ups pretending to know things they don't know are a bore, but six-year-old ignoramuses can be a hoot.

Also, in their ignorance, they can sometimes deliver judg-ments of startling insight. I once showed a visitor's daughter a book full of photos of David Bowie, including early ones in his "mime artiste" phase when he wore pancake Pierrot makeup.

"When your face gets painted," she informed me, "it's hot and itchy. But you can't go home and have a bath until enough people have seen you." As an analysis of fame and its discontents, this is right up there with Bowie's "Fame," I feel.

On an internet blog, a parent reflects: "My three year old is generally fairly uninterested in music that isn't about trains or farmyard animals but since I bought a brilliant two cd ian dury best of a few weeks ago […] he's developed something of an ob-session with 'that funny man' and happily spends hours looking at the picture of him on the front cover while listening. as you'd expect, ['Hit Me With Your Rhythm Stick'] is his favorite […]

and he finds it mind bogglingly comical that a grown up sings 'hit me!' even though hitting is naughty. the first time he heard it, his reaction to the saxophone solo was an excited '…and this must be a mouse!'"*

Indeed, that saxophone solo is very like a mouse, and Ian Dury was exceedingly naughty.†

A *Guardian* journalist quizzes a bunch of six-year-olds on their responses to "classic rock" artists.‡ They opine that Nirvana would win *Pop Idol* for sure, and that The Who, Led Zeppelin, Cream and The Doors are all inferior to the punky-pop "boy band" Busted.§ (I can see their point. Depends what you're looking for, doesn't it?) Holly thinks Johnny Rotten "sounds like the baddie in Scooby Doo" and Sophie thinks Bob Dylan "sounds like he's just smelled something really bad, like cat poo."

These remarks are fine examples of how mercilessly apt children's perceptions can be. The prestigious music critic Simon Reynolds once referred to the "cathartic extremity" of Rotten/Lydon's "muezzin-wail,"¶ while Clinton Heylin admires his "razor edge, suggestive of a man tired of shouting the truth, locked in

* Comment by Pink Champale under review of "Hit Me With Your Rhythm Stick" on *Freaky Trigger* website, August 19, 2008.

† Pink Champale's son possibly understands Ian Dury as well as any grown-up Dury fan. There are, of course, wrinkly intellectuals who can peruse the lyrics of "Reasons To Be Cheerful, Part 3," nod sagely at the mentions of "John Coltrane's soprano, Adie Celentano," and point out that the Scotty in "Elvis and Scotty" is Winfield Scott Moore III (1931–2016). But do they truly appreciate, along with Ian and the three-year-olds, the joys of "being rather silly," "saying okey-dokey" or "sitting on the potty"?

‡ "Under eights v middle eights," Johnny Dee, *The Guardian*, January 31, 2004.

§ Busted's songs rely heavily on the three-note "Three Blind Mice" patterns so beloved by small children, and their music videos show three cheeky pals causing mischief. Prepubescent fans may not get the voyeuristic sex references but they love the sight of the lads constantly jumping around as if on trampolines, misbehaving at school, dancing on tables, throwing cake, falling out of trees and butting each other like puppies.

¶ Simon Reynolds and Joy Press, *The Sex Revolts: Gender, Rebellion, and Rock 'n' Roll* (Harvard University Press, 1996).

to an intensity that suggests this is one singer playing for keeps."*
Under the gaze of little Holly, Rotten stands revealed as a man
who has built his career on sounding like a cartoon baddie. Likewise, six-year-old Sophie has the measure of Dylan's trademark
sneer. On "Like A Rolling Stone" (one of the records that the
kids rated lower than Busted), Bob indeed sounds as though he's
taken a sniff of modern society and decided it smells of cat poo.

o o o

I'm not suggesting that children understand songs better than
grown-ups do. Songs have words, written by adults, and we
fellow adults have a fair chance of understanding what the authors meant by them—unlike a child, who has a small vocabulary and a limited experience of life. Or, as Grandmaster Flash
phrased it in "The Message," "a child is born with no state of
mind, blind to the ways of mankind."

When you or I hear Marvin Gaye's "I Heard It Through The
Grapevine," we know what a grapevine is, and what's meant
figuratively by hearing something through it. We may also have
experienced how it feels to learn of a partner's infidelity from
sources outside the relationship. We have a pretty good idea what
Mick Jagger meant by getting satisfaction. We know that the
jungle mentioned in "The Message" has no lions and tigers in it.

Adults are capable of overcoming ignorance with study. Children jump to conclusions because jumping is something they
can do whereas researching scholarly resources is not. If I played
a six-year-old "Expensive Shit" by Fela Kuti, she might speculate that there are mysterious people out there who try to sell
poo. If I explained to her that the lyrics are a sort of Nigerian
pidgin, she might go on to imagine that the poo came from a
special kind of bird.

---

*   Clinton Heylin, *Classic Rock Albums: Never Mind The Bollocks: Here's The Sex
     Pistols* (Omnibus Press, 1998).

In truth, even at my advanced age, I need to do quite a bit of research to get a grip on the song. The lines "Them go use your shit to put you for jail/Eh! Alagbon!" would mean nothing to me if I hadn't established that Fela Kuti was once detained in the Criminal Investigation Department in Alagbon Close, Lagos, while the cops waited for him to pass a bowel motion containing the joint he'd swallowed. This much I understand, but Fela's heavily accented patois in other lines of the lyric still puzzles me.

For six-year-olds, puzzlement is a scary option. They are small vulnerable creatures in a big world, and they have no way of guessing which things their fellow six-year-olds know and could exploit to assert dominance. So, to avoid being exposed as clueless, they bluff and hope to catch on as they go.

I, however, can assess how serious a handicap my ignorance is. I'm mindful that I'm living in a country where almost none of the people around me are Nigerians. And I know that most of the people I'm likely to meet—even the non-white ones—will have little or no idea who Fela Kuti was, and certainly no familiarity with his imprisonments. So I'm ahead. Moreover, I could win additional respect by declaring self-deprecatingly that I know next to nothing about African music—which is true in absolute terms, but untrue in most contexts I'll find myself in. I can therefore relax: I'm in no danger of being humiliated. Also, I earn extra cultural capital because Fela Kuti is "cooler" than Slade or Justin Bieber.

o o o

This game—a game we all play, with other members of our tribe, and with strangers whose musical erudition we gauge on sight—is far too complicated for children. It relies on a grasp of history and they don't know what history is; they were born yesterday. Also, they haven't learned enough words yet to play the game with. Their vocabulary is a starter kit.

No wonder, then, that a child's brain is a hotbed of mishearings and mondegreens. On the internet you may find numerous websites where people recall what, as children, they mistakenly thought singers were singing. Already primed by fables and fantastical fairy tales, the kids accepted that pop songs were populated with all sorts of grotesques—Elton John's Bennie with her "electric boobs and mower shoes," or the monstrous Eleanor Rigby, who keeps her face in a jar and "picks up her eyes" from a church.*

Such linguistic misconceptions don't mean that children can't tune in to the somber gravity of "Eleanor Rigby," or the jaunty silliness of "Bennie And The Jets." Songs carry meaning in their melodies, tones and textures. One of the first records I ever liked was "Vous Permettez, Monsieur?" by Adamo. At seven, and with no French, I could nevertheless sense the nervousness, the earnest striving to strike a dignified pose, undermined by the absurd grandiosity of the orchestral arrangement, the mocking kettledrums, the wisecracks of comic woodblocks. Do I appreciate the record better now that I understand what Adamo's singing about? No.

o   o   o

Purely instrumental music is, of course, a world in itself, where a listener aged five may be on equal footing with a listener aged fifty. Beethoven's Sixth Symphony sounds joyous and good-natured; his Ninth sounds grand and epic. The adagietto from Mahler's Fifth Symphony sounds terribly sad. Ravel's *Boléro* sounds languid and processional. Holst's "Mars, The Bringer Of War" sounds tense and threatening. Satie's *Gymnopédies* evoke wintry, melancholy tranquility.

Grown-ups can study the classical pieces I've just mentioned and learn more about them, including the historical circumstances of their composition. We can educate ourselves about the

---

* John Jones, posting his recollections to "Misheard Lyrics" on the *Am I Right* website, undated, sometime between 2000 and 2013. "Our church ran a charity to save the sight of children in Africa," Jones adds, "so I guess I made a church/eyes connection."

machinations of the music scene in Vienna in the early nineteenth century, or Paris in the 1920s. We can identify which noises are being made by which instruments. Prompted by Wikipedia, we can speculate whether the perseverating rhythm of *Boléro* might have been a harbinger of Maurice Ravel's dementia.

But does what we've learned allow us to have a response that's categorically more profound than a five-year-old could have? I doubt it.

Sure, no child could compete with the rhetoric that the eminent Prussian critic E. T. A. Hoffmann lavishes on Beethoven's Fifth Symphony, which he claims "leads the listener imperiously forward into the spirit world of the infinite! [...] the soul of each thoughtful listener is assuredly stirred, deeply and intimately, by a feeling that is none other than that unutterable portentous longing, and until the final chord—indeed, even in the moments that follow it—he will be powerless to step out of that wondrous spirit realm where grief and joy embrace him in the form of sound."* Such rhetoric, if we accept that it is more than waffle (and I'm not convinced it *is* more than waffle), boils down to the fact that Ernst Hoffmann felt quite overwhelmed and peculiar—in a good way—when he heard these sounds. That's a feeling uneducated children can have, too.

o   o   o

Being grown-up doesn't guarantee that you understand anything; you merely have the vocabulary to talk as if you do. An adult is capable of phrases like "sinister, stalking guitar riff," which sounds cleverer and more definitive than "Argh! Vampires!" But is it? Whenever we find ourselves feeling superior

---

* E. T. A. Hoffmann, in *Fantasy Pieces in Callot's Manner: Pages from the Diary of a Traveling Romantic* (1813), translated by Joseph M. Hayse (Union College Press, 1996). Note Hoffmann's sneaky disclaimer about the "thoughtful listener." If you can hear Beethoven's Fifth and not feel the way he did, you are obviously not thoughtful.

to a child who is expressing their naive opinion of what music is about, we should ask ourselves: What is it about my own response that's so much better than this child's?

When I was a child, I had no idea where the universe came from, why nobody on our ball-shaped planet falls off, or what a soul is. I still have no idea, but I can now use words like "Big Bang theory," "gravity" and "incorporeal essence." My verbal articulacy allows me to imagine I'm switching on little electric lights all around me, bulb after bulb after bulb, until I feel as though I've illuminated everything.

But the universe remains as dark as it ever was.

SORRY FOR YOUR LOST

Among the first few records I ever bought were Wings' *Band On The Run*, Deep Purple's *In Rock*, and Deep Purple's *Made In Japan*. Typical choices for a white boy growing up in the early 1970s in suburban Australia. I listened to them over and over and over, because I had very little else. Every note and drumbeat became familiar to me.

By my late teens, I'd evolved as a connoisseur. I decided that *Band On The Run* was a fair-to-middling effort, and that those Deep Purple LPs were sloppy, turgid and tiresome. So, I got rid of them. Better works of art took their place.

You may think you can predict where this reminiscence is heading—the fateful day when I reconnected with my love for these companions of my youth; the guilty desire to have them back; the upsurge of joy to hear those deeply embedded riffs again.

Nope. I'm wholly divorced from these records. When I hear them issuing from radios or other audio channels, I recognize their distinguishing features in the same way that I recognize the Pepsi logo or a picture of Napoleon, but nothing happens in my heart. The sounds mean no more to me than the latest unidentified pop confection wittering out of a passerby's phone. The intimate relationship I once had with "Smoke On The Water" has vanished without the slightest emotional trace.

I just don't understand nostalgia.

o   o   o

I'll bet you do.

o   o   o

I had an unhappy childhood, but many people have unhappy childhoods and it doesn't stop them being nostalgic. For most humans, memories are not a cache of happiness stimulants, they're something much more essential—more *existential*—than that. They're the only way of keeping a grip on who we are. They are pieces of a puzzle. Over a lifetime we get shaken about, and our puzzle of self disintegrates somewhat. We feel incomplete. Then we locate a piece we'd thought was lost, and it slots into place, and we feel relieved, restored, confirmed.

I'm using the words "we," "us" and "our" rhetorically here. Memory doesn't work that way for me. My neurodivergent brain has found other methods to hold me together. What methods? I don't know, I can't articulate them, because the language of identity has been devised by other people—people whose brains function the usual way.

o   o   o

I live in the present. I don't mean that philosophically, as if to say I've done work on myself, counseling myself to let go of the past and cease to be haunted by things that happened when I was four or twelve or twenty-three. I mean that my past has no particular resonance for me. It is merely data, most of which has been erased.

People who admire my fiction sometimes ask me why I don't write my *bildungsroman*, the autobiographical novel in which I tackle all the sensational stuff in my formative years. My Nazi dad, my incest-scarred mom, my abandoned siblings, the migrant camp, the bullying at school, the pedophile neighbor, the years of fringe-dwelling poverty. I tell them I don't feel it's my story to write. I'm in possession of some narrative details—some, not many—but I'd be guessing at the emotions. And if I'm going to make up emotions, I might as well write *Under the Skin* or *The Book of Strange New Things*.

o o o

What I lack is the Proustian rush of reconnection, the almost visceral sense of still being the me that once was. Proust got it from a tiny sponge cake, but for most people the most effective madeleines are musical. Songs and tunes are the things that magically unite the past and the present.

"Takes me right back," people say. Or: "The soundtrack of my life."

My life has no soundtrack. Nothing takes me back.

Sure, I recall that I've had good times and bad times, but those times are not linked with any music. Music is its own thing.

This has implications for how I listen compared to how *you* listen. If you are a normal person—and by "normal" I don't mean conformist or dull, but simply in possession of a brain manufactured to standard factory specs—you will relate to music very differently from me. You have to. You can't not.

o o o

In the introduction to this book, and the chapter "Who Doesn't Like Music?", I contend that very few people enjoy music purely for its own sake. For the great majority, music has merit only insofar as it serves a social purpose, or reminds them of their own lives and relationships. You may have felt I was exaggerating. Was I?

Open any music magazine, and you'll find lots of earnest discussion of Art. I'm flipping through the current issue of *Uncut*, and the reviews are full of phrases like "a kinetic, propulsive, riotous fury of krautrock" and "their most ambitious record so far."*

Uncut is a reasonably successful rock music publication. Almost fifty thousand people read it each month. YouTube is rather more successful. Billions of people visit it every day. Millions are motivated to leave comments under the music videos.

Here are some conversations that ordinary humans have had about Bryan Adams's "Summer Of '69." (Very similar comments are posted under virtually every song on YouTube.)

○   ○   ○

Human 1: "Music is such a time machine. It is not the song, rather the memories it touches. With this song, I go back. I go back to the 90s. I remember falling in love with my first girlfriend, I remember learning how to drive. I remember my first kiss. I can't listen to this song without tearing up. The lyrics of 'standing on your momma's porch you told me that you would wait forever and when you held my hand' take me back to my former girlfriend's mothers porch and I remember when she held my hand looked in my eyes and told me she loved me. My gosh what memories music strikes up."

Human 2: "To me it always be one of the best summers of my life. I was 19, had a car, and a girlfriend, and gas was only 30 cents a gallon! Great times."

Human 3: "Life just seemed so innocent and happy back then."

Human 4: "It's sad to see the decline of popular music, but in my opinion, all of the good music has already been made."

Human 5: "times went to shit. its more depressing and full of sex, and digital beats. not much talent nowadays."

---

*   Reviews of King Gizzard's *Omnium Gatherum* by Daniel Dylan Wray, and The Wave Pictures' *When The Purple Emperor Spreads His Wings* by Tom Pinnock, in *Uncut*, June 2022.

Human 6: "Its all down hill from here. Good music is in the past!"

Human 7: "My mom passed away when I was 5. She left behind the cassette tape with this single on it. She loved this song. :)"

Human 8: "Yea, it's so hard when you must grow up without the best woman you ever know"

Human 9: "I'm very sore for your loss. She will always be with you."

Human 10: "RIP mom. Love you."

Human 11: "Summer of '69, with my first love. Danny, 1951–2017, RIP. Best days of my life…"

Human 12: "I am sorry for your lost."

Human 13: "You will see Danny again one day."*

o   o   o

There's no editorial supervision on YouTube. The visitors are free to write whatever the music inspires them to write. They could write about Bryan Adams's guitar riffs, or the quality of his voice, or Tommy Mandel's organ part, or whether "Summer Of '69" is better or worse than other, less celebrated Bryan Adams songs, or, indeed, whether Bryan Adams is better or worse than other, more celebrated singer-songwriters.

Instead, they choose to talk about the things that ordinary people always talk about when music brings them together. They talk about themselves. They signal that they want to be friends. They assure each other that they understand each other even when they don't. They feel sorry for a fellow human when his or her child/parent/partner has died. They remember the times in their lives when they were happiest, and they expound the theory that civilization has gone downhill since then.

"Can someone help me get back to the early 80s?" asks a

---

*   "Bryan Adams – Summer Of 69 (Official Music Video)," uploaded to YouTube by Bryan Adams on November 4, 2008.

human under the upload of Spandau Ballet's grandiloquently nonsensical "Instinction." "The rest of my life didn't work out that well, but from 80–85 I know I was happy."[*]

○ ○ ○

"Pump Up The Volume" by M|A|R|R|S was the first chart-topping pop record substantially made up of samples. Words like "groundbreaking," "revolutionary" and "milestone" are regularly used by critics and historians to describe it. For those who are fascinated to know how it was made, the magazine *Music Technology* has an exhaustive interview with cocomposer Martyn Young, shining a torchlight into the intricate innards of his creative process:

"For the rhythm track we wanted to experiment with high resolutions, which was something we'd never done before. We used an [E-mu] SP12 [drum computer] in step time, which allowed us to shift beats in 96ths. Since then we've got a 192nd-of-a-beat resolution by treating two crotchets as one and then doubling the speed of the drum machine; it gives an even better feel."[†]

Over on YouTube, many thousands of people have added their thoughts about the significance of "Pump Up The Volume." Here is a typical selection:

Human 1: "i was 15 in 1987, now i'm 46. WTF going on?"

Human 2: "yes WTF thinking the same OMG I am old now."

Human 3: "I no how u feel ☹. I'm 43."

Human 4: "Im 48, i feel ya."[‡]

---

[*]   "Spandau Ballet – Instinction," uploaded to YouTube by Spandau Ballet on November 12, 2010.

[†]   Martyn Young, interviewed by Simon Trask for *Music Technology* magazine, November 1987.

[‡]   "M.A.R.R.S. – Pump Up The Volume (Extended Pump Up Mix)," uploaded to YouTube by Ramsey Hagar on May 21, 2016, and "M|A|R|R|S – Pump Up The Volume (Official Video)," uploaded to YouTube by 4AD on March 11, 2009.

The conversation carries on and on. Many other humans join in, revisiting the key events of their lives, reflecting on what they've learned as they've aged, urging youngsters to respect their parents and cherish their good health while they have the chance.

At no point do they venture even slightly in the direction of discussing the role of the drum computer in M|A|R|R|S's "Pump Up The Volume."

o o o

So, does this mean that the specific content of music—the stuff that the artists themselves strove to put into it, and which they hoped listeners might appreciate—is utterly irrelevant? Is the only relevant factor that the listener was at an impressionable age when he or she first heard the music, whereupon the music (whatever it may be) gets bundled into a repository in the brain, forced to mean whatever the individual wants it to mean?

Not quite. Nostalgia can grow on most surfaces, but some surfaces are more hospitable than others.

o o o

For the remainder of this chapter, we're going to dwell in one smoky, bohemian enclave of YouTube, where a combo with a deliberately ugly name can be found. They and their fans are going to prove my argument, and yet, in an odd way, disprove it too.

The Stranglers, fronted by biochemistry postgraduate Hugh Cornwell, got together in the mid-1970s and developed a repertoire of snarling, lurching pop-rock songs just in time for the punk craze of 1977. For several years they worked hard to establish and maintain their image as leather-clad thugs.

Then in 1981 they surprised everyone by releasing "Golden Brown," an elegant jazz ballad with a distinctly continental flavor. Unusually for a British hit record, it's in a minor key and

has a tricky time signature—a waltz interrupted every few cycles
by a toe-tripping bar of four beats. Its dominant instrument is a
harpsichord, and its lyric refers to a variety of heroin.

More than seven thousand fans have left comments under the
YouTube upload of "Golden Brown." In my insanely thorough
way, I've combed through those comments, and classified them
proportionally according to theme. This is the sort of challenge
my brain allows me to tackle, in lieu of allowing me to have a
soft spot for the first records I ever owned, or allowing me to
recall how I felt when my mom put my brother in an orphanage.

o o o

The themes overlap, but I would say that 18 percent of the comments focus on "Golden Brown" as a piece of music. In the
main, they're not what you'd call technical analysis ("When i
was 5 ABBA's super trooper done the same thing. It's so melodic but so desperately sad") but here and there someone mentions specifics:

"Those 'little sounds' that you're referring to is from an instrument called a harpsichord. I LOVE that sound. It's what gives
this song that classic, old, enchanting feel to it."

"It definately changes beat. Try counting the beats per bar
at the beginning and if you dont chage to 4 when you should,
youll lose it."

"Something magical about this cord structure. It pull you to-
wards the end and then throws you back in…never quite fin-
ishes and never let's go. Like a sneeze that is on the verge but
not happening."*

Compared to the 99-percent-proof music-speak that fills
Uncut, 18 percent is not much, especially since it includes a major
detour: a fake "1960s" version of "Golden Brown." Tech-savvy

* "The Stranglers – Golden Brown (Restored Music Video)," uploaded to
YouTube by benski tv on January 16, 2016.

musician Laurence Mason produced a clever mash-up of an archival Dave Brubeck Quartet clip with new saxophone overdubs, making it appear as though the Quartet played "Golden Brown" fourteen years before The Stranglers. Although he was up-front about how he created the illusion, many YouTube visitors are in too much of a hurry to read, so we get lots of "Bet you didn't know…"/"Wow, amazing!"/"No, you are wrong" chatter.

Other threads of discussion might be summarized thus:

"Hands up who else is here because this song was used in the soundtrack of *Umbrella Academy* Season 2/*Snatch*?" (4.5 percent)

"Just learned that Dave Greenfield has died of Covid. Keyboard genius! R.I.P." (6.6 percent)

"Those were the days, the 80s." (3 percent)

General philosophizing, inspired by the notion of nostalgia. (2.5 percent)

The joy of new friends in the atomized emptiness of cyberspace. "I used to think I was the only one that feel's like you!!" "So poetic, so true, thank you, I am in the same life with you, never known you but experiencing the same," "The pub I was talking about was on the Fulham Road opposite the Royal Brompton Hosp. Between Foulis Terrace and Neville Street Sth Ken… Not there anymore ☹," "In the current mess of Corona-19, it's great to connect via music. We are in lock-down here in Dubai, me, wife and kids. We're staying positive, and waiting for it to be over. In the meantime, rock on!!!!!" (9.6 percent)

Murmurs of approval/conversational ballast. "Good answer"/ "Cool story"/"Me too," etc. (10.9 percent)

"Who gives a fuck what you think? Not me, an industri- ous troll who visits many forums expressly to pick fights." (0.3 percent)

"'Golden Brown' was the favorite song of my relative/ loved one who died of cancer/in a car crash." Condolences, of varying levels of sensitivity. ("What sort of car was it? My first car was the infamous Datsun 120Y. Gee I miss that little beast. Sorry about your mate, way too young.") (1.5 percent)

"Yate is Welsh fkd during I Int. Rugby Union innit," and other contributions from individuals who go on YouTube while zonked. (0.6 percent)

"Да, действительно, бывают мелодии…," "Meine Zeit grandios," "Posiblemente no tengas ningún interés…" and so forth. (2.4 percent)

Conspiracy theories about the CIA, covert ops, murder cover-ups, etc., wholly irrelevant to "Golden Brown" or The Stranglers. (0.07 percent). This percentage is boosted to 2 percent if we count the people who feel compelled to insist that Dave Greenfield did not die of COVID.

By far the greatest number of comments concern the song's enigmatic lyric and the relevance it has to the individual listener. As is usual on the internet, hordes of commenters see it as their anointed duty to inform the world of a sensational revelation, not noticing how many other people have already done it. Thus:

"'Golden Brown' is actually about heroin. Not many people know that." (8 percent)

"What?! It's about heroin?? I always thought it was about
autumn/a girl." (2.5 percent)*

"I am a heroin addict/former heroin addict/I know everything there is to know about heroin. I've been clean for X
years/months/weeks/I have relapsed/Every day is a strug-
gle/Wish me luck, people." (13 percent)

Copious wishing of luck. "Hang on in there mate"/"You
can do this"/"Attend to Church activities whenever you
want heroin." (11 percent)

The remainder of the 100 percent, which overlaps somewhat with
the making of new friends and the philosophical meditations on
nostalgia, consists of childhood reminiscences. All different, all
eerily similar, memory after memory after memory—dozens
of vividly specific situations to which "Golden Brown" has become attached.

o o o

"Unforgettable" is a word that's often thrown around. Yet no
one understands how unforgettability *works*. There is presumably a biological process by which the brain decides which sights,
sounds and sensations to store permanently and which to let go
of, but the nature of this process is an enigma. Throughout our
lives, we have tremendously impressive experiences that we're
convinced we'll remember forever—and we swiftly forget them.

---

*   Of which percentage, a subpercentage refuse to accept the evidence. ("What
proof do you have?"/"I once read an interview where Hugh Cornwell said it
was about toast")

Yet we remember, in the most vivid detail, things that seem in-consequential and random. It's as if our tender young brains have a recorder nestled in them that opens its aperture only once in a while, taking an indelible impression of whatever happens to be around at that moment.

"I was 13 when this came out," reflects one of the "Golden Brown" lovers. "My instant memory when I hear this is of a family holiday in the North West of England—Silloth. We stayed on a caravan site with an outdoor pool. There was a short cut to the pool from the caravans through some bushes. Every time I hear this song I am walking through those bushes. This has been happening for forty years now and I still can't figure out why."

It's tempting to conclude that it doesn't matter which song is playing at that crucial moment when the brain's aperture opens—it could be anything. "Agadoo" will do. It's certainly true that even crass, inane, cynically manufactured songs can reduce listeners to tears of nostalgia about their beloved grand-father or a perfect summer day in 1987 or the back garden of the family home since demolished.

But there's a limit to which nuances of emotion can be evoked by which music. "Mr Blobby," if encountered at exactly the cor-rect age and circumstance, may associate itself with Mom or with long-lost school friends or that magic Christmas in 1993 before life went wrong. But it cannot take a listener on the mysterious journey that "Golden Brown" offers.

o o o

"I was 8," recalls Anton, "in England, and it was a miserable late autumn morning, raining, windy and cold. I was waiting for my mother to take me to football practice where I would get very cold chasing a ball around with a group of very rough boys (her idea to toughen me up I suppose). I was waiting in the lounge.

This song came on the telly and I was genuinely transfixed. I knew from that moment that there was a depth to existence that i had hitherto been completely unaware of."

In the other reminiscences archived under "Golden Brown," person after person struggles to articulate the idea that they'd heard the music somewhere before, perhaps in a previous life, or on another plane of existence. Yet it was new and strange, and its sadness seemed profounder than anything they'd previously been able to grasp.

"Mr Blobby" does not conjure this.

"I took a long and lonely London cab ride," remembers Jack, "from a school and friends I dearly loved—to Heathrow airport. We were flying my gravely ill brother home for good. I was a little kid adrift in fields of depth. 'Golden Brown' came on the radio. I have never forgotten that sound, that transparency. All the windows shaking and shifting as time and consequences blurred and magnified."

In these two recollections, so different in content but so similar in spirit, we encounter a word that's seldom used when ordinary people talk about music. One of these children felt himself to be "adrift in fields of depth"; the other glimpsed a previously unimagined "depth to existence." Neither of them necessarily wanted to go so deep. Neither of them was ready. But the music took them there.

o o o

All my life, I've craved depth. Maybe shallowness spooks me. Everyone else in this world seems to have roots, and a helplessly strong emotional investment in their own memories. Somehow, I've survived without those things. My past is not ever-present; it's a few anecdotes told to me by relatives, and a box of photographs that might as well be of someone else.

When I gaze into art, I don't want to see my own reflection.

I want to stare into mysterious waters, and be consoled by not being able to see the bottom.

Band On The Run, which I listened to again this morning, remains shallow. To my ears, *Memory Almost Full*, which Mc-Cartney released when he was in his sixties and I was in my late forties, is more substantial. My "Ever Present Past" and all that.

o   o   o

We will visit my childhood again, in passing, in a later chapter of this book called "The Tracks of My Tears." I don't think I'm spoiling any surprises by telling you in advance that "Il Silenzio" by Nini Rosso, the first record I ever heard,* is powerless to make me cry.

I revisited it just now on YouTube, to make sure. Nini blows his trumpet exactly the way I remember.

"my grandma recently passed away," a human informs us in the comments underneath the video. "this was her faviroute song. one night I remember walking into the kitchen and she was sat at the table with her eyes closed listening to it on her computer. i will never forget it now I do the same and shut my eyes when I hear I miss u grandma."

Other humans confirm that "Il Silenzio" never fails to bring tears to their eyes. "I have told my family this is to play at my funeral, it reaches deep into my soul and warms it," says one.

I do not miss my grandma. I do not miss any of the places I've lived. I regret that my father died so young, because if he hadn't, we might've gone on to have interesting conversations about music and what it was like to be a Nazi. But I can't honestly say I miss him. I don't miss my mother, who wasn't keen on music and chose not to have a funeral service. I paid for her to be buried, and someone told me where it was, but I've forgotten. It's in another country.

---

*   Probably. That I can recall.

I have a soul, I promise, and there are things that warm it. You've agreed to let me be your guide on this musical adventure. Can you trust me?

DIFFERENT STROKES
FOR DIFFERENT FOLKS

When I was growing up, *Sgt. Pepper's Lonely Hearts Club Band* was officially the greatest album of all time. This judgment was promulgated almost as a fact of physics or geography, like Mount Everest being the world's highest mountain.

Oh, I knew there were classical buffs who didn't respect pop—rarefied intellects who dwelled in regions even loftier than *Pepper*'s Everest, thus allowing them to look down at that peak from the heavens above. *They* liked to rank music too, but they didn't think in terms of albums; instead, they argued over which conductor or soprano scored the most points, or which pianist was the greatest interpreter of Chopin. It was all heavily historical and involved a lot of terminology I didn't understand.

Evidently, without even realizing that there had been an exam for admission into the world of classical appreciation, I'd flunked it. Some mysterious natural order had put me in my place. Twentieth-century popular music was what I was fit for.

I could take comfort, however, from a few eminent academics who deigned to recognize the merits of what the plebs liked. Professor Wilfrid Mellers declared that The Beatles were the greatest songwriters since Schubert, while the music critic of *The Times* pointed out that the group's songs employed "diatonic clusters" and "Aeolian cadences," whatever those might be.*

---

* The Mellers quote appears in many Beatles books but I've not been able to pinpoint its original source. Most likely it comes from Mellers's 1973 book *Twilight of the Gods: The Beatles in Retrospect.* The "Aeolian cadences" chap, writing for *The Times* in late 1963, was identified only as "Our Music Critic" but was probably

By the late 1970s, I was an avid reader of music magazines, whose staff were paid to listen to absolutely everything that came out and determine what was worth keeping and what could be safely ignored. Each year, these publications would cast their eye over the landscape of cultural achievement and verify that no newcomers had claimed the top spot. The landscape remained virtually changeless.* In the fullness of time, the supremacy of *Pepper* dropped a notch, giving way to a slightly revised status quo that would last for decades: the best albums, ever, by anybody, were *Revolver* by The Beatles and *Pet Sounds* by The Beach Boys.

Some years, *Pet Sounds* would nudge its way to number 1. That was not a problem; the rivalry between The Beatles and The Beach Boys was quite friendly, we were told. Brian Wilson and Paul McCartney were mutually respectful geniuses. Everyone understood that there was only a hairbreadth between the two *meisterwerks*.

o o o

"Everyone" did not include me. I wasn't keen on *Pet Sounds*.† Songs like "Wouldn't It Be Nice" struck me as cloying, quaint, infantile. The Beach Boys' earlier material was an even worse match for the young Michel. I didn't want a car, I didn't wish all girls could be California girls, and I had no desire to have

---

William Mann.

* As late as 2003, *Rolling Stone* had five Beatles albums in its Top 20, and officially reinstated *Sgt. Pepper* as the greatest album ever made. Public Enemy's *It Takes A Nation Of Millions To Hold Us Back* was the sole hip-hop album in 2003's Top 50— ranked at number 48, well below The Eagles' *Hotel California*. (Intersectionalists may be interested to note that there were almost no albums by women in the Top 500.)

† Later, I would discover *Smile*, the suppressed psychedelic follow-up to *Pet Sounds*, which was more up my street. And in the 1990s, Capitol exhumed its vaults and released a multidisc box set, *The Pet Sounds Sessions*, which featured Brian Wilson rehearsing the instrumental backing tracks with his crack team of session players—a transcendent experience mercifully free of those smarmy glee-club voices.

fun, fun, fun. As someone who suffered migraines in the Australian heat and who only visited beaches in winter when they were safely desolate, I was in the wrong demographic for albums with alarming titles like *Endless Summer*.

The Beatles were a different matter. I loved them. Songs like "The Inner Light," "Flying," "Blackbird" and "Martha My Dear" brought me joy. *Revolver*—which became officially the best album ever at some point during my young adulthood—contained "Taxman," "Eleanor Rigby," "For No One," "Tomorrow Never Knows" and several other fabulous tracks. It was an outstanding effort—dragged down a bit, I thought, by two half-assed Lennon contributions, "And Your Bird Can Sing" and "Doctor Robert." Also, "Yellow Submarine" outwore its welcome if you weren't six.

But, you know, different strokes for different folks.

o   o   o

In a book called *'Every Sound There Is': The Beatles'* Revolver *and the Transformation of Rock and Roll*, cultural historian Russell Reising identifies *Revolver* as a "cultural icon, approaching in its many avatars, its impact and its endurance the status of some of the definitive works of Anglo-American culture such as Herman Melville's *Moby-Dick* and James Joyce's *Ulysses*."* Gosh!

o   o   o

We are now a couple of pages into this chapter, and this may be a good moment to note that everyone mentioned in it so far has been white. All four Beatles were white. All of the Beach Boys, and the musicians who played on *Pet Sounds*, were white. The radio stations on which such pop music was aired were owned by

---

*   "Introduction: 'Of the beginning'" by Russell Reising, in *'Every Sound There Is': The Beatles'* Revolver *and the Transformation of Rock and Roll*, edited by Russell Reising (Ashgate Publishing, 2002).

white people, as were the record companies that marketed Beatles and Beach Boys product. The California girls celebrated in
Mike Love's lyric are "tanned" but we understand that this refers to the lotion-assisted bronzing of naturally white skin rather
than being brown by birth. The journalists who judged *Revolver*
and *Pet Sounds* to be number 1 and number 2 were white. The
publishers of the magazines and newspapers in which these findings were printed were white. The "definitive works of Anglo-
American culture," as name-checked by white historian Russell
Reising, were by Herman Melville and James Joyce—more white
guys. Ditto Wilfrid Mellers, Schubert, Chopin, the music critic
at *The Times*.

    And here I am, white too.

o   o   o

Alienated as I am from list-mongering and conversations about
"the best" and "the greatest," I'm aware that there's a demographic who might feel significantly more excluded from the
conversation than me—people who aren't white. So, I decided
to ask a few people of color what they think about the Top 10
musical artifacts produced by "our" culture.

    I make no grand scholarly claims about my statistical sample.
These are simply half a dozen non-white people I know personally or met in the course of my researches for *Listen*. Most
of them live in my town. Some are musicians, others not. The
only thing they have in common is that they all grew up in a
society where white people decided which sounds were superior.

♩♩

Samenua Sesher was born in North London in 1966, the same
year that *Revolver* and *Pet Sounds* were released. Her family roots
are in Montserrat, West Indies. In 2018, she was awarded an
OBE for services to the arts. She's a culture management con-

sultant and coach, conducts workshops on unconscious bias, and is the founder and director of the Museum of Colour.

o   o   o

Michel Faber: "In Britain, kids are taught by the education system and mainstream culture to believe there's a canon of great music which needs to be checked out. The implication is that if you're a really high-class brain, you'll gravitate to classical music, and the top three in that scene are Bach, Beethoven and Mozart. And if you're not serious or deep enough to appreciate classical music, you'll get into pop music. That's an assumption which isn't overtly stated but it's there. Were you aware of that when you were growing up?"

Samenua Sesher: "Definitely, definitely. My father bought me a piano and said 'You're going to learn' and I was terrible at it. But my parents were typical aspirational immigrants, and my father was very clear that appreciating classical music was a mark of a person, and instilling this in his child was really important. So he did."

MF: "Do you think he might also have felt—on an instinctive level, rather than explicitly thinking it through—that if you were to come up against racist attitudes but could sit at a piano and play a piece of Bach, people would perceive you differently?"

SS: "Well, you're speaking to somebody who does an Unconscious Bias workshop, and in that workshop I quote heavily from a book called *Whistling Vivaldi*,* which is named after a young man who had to deal with the fact his very existence as a tall African American male seemed to pose a threat to white people. And he realized that if he whistled tunes by The Beatles and Vivaldi, it reduced people's nervousness, because he was then perceived as someone who was less likely to stab or mug them.

---

*   *Whistling Vivaldi: How Stereotypes Affect Us and What We Can Do* by Claude Steele (W. W. Norton & Company, 2010).

So, yes, my father may have felt that classical music would in some way protect me, in the future…"

MF: "In pop music appreciation, there's this hierarchical concept—'The Top 100 Albums Ever Made,' a list that builds up to number 1, the best. Depending on the magazine or the journalist, the selection will be a bit different, but not very different—the same albums keep cropping up. At the very top, it's always *Pet Sounds* by The Beach Boys and *Revolver* by The Beatles. There'll be a few albums by black artists in the Top 100—*What's Going On* by Marvin Gaye, maybe one by Jimi Hendrix or Stevie Wonder—but they'll be artists who were signed to huge multinational corporations and who were thoroughly integrated into the mainstream music industry and whose albums were bestsellers. Whereas the albums by white artists don't need to have sold very well; they can be 'left-field' or 'niche.' Were you aware of that ranking process growing up, and how did you feel about it?"

SS: "Yes, I was very aware of it because I was an avid reader of music magazines and music papers. But I was a rebellious young person, so I thought it was bollocks, fairly early on… Still, that bullshit actually helped shape me, because a lot of my own musical journey was in reaction to that. A refusal to engage with those [culturally recommended] things all through my life.

"It's funny: for my fiftieth birthday party, I knew I'd have friends in their sixties, and their children, a real wide range of ages, so I decided to organize the music playlist by decades. Which made me listen to music that I'd ignored when I was in my teens. And I'd go: 'Oh my God—I love it! These people were so *talented*!' It meant I was discovering stuff by The Rolling Stones and The Beatles at forty-nine."

MF: "OK, let's go through a very typical Top 10 from the era when you and I were growing up. This one comes from *Rolling Stone* magazine,[*] but it could just as well have come from *Q*,

***

[*] In 2020—a preposterously late date—the list was finally overhauled to include

Mojo, *The Guardian*, anywhere in our mainstream culture. It's a list which most white music fans of a certain age would instantly recognize as a list of the greatest albums ever made.

"First off, supposedly the greatest album ever, the pinnacle of musical perfection—*Revolver* by The Beatles. Do you know this album?"

SS: "I know it. I heard a few of the songs when I was in my teens, when I was hungry to know what was out there, and I thought [shrugs] *Ew, they're OK*. I was just very underwhelmed. I still don't think, even amongst Beatles albums, that *Revolver* is the best one."

MF: "How did you feel about the light in other people's eyes, as they expounded the album's importance?"

SS: "I've always been naturally mistrustful of the idea that a certain set of people had this taste that was to be lauded above other people's taste. It confused me that large groups of people found things that *I* thought were really average so amazing. I'm like *Really? You're all thick*."

MF: "What age are we talking about here?"

SS: "Twelve, thirteen."

MF: "Most kids at that age are desperately trying to figure out what they need to do to be accepted into a peer group, a gang…"

SS: "Yeah, I obviously made a choice: *Fuck that*. But I think my bloody-mindedness is also partly laziness, because I would've had to pretzel myself in order to fit in."

MF: "Many kids *do* pretzel themselves. They spend a colossal amount of energy on that project."

SS: "I just could not spare that energy, because it would've been so convoluted. How could I pretend to *this* group that I didn't love Prince, but pretend to Prince fans that I didn't love ABBA? I just wasn't capable, it would've been too big a project for me, because, you know, I also loved Bach… And headbang-

---

more people who weren't white males. Marvin Gaye's *What's Going On* was moved to the top spot, with *Pet Sounds* at number 2 and *Revolver* at number 11.

ing music: the Dead Kennedys, Iron Maiden... And then in the 1990s, a friend of mine introduced me to African music and the WOMAD festival, and oh my God, it was like an expression of a self I didn't know I had. I felt like a newborn...like a born-again Christian. I felt like it unlocked and liberated some part of me."

MF: "Does this raise the issue of white people being custodians of black music? Because WOMAD was founded by Peter Gabriel. And the most powerful champions of African music in Britain have been people like John Peel, Andy Kershaw, Joe Boyd..."

SS: "Well, there's a couple of dynamics here. One is that we are a minority. So the majority of the gatekeepers are going to be white, for no other reason than the numbers. But there are other reasons. [laughs] Because as a black person, you're allowed to be an expert on your own thing but you can't be an expert on anybody else's thing. As a white person, you get to be an expert on everybody's thing because that's your purview. There's also the monetary issue—the money that enables you to do the thing that you want to do."

MF: "*Pet Sounds*. Do you know this album?"

SS: "Love it!"

MF: "How did you become aware of it?"

SS: "Don't know. This is one of those things I talk about in my Unconscious Bias workshops—the way you're informed of something without realizing you're being informed of it. I suspect many if not all of the albums on that list might qualify. You know *of* them; you may even know all the lyrics, but you have no idea how it got in. You don't own the album, you didn't consciously learn the lyrics, but somehow you just did. And *Pet Sounds* is in that category. Especially [sings] 'Wouldn't It Be Nice...' I mean, I have no idea where I heard it, but I did, and I loved it, it made think about sunshine and happiness. I've never bought it, I've never owned it, but... Do I like most of the tracks on *Pet Sounds*? Yes."

MF: "Here's a question about cultural appropriation, depending on how you conceive of that issue. One of the tracks on *Pet Sounds*, 'Sloop John B,' is a version of a folk song from the Bahamas. The song was originally composed and sung by descendants of the slaves that the British brought with them when they colonized the archipelago."

SS: [aghast] "Noooo…"

MF: "It was 'collected' by a wealthy white cartoonist who 'owned' one of the islands, and that was heard by the white poet Carl Sandburg, who included it in his 1927 sheet music book *The American Songbag*, which made its way into the repertoire of a white 1950s Californian folk trio called The Kingston Trio, whose version was liked by one of the Beach Boys, who played it on the piano to Brian Wilson, who then decided to do it for *Pet Sounds*.

"Now, some people would say that this is just the way folk music works, and it's got nothing to do with race. Musicians in ancient times sing songs, subsequent generations of musicians copy and preserve and adapt them, and this is how music survives. Other people argue that this is cultural appropriation. Black people create something, white people take it, the black originators get forgotten, the white adapters get celebrated. It's a complex topic, but what's your gut response as I'm talking to you now? What are your thoughts as you hear the story of 'Sloop John B'?"

SS: [deep sigh] "Disappointment."

MF: "Disappointment in what or who?"

SS: [very long pause] "I'm just so sad."

MF: "Sad about humans?"

SS: "Sad about the way people who are supposed to be intelligent can't understand this stuff. Sad about the fact that it's so difficult for us to understand that both of those truths can be the case. That, sure, this is absolutely the way music travels, and the way lots of culture travels, but at the same time, we live in a capitalist world, where people make millions of pounds from something that was created by somebody else, and if that creator comes from a group of people who've been oppressed for hundreds of years, and who've been culturally denuded, this has implications. And those implications will continue perpetually, and that's going to impact on the oppressed people's ability to live their lives and survive. And that those two truths are in conflict."

MF: "Who is the 'we' that can't understand this?"

SS: "Actually, all of us. I quoted Angélique Kidjo on this, last year, for one of my workshops. She talks about acknowledgment. She says that if you don't acknowledge where it comes from and you're getting the money then that's theft. Whereas if you acknowledge that you're influenced by something, that it took you to where you are, then that's part of the creative journey. That's respect."

MF: "The credits on 'Sloop John B' are 'Trad, arr Brian Wilson...'"

SS: "Well, the word 'trad' is a whole exhibition in itself. Trad, i.e. nickable. We can *use* that, because somebody who doesn't expect to get paid for it created it some time ago."

MF: "Do you believe that a way forward might be, instead of saying 'trad,' saying 'Unknown person from the Bahamas'?"

SS: "Absolutely! Give the credit to the place, give the credit to the island. It's hugely important. It blows my mind that people can imagine that it isn't."

MF: "The other albums in *Rolling Stone*'s Top 10 are *Sgt. Pepper's Lonely Hearts Club Band*, *Rubber Soul* and the double White Album by The Beatles, *Highway 61 Revisited* and *Blonde On Blonde* by Bob Dylan, *Exile On Main Street* by The Rolling Stones, *London Calling* by The Clash, and the solitary album by a non-white artist, Marvin Gaye's *What's Going On*. How do you feel about that mix?"

SS: "I don't feel any way about it, because I don't have a Caucasian-centric worldview, it's not the way I see the world. But I know it's the way most people see the world, and many people who look like me are going to have that way of seeing the world too. It's not surprising to me. It is what it is."

MF: "There are two—at least two—possible ways forward. One is to work to change popular culture so that there are more people of color in that Top 100 list. The other way is to say 'What's the point of this "Top 100" stuff anyway? Why do we need to grade and rank things? Can't we evolve beyond needing to make these sorts of lists? It's so blokey.'"

SS: [sighs] "I think the desire to make these lists is up there with the desire to be in a pack, quite frankly."

MF: "In women as well?"

SS: "Yeah… I think we just list different things. Favorite handbags and perfumes? We'll rank music too, and our favorite artists. I'm thinking of how *Songlines* [the UK's foremost 'world music' magazine] would do their lists of the top African artists, and they would always have Youssou N'Dour at the top and I'd think *Really? Where the hell is Oliver Mtukudzi?* He is *bettah*, end. We can talk about all the different ways, lyrically and so on, but…he's just *bettah*.

"I think ranking is a need to organize our thinking, and our music appreciation is part of our thinking, part of our emotional lives. We need to ascribe value. 'What's my favorite stuff? What would I leave to my child?'"

MF: "It's all those things, but I think it's also, particularly in the modern world, a way of keeping the sheer unmanageable profusion of everything at bay."

SS: "Yes, that's exactly what I mean, it's a need to order."

♩♩

Singer, songwriter and keyboardist Art Terry grew up in Los Angeles and lives in London. He presents the radio show *Is Black Music* on Resonance FM. As well as fronting his own ensembles, he's a member of Stew & The Negro Problem. He tunes pianos on the side.

o   o   o

I began by asking Art to name the last piece of music he'd se-lected for his own enjoyment. "Donovan's *Mellow Yellow* album," he replied. "Though I chose it because the producer I'm cur-rently collaborating with said he has been listening to it recently."

In response to the question about the education system and the implied hierarchy with classical music at the top:

AT: "I was somewhat aware that some art and culture was being forced on us (Shakespeare, European Classical). Yet I couldn't square that with the fact that there was so much rele-vant, deep and beautiful work happening right then and there which was being frowned upon, for instance soul music.

"There was a general counterculture spirit in the air that en-couraged the questioning of authority in the 1960s. And as the 1970s set in, that spirit helped fuel a quest for identity within Black Nationalism which began confirming some of the African American folk tales. I was around eight years old when some-one casually pulled me aside and said you know Queen Victo-ria's grandma was Black."

In response to the white-dominated Top 100/Top 10 lists:

AT: "I never really listened or paid attention to 'White' music till 1976. When I was a kid I wouldn't miss the Beatles cartoons or the Monkees TV program. And you would hear the hit songs in the street. But it was such a creative time for Black Music, that you didn't dare change your radio dial away from the local soul station KGFJ!*

"The only two exceptions I remember to this rule were Elton John's 'Bennie And The Jets' and Bowie's 'Fame.' For some rea-son those two songs crossed over onto the Black radio stations. Perhaps because both tracks utilized falsetto vocal techniques

---

*   The radio station formerly known as KGFJ is nowadays known as KYPA and broadcasts solely in Korean. There is an unrelated KGFJ broadcasting Christian content to white people in Montana. Bad news for soul fans in either case.

which were popular in soul music at the time. We certainly didn't have any time for rocky music. That was 'White boy' stuff.

"That all changed for me in 1976 when it was clear that Black Music had become co-opted by big money and was being watered down to disco. So for the first time I turned the dial away from KGFJ and opened my ears and mind."

The mention of *Revolver* sparked a reminiscence illustrating how The Beatles were intertwined in Art's family history.

AT: "I'm actually not the first person in my family to live in England. My Uncle Jack was in the service and based in Liverpool during the 1950s. He married Aunt Hilda, whose mother was white English and whose father was from Africa.

"In 1976, I was on a family holiday trip. I was just beginning to be interested in 'White' music. So when we went to visit them in the summer of 1976, I went straight to my older cousin's record collection, put on the headphones and The Beatles' White Album. As 'Martha My Dear' began I started to realize what The Temptations meant when they sang 'The Beatles' new record's a gas!' on 'Ball Of Confusion.'

"*Revolver* means less to me. I am more affected by psyche-pop, so *Sgt. Pepper* (particularly the art-song masterpiece 'A Day In The Life') has been a bigger influence than *Revolver*. But I can appreciate *Revolver*'s comparative simplicity.

"Actually, I came to adore all The Beatles' work. I still consider their albums as the ultimate pop prototype.

"*Pet Sounds* and The Beach Boys are totally different for me. Being a native Californian, The Beach Boys were on the radio and in the air everywhere. It was just part of the culture. So you took them for granted. I didn't like them or dislike them. They were just another cute thing about living on the West Coast. Like tacos, hot weather or gospel music. But for that reason they were more personal than the British bands.

"The first time I heard the name Brian Wilson I must have been at least eighteen years old. It was an interesting late-night

TV program which basically proposed that The Beach Boys were as great as The Beatles. At that point I felt there was no comparison, and that there was no way The Beach Boys were as cool as The Beatles. I thought it was ridiculous!

"The thing was, I had never listened to a Beach Boys album. Did they actually even make a real album? I assumed it was all greatest hits compilations. Surely nobody took them seriously? And what was *Pet Sounds*? An album or some kind of bikini beach film?

"Then it hit me one day when I was driving down the Pacific Coast Highway by the beach. 'God Only Knows' came on. And God only knows I must've heard that goofy song hundreds of times to no effect. But instead of turning the dial like I normally would whenever a silly Beach Boys song came on, I turned it up and really tried to listen for the first time.

"I don't know how I continued to drive. I may have pulled over. But what I do remember is it lifted me out of my seat beyond the sunny LA skies, and I had to press my mental body back down in my seat to stop it from floating away with their French horn player and vocal harmonies.

"Now I realize that The Beach Boys have been a subliminal and powerful influence on me. Even before they cut records. What they represent is part of what and who I am as an artist. That is, they have what was best about the West Coast musical landscape. The doo-wop, rock 'n' roll, dreamy prepsychedelic vision of Californian pop culture. *Pet Sounds* confirmed that for me."

My question about "Sloop John B," and whether the copying of "traditional" songs is just the way folk music naturally works or whether it's racist appropriation, prompted the following:

AT: "As an ignored Black artist my gut response is 'I'm not surprised.' But actually I believe the two truths can coexist together comfortably. I think we all borrow from each other artistically, and reshape and expand things into new creations. I don't have a problem with that.

"The separate question is one of economics. Why do we allow people of European origin to dominate us economically? Or is the question: Why do we allow them to dominate us culturally? I have always believed that America has been the culturally dominant force since the 1920s. And that Black culture is the most influential in America.

"As a radio producer I love to discover these connections. That is what my radio show *Is Black Music* is all about. I will definitely be following this up and adding 'Sloop John B' to our playlist alongside the Black Beach Boys album *Holland*, which features Blondie Chaplin and Ricky Fataar."*

MF: "Staying on the cultural appropriation point for a moment—Samenua Sesher pointed out that the whole notion of 'trad' is deeply problematic. She feels that a song like 'Sloop John B' should be credited to the people of the Bahamas. I'm not sure what I think about that. On the one hand, I feel that when songs go back as far as ancient Persia or medieval Europe, it becomes impossible to link them to a specific place or community—which chimes in with the idea of folk music being something that evolves organically. On the other hand, I'm well aware that when Jimmy Page and Robert Plant of Led Zeppelin credited some of their songs as 'Trad, arranged Page & Plant,' they did so in the full knowledge that those songs were written by black blues artists to whom they didn't want to pay royalties."

AT: "Crazy, isn't it? The music business is so screwed up and

---

*   Guitarist Blondie Chaplin and drummer Ricky Fataar are both South Africans. "Sail On, Sailor," on which Chaplin sang lead vocals, is as soulful as The Beach Boys ever got, and the two new black members also contributed an anti-apartheid song—which predictably was bumped off the final track list. In any case, *Holland* would prove to be The Beach Boys' last artistically credible album. Chaplin and Fataar left, and the band was restructured into a nostalgia act.

dodgy. There is so much that is problematic, including the way 'trad' is used.

"I'm sure you know that the reason why the 'songwriter takes all' thing was established way back in the 1920s was so that the White producers could claim all the royalties from the Black performers. Have you ever read *Rhythm and Business* by Norman Kelley?"*

I hadn't, then, but I sought it out after my interview with Art. Kelley's overview of the ways black musicians have been used as "plantation labor" by the music industry makes depressing reading, although, arguably, it's an insight not so much into racism as into corporate capitalism's merciless disempowerment of creative humans generally.

MF: "At number 4 in the best albums ever, we have *Highway 61 Revisited* by Bob Dylan. Again, do you know it? How familiar are you with it?"

AT: "We didn't discover till fairly recently that the man behind Bob Dylan was his Black producer Tom Wilson.

"Tom Wilson represents better than anyone what our radio program *Is Black Music* is all about. Here is the one producer who seems to have been at the turning corner of almost every artistic leap that music made from the early sixties to the midseventies.

"He produced the first record for Sun Ra, Cecil Taylor, The Velvet Underground, The Animals, Frank Zappa and Soft Machine. And he produced four of Dylan's first five albums as well as guiding him into the world of electric guitars.

"Something separated them midway through the making

★ *R&B: Rhythm and Business: The Political Economy of Black Music* (Akashic, 2002). The bit Art is recalling is Kelley quoting from Simon Frith's *Sound Effects: Youth, Leisure and the Politics of Rock 'n' Roll* (Pantheon, 1981): "It is songwriters who get royalties when records are sold or broadcast, not their performers, and black singers who were popular in the 1920s and 1930s were systematically cheated out of their due returns. Their music, however distinct, was in a legal sense 'composerless,' and it was white publishers who rushed to copyright the resulting 'spontaneous' compositions."

of the *Highway 61* album. But not before he produced 'Like A Rolling Stone,' which was a turning point for Dylan.

"I love Dylan, but *Highway 61* is not one of my favorites. I think my favorite would have to be *Blonde On Blonde*. 'Sad Eyed Lady' is an incredible feat."

MF: "Highway 61—the highway, not the album—runs all the way from Ontario to New Orleans, passing near the homes and birthplaces of some of the blues pioneers like Muddy Waters, Son House and Charley Patton. Dylan was born in Duluth, Minnesota, right by the highway, but was actually raised in Hibbing, a mining town seventy-five miles inland. In any case, both towns were pretty much all-white.

"Yet, in his memoir, *Chronicles*, Dylan talks about his origins like this: 'Highway 61, the main thoroughfare of the country blues, begins about where I began. I always felt like I'd started on it, always had been on it and could go anywhere, even down in to the deep Delta country… It was my place in the universe, always felt like it was in my blood.'

"This is Dylan positioning himself in a blues tradition, taking his place amongst Son House, Muddy Waters and the rest. What we see here is one of the most common practices in pop-rock music—the attempt by white artists, usually from comfortably-off backgrounds, to align themselves with a blues or folk tradition founded in poverty and hardship. We see this even more in what's supposed to be the seventh-greatest album of all time, *Exile On Main Street* by The Rolling Stones.

"This was recorded in a luxurious rented villa in the south of France where the Stones were staying as tax exiles at the time. Keith Richards was spending thousands of pounds a week on heroin and Mick Jagger had just married Bianca in a lavish ceremony in Saint-Tropez. *Exile On Main Street* was full of songs about being low-down, poor and dirty, sung in an imitation of the old black blues singers' diction. There was some Southern gospel as well, pulled off with great panache by Mick Jagger, a former London School of Economics student from Dartford, Kent.

"How do you feel about these white guys trying to position themselves as honorary members of the black community? Do you feel it's OK?"

AT: "I do dig the Stones. I agree with everything they've been accused of. But I think they created something new and different to the music they stole from. Ironically, if it wasn't for people like Jagger and Richards, I may never have known the far-reaching value of Black Music. I think it's part of the 'prophet is never appreciated in his own country' syndrome.

"So many Black American artists have first found acceptance in Europe through the decades."

Art's observation is well-documented. European respect for African American art forms goes back to the late nineteenth century. By the mid–1960s, many of the American blues and gospel pioneers were considered has-beens in their native country, trapped in a worst-of-all-worlds situation: still hampered by racism, yet no longer considered a thrilling novelty by white audiences, and rejected by black audiences as a reminder of the low status and rural poverty that aspirational African Americans were at pains to leave behind. Sharp tailored suits in rich colors, choreographed dance routines and the exultant beat of Motown were the signifiers of Now. Those old guys were signifiers of the past.

In Europe, however—particularly France and Britain—young hipsters and scholars alike were hungry to see the original exponents of the music they'd taken to their hearts. Black artists who could no longer fill a club in Chicago or Mississippi were given rapturous receptions in Paris and London.*

---

* Among the barely believable—but glorious—musical events that occurred in Britain in the sixties was *Blues and Gospel Train*, a concert filmed for Granada TV in 1964, featuring Sister Rosetta Tharpe, Muddy Waters, Sonny Terry and Brownie McGhee, Otis Spann, and the Reverend Gary Davis strutting their stuff on a disused railway station in Manchester. As The Supremes and

MF: "The only album by a black person in the Top 10 is *What's Going On* by Marvin Gaye. What's your history with it?"

AT: "Marvin and Motown are so ingrained into my experience of soul music. *What's Going On* definitely made us shut up and listen. The song was on the radio and it was a hit. I had the album at my house as a young teen. I didn't totally get it as I do now. I knew 'Inner City Blues' was great, and it was played on the radio and was just as popular as 'What's Going On.' But the rest of the songs kind of went over my head.

"It was only when I performed the entire album as a duet with saxophonist Mussinghi Edwards that I recognized that 'What's Happening Brother' must be the most profound piece compositionally. It just continues to modulately ascend."

MF: "If you were made responsible for choosing one album by a black artist to insert into a mainstream magazine's Top 10, what would it be?"

AT: "Blue Magic's second album, *Magic Of The Blue.* Though it was fairly popular in the Black community, it is relatively unknown here and a personal favorite of mine. It was produced by the guitarist Norman Harris. I like their confidence coming off of the first album, which was a hit. Every song is strong. It's kind of like Arthur Lee meets Gamble and Huff. Ted 'The Wizard' Mills is the lead vocalist and shares in some of the songwriting…

"I think critics listening from outside Black culture don't quite get how this type of feminine and elegant vocal falsetto is as important a part to Black expressiveness as the more macho and gritty approaches that an Otis Redding or James Brown might take.

"I think a lot of critics foreign to Black America don't understand that our value system isn't simply reflected in gritty art

---

The Four Tops were carving a new space for black performers in the States, Sister Rosetta was showing off her hugely more accomplished artistry in the northwest of England, with Eric Clapton, Jeff Beck, Keith Richards and Brian Jones goggling at her from the pale-faced crowd.

forms like blues. We are complex, and are anxious to transform our horrible past struggles into a new glamorous future while somehow being true to our roots.

"This album does that somewhat. *Magic Of The Blue* culminates with two exquisite pieces, the last of which—'Looking For A Friend'—is comparable to Brian Wilson's 'Surf's Up' moment in its climactic resolve."

Asked whether he thought the best way forward was to get more non-white people into the Top 100 or to discredit the whole idea of authoritative rankings:

AT: "The latter, ideally. It's fun to talk about these things and make lists, but it doesn't reflect the reality that art is not a competition and that truly original art is incomparable."

♩♩

Maria Uzor, aka Girl In A Thunderbolt,* is a singer and composer who mixes electronica, soul, pop, dub and Caribbean rhythms. She's one half of Sink Ya Teeth, who describe themselves as an English post-punk dance-infused duo. Uzor is based in Norwich, with roots in Nigeria and Barbados.

○ ○ ○

In response to the question about youngsters being educated to feel that classical music was superior to pop:

MU: "I think that may have been the case at some point, but when I was growing up the canon seemed to be less about 'classical versus pop' and more about music made by white men with guitars versus music made by people of color, with the only exception being jazz (which I think is quite cerebral and, as such, probably is identified closely in some people's minds with classical music). I never really mixed with people who were

---

*   A nod to a T. Rex song, "Girl In The Thunderbolt Suit."

bang into classical music so I'm not really aware of that divide, particularly among my contemporaries.

"I don't mind a bit of that stuff, though. Chopin's pretty decent. And Mozart's got a few tunes!"

Commenting on the Top 100 albums ever made:

MU: "I would hazard a guess that most of the journalists who compiled these lists (and indeed the readership) are white men, and I guess they just want to see themselves reflected back. It reinforces their sense of identity and strokes the ego a bit.

"There are some great albums on those charts, and I'm hugely inspired by all the bands and artists that you give as examples. It would be good if people felt able to delve further afield, though. I think people are lazy. I think journalists are *very* lazy! [grins]

"I love *Revolver.* I'm still eternally enchanted by the soundscape of 'Tomorrow Never Knows.' I discovered the album when I was about sixteen, and I still find myself rediscovering it every couple of years and being completely and unequivocally floored by it every time. I was obsessed with The Beatles (and the 1960s) when I was a teenager so it holds very fond memories.

"*Pet Sounds* is another great album (with the exception of 'Sloop John B'!). In my final year of art school I painted all my canvases with that album on repeat in my headphones! It's not an album that I come back to much, though, not like The Beatles or *What's Going On.* Maybe I overdid it at art school."

On the problematic history of "Sloop John B":

MU: "Cultural appropriation is definitely a thing, and I think it was exploited a lot more in the past. I think today white people are a bit more aware of their history of imperialism and of the need to pay homage to the originators so as not to perpetuate that rhetoric. (I know The Rolling Stones paid homage some in the 1960s, but I think they were one of the few bands who did at the time. Led Zeppelin were terrible for it.)

"By the same token, though, I do also think that a lot of people mistakenly accredit certain types of music to white originators without being aware of the black origins. I think that's to do with the stories that were being told around music. Who was it who said that history is written by the victors?

"I've found that most of my friends of all colors who are into music are aware of the various origins, though."

On the supposed number 4 in the Top 10 albums ever made, *Highway 61 Revisited* by Bob Dylan:

MU: "Haha! I used to bike around my hometown of Norwich at nighttime drunk to this! Good times! I'm not a huge Dylan-head but I'm glad he went electric for that album."

On the attempts by The Rolling Stones to obscure their middle-class whiteness and claim a place in the black blues pantheon:

MU: "They're not the first white boys to want a bit of the dark allure of something beyond the confinement of middle-class suburbia. Rock music was built on this very thing. It strokes their ego and gives their art a fleeting authenticity which they can dip in and out of. (Pulp wrote 'Common People' about a similar thing.) I don't have a problem with it. It's pantomime. Performance. I guess the problem arises when one is not able to see through it.

"In 1960s America things were very different to how they are in 2020s UK though. I imagine if I lived in Alabama at that time I'd have a very different take on it."

On Marvin Gaye's *What's Going On*:

MU: "I was playing this album again earlier today! One of my all-time favorites! I don't remember when I first came across it. It's been a constant companion throughout my life.

"If a *Rolling Stone* journo asked me to suggest the greatest albums ever made by black artists, which ones would I put forward? Cor, that's a tough one! I don't listen to music in terms of 'greatest album ever made.' There are some albums by black artists that I always come back to, such as *What's Going On*, *Otis Redding Sings Soul*, Coltrane's *A Love Supreme*, *3 Feet High And Rising* by De La Soul, *Nightclubbing* by Grace Jones…"

On the need to rank and list:

MU: "Haha! It *is* a bit blokey and reductive, isn't it! It's the equivalent of collecting trainers, or likes on Instagram. I think it comes down to the ego again, doesn't it? Everything comes down to the ego in the end!"

♩♩

Ilā Kamalagharan, formerly known as Anil Sebastian, is co-founder and director of the London Contemporary Voices choir, who've worked with Grammy-winning artists including Imogen Heap and U2. She has composed soundtracks for films, ballets and fashion shows. I first heard her beauteous voice at a gig by Hrím, a trio whose other members were Icelandic and Japanese. Then she turned up on a favorite album of mine in 2018, Nakhane Touré's *You Will Not Die*. Malaysian in origin, and nonbinary, she is also cofounder and director of Trans Voices.

o o o

MF: "Were you aware of this ranking/grading and 'best thing ever' stuff as you were growing up, and how did you feel about it?"

IK: "Structural racism in the music industry is rife. This is unsurprising when the people deciding what music we listen to are near on 100 percent white, privately educated and male both in the US and the UK. BAME and queer artists have been used by brands and labels for years to give an impression of diversity and political values that appeal to younger audiences. But behind all that sits quite a different beast. I think those rankings/gradings are interesting for these reasons.

"I'm also aware that they're usually compiled by white male journalists for a white male audience so it's unsurprising to me that they'd represent what you'd typically see in the record collections of those people.

"Don't get me wrong—I have a great love for most of the music that frequently appears in these rankings—but I think they're becoming considerably less important to younger audiences. I'm not sure they read [those articles] at all in fact."

On The Beatles' *Revolver*:

IK: "I am indeed familiar with it—it's pretty hard to escape I think. Interestingly, 'old music' is outselling 'new music' for the first time—and The Beatles rank extremely highly among young audiences who are only just discovering their music. It's undeniably incredible music. The song writing and production is pioneering and utterly magnificent."

On The Beach Boys' *Pet Sounds*:

IK: "Yes, this is an absolutely incredible piece of work. The vocal arrangements are phenomenally intricate and performed extremely well. I think it's remarkable and unlike anything else. For the time, to get vocals that in tune and that tight can only really be done through masterful arranging and musicianship."

On "Sloop John B," cultural appropriation and the "organic" evolution of folk music:

IK: "It is impossible to not be heavily influenced by black music in modern popular music and that should be celebrated—whether that be rock 'n' roll or techno. What is unacceptable to me is how music is appropriated by white artists (and more importantly their record labels and publishers) and then sold on as white music with very little recognition or return back to the original creators of it.

"If we lived in a more equitable world, I think it would be absolutely right to say that it's the way folk music is and should be—it's essential for its evolution."

MF: "Do you think blues is merely a style which anyone should be free to have a go at?"

IK: "I think The Rolling Stones are undeniably brilliant, but yes, I do find this problematic. I think everyone should be able to sing the blues regardless of their race—but I don't think profiting from that is really OK in a world where such huge inequality remains. I think artists like that could have and could still now do a huge amount more to recognize the roots of their music, acknowledge their privilege and help foster a more equitable world.

"I'm reminded of Eric Clapton's racist rant during one of his shows. Not only did he appropriate black music and build his career on it, he then went on to actively discriminate and incite violence toward the same group of people. It's so incredibly sad to me that such a gifted musician would so vehemently attack his teachers. He should have been honoring those people, giving back—celebrating—collaborating—using his great privilege to celebrate that music and those people and challenge the world around him."

♩ ♩

Lee Desai is an activist and restaurateur. He was born in Cape Town, South Africa, and has been closely involved in the cultural life of Folkestone. He cofounded and still cooks at Dr Legumes, my favorite restaurant, where you can scarcely believe what deliciousness has been conjured with plants you've never even heard of and where the music coming out of the speakers likewise eludes identification.

Lee and I conducted our conversation years ago, recorded on a cassette. I've since searched my flat several times for that tape and failed to find it. I can't recall what Lee's opinions on *Revolver* or *Pet Sounds* were, or his thoughts on the other issues that these interviews tackle. But I do recall two things about our session with great clarity.

As we discussed his tastes and the records he felt might merit inclusion in a putative Top 10, Lee opened his laptop and accessed his cache of downloads. Each was tagged with a small picture of the relevant promotional artwork—hundreds of thumbnail images as he scrolled through them to pick out special favorites.

Usually when I glimpse someone's music collection—regardless of the person's age, gender or ethnicity—I recognize many of the items. One person will have a lot of punk and hardly any funk, another person will have a lot of funk and hardly any punk. Usually the approximate year they were born will be obvious from the fact that they possess a lot of stuff that came out when they were in their late teens/early twenties, or they may have a surprising predilection for prog or Indian classical music or bubblegum pop. But in all cases, I'm accustomed to being able to take the measure of the person within seconds.

Lee's cache bamboozled me. Nudged by his finger, the thumbnails flitted by, dozen upon dozen, all of them depicting non-white faces, or imagery suggestive of non-white experience. Not only was I unfamiliar with the tracks, but in most cases I'd never even heard of the artists. Here and there something would flash past that I knew, but mostly I was peeking through a portal into a foreign world.

Late in our interview, it emerged that Lee's partner—his girlfriend, not his business partner at the restaurant—was white.

"Has she had an influence on what you listen to?" I asked.

Lee has a charming smile—self-confident, relaxed, a little impish. "Oh, I don't think so," he said, shaking his loc-topped head just a fraction.

♩♩

Johny Pitts is a writer, photographer, musician and broadcaster from Sheffield, with roots in Brooklyn and South Carolina. He's a member of the Bare Knuckle Soul collective, and the author of *Afropean*, an award-winning examination of diasporic black communities in Europe.

The piece of music that Johny was listening to just before our interview was "TwoThousandAnd5" by the Runcorn-based white rapper Lee Scott.

o o o

JP: "I grew up during that whole BritPop boom, and my group of friends were a motley bunch. There was Ady, whose ethnic heritage was Tanzanian, who loved Oasis and Ocean Colour Scene—and, by extension, The Beatles; Leon, who was white but grew up in Pitsmoor, surrounded by Caribbean culture; and Mohammad, who was Yemeni and loved underground hip-hop. I was listening to a lot of the Motown and Atlantic Records stuff my mum and dad played at home—my father is African American and came over in a northern soul group. So for me the notion of good music was always something to be debated and contested.

"During the nineties, hip-hop felt essential, and didn't belong in any officially recognized canon. The whole point was to make sense of the unofficial, of life at the periphery, outside the canon. And even within hip-hop, there was what I call a B-side culture, where we'd turn our noses up at official A-side singles and only check for the remixes on the B-side. The B-side of an LP represented the B-side of Britain.

"It was only when I left my little enclave of multicultural Sheffield that I came upon a hierarchy of taste. I presented *cd:uk* [a music TV show originally presented by Ant & Dec, running from 1998 to 2006] with Lauren Laverne and Myleene Klass, and we were all asked who our dream guest would be. Madonna and Paul McCartney were mentioned, and my pick was Stevie Wonder. Both Madonna and McCartney ended up on the show, but I was told Stevie 'isn't really on the same level.'"

MF: "That's jaw-dropping, in more ways than one. There's

the obvious racism issue, where a black person is asked by white people to name a significant artist, picks a black artist, and is told to go away and think again until he can come up with a white one. But there are other weird things about it as well. Whatever Madonna's merits as an artist may have been, she was a repackager rather than an originator. She kept her eye on trends and cherry-picked other people's ideas. Stevie Wonder was an innovator."

JP: "I was so angry, but operating in an environment where this kind of thing had been normalized. Lauren Laverne, as smart as she is, was so patronizing about black music. She would mock UK hip-hop, and loved all those awful folky guitar comedy parody covers of gangsta rap that were so common during the noughties, when black music was being persistently undermined.

"It wasn't just Lauren, it was an entire toxic culture that devalued black music from the streets, and hailed The Rolling Stones and The Beatles without recognizing the black cultural roots of either band's musical output."

On the notion of Top 100 albums ever made:

JP: "I wasn't aware of all that stuff, really. I had an abundance of great music at home, stretching from John Lee Hooker, through Marvin [Gaye] and Donny [Hathaway], into BeBe and CeCe Winans, and then through to people like D'Angelo, J Dilla, 2Pac, Soul II Soul, Omar and the extraordinary output of Teddy Riley and DeVante Swing, the two authors of the sound of nineties soul and R&B. I thought people like Lou Reed sounded amateur, both as musicians and singers. It's only as I've grown older and made my way through the black music canon, and wanted to explore other sounds, that I've acquired a deep respect for some of those white artists you mentioned, and can see how the traditions have and always will crisscross.

"I didn't know *Revolver* directly until I was in my twenties, but of course most of the songs had made their way into my psyche through popular culture. I don't want to be too separatist or divisive, because The Beatles were incredible, but I see them a bit like I see Eminem. People talk about Eminem as though he is the God of hip-hop, but to me he's maybe somewhere in the Top 200, because I know all his references—I know what he's trying to do and where he got his source material from. If you listen to Pharoahe Monch and Kurupt, they were Eminem before Eminem. When I hear The Beatles I hear Harry Nilsson, and when I hear Harry Nilsson I hear people like Ray Charles and Chuck Berry. The Beatles deserve to be canonized, but then so do so many others who aren't.

"I'm not as familiar with The Beach Boys. If I'm being honest, I find it hard to take them seriously because the first Beach Boys song I ever heard when I was a kid was 'Kokomo,' from the *Cocktail* soundtrack (which I do love, by the way). But they weren't in my orbit and still don't resonate hugely."

On "Sloop John B," cultural appropriation and the "organic" evolution of folk music:

JP: "I'm torn on this one. On the one hand, as an autodidact I hugely appreciate artists bringing important information and art from obscure places into popular consciousness... On the other hand, I do think there is something gross about how white people continue to make money born from the suffering of black people. So while I don't think we need to cry cultural appropriation every time a song born of struggle is covered by somebody who isn't from the struggle themselves, it's imperative artists use their platform to draw attention to and acknowledge the source material."

MF: "Do you believe that a good way forward, instead of saying 'trad,' would be to say 'Unknown person from the Bahamas'? This was a policy suggested to me by one of the other people I interviewed, Samenua Sesher, who's setting up a museum of black history."

JP: "I absolutely agree with Samenua, and it ties back into

the idea of helping anyone interested in the song to discover the original context.

"It's a question of who gets to control the narrative. The historian Adam Hochschild, when he wrote the brilliant *King Leopold's Ghost*, about King Leopold's Congo Free State, mentioned how hard it was to get written word and stories from the colonized, the poor and the powerless, which was constantly overshadowed by documents by the colonizers, the rich and the powerful. Even if we have to make a bit of an imaginative leap, I think we do need to find ways to sing communities who have been woven out of history back into existence somehow, and 'trad' doesn't really cut it, especially when a song has roots tied to enslaved peoples."

On Bob Dylan and *Highway 61 Revisited*:

JP: "Dylan's another one of those characters that took me a long time to understand, and I still feel he's a bit overrated. Over the years he's been forced down my throat so often that I now have a certain appreciation for his music, even if I feel the struggle he's supposed to represent with his wonky vocals is really just indicative of someone who can't sing."

On The Rolling Stones and *Exile On Main Street*:

JP: "It's fascinating that *Exile On Main Street* was recorded only a couple of hours along the same coast where Picasso lived and died, and said 'I want to live like a pauper with lots of money.' The same thing is happening with hip-hop in the twenty-first century. Initially, I think black artists saw [white identification with black music] as a symbol of power. KRS-One rapped 'now we got white kids calling themselves niggers' somewhat triumphantly. But I think all meaning gets stripped when the appropriation is being done cynically, to make someone a lot of money. It's led us to a place where, to paraphrase Simon Reynolds, music is no longer where important social and political ideas are worked out in public. And that's fine for a lot of people in the system we currently live under."

On Marvin Gaye's *What's Going On*:

JP: "*What's Going On* loomed large during my upbringing. I can't remember the first time I ever heard it because it's likely that it was being played while I was in my mother's womb."

MF: "If you were made responsible for choosing one album by a black artist to insert into a mainstream magazine's Top 10, would it be Marvin Gaye's *What's Going On*? If not, what would it be?"

JP: "I'm not going to argue with *What's Going On*, it's a great album. But I would point to some more contemporary albums by black artists. I think D'Angelo's *Voodoo* is still one of, if not the greatest album of the twenty-first century. It's astonishing to me that people such as Gil Scott-Heron and Donny Hathaway are rarely mentioned in these lists. One of my friends boldly stated that James Brown was the most important musician of the twentieth century, but after some thought it's hard to argue— Hendrix, Fela Kuti, Gaye, Prince and Michael Jackson etc. all owe something to James Brown. Speaking of which, why haven't Prince and Michael Jackson been mentioned yet!?...

"I do wonder how long lists such as these will hold weight. They're for people to whom a 'Top 10' felt and indeed was important in a popular culture that was top-down, where you were told what was good by mysterious behind-the-scenes figures and they were broadcasted to you—you couldn't broadcast back. You had to make a journey to the record store and think carefully about what you were going to spend your money on.

"I find someone like Ed Sheeran interesting, because if he'd have been around in the nineties he'd have been positioned as maybe a David Gray type of singer-songwriter, or maybe even a Michael Bublé, but you see him getting into bed with people like Pharrell Williams and Stormzy, because he doesn't need to worry too much about being a category in a record store.

"If you're twenty-two and into music, do you give a shit what *Rolling Stone* thinks are the best albums ever made? Do you even listen to albums? Care about genres? There's a trendy café opposite where I live in Peckham, and the staff are these young creative types who are also students at Camberwell College of Art. Sometimes they play really great music, and when I ask what's playing, eight out of ten times they'll say they don't know, that it's just from a random playlist they liked and added to their SoundCloud."

MF: "Here's a question I didn't ask my other interviewees (who were all British or American) but which I will ask you because of your special interest in Europe. The whole conversation surrounding the 'best/greatest' music ever made is an almost exclusively Anglo one. Listeners in Britain and the USA are completely unaccustomed to considering anything that's not sung in English. It doesn't even occur to them that great musicians may be operating in other languages. Have you encountered this attitude?"

JP: "Absolutely. When I was a DJ on BBC Radio 1Xtra, I wanted to set up a show that played black music from across the Afro-European diaspora. I'm not talking here about some fuddy-duddy conception of 'world music,' but very fresh, contemporary sounds—French hip-hop, German grime, Swedish soul, avant-garde artists who these days would be people like Stromae, Dream Koala or Ibeyi. They looked at me as if I was bonkers. They wanted me to talk about what Rihanna was wearing on the red carpet, and the 'shade' she threw at Beyoncé, or whatever.

"The management at the BBC at that time were all these middle-class, white, ghetto-fabulous execs who had been given a job and maybe wore tracksuits to work for the first time in their life. People exemplified by the likes of Seb Chew, who brought Lily Allen and Mark Ronson through at Universal. They were obsessed with two things: London and America. Anything outside of those two places was 'niche.' I honestly think it's a hangover from British Imperialism."

♩♩

London-born, Randolph Matthews is from a family who emigrated from Grenada as part of the Windrush community. As a young man he worked as a telecommunications engineer and was laughed at by Job Centre staff when he told them he wanted to be a musician instead. Now forty-nine, he has forged a busy international career as a singer, composer, percussionist, dancer and educator, mostly under the mainstream's radar. His music ranges across soul, jazz, African, Caribbean and avant-garde electronica.

o o o

MF: "When you were a kid, what messages were you given about classical versus pop?"

RM: "I didn't really get many messages, because my primary school was pretty much a convent school. So most of the music was church music. But in any context that we're put in, it's really about who holds the narrative. The narrative of what music *is*, what it stands for.

"From the beginning, for me, there was an undertone of a slightly warped view. Coming from the Caribbean, you conceive of tones differently. [Randolph demonstrates, by singing a conventional western scale, then singing a similar sequence of notes shot full of syncopation, melodic embellishments, ad-libbing, tone-bending and rhythmic excitement.] So already you're split. Even just singing a popular song—which, for me… popular equals white. Without even realizing it, you're already subtly shifting out of the connection with sounds that are relative to your race.

"When I went into secondary school, I didn't get the opportunity to play an instrument because I wasn't one of those children that was able to get a trumpet, when all the trumpets were taken, and we didn't have opportunities to sing, and I think I was probably too self-conscious to go down that road. It wasn't until afterward that I reidentified myself through my own influences—my brother playing music, my mother playing reggae tunes or soul music in the house, for example. My sister was into Al Jarreau, so I was getting these kind of reverberations…"

MF: "Al Jarreau? You've got something to thank your sister for…"

RM: "Of course! And she played the flip side. She played things like Depeche Mode, and I really liked that part as well. But it wasn't until I met other musicians that I started just listening to more music, started to feel this connectedness, to music itself as opposed to particular artists. Music is very cultivated and you can learn from any number of approaches what it is and how it works."

MF: "One of the pieces that I listened to on your SoundCloud was 'Momento (Live In Zanzibar).' Seen through a certain lens, 'Momento' is African music, but if you put a different lens to it, it's Baroque counterpoint."

RM: "Yes! Yes."

MF: "Is that what you're getting at? That depending on the lens you're using, you can learn the same stuff…?"

RM: "Totally. There are underlying principles for how that sound is manipulated. A jazz musician would listen to Bach and go 'I get it: he was an improviser, just like we are.' So that's one aspect of it. But the other aspect is indoctrination, associating music with dexterity and mastering a score, learning something that people will recognize as A Quality Piece of Work. A cue for them to say 'Oh, that's a complicated piece that you learned there: well done.' So, learning a Beethoven piece, learning a Bach piece, is given a status, given a class."

On the grading of pop music into a Top 100 hierarchy, almost all of them white:

RM: "I wouldn't say I was particularly aware of it, because when the TV wasn't on I didn't have that music in my house.

But once the TV was switched on and we had *Top of the Pops*, then you got this sense, from presenter all the way through, of [whiteness]. But I already knew, from being a young person in a primary school, that I was the one black child in that school. So, to look at the TV and see the one black band, or the two black bands—that was nothing new for me.

"I didn't have any conscious understanding of which one was 'the best,' I just knew what I liked, you know, and everybody else would make their decisions. The top tune, or the Top 10 tunes, as *Top Of The Pops* used to present them, was whatever was bangin' at that time. I couldn't see that it was a biased view, I didn't understand that it was down to who held the narrative and which artist was able to sell. Everything was about the business; the artist as a cog of the business. And still is, today."

On *Revolver* and *Pet Sounds*:

RM: "Yes, I'm aware of *Revolver*, and I'm aware of…well, actually no, I wasn't aware of *Pet Sounds* by The Beach Boys as a 'best' or 'second-best' album. I've heard of *Revolver* but never actually listened to it. Again, it all depends who's holding the narrative."

On Marvin Gaye's *What's Going On*:

RM: "That album came later. I think I must've been about twenty-one, twenty-two years old. Marvin Gaye had been around as part of Motown, but it wasn't until I went on my own search for myself as an artist, and reading [David Ritz's biography] *Divided Soul: The Life of Marvin Gaye*—it sounded so familiar, just so familiar, what was going on around his relationship with his father, and his relationship with the church, you know, quite symbolic things about black community."

On "Sloop John B" and cultural appropriation:

RM: "We are the starters. Black people start the trends. Black people start it because of where it comes from within us. Music is something that we really deeply feel. We feel…not in an intellectual way, we feel it because it's linked to our spiritual emancipation, it's a communal expression for birth and for death, it's a rite of passage. The evolution of anything artistic in music has always been one of our key expressions. The rest is just down to where we are socially, our place in the world, and how that permits our music to be manipulated and popularized and also, you could say, copied."

Randolph and I talked at length about due credit for influence. He cited a recently resurfaced interview in which an exasperated Ray Charles dismissed notions of Elvis Presley as an exciting phenomenon or any sort of "king." I mentioned a very early interview with Elvis, done in 1954 when "That's All Right" was creeping up the charts:

Louisiana Hayride presenter: "I'd like to know how you derived that style, how you came about that rhythm-and-blues style."

Elvis: "Well, sir, we just stumbled upon it."

Louisiana Hayride presenter: "You're mighty lucky, you know. They've been looking for something new in the folk music field, I think you've got it."*

---

* Frank Page interviewing Elvis Presley on *Louisiana Hayride*, October 16, 1954, quoted by Colin Escott, in "Come On, Let's Go!", *Mojo*, December 2004.

The thing Elvis had "stumbled upon" was Mississippi bluesman Arthur Crudup, who wrote "That's All Right" and recorded it in 1946. Presley's hit record credited Crudup as the composer, but, by the magic of music industry accountancy, none of the royalties ever reached Crudup, who supplemented his meager touring income with field labor and hawking bootleg whiskey. He died of heart disease in 1974, a veteran of many failed attempts to sue the industry into doing the right thing.

What we see here is systemic racism in its commonest form. Elvis Presley, a flawed young man who meant no harm and wanted to be decent, didn't claim to have written "That's All Right." He merely kept silent when the white folks around him praised him for innovations that had supposedly come out of nowhere and germinated in a depersonalized environment—a murky genre on which Elvis could impose a name and a personality. As a child, I grew up with the mythic narrative that rock 'n' roll was invented by Bill Haley but that Haley was old and pudgy, so the genre had to wait for a sexy, charismatic youngster—Elvis—to bring it to fruition. This fable was sold to me as sociohistorical fact.

By 1974, when Crudup was buried in a nondescript plot in Virginia, Elvis was living at 3764 Elvis Presley Boulevard (a stretch of Highway 51 South

RM: [sardonically] "He just 'found' it, yeah. He didn't talk about going to a gospel church, and seeing people getting the spirit…"

MF: "But what's the answer? What about Samenua Sesher's suggestion to credit a community? Is that impractical?"

RM: "People can only do what they feel personally compelled to do."

MF: "There are different levels of moral decision… For example, there's this amazing electronic piece called 'Electro Blues For Bukka White' by Recoil. Recoil is Alan Wilder, an ex-member of Depeche Mode. Judging by the music you made for *Shadows* [a Terry Smith dance piece performed in Folkestone a few months before this interview], I think you'd love it. Anyway, it uses samples of Bukka White, mostly just him talking, and a bit of a cappella singing. Now, Wilder could've just credited the piece to himself, because he's using samples in the service of a wholly new piece of music, and anyway, Bukka White is long dead. But Wilder chose to cocredit Bukka White. Whereas you've got cases like Led Zeppelin, where they claimed to have written blues songs that had been around since the 1920s—and some of those original artists were still alive. So that's two different moral compasses…"

RM: "There can be no evolution unless we honor the originators. You look at the great jazz musicians, and they're all broke. They're the ones who wrote these amazing pieces, the pieces we regard as the rule book. White musicians are playing this beautiful work, and yet the musician who invented it has not received a cent."

MF: "This is a capitalism issue as much as it's a racism issue, because the industry is deeply corrupt. When the record com-

---

renamed in his honor) in an opulent mansion that has since been designated a National Historic Landmark. He was rich beyond the dreams of avarice, surrounded by sycophants and servants, eating himself to death.

pany's legal team see naive young musicians coming up, they're rubbing their hands…"

RM: "Of course. Because they know they'll do it for tuppence."

MF: "But when the artist finally wakes up, and goes into litigation, that's when it becomes relevant what resources you have as a litigant."

RM: "Yes. Yes."

MF: "So even though the industry is screwing *everybody* over, regardless of color, once you're trying to do something about the fact that you've been screwed over, your blackness or whiteness comes into play again."

RM: "Yes. It determines how much the authorities listen, how much the case moves forward, how much it gets side-parked."

MF: "And then, eventually, Bonnie Raitt finds out you've been buried in an unmarked grave and she buys a headstone for you."

RM: "Yes. That's the one. There's definitely a difference in people's moral compass. I can appreciate The Rolling Stones more than I can appreciate Elvis, because they explicitly made their influences very clear. They said 'This is some of the stuff we've heard. Check this out.' Whereas Elvis was in denial."

Randolph and I finished up with a discussion of the big life questions—religious faith, alienation, and how we can deal with the otherness of others.

RM: "I think the fundamentals are the human values of connectivity, how we can learn to listen to each other and appreciate the essence that we are human beings together. The best conversations are the ones where two very conflictual viewpoints can get to that point where they just realize 'Yeah, but we're both here at the same time, aren't we? We're both humans on this earth, and if you just pulled away all the skin, you'd see that we've both got the same muscular tissues, framework, everything is just built on that…'"

♩

This chapter was the last to be added to *Listen*. I finished it during the painful process of cutting the book down from 249,000
words to whatever it is now.

I'm aware that this chapter is long. It was an obvious candidate to be cut when my editor and I were hunting around for
things that could be cut. I'm also aware that my interviewees
had a great deal more to say, which you haven't heard. And that
they were just a randomly chosen few people of color among
all the multitudes who are routinely ignored and omitted when
white people write books about music. Not for *racist* reasons, oh
no. Just because space is at a premium and there's a lot to discuss and the experience of people who aren't white doesn't fit.

o   o   o

For at least forty-five years of my life, mainstream society reassured me that I was familiar with the best albums ever made.
At one time or another, I owned all of the Top 20.

But since 2020, when *Rolling Stone* was finally shamed—or
embarrassed—into revamping its list to reflect the ethnic and
artistic reality of modern-day America, an album has entered
the Top 20 that I haven't heard—Kanye West's *My Beautiful Dark
Twisted Fantasy*. It is ranked seven places above *Sgt. Pepper*, and
one place higher than *Highway 61*. Is it worth my attention? I
don't believe in ranking music, but maybe I should check it out.
Maybe I'll find it's not for the likes of me. Lots of things aren't.
None of my favorite albums are even in the list. The compilers
seem not to have heard of Germany. Or Africa, for that matter.

Seriously, my taste has its limitations and parameters. How
much of the music I love is by artists the same color as me? I don't
know. A big percentage. Smaller than when I was a teenager. But
still big. My music collection will never resemble Lee Desai's.

Nor will I ever truly understand what it feels like to have just performed a terrific gig to great applause, and to be walking home in my sharp purple suit, and to be called a fucking black bastard by strangers on the street—as happened to Randolph Matthews shortly after he settled in my town. Not only did Randolph and I grow up in different worlds, but we continue to live in them, despite being almost neighbors.

I had to get Samenua Sesher to spell "Mtukudzi" for me, and she introduced me to the word "Maafa," which I'd somehow never come across. Yet by the age of fourteen I knew who minor white artistes such as Peter Skellern and Jim Croce were, despite not even liking their music, and I was extremely well-informed about the Holocaust. That's racial tribalism in action.

Listen has conscious and unconscious biases, some of which I couldn't address if I wanted to, others of which I prefer to stick with. My lifetime habit of keeping my ears open has not guaranteed that I'll hear sounds from outside my appointed space. I can only hope that this book has more to offer you—*all* of you—than the same old canons of white noise.

THE SIREN CALL
OF HORRIBLE DIN

One of the most transcendent pleasures I've ever had was granted to me on the morning of November 14, 2018, in the street right outside my flat. I was indoors at the time, sitting at my desk, working on this book, when suddenly the heavens opened. Not with rain, but with music. Over a sonorous industrial growl of unknown origin, a melodious skirling pierced the air. Pitched somewhere between a piccolo and a Northumbrian pipe, it improvised melodies of exquisite grace.

I'd lived in Folkestone long enough to know that it is full of cultural surprises. I guessed that an experimental musician was playing a concert on the Leas, the promenade just round the corner. I rushed out with a camera and a portable cassette recorder…only to find a gigantic builders' crane parked outside the block of flats across the road.

Necessary repairs were being carried out to a damaged roof. Men in hard hats and yellow reflective clothing were making the crane swivel about. When the task was accomplished, the crane folded down onto the truck like a swan settling to sleep, its song exhausted.

"You're not going to believe this," I told the supervisor. "But I love that sound."

"What sound?" He squinted at me mistrustfully, perhaps thinking this was sarcasm and I was all geared up to report him to Environmental Health for noise pollution.

I imitated the skirling tones, contorting my face in a way he no doubt found bizarre. "What exactly *makes* that sound?" I asked, a bit tongue-tied because I was still dazed by the beauty of what I'd just heard.

"Lack of lubrication," he said, in a tone of voice he might reserve for an imbecile who asked which part of a building, exactly, the roof is. "It's going in for a service tomorrow."

"But I *love* that sound!" I protested.

It was one of those moments of basic attitudinal collision, a meeting of minds that cannot meet. Like when you cross paths with someone who regards it as self-evident that England should get rid of all the bloody immigrants.

"Drives you mad," he muttered, turning away from me.

o o o

The allusion to xenophobia above is not a rhetorical flourish, irrelevantly inserted into a book about music because I can't keep my political values to myself. Mistrust of strangers is not just a social issue but also an aesthetic one.* Over the years I've found that a listener's openness to different conceptions of music is part of a more general relationship with deviance and diversity. The mind is a border. Some people hold very strong views about what should and should not be allowed through the checkpoint.

o o o

---

* In 2018, the *British Journal of Sociology* published the results of a study done by researchers from Oxford University, who'd surveyed 3,607 members of the British public seventeen months after they'd voted in the 2016 referendum on EU membership. The participants were shown four pairs of artworks—traditional, realistic paintings on the one hand and more abstract or avant-garde images on the other. A clear majority of people who supported Britain's divorce from the European Union (and the tougher stance on immigration that was sure to follow) also had a pronounced dislike of "abstract" or challenging art. By contrast, the people who were happy to identify as Europeans (and, by implication, hospitable to foreigners) preferred the avant-garde stuff. Remarkably, these were the results despite the method controlling for gender, age, levels of education or ethnicity.

The term "avant-garde" derives from the language of warfare. The avant-garde, or vanguard, was the first wave of soldiers who prepared the way for the larger conquering army to over-run the terrain. This vanguard included "harbingers" or *her-bergeres*, whose job was to find accommodation for the troops that were coming.

The symbolic resonance is clear: avant-garde art will swamp us if given half a chance. Parochial art that harks back to a by-gone era is a bastion against the dangerous incomers. The fa-miliar sounds of which our tribe approves are Music. What's not Music is Noise. We don't want any of those noisy harbingers coming over here, stealing our time and violating our brain cells.

o   o   o

From birth, our most anxious wish is to be safe. We like simple and we like familiar. In surroundings, in food, in melodies. Our infant brains are not equipped to handle anything else. And even when we're a little older, and we want to see ourselves as adven-turers, it's still hard to venture far from the cradle. Outlandish sounds don't tend to be available in the home; they're exiled to the obscure peripheries of culture, and kids lack the skills and autonomy to go in search of them. Mostly, what we "discover" on our aesthetic adventures is what is put in front of us.

The odd kid has bohemian parents who play them freaky stuff. Freaky stuff is thereby made familiar—literally. My fam-ily was not bohemian. My parents had a modest collection of easy-listening LPs by The Vienna Boys' Choir and The James Last Orchestra and so on. They didn't even play them for their own pleasure anymore, let alone for me. They watched TV or leafed through magazines. Music, for them, was something that had happened a while back, and was over now.

I have no musical memories of my early childhood. My first seven years, in Holland, are a blank. By the end of the sixties, I was living in Boronia, an outer suburb of Melbourne on the foothills of the Dandenong Ranges. Our street had tarmac, but the next road along was still dirt, because we were on the edge of "the bush." Civilization, for our tribe of settlers, was symbolized by a lawn mower.

What would my response have been, as a boy growing up in that environment, if I'd been exposed to revolutionary auditory weirdness? I can't know, because there wasn't any.

At least, not until the formative encounter that happened when I was about ten.

One of our neighbors owned an album by a group I didn't know much about except that they were extremely famous and had just broken up. Its cover was lustrous white, and it didn't seem to have a title. Our neighbor kindly allowed me to borrow the record and I played it over and over on my parents' stereogram.*

The Beatles' White Album was recorded in 1968, as the band's musketeer ethos was unraveling and quality control was allowed to slip. It has always caused division among listeners. Confronted with the sprawling double LP's multiple self-indulgences, most people (including producer George Martin) felt that the album should've been edited down to a superior single disc.

The most controversial track was "Revolution 9," an eight-minute tape collage that looped harsh static, angry crowds, gunfire, screams, incoherent babble and random bursts of backward classical music. We can safely assume that, for the vast majority of the tens of millions of people who've owned the album, "Revolution 9" is the only piece of musique concrète they've ever heard. And they're pretty unanimous in their agreement that the White Album would have been better without this rubbish.

Even music journalists—usually keen to demonstrate how

---

*   My parents did own a Beatles record—a 7" EP on the German Odeon label, issued in 1963. The back cover featured photos of Trini Lopez, the Swiss mountains and an accordionist, but there was no photo of The Beatles anywhere. On "Thank You Girl," the boys kept singing "Auw! Auw!" and I thought they must be Germans.

much hipper they are than the person in the street—spat their disdain. Reviewing the album at the time of its release, Alan Smith, soon-to-be editor of *New Musical Express*, decried "Revolution 9" as "a pretentious piece of old codswallop which is no more than a long, long collection of noises and sounds seemingly dedicated toward expanding the sale of Aspros [aspirin]. I am angry at this because the 'Listen to me, I'm being mysterious' bit is a piece of idiotic immaturity and a blotch on their own unquestioned talent as well as the album."[*]

Reader, it's fairly likely that *you* have heard "Revolution 9." What did you think?

o   o   o

My ten-year-old self was electrified.

Many aspects of the White Album failed to connect with me—Ringo doing his country & western shtick, Paul crooning "I Will," John's wimpy "Julia," the oafish pummel of "Birthday," the sentimental gloop of "Good Night." Ninety-three minutes of new music, borrowed from a neighbor, was a lot for a kid to take in, and I lacked various kinds of cultural capital. I hadn't yet heard any Beach Boys, for example, so the Beach Boys pastiche of "Back In The USSR" flew right over my head. On the 1920s homage "Honey Pie," Paul McCartney fruitily interjects "I like-ah this kinda muu-sic!" but I'd heard no vaudeville yet, so "Honey Pie" was my introduction to that genre rather than an homage to it.

"Ob-La-Di, Ob-La-Da" was another learning curve for the boy Michel. There were no black people where I lived, not even any indigenous Wurundjeri (all dispossessed and scattered by the time I got there), and I'd never heard of ska, so "Ob-La-Di, Ob-La-Da" struck me as a whole new thing. Even so, its jollity

---

[*]   Alan Smith, *New Musical Express*, November 9, 1968.

irritated me. As the son of traumatized expatriates haunted by the Nazi era, I wasn't shaping up to be a cheery chap.

But "Revolution 9"…that was something else. It made my brain light up with strange thrills. I couldn't even say if I liked or hated it. The piece seemed supremely indifferent to what I thought of it, as indifferent as a giant alien organism might be to the opinions of puny earthlings. There was stuff going on here that I didn't understand, and I simultaneously enjoyed the incomprehension and glimpsed a future Michel who might comprehend it.

In that moment, the path toward surrealist provocateurs like Nurse With Wound opened up, and I set foot on it, and other paths I might've trod disappeared from view.

o o o

What makes that attraction possible? What makes some people who encounter "Revolution 9" get excited, and other people decide that they must prevent such ugly muck ever soiling their ears again?

Over and over, this book contends that the musical tastes that seem to us so instinctive and hardwired are, in fact, the products of enculturation—the way we're brought up, the tribes we wish to identify with, the rewards and punishments associated with the allegiances we choose. Where is the cultural benefit in adoring the sound of a badly maintained builders' crane? Why on earth would my brain give me an appetite for noises that the vast majority of my fellow citizens find distasteful?* Why, when I could take my seat among hordes of happy pop fans and sing along to a tune we all know, do I pass up opportunities

---

* This is as good a juncture as any to acknowledge that when I refer to "my fellow citizens," I'm referring to people who've been brought up with European or African music. Certain kinds of Asian music sound "avant-garde" to my ears simply because they arise from tuning systems and compositional traditions that are alien to the ones I grew up with.

for such companionable entertainment in favor of checking out albums with titles like *Chance Meeting Of A Defective Tape Machine And Migraine*?

A psychologist might argue that the taste for avant-garde music—the taste for a thing that almost nobody else can stand—is an expression of anger and alienation, a peevish rejection of the values cherished by "normal" society.

Was that what motivated me? I don't recall wishing to reject societal norms when I was intrigued by "Revolution 9." I do remember being called a weirdo when I told some kids at school that I'd rather listen to Joni Mitchell than Suzi Quatro, but Joni Mitchell was hardly a scarifying racket.

One person I know who definitely used avant-garde music to bolster his identity is Jake Pilikian, the only person in my town with whom I can share my love of the pioneering Australian electronica project Severed Heads.

"When I was about fourteen, fifteen," he told me, "I was at a school where I was a total fish out of water; I really didn't belong there. Everyone else was quite wealthy, the privileged media kids of North London, and then there was me, who got in on a scholarship and took the bus. I was a natural outsider anyway because I looked foreign, and I had this giant, almost Afro-ish hair, so I got called 'Shirley Bassey.' Everyone just took the piss. I wasn't a threat, so they teased me in a half-hearted way; they weren't trying to destroy me, I was just a bit laughable.

"At break time, some of the kids would gather in the basement of the school around a cassette player, and they'd bring in a tape and play a few tunes. I stuck my head round the door a couple times and heard what they were listening to, which was eighties middle-of-the-road stuff, you know, Huey Lewis & The News, that kind of thing. I thought, *Right, I'm gonna do something here, I'm gonna bring a cassette tomorrow*. And I went home and stared at my cassettes and picked one.

"Next day, I went into that basement, where everyone had

convened, and I said, 'Can *I* play something?' A really patronizing air arose from the sea of faces, kind of 'What's this tosser
gonna bring to the party?' I'd chosen *Locust Abortion Technician*
by the Butthole Surfers, axnd I announced that this was what I
was going to play, knowing that none of them would even have
heard of it. Just the name already caused a frisson. And I started
getting this really weird feeling; I was quite excited as the opening track started. There's a long spoken-word intro, where Gibby
Haynes, the singer, is acting the part of a folksy dad impart-
ing wisdom. His kid asks, 'Daddy? What does "regret" mean?'
and he says, 'Well, son, the funny thing about regret is that it's
better to regret something you *have* done than to regret something you haven't done. And, son? If you see your mom today,
will you tell her... *SATAN! SATAN! SATAN!*' And then the
whole band crashes in with this heavily distorted sludge rock.

"The instant that happened, everyone backed away from the
tape player, and they were looking at me as if...as if they were
afraid. Of me. It was a feeling of power, for the first time, ever.
I think they were wondering if maybe I was gonna kill them—
this weird guy who'd been moving amongst them silently, quietly, day after day... I didn't say anything, I just let this thing
play, then I picked it up and left. No one said a word. And in
my head I was just thinking *All of you: go to hell. Fuck you all.
You can all fucking die.*

"It was glorious. I was fourteen years old, but you can see that
the euphoria is still in me, so a part of me has clearly never re-
covered from this experience. The Butthole Surfers' *Locust Abortion Technician* served a dual function, in that it was an album I
genuinely loved, aesthetically, but at the same time it had this
extra meta-level of being a cultural weapon with which to attack people, because I knew they couldn't cope with it."[*]

---

[*]   Interview with Jake Pilikian, March 2020. I should mention that as Jake told
       this story, he was smiling and his eyes twinkled with good humor. When he
       got to the part about his schoolmates fearing him, his wife, the composer and

o   o   o

An anthropologist might observe that the people who refuse
to enjoy what everyone around them enjoys are members of a
tribe all to themselves—the tribe of tribe-rejecters, supporting
each other in their alienated outcastness. When Jake and I met,
was it a meeting of two self-defined outcasts? I'm not convinced
it was. Sure, we both like obscure music that the majority of
people would probably dislike, but we haven't pursued a life of
misanthropic passive-aggression. Jake is a teacher and sometime
screenwriter, a devoted father, amiable company. I live a hermit-
like existence most of the time, because of the writing and other
private passions, but I can be sociable when I want to be. Neither of us has become the embittered incel, the troll, the serial
killer who, according to the neighbors, "kept himself to himself."

Over the years, I've certainly observed some individuals who
fit the sociopath clichés. People who wore Charles Manson
T-shirts and subscribed to murkily photocopied fanzines discussing music inspired by Nazi death camps, sadomasochism
and necrophilia. I could've subscribed to those fanzines myself.
I could've corresponded with all sorts of crazed loner artistes
who printed their home addresses on the LPs and cassettes that
only I and a few other oddballs worldwide bothered to buy. I
could've had a pile of handwritten letters from avatars of alienation, and regular updates on the activities of Thee Temple Ov
Psychick Youth. But I didn't.

If the self-conscious outsiders *were* my tribe, I clearly failed to
avail myself of the benefits of membership.

o   o   o

What I loved, and still love, about avant-garde music was the
sounds themselves. The musicians who made those sounds might

---

singer Anna Braithwaite, broke out in giggles.

be interesting, or not, but ultimately they were less important than the precise way the airwaves vibrated.

Which leads to the question: What is an "avant-garde" sound? How does it differ from a sound that's not avant-garde? There are dozens of genres that are considered "normal." What does it take to be classified as "abnormal"? If Vivaldi, Van Halen, The Wombles, Luther Vandross and Dolly Parton are all safely not avant, what is the element that pushes an artist over the line?

It's not noisiness per se. Tchaikovsky's *1812 Overture* is noisy. Cannons go off in it. But it's one of the best-loved chestnuts in the classical repertoire. AC/DC are very noisy. But millions of fans have sung along to "Rock And Roll Ain't Noise Pollution" and AC/DC are one of the bestselling music acts in the world.

Avant-garde music, by contrast, needn't be terribly loud; it can noodle quietly in the corner of the room and still people will jump up and say *what is that horrible din*?

o   o   o

On the face of it, lack of melody may seem to be the deal-breaker. When people who detest avant-garde music are challenged to articulate what's wrong with it, they will often point out that it has "no tune."

Undeniably, there is a certain kind of avant-garde piece—by Merzbow or Controlled Bleeding, for example—that consists of a relentless barrage of abstract noise. "I don't want to make music," N. U. Unruh, a member of the aptly named Einstürzende Neubauten[*] once declared. "I just want to torture people." His colleague Frank-Martin Einheit brandished an electric drill and agreed: "All great music is torture of some sort."[†]

A few masochistic individuals enjoy being tortured. Not

---

[*]   In English: Collapsing New Buildings.

[†]   "Trans-Europe Excess" by Don Watson, *New Musical Express*, April 6, 1985.

many. Here's a gentleman from East Arcadia, California, writing in to an internet forum dedicated to concerts that attendees felt compelled to flee from. He nominates Throbbing Gristle at Culver City Veterans' Auditorium on May 22, 1981. "The show started out with their typical 130dB 'Wall Of Sound' with the curtains closed and B&W 1950's full-on porn movies playing on the curtain. That was followed by the curtain opening up about 12″ and a series of aircraft landing lights were turned on, facing directly at the audience. I left after a while with a really, really bad headache."* It hardly needs mentioning that the piece in question, "Scorched Earth," had no melody whatsoever.

This sort of experimentalism is part of an evergreen tradition of "art terrorism" that stretches back to Dada, if not further. But we should keep in mind that it occupies only a small corner of the landscape of unpopular music. Sheer noise is rare, and avant-gardists seldom intend to torture their audiences. Most of the stuff that people consider ugly and indigestible contains plenty of notes, arranged in careful sequences. Whereas a recent, not at all avant-garde rap record like "Jump" by DaBaby & NBA Youngboy has no clearly identifiable notes at all, let alone a tune. Quite a lot of today's rap, in fact, is defiantly uninterested in melody, as hit after hit—by Drake, Pop Smoke, Tory Lanez, King Von, Ski Mask, CJ, 21 Savage, Lil Loaded, Blueface and dozens of others—focuses doggedly on the rappers' monotonous speechifying.

If "tunes" are what the public is supposed to want, what do we make of the fact that millions of listeners in the contemporary marketplace evidently don't need them?

In the twenty-first century, even those records that are deemed

---

* "Ralf Hutter" (a pseudonym) from East Arcadia, CA, writing in to "Concerts That You Walked Out On Early," Steve Hoffman Music Forums website, February 18, 2013.

   I like Throbbing Gristle but I have not experienced them at 130 decibels, which is well above the pain threshold; nor am I confident I would cope with having tremendously powerful lights shining into my eyes.

to be "catchy" are seldom melodious in the way that songs by Cole Porter or The Beatles or even Nirvana were. Typically, they rely on a perseverating pattern of two or three notes, which the songwriters of yesteryear would've regarded as a mere fragment rather than a tune or riff worthy of the name.

o o o

So…if the masses are OK with music that's noisy, and OK with music that has little or no melody, why is the avant-garde still considered unlistenable?

I think it comes down to familiarity. The music most people like conforms to rules and preconceptions. Whether it's rap, reggae, rock 'n' roll, Baroque sonatas, country & western, classical symphonies, South African township jive, jazz (hard bop, smooth, swing, Dixieland, Latin…), Ghanaian highlife, Gothic plainchant, Indian ragas, Bollywood sing-alongs, J-pop or power ballads, the listener knows how this thing will go. Knowing how this thing will go is clearly terribly important to the average human.

Some genres are very rigidly formalized, others less so, but the mere fact that we can put a label on the music in the first place shows how well-trained we are in our expectations. A given piece is "funk" (no, not "disco" and, no, not "boogie") because it makes the stylistic choices that allow us, within seconds, to identify it as funk, and chooses against the stylistic elements that might tempt us to define it as disco or boogie.

Our formalistic expectations apply not just to questions of style, but to structure. We want compositions to cohere rather than "fall apart." We have strong opinions on which notes "go well together," which chords we think "should" follow after which. In western classical music, from which much jazz and pop is descended, we cherish the tonic—"the note upon which all other notes of a piece are hierarchically referenced."* When

---

*   Wikipedia article on "Tonic (music)."

a piece of music wanders away from the note or chord that impressed us as the dominant one, there's said to be "tension," which must be "resolved" or "released" when the piece finds its way back where it "belongs." Tellingly, this place that the listener is waiting to arrive back at is often called the "home" key, or simply "home."

The music people fear is the music that stops them going home.

o   o   o

In the mid-twentieth century, a group of composers and music theorists decided that it was time for humanity to cast off its bourgeois shackles and go adventuring in regions of alternative tonality. No progress would ever be made if listeners clung to their safe havens.

Unsurprisingly, the listeners put up a fight. They didn't want the vanguard and its harbingers to evict them from their cozy burrows. Throughout the 1950s and 1960s, in the concert halls and on cutting-edge record labels, there was a war on. You had to choose a side: Were you part of the future or were you determined to cling to the past? The rhetoric got mighty strident. Collaborators with the enemy were viciously denounced.

Pierre Boulez, the major general of atonal music, refused even to speak to tonal composers.[*] In 1958, Milton Babbitt wrote an essay for *High Fidelity* magazine called "The Composer as Specialist" (published with the more provocative title "Who Cares if You Listen?"), in which he argued that the reason the public rejected modern music was that they were too ignorant to understand it, and that serious composers should keep composing difficult material even if nobody came to the concerts.[†]

---

[*]   This claim is made in Philip Ball's review of a book I haven't read—David Stubbs's *Fear of Music: Why People Get Rothko But Don't Get Stockhausen* (Zero Books, 2009), reviewed in *Prospect*, October 21, 2009.

[†]   The author and baritone singer Jo Falla, a friend of mine who read this chapter before publication, pointed out: "You don't mention that much experimental

It's easy to poke fun at the modernist hard-liners. Boulez with his formal suits and ridiculous comb-over, fretting that his status as the Grand Fromage of experimental music was being threatened by that young German Karlheinz Stockhausen. Babbitt, the former mathematician, writing obsessively precise electronic pieces that I—a huge fan of electronic music—find insufferably boring.

Besides, looking back from our decidedly tonal twenty-first-century vantage point, we know that Boulez and Babbitt lost the war. The "ignorant" public stubbornly stayed home and the discordant clamor died down. The chords that Vivaldi and Puccini thought should follow each other are following each other once more. It's in the God-given natural order of things, we're told.

Yet there is a part of me—the part that was excited by "Revolution 9" when I was a kid, the part that slumps with ennui when I'm subjected to the facile music that everyone around me seems to like—that admires those crusading losers, waving their revolutionary flags. In a 1967 interview with *Der Spiegel*, Boulez declared (jokingly, he later claimed) that it was time to "blow up the opera houses" because they were "full of dust and shit."*

Forgive me, opera-loving friends, but I feel like raising my fist in the air. Yes! Death to those overacting Carmens and pompous Don Giovannis!† I'm not in favor of blowing up nice old architecture, but I do wish these palaces were not subsidized to the hilt and used for endless reruns of *La Traviata* and *The Marriage of Figaro.*‡

---

music is very difficult if not impossible for others to re-create or perform. I like listening to Stockhausen's *Gesang der Jünglinge* but I could not perform it myself—it's a recording. For very many music lovers, it is the performability of classical music that is a major part of its attraction. They can join in, take part."

* Many citations, but Boulez's perspective on the controversy can be found in "At 80, Boulez Makes a Grand Tour," an episode of *All Things Considered*, National Public Radio, May 22, 2005.

† Not literal death, you understand.

‡ At which point, my opera-loving inamorata Louisa scribbles "HANDS OFF

Babbitt's contention that artists should create brave new art even if the public aren't ready for it likewise resonates with me. Much of the music I love is not to the average person's taste, and I would be horrified if my beloved sonic explorers had decided to abandon their vision just because there weren't many supporters. My own books invite people on journeys they didn't expect to make, and the one you're reading at this moment has an unashamed agenda to pull you out of your comfort zone.

However, as I head into old age, I get increasingly pragmatic about what it takes for people to open their minds. Much as I've always admired the uncompromising stance of artistic revolutionaries, and ascribed nobility to the voice in the wilderness, I've come to appreciate that there's nothing noble about not being heard. What's the point of telling people that they should listen, if they can't or just don't want to? Can the vanguards and the harbingers do their thing without causing pain?*

o o o

When I first shared my unpublished fictions with the woman who would become my wife, she recognized their potential but found some aspects of my approach alienating. In those days, I was arrogantly indifferent to any putative audience. Writing

---

TRAVIATA!" in the margin of my typescript, adding a skull and crossbones. We can agree to disagree about Verdi and Mozart, but she makes the valid point that there are a lot of contemporary operas, most of which I haven't heard. The ones I *have* heard often seem to me to fall between two stools, being neither avant-garde enough to take listeners to new realms nor tuneful enough for the majority of operagoers to like them. However, my ignorance of the territory is vast, and my irrational prejudice against the operatically trained voice is nakedly obvious.

*   John Cale liked to think so. The former Velvet Underground violist, who'd already had a substantial career in New York's avant-garde scene before joining the group, spent the rest of his career trying to lure listeners with his ballads and his rock 'n' roll, so that they would get a taste for the weird stuff too. His 1994 "best of" collection was called *Seducing Down The Door*, a splendid title.

was a communion between me and "the God of Literature," as I called it. Readers were irrelevant.

Eva kicked back. She thought the notion of a "God of Literature" was bullshit, and she was not content to be an irrelevance. Moreover, as a schoolteacher, she knew that kids learn better if you make them feel included and valued. Her mission, as my de facto editor, was to make my stuff reader-friendly. We had some vigorous discussions, over the years. Now here I am. And here you are.

o   o   o

It's in the nature of revolutionaries to be absolutist, and it's in the nature of society to reject absolutism. Society evolves and moves forward, and incorporates some new ideas here and there, but not if what's called for is a fundamental redesign of everything. If it ain't broke, why fix it?

The twelve-tone serialists, like the anarchists and Communists in the political sphere, jump up and protest that it *is* broke—the old ways must be swept away and a brave new world established. For a while, that new world may seem to be dawning; the firebrands may appear to be winning the battle. But in the long run, the masses do not relish being jolted, disturbed and discomfited. The "groundbreaking" atonal composers grow old and die, and take their rebellions into the grave. Tonal music rules. Deflated, the revolutionaries cry into their beer, mourning the superior form of human that so very nearly, or so very briefly, existed.

I mourn with them, sometimes. I'll be walking through a shopping center, plagued by universally loved pop "classics" that I do not love, and Bob Seger and The Silver Bullet Band will come on the public address system, and Bob will be telling me that he likes the kind of music that just soothes the soul and makes him reminisce about the days of old, and I will want to tie Bob to a chair at the bottom of the Grand Canyon and toss eight squillion rock 'n' roll records down upon him until the canyon is full.

o   o   o

When I'm in a more tolerant mood, I remind myself that people need their sentimental tunes and festive beats, because they're only human, and I'm human too. I may not need that old time rock 'n' roll, but there'll be times when Coil's *Constant Shallowness Leads To Evil* won't soothe my soul, and when I fancy shaking my bum to The Sweet's "Blockbuster."

Maybe the optimal outcome for avant-garde music is what The Beatles achieved in their glory years. Inspired by Stockhausen, Luciano Berio and John Cage, as well as by even more obscure figures like synthesizer pioneer Peter Zinovieff and "free improv" group AMM, The Beatles introduced the mass public to experimental orchestral cacophony on "A Day In The Life," exotic new instruments like the Mellotron and the clavioline, and mind-altering tape collages on "Tomorrow Never Knows," "Being For The Benefit Of Mr Kite," "I Am The Walrus" and "Revolution 9."

They got away with it because they were the most popular group in the world, and the media didn't dare to ignore them the way it ignored the professional avant-gardists. As a ten-year-old boy growing up in an antipodean suburb, I had zero chance of ever hearing Stockhausen or Berio or AMM. But, like just about everyone else on the planet, I had access to the Beatles' White Album—and therefore heard my first piece of musique concrète.

This is true seditious activity. *Don't talk about it, just do it.* The Beatles smuggled revolutionary ideas into entertainments that the general public—the grandparents, the parents, the teens, the tots, everyone in the street—eagerly consumed. Hallucinogenic substances in the breakfast cereal. Here, have some "Ob-La-Di, Ob-La-Da" and "Mother Nature's Son" and, while you're at it, have "Revolution 9," the most alarming and challenging sonic phantasmagoria your impressionable little mind has ever encountered. And when it's over, Ringo will sing you a lullaby.

o . o . o

Never again would The Beatles have the same subversive power. For one thing, like any conquering army, they lost the element of surprise. Second, once they founded their ill-fated Apple business empire, they kept their avant-garde music separate from their pop fare, creating a subsidiary label—Zapple—especially for "difficult" material. Had they not done so, and had they not lost their solidarity as a group, the freaky experimental sounds that got issued (to instant commercial oblivion) as *Unfinished Music No. 1: Two Virgins*, *Electronic Sound* and *Unfinished Music No. 2: Life With The Lions* might have been sneaked into regular Beatles LPs like *Abbey Road*. Many tender, unsuspecting brains would've been penetrated by bamboozling noises.

Instead, the experimental Zapple LPs by George Harrison and John and Yoko trickled into the same obscure niche where albums by Stockhausen or Berio could be found, sought out by intense hipsters who were not you or your mom or your auntie or your neighbor or maybe anyone in your town.

For a while, John Lennon cherished the notion that his music was revolutionary. "You can change people you know, change their heads," he told Maurice Hindle, a student at Keele University. "I've changed a lot of people's heads and a lot of people have changed my head—just with their records."*

This was no doubt true, when The Beatles were delivering "Revolution 9" into every home in the land. Popularity is power. When the White Album was released in the UK, it went straight to number 1 and spent seven weeks there, selling hundreds of thousands of copies.† Whereas *Two Virgins* failed

---

* "Christmas with John and Yoko," interview by Maurice Hindle at Kenwood, December 2, 1968.

† By coincidence, 1968 also saw the release of the soundtrack album of *2001: A Space Odyssey*. What sold the LP—hundreds of thousands of copies of it— was the connection with the movie, and Johann Strauss II's waltz "The Blue Danube," a romantic chestnut that was given a new lease of life here. Richard

to chart, and sold a meager five thousand copies, despite being made by one of the most famous pop stars on the planet, at the height of his group's celebrity, and being reviewed in every major newspaper.

The fatal error was to give people a choice as to whether they wanted it or not.

"Drives you mad," muttered the people, and turned away.

Strauss's majestic prelude *Also sprach Zarathustra* (soon to be turned into a disco/funk hit by Deodato) was a big drawcard too.

But the LP also contained some hardcore experimental music, by György Ligeti. Ligeti, mindful of his cred as an avant-garder, was miffed that his compositions had been thrown into the demeaning company of the Strausses', and he sued Kubrick for unauthorized use, eventually settling out of court.

But in truth, the exposure did Ligeti's career a lot of good. As with The Beatles' "Revolution 9," avant-garde music that the public would normally have avoided like the plague ended up in the homes of the masses. How many of those purchasers actually listened to the excerpts of "Atmospheres," "Requiem For Soprano, Mezzo-Soprano, 2 Mixed Choirs And Orchestra" and "Lux Aeterna" more than once? We'll never know.

A NEEDLE THROUGH
YOUR BROW

The brain is an awesome device, but should've been packaged in a much larger, better-protected container, or made of tougher stuff. It's squishy, quite easily damaged, permeable to harmful chemicals, and tends to shrivel up with age. One of the ironies of human existence is that we hatch our dreams of immortality inside a perishable camembert.

The brain has an impressive—you might say mind-boggling—number of functions. Some of them keep working no matter what. Breathing, for instance, happens without us needing to remember to do it. Our cerebral cortex instructs the concertina of our rib cage to keep pumping our lungs, hundreds of millions of times in a lifetime. It's pretty much guaranteed to be the last thing to go.

Many of our other brain functions, however, are not robust and there's no backup. Our recollections of facts, routines, the names of our friends and relatives, how to read, how to button up a shirt, how to recognize our children or our own faces, how to talk, how to feed ourselves, how not to soil ourselves, are stored in very specific pockets of the brain. When those parts get ruined, we lose what was logged there, and we can't find it anywhere else, and there's nowhere to reinstall it.

Stick a needle through your brow into your frontal lobe, and you may instantly forget how to climb a ladder. An inch to the right or left, and you may see double, laugh uncontrollably, start masturbating in public, become weirdly placid, or gain sudden insight into the evil worldwide conspiracy that connects the Illuminati, 9/11 and your neighbor's dog.

A place for everything, and everything in its place.

o   o   o

Music is a different matter. It's too complex a thing to be housed in just one location. There is no single body part where music lives. It commandeers.

Magnetoencephalography (MEG) and functional magnetic resonance imaging (fMRI) machines can scan and measure our brains' real-time responses to stimulus. When you're challenged to complete a nonmusical task—recall a password, for example, or recite the days of the week—only one tiny spot reacts. Whereas, when music enters our ears, multiple spots in the brain light up. You switch on all over.

The response is most lively if you love the music. But even if you're not wild about it, your brain is still stimulated. Music rouses us whether we approve of it or not.

You may, for example, detest Kylie Minogue's "I Should Be So Lucky" (or think you do). Nevertheless, if you're a pop-aware UK citizen of a certain age, it'll be in your system. The posterior lateral temporal region of your brain—the bit of the lobe that sits right behind your ear—houses your vocabulary, so the words of "I Should Be So Lucky" are lodged there.

Remembering words is not the same, however, as remembering their definitions, and remembering what words mean is not the same as noting how they rhyme. Different bits of the brain specialize in those functions.

Speech (should you wish to recite the words) and singing (should you wish to sing them) are also administrated in separate departments.

Singing involves the sinuses, tongue, throat, lips, jaw, chest and abdomen, as well as less easily identified bits like the planum polare, the superior temporoparietal region, the left and right premotor cortex, the anterior superior temporal gyrus, and the lateral aspect of the VI lobule of the posterior cerebellum. These are the tools you're using when you find yourself humming a tune you didn't mean to hum, a tune you don't even like, a tune that, when you force yourself to identify it, turns out to be "I Should Be So Lucky."

Then again, "I Should Be So Lucky" is a dance record, so you also access the part of your brain that controls motor movements. Messages are sent to your glutes, your hip adductors, your calf triceps, the dozens of muscles in your toes, and many other myopropulsive tissues, so that you'll be able to dance to Kylie if called upon to do so. (Etched somewhere in your brain may be memories of all the clumsy dance moves you made on your journey toward a less clumsy mode of dancing that you judged suitable for public display.)

But it's not all about vocabulary and calisthenics. The 116-beats-per-minute rhythm program devised by producers Stock, Aitken & Waterman resembles the rhythm program of many other dance records, which means that being reminded of "I Should Be So Lucky" will remind you of many other songs, each with its own associations.

The production values and sonic textures will evoke 1987, and this will in turn lead you to that year in your life—what 1987 meant and felt like to you. To your surprise, "I Should Be So Lucky," which you would not describe as a record you care for, may nevertheless remind you of the summer when you were first in love, or the afternoon when a removal van took your belongings out of the family home, or the theme tune of Kylie's soap opera *Neighbours*, which in turn reminds you of those funny neighbors you had back then. All sorts of significant moments in your history have been impregnated, it seems, by sticky spores of Kylie.

If you're gay, other gay people may have made you feel that you should adore Kylie Minogue because she's a "gay icon." This may have helped you decide to what extent you wished to be part of a gay "scene" or not, and this, in turn, will have shaped the subtleties of your sexual response.

If you're straight, the fluctuations in Minogue's cultural capital—first hopelessly uncool, then forgivably harmless, then ultra-cool, then passé, then a "guilty pleasure"—will have poked and prodded your social identity, honing your capacity for shame or self-confidence.

You may have had a boyfriend who considered Stock, Aitken & Waterman an unforgivable blight upon civilization. You may have *been* that boyfriend. A war was waged around tolerating or not tolerating "I Should Be So Lucky," and you took a side, because however little you may have cared about Kylie, you cared quite a lot about your own status within your tribe.

o   o   o

As for the songs you *really* love, the sounds that *really* thrill you, those have an almost comically extreme effect on your brain. You get so excited that you light up like a lava lamp. Externally, you may look calm, but on the inside, it's all go. None of us can have any secrets from the measuring equipment: we are visibly turned on. The Beatles or Beyoncé may be nothing more than sparks in our neurotransmission, but we feel them (or think we feel them) in our hearts, our guts, our tear ducts, our sex organs, our souls, our mysterious "core."

What this means is that when parts of the brain get damaged or corroded, the music that was embedded in those parts is also embedded somewhere else. It's like finding "lost" files after a computer system crash. Maybe not the best or most complete versions of those files, but a hell of a lot better than nothing.

o   o   o

In a nursing home in the USA, an ancient African American man called Henry sits hunched in his wheelchair. Staring dully into the tray table on which he's fed, he's unwilling or unable to answer even "yes" or "no" to the simplest questions. Dementia or some such neurological curse has eaten away at his brain.

But as soon as a few choice recordings from the 1940s enter his ears from an iPod, a light comes on behind his eyes. He straightens up; his gnarled hands uncurl to wave in time to the rhythm.

"I'm crazy about music," he volunteers. "You play beautiful music, beautiful sounds."

The playlist is a bunch of educated guesses, based on his daughter's recollections. But now that Henry is switched on again, he's able to reply when the researchers ask him what his favorite music was when he was young.

"Well, I guess Cab Calloway was my number-one band guy I liked," he says, then does a bit of scat-singing in imitation of Calloway, then launches into "I'll Be Home For Christmas."*

In another nursing home, in Arizona, we meet Orma. Her language skills are horribly eroded. The sentences she comes up with in response to questions are incoherent strings of verbiage. She is too befuddled even to be frustrated.

The therapists put headphones on her ears and play her "As Time Goes By." Orma's face, which had been vacant, goes through a range of expressions.

"Where is he?" she asks, referring to Bing Crosby. "Tell him not to stop."

Afterward, the therapists ask her the same questions she was unable to answer before, but now, it's as though the neural pathways have been refurrowed by Crosby's crooning. She recalls the names of her mother and father, then chuckles as she reveals that she "wasn't an honest kid." She seems relieved to have been able to nuance her visitors' overly sentimental picture of her childhood.

"Such was life," she concludes.†

---

*   "(original) Man In Nursing Home Reacts To Hearing Music From His Era," from *Alive Inside*, uploaded to YouTube by Music & Memory on November 18, 2011.

†   "The power of music in dementia," uploaded to YouTube by Katie Reed on December 11, 2015.

∘ ∘ ∘

For a brief time, while the effects of the music last, Henry and Orma are "back"—back from wherever it is they've gone. It took them ages to get so lost. But some people—thirteen million per year, to be precise*—get lost abruptly. At a stroke. Strokes can rob the sharpest, wittiest people of the power of speech. The lips and tongue and vocal cords, all the equipment with which they previously made conversation, remain in perfect working order, waiting only for coherent instructions from a part of the brain that has died.

A person who can no longer speak, or whose stroke-afflicted speech sounds like a tortured animal, may, however, be able to sing. Stroke victims who've been rendered mute have been known to startle the hell out of their family by suddenly joining in with Gloria Gaynor's "I Will Survive" when it comes on the car radio.

Speech is a pushover, but the music in us is damn near impossible to kill.

∘ ∘ ∘

In November 2019, as the center of my town sprouts tinsel in anticipation of Christmas, I walk to the suburban outskirts, near the motorway to Dover. Nestled among the bungalows is a drab, underfunded public library. It's here that Duncan Moris and Helen Evans rehearse their group—the HeadStrong Singers, a choir of people with brain injuries.†

Helen is a coordinator for the South Kent division of the Stroke Association. She had "a pot of money" to allocate and decided that this choir was a worthwhile project. Other bits of

---

★   "Learn About Stroke," on World Stroke Organization website, 2021.

†   My thanks to Duncan Moris and Helen Evans for agreeing to be interviewed, at the HeadStrong rehearsal on November 25, 2019, and in follow-up emails in December 2019 and January 2020.

support came from unlikely sources—like the local police, who supplied the digital projector that displays the song lyrics on the library wall.

Duncan is a guitarist, songwriter and humanist marriage celebrant. He's spent a lifetime in the music industry without becoming famous. His other group, The Slammers Maximum Jive Band, who play in places like The Sands in Lincolnshire and the Mundesley Rock 'n' Roll Weekender in Norfolk, may get reviewed in the *Rockabilly Chronicle* but probably not in *Mojo* or *The Times*. Duncan has been leading choirs for many years, together with the composer, producer and music director Alex McNeice.

"Alex and I grew up together. It occurred to us when we were coaching football and PE that we should start up some local choirs. We started with a primary school choir. At the same time we were running singing groups at aged care homes, a dementia center and so on."

I sit at the back of the room while the choir members come in—some walking independently, some with walking aids, some in wheelchairs. A vivacious woman called Tracey welcomes everyone and offers them tea. (I learn later that she's had a stroke herself, and an aneurysm.)

"We've got your chair ready for you," says Tracey to the latest arrival.

"Oh, bless you," says the lady inching in with the four-wheeled stroller.

Duncan knows them all by name. "Hello, Poppy. Is it just you today, no Dot?" Dot's unwell. "Oh, that's no good."

The HeadStrong choir is not here for therapy alone. They're preparing to sing in public, for other people's entertainment. Their next gig is at the Richard Stevens Stroke Unit at William Harvey Hospital in Ashford, three weeks hence.

"We always go on the day of the staff party," says Helen. "Everybody loves it. I don't know anything about highbrow music. But I do know that people like to sing and it does them good. And when you've had a head injury, it's tremendously inspiring and empowering to be doing something as a team, something normal."

The forthcoming concert, on December 12, will have a Yuletide theme. The choir tackles "Silent Night" (first in German, then in English), "Once In Royal David's City," "The Little Drummer Boy," "It's Beginning To Look A Lot Like Christmas" and "All I Want For Christmas Is You." ("There's been some terrible versions of this over the years," remarks Duncan. "But the way we do it is brilliant.")

The choir struggles with Elton John's "Step Into Christmas," whose clunky words hang mercilessly exposed on the library wall. By contrast, the choir has no trouble learning Duncan's own ditty "Head Over Heels For The Holidays," which he finished writing a few days ago. "With my head strong/My feet can't go wrong," they sing, to a tune that sounds like an old standard.

"OK, we're moving on now, otherwise we'll be all Christmased out by Christmas," says Duncan. They move on to "Blue Moon," "Me Ol' Bamboo" and "Puttin' On The Ritz," whose rhythmic syncopations provoke fumbles and giggles.

"I used to hate ABBA," Duncan confesses as they prepare to sing "Mamma Mia." "I was wrong."

Sitting at the back of the library on that gray November afternoon, I'm blown away by a song I've not encountered before: "This Is Me," from the soundtrack of the movie *The Greatest Showman*. Friends of mine warned me off the film, for all sorts of good reasons, but this song, written by Benj Pasek and Justin Paul, lights up the room with grace. It's about society's pressure to be ashamed of being scarred and broken, to concede that you're unlovable. But no! No more apologies! "I am brave, I am bruised/I am who I'm meant to be, this is me." Halfway through the song, I realize I'm experiencing as transcendent a moment as I've ever experienced at a concert.

"Did you enjoy that?" the lady who came in on the stroller asks me, when it's all over and the choir members are leaving the building, going back to their maisonettes, their adapted flats, their beds. "Will we see you again?"

I stay behind, chatting to Duncan and Helen as the tea mugs are washed and the biscuit crumbs are cleared away.

"'This Is Me' is another one I had a prejudice against," Duncan reflects. "I'd never really listened to it, hadn't taken notice of the words. Alex introduced me to it. As soon as I brought it into the HeadStrong session, they were like 'That's our song. That's about us.' And then we all cry."

I ask Duncan and Helen if they have religious faith. Helen does, Duncan doesn't. He says that even at Christmas he tries to keep the repertoire "as secular as possible, to be more inclusive." I say that the reason I asked is that his involvements in the community seem so altruistic.

He smiles. "Well, I'm being paid for this. Is it altruism if you're being paid?" He thinks a moment. "I suppose if I won the lottery and didn't need money, I would do the exact same things with my week."

o   o   o

I don't spend my week restoring the dignity of the disabled. Reviewers and academics may write flattering articles about how "important" my books are, but I do wonder sometimes if my greatest contribution to society was the years I spent as a nurse, before my writing made it possible to quit that job. An old lady died in my arms once. I'm not convinced a novel can compete with that.

One of the ways I spend my week is conducting correspondence with artists and musicians. In my conversations with the violinist Judith van Driel, of the Dudok Quartet Amsterdam, we mostly discuss my lifelong lack of passion for classical music, and why people respond to some kinds of music and not to others.

One day, she mentions that she used to play in a street orchestra called the Ricciotti Ensemble. "We played everywhere where a normal orchestra doesn't play: in hospitals, prisons, psychiatric homes, for children with special needs, on the street... I remember playing Puccini's 'Crisantemi' for severely handicapped children. Because these children couldn't handle too much stimulus, a whole orchestra was too much, so we went as a string quartet. The children were making a lot of animallike noise (the only way to express themselves, but a little frightening for an outsider), but as soon as we started playing, they became silent. The atmosphere turned into something totally serene. The fact that music can do this is something extraordinary and unique, I think."*

o   o   o

In my former career, I was all too familiar with the Parkinson's walk. Patients would stand at my side, slightly hunched over, glancing nervously at the end of the corridor, their desired destination. I would hold their elbow as they attempted to launch themselves. At first they would seem glued to the spot, and then they would shuffle forward, taking very small steps, almost toppling over.

On YouTube, I watch a man called John go through this same indignity. His shoes seem nailed to the floor. He could fall on his face any second. Then music starts playing. Without hesitation, he takes his nurse by the hand and smoothly, gracefully, dances the tango with her. It's a miracle.

Except, physiologically, it's not. To walk with big, confi-

---

* Email conversations with Judith van Driel. Having read this chapter, my friend Jo Falla (formerly the baritone in a singing quartet, and father of a horn player) commented: "This is a little unjust to 'normal orchestras' most of which these days (in the UK at least) have 'outreach' or 'connect' education or community programmes, and play all over everywhere. They have to do this to secure their funding from arts councils and other funding bodies. [My son] as a child used to greatly enjoy 'play-away days' with the Scottish Chamber Orchestra."

dent steps, we need dopamine, which is produced in nerve cells that have died off in Parkinson's sufferers. They're rummaging around in their substantia nigra looking for something that's not there. The brain, as I said at the start of this chapter, is an awesome device, but, like any overcomplex piece of tech, it can get stubbornly attached to problem-solving processes that don't work. Headstrong, you might say.

"What we think music does," explains Professor Meg Morris of La Trobe University's Human Movement Lab, "is to bypass the defective basal ganglia, to activate what's trapped inside. The music provides an external rhythm, to compensate for the defective rhythm inside the brain."*

John dances like a dream. It's a pity he can't tango his way down the street.

o o o

Grenville Hancox, musician, humanitarian, founder of the Canterbury Cantata Trust, conductor and professor emeritus at several universities, was awarded an MBE for his services to music in 2005. He's easy for me to find—in a church three minutes' walk from my home, conducting a choir of local people with neurological afflictions, mostly Parkinson's disease.

Hancox started the sessions in May 2019. Seven months later, the ensemble has swelled from twenty to sixty, just from word of mouth. There's room for them all, though. It's a big church. Victorian Gothic. Good acoustics, chocolate biscuits, tea and orange squash.

The drill here is similar to what happens at Sing to Beat Parkinson's gatherings all over the country. Everyone sits in a circle, facing each other. They're a team, not a congregation. They're here to work out.

---

*   "Power Of Music On The Brain | Dementia & Parkinson's," uploaded to YouTube by ABC Science on June 7, 2016.

The youngest person is Sophy, whose promising career in a youth orchestra was cut short by a car accident. She's now in a motorized wheelchair, bundled up in scarves. Most of the others look to be in their sixties and seventies; one man is ninety. But then, the silver-haired Hancox himself is seventy, and, despite his smart floral shirt and fashionably baggy jeans, walks with a gait that suggests his musculoskeletal system is no longer tip-top. At one point, reattaching a lapel microphone that fell off his breast, he jokes, "This is a pacemaker, really."

Even so, Hancox is turbocharged, managing the crowd like a Mick Jagger sans hair dye. He warms them up with what might appear to be nonmusical exercises: "Massage your left arm. Massage your right arm. Stamp your feet. Massage your left thigh. Massage your right thigh. Punch the air with your left leg..." and so on. The exercises evolve into clapping games, and before long, sixty souls are performing the unmistakable clapping/stomping intro of one of Queen's big hits, while Hancox leads the chant of "We Will Rock You."

From there, the vocal workouts get more complex. Scales, tackled not in do-re-mi fashion but as mathematical sequences: 1-2-3-4-3-2-1, then 1-2-3-4-5-4-3-2-1, and so forth, stretching the voices toward an octave. Next they do the alphabet, reaching their top note with M and then scaling down again. "See if you can do it with one breath," urges Hancox. "Use your diaphragm to push the air out."

Next, Hancox divides the group into two halves of about thirty each. He gets one half to start singing the alphabet, and the other half to start a few seconds later. The church resounds with the ancient canon known as a rondellus.

Next, Hancox divides the group into four, all starting at different points. I expect them to dissolve into hapless chaos. They don't. They sing their appointed parts unwaveringly, without being thrown off by what their companions are doing.

They move on to "Land Of The Silver Birch," an early

twentieth-century Canadian song celebrating the ancestral home of Indigenous peoples. "It's full of consonants which are quite difficult to get out," forewarns Hancox, but within minutes the group is singing "My paddle's keen and bright/Flashing with silver…" in several discrete overlapping parts.

"Fantastic!" crows Hancox when they've pulled it off. "We're doing all these new pieces and your brain is being exercised like mad. You know that phrase: use it or lose it? This is absolutely brilliant for that." And he pats his head and rubs his stomach simultaneously.

Hancox grew up with classical music and its veneration of elite skills, but is remarkably democratic in his values. He seems to have no time for virtuosos.

"Training is of minuscule importance in terms of our human development," he tells me during the refreshment break.* "We've always been performers, all of us, but at a certain point we gave other people responsibility for doing it on our behalf. That performance tradition is taken to its isolated extreme in Romanticism and post-Romanticism. *Our* sort of group is just rekindling the whole point that we're hardwired to sing. Everybody can do it."

Everybody can indeed do it, but not as well as Dolly Parton or Pavarotti. The way ordinary people sing can be charming, even moving, but compared to the finest practitioners of Art, it falls audibly short.

"I'd dispute that," insists Grenville. "These people are singing from the heart and they're singing with conviction. Also, their pitch and their sense of rhythm and pulse are quite remarkable. Besides, this isn't a professional choir. This is a singing group coming together specifically to feel better."

Hancox has campaigned to have singing prescribed on the

---

* My thanks to Professor Grenville Hancox and his program director Matthew Shipton for allowing me to witness the session at Holy Trinity Church, Folkestone, in December 2019, and for the interviews.

NHS. His many scholarly articles attest to the power of music to heal trauma and promote well-being.

"Alan over there is a fantastic example," he says. "He's profoundly deaf; he was convinced he couldn't sing because of his deafness, and now he's pitching really quite well. His wife's got terrible Alzheimer's and is in a home and is violent, so emotionally he's really suffered, and these sessions have become for him a salve, a sanctuary."

I ask Grenville if he's a person of faith.

"Faith in music, yeah. I don't have faith in the sense of a belief in God. I believe in good. There's so much good, but we don't let it surface as often as we should."

o   o   o

One music therapist who definitely believes in God is Adrian Snell. In his younger years, he was one of the luminaries of the Jesus rock movement, making orchestrally enhanced prog albums like *The Passion, The Virgin* and *Alpha + Omega*. In more recent decades, he has laid aside the grandiloquence to work with disabled and discarded people, not just in Britain but in Nepal and Albania.

His musical tool kit these days is portable noisemakers that can be shared with nonmusicians. The kalimba, or thumb piano, makes lovely sounds even when plucked by spastic fingers. Handheld wind chimes, harmonicas, swanee whistles, touch-sensitive iPads, HAPI drums* and other gadgets can all bridge the gap between performer and audience. Laughter and touch—hand in hand, sometimes forehead to forehead—have taken the place of choreographed light shows. Often, Adrian tenderly sings the person's name—Kasandra, Romi, Koli—while looking into their eyes.

In the post-Communist shambles of Korçë, Albania, poverty is

---

*   HAPI = Hand Activated Percussion Instrument.

rife and there's no NHS or welfare system to give a damn about the losers at the bottom. The church and what Snell describes as "the goodness of people's hearts"* fill the vacuum.

The work that Adrian and his daughter Carla do with orphans, prisoners and street kids is outside the scope of my chapter, but for the Snells it's no different from the work they do with the severely disabled. It's all honoring the belief that God loves everyone, no matter what their situation.

And anyway, in the high-rise asylum that Snell calls The House on the Hill, the dividing line between social destitution and physical disability is very hard to see. The admission criteria seem to be that you have nowhere else to go; ages range from teens to eighties. Some are alarmingly emaciated, others shuffle on elephantine legs. I spot some Down syndrome folks. I watch Carla Snell dancing madly with a vivacious kid called Voltisa. What's Voltisa's health status? I can't guess. Her teeth are bizarre, but maybe that's just the miserable diet.

I ask Adrian to choose one incident that embodies for him how powerful a difference music can make. He recalls his work with Cindy, a girl with cerebral palsy. Cindy, unlike most of the Albanian children Adrian and Carla have bonded with, lives with her own family in a haven of nurture. But her brain is so severely impaired that she struggles to even touch the instruments Adrian shares with her. She does breathe, so in principle it's possible for her to make a noise with a harmonica, but for ages she was "just unable to find the amount of 'blow' needed to find the sound… And then, *suddenly*…it's there. The joy on her face, and the face of her mother, is impossible to describe."

In conversation, Snell occasionally mentions a Bible verse that resonates with him, or speaks of his sometimes troubled faith in

---

*   From *Beyond Words: Music Therapy in Albania* (Rachel Bunce Films/The Coverdale Trust, 2012). My thanks to Adrian Snell for sending me this DVD, which I don't think is commercially available. The other quotes in this chapter come from Adrian's email interviews with me.

God. Mostly, though, he's a practical humanitarian, worlds away from the old-school Christian missionaries who would travel to "exotic" cultures to win souls for Christ. He never mentions miracles of healing. He knows that his brain-damaged friends are not going to leap up from their wheelchairs or throw away their crutches. He wants them to have fun fooling around with a swanee whistle. He wants their contorted fingers to make sweet music on the kalimba.

o   o   o

I reach out to Dr. Maggie Haertsch, an Australian consultant who has spent decades studying and promoting recorded music in health care. I'd been struck by her observation—made in a documentary for ABC television—that "music is a human right."* What exactly does she mean by that?

One of Haertsch's principles, in the Music & Memory sessions she does in care homes, is that the playlists should be specific for each person, and channeled directly into their ears rather than broadcast into an open space they share with others. Henry, the Cab Calloway fan we met near the beginning of this chapter, is a classic Music & Memory beneficiary, coaxed out by sounds meant for him alone.

"I find that music delivered through a speaker rather than headphones can easily become muzak, caught up in the humdrum of the day," she tells me.† "It often becomes irritating if the volume is high and the other noise in the room is noticeable."

I ask Haertsch to describe the most moving or extraordinary reaction to music she's ever observed. She describes two.

"I recall one woman, 46 years old with advanced Multiple Sclerosis. She relied on help for every aspect of living includ-

---

*   "Power Of Music On The Brain | Dementia & Parkinson's," uploaded to YouTube by ABC Science on June 7, 2016.

†   Email exchanges between Dr. Maggie Haertsch and me, July 2020.

ing bathing, dressing, positioning and repositioning her body... Sadly she was nearing the end of her life. Her husband had given us her playlist of songs. Spandau Ballet's hit 'True' was played for the first time through the iPod. She erupted in a flood of tears with the lyrics: 'I bought a ticket to the world/But now I've come back again...' She recounted the memory of her once vibrant and independent life. They were good memories and good feelings.

"I remember another couple, the husband had dementia living at home with his wife as a full-time carer. She was exhausted, he would be up at all hours, wandering, checking all the doors and windows to see where he could leave the house. He also developed a keen interest in eating anything that looked attractive, including cleaning products, which of course needed to be hidden.

"His advancing dementia resulted in many other changes in their lives, including his inability to speak, which caused him a lot of frustration. The couple originally met when they were 21 at the town hall dances in the 1950s, both were very talented dancers and loved to do the Jive. When we put the headphones on them both and turned up the iPod with Bill Haley and His Comets' classic hit, 'Rock Around The Clock,' he started to laugh, took his wife by the hand and they danced together around the lounge room, both working up a sweat. The pace was fast and the mood was uplifting. He started to sing: 'When the clock strikes two...'

"A small miracle happened, the love was alive and they connected in a way that was not about illness, caring or a dynamic of dependence. It lasted for about 20 minutes after the music finished and was a cherished moment that gave them back each other."

I'm all for people swingin' to Bill Haley, but the first of Maggie's anecdotes is challenging for me. Spandau Ballet are a group I particularly dislike, and "True" is the song of theirs that irritates me most. Of course I'm aware that there are women who found Spandau Ballet handsome and debonair, and who, at a tender age, swayed to their songs. But the idea that a song as empty and smug (to my ears) as "True" should ring so true to a woman dying of multiple sclerosis—and that its words may have profound meaning if given a chance—takes me aback.

I suddenly appreciate what Maggie Haertsch (who confesses to me that she can't stand Spandau Ballet either) has long argued—that a personalized playlist is crucial. The likes and dislikes of the nursing staff or the therapists are irrelevant; what's important is the taste and associations of the vulnerable person stuck in an institution.

Indeed, Haertsch tells me she cringes at the concept of "therapizing" music. "I see this in aged care a lot," she says. "Everything that has anything to do with enhancing well-being becomes a 'therapy.' We don't need to medicalise the enjoyment we try to create for everyday living. It only reinforces institutionalisation. All this is about is helping people to access and enjoy their own music. They're simply listening to what they would listen to if they were well."

I imagine myself trapped in a body ruined by some neurological horror show like motor neurone disease or Huntington's chorea. I imagine myself in a home that is not my home, being cared for by nurses. I imagine them playing me Spandau Ballet, or, if they've taken the trouble to research the music that was in the charts when I was a teenager, Thin Lizzy or KC & The Sunshine Band. Would I ever hear Moebius & Plank's *Rastakraut Pasta* again? How likely is it that the staff would pipe Coil's *Astral Disaster* into the communal sitting room after lunch?

o   o   o

Reading between the lines of this chapter, you can probably tell that different music therapists have conflicting ideas about how to help those who can't organize their own sounds. Which is the best approach? What counts as evidence that someone has been helped? If the person to whom we offer the music is moaning and grimacing and squirming, or sitting blank-faced, because moaning and grimacing and squirming or sitting blank-faced is all their condition allows them to do, how do we know if they've been "reached"? What about the hopeless cases, the ones who are too far gone?

Arguably, our focus on a certain kind of "result" may be more about how *we*, the onlookers, want to feel than anything else. The responses we're looking for—the kind that go viral on YouTube if a camera captures footage of demented or disabled people "coming alive"—play into our normative attitudes. Strangers who are no longer like us (or who never were like us) seem to demonstrate, even for a moment, that they can be like us after all, and we applaud. Thanks to the magic of music, these abnormals can be almost normal.

The general public loves feel-good stories, little narrative orgasms. A juicy video in this genre will attract tens of thousands of comments, most of them along the lines of "OMG, I'm crying!" I hope that you, or I, never end up in a YouTube video that gives web-surfers their fix of sentiment for the day.

o   o   o

As I write this, I'm still in reasonable neurological shape. I live alone, and need no assistance. My flat has thirteen concrete steps leading down to it; I nip up and down them without a thought. That won't last. But it's fine for now.

If I feel like hearing Coil's *Astral Disaster*, I'm capable of making it happen for myself. I know that the CD is filed in one of the bookshelves in my music room, about ten feet to the right of where I'm sitting. I know that if I got up now and walked there—which nothing hinders me doing—I would find *Astral Disaster* among the other Coil albums in the Cs.

So far so good, cerebrally speaking. I remember that C comes after B and before D, and I remember what the album is called and who it's by. This suggests I don't have dementia yet, although the evidence for that is not conclusive, because I do forget other musicians' names and album titles with much greater frequency nowadays than I used to.*

People with dementia remember the distant past better than the day before yesterday. Should I worry about the fact that I can recall virtually every word on Leo Sayer's *Just A Boy*, and the names of the session musicians who worked on it, even though I haven't played the album in forty-five years, whereas I had to do a Google search for "African"/"electronica"/"1980s" to retrieve the name of Francis Bebey, whose music I've loved more recently and consider more remarkable than Sayer's? Each time I play Bebey's stuff, it's as though I've never heard it before. Is that the magic of his music, or my cerebellum shriveling up?

Having been reminded of Leo Sayer's *Just A Boy*, I experience it replaying in my mind, as though there's a turntable inside my skull that has a black platter revolving on it, its stylus

---

*   This morning, I couldn't remember the name of a CD I own celebrating the philosophies of Scientology supremo L. Ron Hubbard. I thought it might be by Chick Corea, the most famous of L. Ron's jazz converts, but I checked under C, and no luck. So I typed "Scientology" and "musicians" into Google. (That's cheating, of course: using the internet as an external brain to compensate for the misfired synapses of your own.) The usual suspects came up, but none of them suggested the item that was hiding somewhere on my shelves (i.e. somewhere in my mind). I finally found the damn thing on Discogs, by perusing the cover art of all the albums that name-check Hubbard. The CD I'd been looking for was credited to "L. Ron Hubbard and Friends" and safely stored on my shelves under H.

       Was my memory failure a sign that my brain is being eroded by Alzheimer's? Or was it because I refuse to believe that Hubbard—who was not a musician—truly composed the material on *The Road To Freedom*? Or was it simply a sign that I own far too many albums, including some I should've got rid of ages ago?

       I prefer these alternative explanations, of course. That's only natural. But the inescapable fact is that my brain doesn't work as well now as it once did. The camembert is past its best.

riding in the groove of side two, track five. Twenty-six-year-old Leo from West Sussex, doing his best to sound like a black soul singer who's lived a long life of trouble.

In my teens, I found all sorts of things about *Just A Boy* worthy of filing in my brain. It had Mike Giles, formerly of King Crimson, drumming on it. Andrew Powell, who'd done the orchestral arrangements for Cockney Rebel, put strings on Leo too. Backing vocals were supplied by session singers Barry St. John and Liza Strike, whose names I'd noted on lots of other LPs.* Nowadays, my brain declines to log the names of backing singers and orchestral arrangers. I'm lucky if I can remember the name of the star.

Just A Boy is still in my collection, because I've lacked the impetus to get rid of it, and because I like the booklet with its sweet illustrations. I haven't played the LP for decades but I don't need to, because every note and vocal inflection is etched in my brain, a legacy of the time when I only owned about thirty or forty albums.

I currently own thousands of hours of music that I will never get to know as intimately as I got to know *Just A Boy*. Much of it is avant-garde and "challenging." I'm not yet challenged by Parkinson's disease, or a massive stroke that maims half my body. That phase of my life may begin next month, or this afternoon.

If I'm hit by such a misfortune, maybe the thing that will make my brain light up like a Christmas tree, make me rear up in my wheelchair, free my stifled voice to sing along, exorcising all my anger and sorrow as my dreams of immortality die, is Leo Sayer bitterly crying "I was just a boy/I know better now."

I prefer to imagine that the cosmic melancholy of Coil's *Astral Disaster* will bring me consolation. Maybe I will spend my

---

*   In the early 1990s, before I was a published author, I wanted to write a book about backing singers and corresponded with Barry about this. I failed to convince her and then she had a stroke and then she died.

final years on earth with a pair of headphones on, grooving to all the weird shit I've collected.

I should be so lucky.

SOMEWHAT MARRED
BY AN ECHO

In the olden days before amplifiers, digital delay units, volumetric diffusers, membrane absorber modules and fiberglass-reinforced gypsum (i.e. all of history up to a few minutes ago, proportionally speaking), people used to travel to real places and make music there, just because they liked how those places sounded. A place would get a reputation, and the musicians would come. From the moment the first hominid Caruso unleashed his yodel in the big cave underneath the short trees, music-makers have been enchanted by how different environments add magic to their warblings and hootings and pluckings.

That magic is science, actually, but there has always been a gulf between the two.

In the beginning, we weren't equipped to understand how sound works, and later on most of us preferred to maintain the mystique, treating an eerily reverberant cathedral almost as if it had been formed by natural forces, like a cave or a canyon.

Also, to be fair, buildings are complicated ecosystems that often behave in surprising ways. Time after time, architects and stonemasons have gazed up in bafflement at the auditory ghosts hanging around the rafters.

How do those ghosts get there? We invite them in. In our vision of the homes and palaces we wish to build, optics always win out over sonics. There are technicians who are happy to explain to us the geometry of sound waves and the absorptive properties of chair upholstery, but unless we are technicians ourselves, our attention will wander as soon as the numbers and graphs get too complicated. We may even cover our ears, not wanting magic to be reduced to mathematical formulas.*

If we regard the acoustics of an environment as some sort of supernatural mystery, then we're bound to note that the magic can sometimes work in reverse. Some spaces kill music stone dead. You can be the world's greatest singer yet when you unleash your utterance upon the airwaves in a particular room, you will barely be heard by people just a few feet away from you, and everyone will be distracted by the chatter of people at the back, or by the hum of the air-conditioning, or by a distant coffee machine, or by invisible clouds of despair.

This, too, is science.

o   o   o

The sound you hear when you speak while wearing a woolly hat on a snowy day is what recording engineers call "dry"—devoid of reverberation. Your voice is trying to make the atmosphere

---

*   I mean no disrespect to scientists in quoting the material below, I mean only to note—in all humility, and with gratitude for their expertise—that scientists have traveled very far down roads I took only a few steps on before turning back.

First, from *An Introduction to Acoustics* by S. W. Rienstra and A. Hirschberg (Eindhoven University of Technology, December 2021): "Consider in the 2-D half space $y \geq 0$ the harmonic sound field $p(x, y,\omega)$ e $i\omega t$ satisfying the Helmholtz equation $\nabla^2 p + k^2 p = 0$. where $k = \omega/c0$. If p, generated by (say) the surface $y = 0$, is given at $y = 0$ as the Fourier integral $p(x, 0) = p0(x) = \int\infty -\infty A(\alpha)$ e $-i\alpha x$ dα, it is easily verified that the field in $y \geq 0$ may be written as $p(x, y) = \int\infty -\infty A(\alpha)$ e $-i\alpha x -i\gamma y$ dα with the important square root (with branch cuts along the imaginary axis, and the real interval $|\alpha|$.)"

Second, from "Concert hall acoustics: Recent findings," by Leo L. Beranek, in *Journal of the Acoustical Society of America*, Vol. 139, Issue 4, April 2016. The author is discussing the acoustics in Boston Symphony Hall: "If Area $(B+C)$ is larger than Area $(A+C)$ the direct sound should be clearly heard, i.e., is not masked by the reflections. Since Area $(B+C)$ for this position in Symphony Hall holds the equivalent of about 600 closed circles and Area $(A+C)$ about 416, the difference between the two is 184 closed circles. The number of circles along the abscissa is equivalent to 37… A value of LOC of $+3$ dB predicts reliable detection of the direct sound and good clarity."

vibrate, but the atmosphere is in no state to comply. The famous promotional poster for the sci-fi movie *Alien* summed up what happens in the airless, boundless void outside our planet's gaseous halo: "In space no one can hear you scream."

By contrast, if you go to the Hamilton Mausoleum fifteen miles southeast of Glasgow, shut yourself into Mr. Hamilton's Roman-style tomb and shout "Boo!", you will hear that boo reverberating for up to fifteen seconds. Better still, if you can get permission to crawl into the formerly secret Royal Navy fuel depot in Inchindown, Invergordon, you can bask in the aftereffects of your sounds for seventy-five seconds—the longest reverberation in the world. My friend Lucie Treacher, a composer who grew up in the area, went down there in 2019, stood in tunnels that were once filled with millions of gallons of oil, and sang.*

Echoes are tremendous fun. Kids love them. Several times a week, I go on a walk that takes me through a railway underpass. It's not uncommon for me to encounter mothers with small children taking that same route. The children shout and stamp their feet, delighting in how resonant these noises are in that hoodoo hollow. Sometimes they keep hooting and stamping when they've emerged into the sunlight on the far side, and they look up in disappointment. "It only works when you're in *there*," explains Mom.

Edward, Prince of Wales, the son of Queen Victoria, was not quite as keen on echoes when he officially opened the Royal Albert Hall of Arts and Sciences in 1871. "The address was slowly and distinctly read by his royal Highness," noted *The Times*, "but the reading was somewhat marred by an echo which seemed to be suddenly awoke from the organ or picture gallery, and re-

---

*   Footage of Treacher's performances can be seen in *The Lucie Sessions*, a bonus feature released with the documentary film *One Shot: Inchindown* made by Simon Riddell and David Allen. Treacher also made her own more impressionistic film *Cryosphere*, and an album of the same name. See: "the Lucie Sessions | One Shot: Inchindown," uploaded to YouTube by David Allen on June 3, 2020.

peated the words with a mocking emphasis which at another time would have been amusing."[*]

The Royal Albert Hall was built to memorialize Victoria's beloved husband, who'd died a few years before of a mysterious ailment—possibly gastric cancer, possibly Crohn's disease—that nineteenth-century medicine was not advanced enough to diagnose. Nineteenth-century audio science was similarly clueless, it seems: the architects could've copied the design of spaces in which music had been noted to sound good, but chose instead to build an imperial edifice that *looked* awesome. Those infernal French might have their Cirque d'Hiver, but the English would outclass that Parisian indoor circus with a triumph of amphitheatricality.

The echo was so intrusive that the hall's owners soon compromised on the visual splendor of the domed ceiling by hanging a canvas awning under it. This dampened the worst of the reverberations. In the 1940s, the awning was replaced with a state-of-the-art aluminum curtain. Still the wisecrack persisted that the Royal Albert Hall was the only place where you were guaranteed to hear a new British composition more than once. It wasn't until the 1960s that the ceiling sprouted dozens of fiberglass mushrooms—pop art monsters invading the sacred dome of Victoriana—which stopped the echoes causing their mischief.

Unwanted echo is not the only problem the hall has, however. The building misbehaves when certain performers appear in it, because different spaces are suited to some kinds of music and not to others. In recent decades, the RAH has been opened up to all sorts of things, from violin concertos to African troubadours to Nine Inch Nails. Each thing vibrates the air in its own unique way and suffers its own peculiar sonic humiliations.

Diversity is the buzzword—good for business as well as for sociological progress. A part of me is tickled that the Royal Al-

---

[*]   *The Times*, quoted in *Sonic Wonderland: A Scientific Odyssey of Sound* by Trevor Cox (Vintage Digital ebook, 2014).

bert Hall is no longer the exclusive preserve of neoclassical white culture. I'm not convinced that the part of me being tickled is my ears, though. There are better places to see Patti Smith or Angélique Kidjo.

o   o   o

See? Or hear? Our terminology betrays our confusion about what we're actually doing when we witness musical performances. Do we want to aud or do we want to vid? Ideally we do both at once, but here again the acoustic properties of the space can make things complicated. Once music is electronically amplified, it no longer travels from the performers' mouths and hands directly to our ears; it is first conveyed into machinery, the machinery converts it into electronic impulses, and those impulses are then conveyed to loudspeakers that agitate the air around our heads.

One of the many potential problems with this setup, in a venue that's enormous like the Royal Albert Hall or Wembley Stadium, is that there may be a synchronization lapse between what we see and what we hear. The singer's lips move and the guitarist's fingers strum the strings, but the word and the chord arrive in our ears a moment later. This can be wildly discombobulating— a disconcert in every sense.

The scientific solution is to install multiple smaller loudspeakers at strategic points in the venue rather than relying on a few very large ones to project the sound the full distance. Thus we resort to increasingly sophisticated technology in order to preserve the illusion of something natural. And the quality of the listening experience we enjoy in any given building may depend on how much money the owners are willing to splash out on tweaking the sound waves. Even a new paint job—replacing a shiny reflective surface with a textured one—can make an audible difference.

o o o

I've seen/heard the experimental post-punk group Wire quite a few times over the years, including at the Royal Festival Hall, a concrete cavern that, unlike the Royal Albert, was designed with acoustics in mind. The music Wire play is sharp and un-sentimental, all angles and interlocks, and it came across well in the RFH. The symphonies of Elgar, Sibelius and Schubert fared less well, I gather. The classical conductor Sir John Barbirolli once complained (along with many other fans of orchestral music) that the hall was too dry: "Everything is sharp and clear and there is no impact"*—impact meaning, in this case, reverb. When a crescendo climaxes, the classical lover craves a bit of sonic afterglow, a postorgasmic throb in the auditory canals. In the Royal Festival Hall, it was all over just a second too soon.

A few years after the Wire concert, £91m was spent on the hall to make it friendlier to music that wasn't Wire. Canopies and ceiling panels were installed to stop the building swallow-ing so much reverb. The number of seats was significantly re-duced, because chairs, human bodies and clothing all absorb sound too. Just by being in the room, you alter the experience that you and your fellow concertgoers will have. It could there-fore be said that nowadays, whenever you miss out on a ticket for a sold-out classical gig at the RFH, it's because the refurbishers decided that everyone would have a better time without you.

o o o

I saw Wire twice in 2018, in smaller venues on the Kent coast.

The Booking Hall in Dover is a disused train station, with standing room for two hundred and eighty people. It's a high-ceilinged oblong that, from an aesthetic point of view, is at its best in pitch darkness. Wire made a raucous din in there,

---

*   Quoted in *Music, Acoustics & Architecture* by Leo L. Beranek (John Wiley & Sons, 1962).

which was OK because they're not averse to making a raucous din. Nevertheless, I always feel pity for musicians when they're frowning intently over their instruments, teasing out details and nuances that nobody in the audience has the slightest hope of hearing.

The Ramsgate Music Hall, likewise seatless, can squeeze in a mere one hundred and twenty punters. The owners bought it at auction when it was a dilapidated comedy club, and they spent £300,000 rebuilding it from the ground up. Quite a lot of that money must have been spent on the sound system and acoustic infrastructure. Wire played much the same set as they'd played in Dover, but sounded fabulous. Everything sharp and clear with plenty of impact. No doubt an acoustician could explain exactly why, with the help of a diagram crowded with arrows and geometric symbols. But what it boils down to is that the musicians' instruments were plugged into amplifiers and a mixing desk that were then, in effect, fed into an even larger "amplifier" and "mixing desk"—the Ramsgate Music Hall itself. The venue was one big high-spec gadget.

o   o   o

Before the rise of technology-driven capitalism, humans poured their ingenuity into adapting themselves to the world; from the twentieth century onward, we've been adapting the world to us. And nowhere is this more so than in the area of sound.

Our relationship with concert halls, as discussed above, is just one aspect of our changed relationship with acoustics. It is no longer necessary for us to make pilgrimages to the cave where our voices sound glorious, or to the palatial Baroque parlor where the tinkles of the harpsichord bounce off the walls just right. We make music wherever it suits us, and expect to be in control of the sound—to have dominion over it, as Jehovah puts it in the Book of Genesis.

o   o   o

The final phase of our journey—the final echo, if you like, of the Big Bang of the Industrial Revolution—is recorded sound. Sound was once an evanescent phenomenon, existing only in the moments it took to vibrate and decay. Now we conceive of it as an immutable object we can manufacture, collect, possess. Whether it's a shellac disc, a vinyl LP, a CD or an mp3 doesn't much matter: the crucial thing is that it seizes and preserves what was once unseizable and unpreservable.

o   o   o

Yet our scientific magic exceeds even this.

When we first invented audio recording, we set up our microphones and our wax acetates and our tape machines in reverberant spaces—magic caves whose properties we hoped to capture. That state of affairs didn't last. Soon enough we discovered that the uncanny acoustics we prized could be supplied by our equipment. We'd been doing things the hard way. "Echo" could be a knob on a console.

In a modern recording studio, virtually any physical environment can be mimicked. An urban underpass, the Alps, a submerged submarine, a Gothic cathedral—you name it, there's a way of simulating it. Nor do you need to pay for an expensive professional studio to work those wonders. The home equipment that any indie rock or folk musician can afford will offer her the option of cavernous reverb even in a tiny bedroom stuffed with sound-muffling cushions and knitwear. If you fancy sounding like a pixie or an abbeyful of Gregorian monks, you can. If you want a vibe reminiscent of a smoky blues club in 1948, there are settings for that. Or, if you fancy being the caveman in the echoey cave, you can choose how many times your whoop whoops back at you—once, twice, endlessly.

At long last, we are free of both time and space.

o   o   o

I love that freedom. This book of mine arises almost entirely from my love of that freedom.

But I can't help feeling the itchy discomfort of hubris in the glue that attaches the wings to my back.

THE FORCE OF THE BLOW

You know about my tinnitus, although it has probably slipped your mind by now. It has not slipped *my* mind. It's been whispering to me tirelessly since you began this book.

It hasn't stopped me listening to music or hearing the exquisite sounds that the world lays on for us every day—birdsong, the rustle of leaves, the prattle of small children. As I type, my fingers make noises on the keyboard, unmistakably "plastic" noises compared to the "Bakelite-on-metal" clacks made by an old-school typewriter. I wouldn't say they're beautiful noises, but I'm grateful to be able to hear them.

I'm grateful for all the physical capacities that still work. I hope you are, too, whatever your health status may be. My friend Jen has a genetic condition that will render her blind at some point; the question is not *if* but when. Other friends have had strokes and can no longer speak. My late wife was humiliated by the twin evils of cancer and chemotherapy, which made walking difficult and ultimately impossible. This has left me, years after her death, with a deep gratitude for my own mobility. Every time I tackle a flight of steps, I vividly recall her upward glance of despair.

As part of my nursing training, I learned how to fingerspell in British Sign Language. I'm a bit rusty now, and Google tells me that Americans use an entirely different and much more complicated system, which makes me hope that I never need to communicate with deaf Americans.

What I haven't told you yet is that I was once a deaf Australian.

o o o

I remember a tranquil sunny afternoon, June 10, 1983, in my old Melbourne neighborhood. The seaside suburb of St Kilda, to be exact, a decade or so before it gentrified. Lots of kebab shops, pawnshops, souvlaki joints, pornographic bookstores, brothels, and the Seaview Ballroom, where I'd seen The Birthday Party the night before. It had been the band's last-ever gig, although I didn't know that at the time. All I knew was that when I woke up the next morning, I was deaf.

Deafness, like blindness, is a spectrum and can manifest in all sorts of ways. But the main thing is the awareness that the people around you are living in a different world from the one you're in.

As I walked along Fitzroy Street, the pensioners and the junkies and the Goths ambled in the sunshine, chatting to each other. They were evidently untroubled by the rushing sonic wind that gusted all around me, the unrelenting muffled buzz that prevented the ordinary street sounds from entering my brain. I walked strangely, not convinced my feet were connecting with the pavement as they should. My head swiveled, in the hope of finding an angle where the squall of deafness would quieten, where the buzzing would go away. The junkies probably thought I was suffering withdrawal.

As I approached the grocery store, I saw a thin young man walking toward me. He had a very small dog on a leash, which trotted ahead of him on its twitchy little legs. He was Des Hefner, the drummer from last night. I considered congratulating him on the fine job he'd done, as he was an eleventh-hour replacement for The Birthday Party's regular drummer Mick Harvey, who'd refused to fly down from England for this tour, and he'd had to learn all the songs in a big hurry. But I decided against it, and let Des and his dog pass.* I'd already spoken to a few people that day, and couldn't really hear them or myself.

I was pretty sure I'd get better soon, partly because I was twenty-three, and a twenty-three-year-old *would* think that, and partly because I'd read articles about people who'd attended loud gigs and been deaf "for days afterward." That meant forty-eight to seventy-two hours, I figured.

I'd been to loud concerts before, but I'd always had a choice how close to the speakers I was. At the Birthday Party gig, which was unseated and chaotic, I was at the front, and the people behind me were pushing forward. There was no way I could've retreated even if I'd tried to. Indeed, at some point during the performance, the crush of bodies became so severe that my chest was being shoved against the hard edge of the stage and I was worried I might break a rib.

So I clambered up onto the stage and sat on it, hunched as low as possible to signal that I was not some attention-seeking stage invader but an innocent patron in a tight spot. I was less than a yard away from Tracy Pew's black-booted feet as he hammered the bass. Pew looked mean, and the tips of his boots were sharp. Fortunately, he couldn't be bothered to kick me.†

The real harm, in any case, was being done by the music. I was about a body's-length from the speakers, whose cones pulsed visibly with the seismic impact of "Hamlet (Pow Pow Pow)." The din was so all-enveloping that I couldn't comprehend the connection between those shivering speaker cones and the sound pummeling my head.

---

*   Niggled by doubts raised by the fact that the Birthday Party gig was in the middle of winter whereas my memory of the encounter with Des Hefner in the street was of him sunlit and short-sleeved, I tracked Des down and asked for clarification. Amused, he informed me that the incidents occurred three years apart.

†   As it happened, the only kicking on that stage occurred when Nick Cave fell on his back in the middle of a song and writhed there for a bit, provoking an incensed Rowland Howard to kick him and yell, "Get up, ya cunt!"

o   o   o

Were The Birthday Party too loud? From a medical perspective, yes. That is, my auditory system obviously took a battering and it is not healthy to batter one's auditory system. But I lived to tell the tale and I wasn't unhappy with the volume the band employed. The Birthday Party were a feral post-punk group whose explicit purpose was to channel rage and delirium. It would've been wrong, I reasoned, for them not to assault the senses. Besides, the experience made a good story to tell my British friends twenty years later when the non-Australian world had begun to worship Nick Cave, and anecdotes of his mythic origins were suddenly gold.* "I've read that those gigs were ferocious." "Yes, I suppose you could say that they were," I murmur.

o   o   o

At home, I play music quite soft, usually while I'm writing or researching. I don't cause nuisance to the neighbors. If you look at vintage record sleeves, you'll often find that they display an ostensibly defiant but actually quite nannying instruction: PLAY LOUD. I routinely ignore it. Diamanda Galás's *Plague Mass* (*Give Me Sodomy Or Give Me Death*), a scarifying exorcism of the discrimination suffered by AIDS victims, is stamped PLAY AT MAXIMUM VOLUME ONLY. Who is she kidding? Does anyone ever play anything at maximum volume through their home stereo? On rare occasions, I've turned the knob halfway, and worried that the speakers might blow.

As I write this, I'm playing *Information Overload Unit* by SPK, a pioneering release in the genre of industrial or "power electronics." There are no instructions on the cover but if any album

---

*   I'd actually interviewed Nick Cave in 1979. Nobody regarded his origins as mythic then. The local record company to which his group The Boys Next Door were signed gave me his mom's phone number, in case I needed to get in touch. See the chapter "Overcome with All The Excitement."

demands to be played loud, it's this one. Yet I'm playing it very soft—the amplifier dial barely above minimum—because I'm expecting a package and I want to hear the postman when he rings the doorbell.

o   o   o

I'm not alone in exerting this sort of control over how much I allow the music in my home to claim my attention. We buy the thing and then feel we should be allowed to use it in whatever way we wish. The musicians plead in interviews that the only way to appreciate their masterpiece is to surrender to it utterly, and we put it on in the background while we do the washing up or prepare our tax return. Tough.

In a concert situation, however, we expect to be at the mercy of the performers. All other concerns we might ordinarily be distracted by are supposed to be banished by the authority of what's happening onstage. In a classical context, this might be operatic bombast, or it might be something barely audible—the highest string of a violin played with exquisite restraint. ("You could hear a pin drop.") In a rock or pop context, it's more likely to be an almighty racket.

My most recent rock gig was at the 100 Club in April 2022. It was a celebratory reunion of Red Guitars after thirty-five years apart. Many members of the audience were, to put it diplomatically, not whippersnappers anymore. Polyvinyl earplugs were handed out at the bar. I tried them for the first couple of songs, but got frustrated by the dulling of the treble registers. I wanted the zing and sizzle of that top end.

So I ditched the protection and let the din do its stuff. The sound balance organized by the band's mixing engineer was excellent, which always helps—bad mixes inflict damage without any compensatory benefits. By the end of the gig, the audience was shouting along with the chorus of Red Guitars' greatest hit "Good Technology."

o   o   o

It's technology that has given us the means to deafen ourselves with music. In centuries past, you could conceivably have your eardrums perforated by someone clashing cymbals right next to your head, but that was an unlikely encounter. Whereas we are using electricity and sophisticated gear to damage our brains, whenever we go to an amplified gig.

Humans can be stupid when it comes to assessing risk. They refuse lifesaving medicines or vaccinations because of the (vanishingly small) possibility of serious side effects. They lecture their friends about how meat or dairy products are ruinous to health, while continuing to smoke and drink. They fret about toxins in tap water, but unthinkingly get into cars every day, despite the fact that the risk of dying on the roads is alarmingly high.

A favored pastime of seasoned rock fans is to swap stories of the loudest gigs they ever attended. It's yet another way that humans can bond over music chatter without necessarily talking about Art. The focus, instead, is on the physical effects wrought by sound waves upon the hapless attendees at this or that venue on such-and-such a memorable occasion. Dental fillings shaken loose. Sonic punches to the guts. Nausea, vomiting. Handbags moving eerily along the floor. Chunks of plaster falling off the ceiling. Vibrating eyeballs. Pain, pain, pain. Morning-after visits to the hospital. "Great, though. Wouldn't have missed it for the world."*

My ears are very precious to me. Yours, too, to you, I imagine. We all want to be able to hear birdsong, rustling leaves and

---

*   Andrew Male, my editor on this book, wrote to me after reading this. "While I was walking the dog I was asking myself what I was looking for in those loud gigs by Swans, Boris, My Bloody Valentine, Dinosaur Jr, etc. Maybe, when we're young, we want loud music to act on us like the Holy Spirit might act upon a worshipper in a Pentecostal church. But also…hearing loss worn as a proud souvenir, a mark of pain to prove that *something happened*?"

chortling babies. Yet I thought nothing of taking my ears into the Seaview Ballroom to be bludgeoned by sounds that made metal fixtures tremble. What made me so confident that no harm would come to me? It seems as foolhardy an act as sauntering onto a rope bridge across a chasm, or diving from a height into murky waters.

Herd mentality must have been part of it. We tend to adapt our behavior to what the people around us are doing. A couple of years ago, when the COVID epidemic was far from over, I attended an arty event in my town, wearing a mask, as instructed by the NHS guidelines of the time. Nobody else in the room was wearing one. Within minutes I'd taken mine off. Nonconformist though I may fancy myself to be, I felt weird respecting a danger that everyone else didn't regard as serious. Was anyone in the Seaview Ballroom wearing any ear protection? No.

Then there's the machismo, the gladiatorial bravado of the performers, with which the fan is invited to identify. "The only way to feel the noise is when it's good and loud!" sang Lemmy in Motörhead's "Overkill."* "Everything louder than everything else!" caterwauled Meat Loaf (who would end up wearing hearing aids). "Rock and roll ain't noise pollution!" crowed AC/DC. (Thirty-six years later, they had to cancel a tour so that the singer who screeched those words wouldn't go totally deaf.) During The Who's 1989 reunion tour, Pete Townshend, who'd once smashed electric guitars in front of giant Marshall amplifiers blasting out monstrous excesses of sound, opted to sit inside a glass partition to protect his horrendously degraded ears. In 2012, at a gig in Florida, the volume drove him to flee the stage altogether.†

---

*   Lemmy never wore earplugs, and never went deaf. In later years, he did write a song called "Deaf Forever," but its lyric referred to fallen warriors no longer hearing the battle's din.

†   "Pete Townshend Walks Off Stage During Encore After Complaining Of Too Loud Music" by Roger Wink, *Noise11.com* website, November 5, 2021.

Townshend's paradoxical behavior—trademarking the essence of heedless youthful rebellion while exhibiting more and more of the frailties and compromises of old age—is actually not a bad fit for the twenty-first-century entertainment business. The current generation of rock, rap and pop stars are not the naive adventurers of yesteryear. They approach the concert stage the way construction workers approach a building site. If their act involves falling passionately to their knees, they wear shock-cushioning knee pads. The soles of their shoes are lined with textured tape to give them extra grip on slippery floors. They all wear earplugs. And they use all manner of sophisticated wizardry to ensure that the most harmful sound waves are directed out at you, not at them.

The ultimate in contemporary absurdity is a concert where the performers and the audience are all wearing earplugs. Such concerts are already happening, partly because capitalism just loves to create new problems with expensive solutions. You can accept the crappy little earplugs that venues hand out for free, or you can get serious and buy proper equipment, researching the myriad options in the NRR (Noise Reduction Ratings) marketplace. Vibes Hi-Fidelity Earplugs can be had on Amazon for £10.99, and they're discreet so nobody need know you're using them—thus preserving your "gimme danger" cred. Or there's the Flare Audio Isolate Pro, the Alpine MusicSafe Pro, the Ear-Labs dBud, the Wowteech Super Soft, and many others. At the top end of the market, we find the Etymotic Music Pro plugs, which one website acknowledges are "an expensive option—but how much do you value your hearing?" The answer to that question is £349.95.*

Unnecessary commercialism aside, there's something inherently stupid about paying lip service to the tradition of Dionysian abandon, while taking prudent precautions. Music should

---

*   "Best earplugs for concerts 2022: Protect your hearing and get your ears gig-ready" by Chris Corfield, *Louder* website, October 18, 2022.

be unfettered and alive, with the potential to be frightening or overwhelming. Shattering, even.

A much better alternative to an "arms race" of hearing protection was suggested at a King Crimson concert in Arlington, Texas, in October 1973. The band had just performed "Larks' Tongues In Aspic," a piece with wide dynamic range, in which the ensemble attack sounded all the mightier for its contrast to the bits where bells tinkled delicately in the hush—had there *been* any hush, that is. The restless Texans, as was their wont, hollered utterances like "Wah-hoo!" and "Louder!"

To which guitarist Robert Fripp replied, in his droll Dorset tones: "I heard a request from a gentleman over here to play louder. I'd make one suggestion: If we're not loud enough, sir, perhaps you'd care to listen more attentively."*

I'm quite prepared to listen more attentively.

Looking back on my gig-going life, I always was, even in the days when I'd glance down at my T-shirt and notice that the fabric was flapping against my abdomen with every bang of the drums. I wanted—and still want—such dramatic effects to happen within my invulnerable soul, not in my fragile, irreplaceable capsule of flesh.

---

* Originally on a bootleg called *Senabular*; since officially released on the twenty-seven-disc *Starless* box set.

ON HAVING NO VOICE

For a few months in 1985, I could sing!

Then I lost the knack. But while I had it, it felt pretty good, I must say.

Here's how it happened.

I'd just moved from whatever rented dump I was living in before, to another rented dump, in Tempe, a poor suburb of Sydney. My new abode was actually a freestanding house, but small—smaller than the flat I live in now—and in shabby repair. It was perched on a scarp above the Cooks River, known as "the river that died of shame" because of its unique blend of sewage, diesel, mercury, battery acid, cyanide and dead things. It was also right underneath the flight path of Sydney Airport.

Even so, I was moving up in the world. I had a house and a boat (a wee inflatable plastic dinghy). I was no longer an unemployed literature graduate. I'd qualified as a nurse and had full-time work.

One of the things I spent my amazing new wage on was a piano. I bought it at the Tempe Tip, a large Salvation Army charity shop nicknamed after the landfill site nearby. It wasn't a grand piano, obviously; it was a small upright. But it was made of varnished wood and ivory* and looked appropriately olde-worlde. It had castors, which allowed me to push it up the hill

---

* Yes, elephant tusks. Few people even paused to ponder the implications, in those days. Occasionally, in antique shops, you would see a hollowed-out elephant leg for storing umbrellas in.

all the way to my house. I was fit and strong in those days, from lifting sick and paralyzed people.

Having installed the piano in my living room, I tackled the next challenge, which was that I had no idea how to play it. But with a wage, everything seemed possible. I hired a piano teacher to visit me once a week.

Before long, I'd learned to sight-read a simple score and play the first few études in Béla Bartók's *Mikrokosmos* series. My teacher encouraged me to sing along with what I was reading and playing. To my surprise, the notes that came out of my mouth were accurate. They were even quite pleasant. Who was this warbling stranger that had possessed me?

I'd sung soprano in a choir when I was a child. We were called the Maroondah Singers.* I wore a cummerbund and sang chestnuts like "Raindrops Keep Falling On My Head," "If Ever I Should Leave You," "My Favorite Things" and that Swingles arrangement of the Bach bourrée that goes "doob-*dooo*, doob dooby-dooby-doo." After my voice broke, my ability to hit the right notes collapsed, a sad state of affairs that persists today. I know what notes I want but my throat won't go there. I quaver, I croak, I bleat, and I'm so off-key you would think I was doing it deliberately to disqualify myself from being chosen for the team. I'm not. I would love to sing, but I just can't.

Except for those few months in 1985, at my junk-shop piano, with the jet planes roaring overhead.

Not long afterward, I moved again, to a minuscule flat near a different body of water—Sydney Harbour. The piano didn't come with me. I promptly forgot how to play Bartók, forgot how to sight-read music. And forgot how to make music come out of my mouth.

---

* Still going, half a century on, and still very much the same sort of proposition. No more cummerbunds, but the males get to wear long dangly red ties, like Donald Trump.

o   o   o

Never mind: I may have forgotten how to do it, but I'll never forget that I once could. And that's why I know that music teachers and vocal coaches are right when they insist that everyone can sing. It's not like glibly supportive parents assuring inept, clueless children that they're marvelously clever and can do anything. It's just biological fact.

o   o   o

I shouldn't need the memory of my piano-playing year to know this. All of us with functional throats should take it as a given that we can sing. If you can talk, you know how to push air through your lungs, larynx and vocal cords to make modulated sounds. It may not sound like music to you, but it's the same stuff that songs are made of.

Also, we have sophisticated stylistic skills we seldom use in earnest but often use in jest. If you can sarcastically imitate the voice of a person who annoys you, or use tonal inflection to signal that you're speaking ironically, or recite a Monty Python sketch or even a catchphrase like Arnold Schwarzenegger's "I'll be back" or Homer Simpson's "D'oh!", you are capable of using your instrument in a virtuoso manner. With talents like that, you could tackle Mozart next.

Except most of us can't. Singing is a locus of ridiculous anxiety. Many of us find it as exposing as being stripped naked in front of strangers. An inner Simon Cowell, supercilious and smug in his Olympian authority, fixes us with a withering stare and says, "You must be *joking*, honey. Get out of here."

o   o   o

There are born singers, in the same way that there are born sprinters and dancers and woodworkers and so on. Particular designs of hand or foot or nose or throat—and brain, of course—make some individuals more suited to particular pursuits. From a very early age, without being taught, they show a natural aptitude for activities that other people need a lot of training to master.

Nevertheless, even those with an innate talent for singing need a bit of luck in their journey toward being a confident vocalist. A voice can be forced to do things that are wrong for what it's naturally suited to do. And when we're forced to do things that are wrong for us, we perform badly, and when we perform badly, we're liable to avoid performing at all.

In Orson Welles's cinematic masterpiece *Citizen Kane*, tycoon Charles Foster Kane meets a woman who wins his heart by singing an aria from Rossini's *The Barber of Seville* at her parlor piano. Her voice is light, a little wobbly, but sweet: she could sing heart-melting lullabies for children; she would be an asset to any choir; she might even, with the right material, find a niche in musical comedy. Kane decides to make her an opera star. He buys an opera house, pulls strings, bribes critics, and propels his protégé into concert halls across America, despite the fact that her voice is woefully unequal to the challenges of coloratura. Her screeching is painful not merely because it is incompetent but because her vocal cords vibrate with her inner misery.

Emma Kirkby, one of the world's most celebrated sopranos, realized early in her career that belting out Wagner or Bizet with lots of vibrato and cleavage was not for her. Medieval and Renaissance repertoire proved a perfect match for her pipes. I met her at a talk she gave at an intimate venue. She did brief impersonations of the grandiloquent singing styles she'd chosen to avoid, but was careful to claim no superiority for any one form of music over another. The important thing was to find what your voice was meant to sing.

She related the story of a schoolboy who was told to keep quiet in singing classes because he was a "groaner." A kindly chorus master insisted on auditioning him, along with all the other kids, for the choir. Asked to sing a treble note played on the piano, the boy responded with a deeper sound, whereupon the chorus master said, "That's interesting. You want to be down *there*, don't you?" and gave him permission to sing in that range—and Philip Langridge, future star tenor and CBE, was on his way.*

○ ○ ○

How many people are born to sing superbly? Not many, I suspect. As many as are born to compete in the Olympics, perhaps, or play professional tennis. The others make do with what they've got, and sometimes manage to turn their humdrum pipes into distinctive, emotive instruments that compensate for their lack of might and purity with bags of character.

Leonard Cohen, the man who wrote the wickedly self-mocking couplet "I was born like this, I had no choice/I was born with the gift of a golden voice," took decades to find the sweet spot. The droning, whiny quality of his early efforts attracted much derision, and his material attained its stature not through his own recordings but through cover versions by "proper" singers. By the late 1980s, however, he developed the baritone *sprechgesang* (often ghosted by mellifluous female co-vocalists) that served his songs best.

Richard Thompson's voice is nowadays a supple instrument capable of teasing out all the emotional nuances of his audaciously broad repertoire. It wasn't always thus. His early efforts with Fairport Convention and on his solo debut, *Henry The Human Fly*—the lowest-selling album ever on the Warner Brothers label, reportedly†—were sung in a faux rustic bray.

---

*   My thanks to Emma Kirkby for our subsequent email exchange in which she refreshed my faulty memory of this anecdote. I've partly quoted, partly paraphrased her reply here.

†   Thompson has chuckled over this in several interviews. Note, however, that Reprise/Warner Brothers was his American label and that *Henry The Human*

Of all the marketplace-conquering pop divas of the last half century, Madonna was arguably born with the puniest vocal equipment. Her self-belief was ferocious but her pipes were feeble, and the records on which she built her fame, like "Holiday" and "Material Girl," were confected from nasal squeaks. Then, in the 1990s, having signed up for the lead role in Andrew Lloyd Webber's quasi-operatic *Evita*, she took formal singing lessons under Joan Lader, a proponent of the Estill Voice Training system. Lader coached Madonna in such skills as thyroid cartilage control and aryepiglottic sphincter control, and the results were displayed to impressive effect on *Ray Of Light*, a career peak that charmed her detractors. Silky performances like "Mer Girl" and "Frozen" proved beyond doubt that the voice is a utensil that anyone can learn to use better.

o   o   o

Frankie Armstrong, in her late seventies by the time I interviewed her, has been a singer, workshop leader and vocal coach for many decades. The music industry is well-stocked with tutors whose specialty is showing the Adeles and Beyoncés how to ululate on demand without doing themselves harm. This is not Frankie Armstrong's mission. She has devoted a lifetime to liberating ordinary people's voices.

In the 1960s, after going blind, she trained as a social worker and worked with the visually impaired, then with street addicts and juvenile delinquents. At the same time, she pursued a parallel career as a folk singer, excited by traditional singing as a conduit for common experience. Eventually, the two strands coalesced: folk singing as an environment in which damaged and disrespected people could "find their voice." Perhaps inevitably, Armstrong's practice became vigorously political and

---

Fly's sales were not quite so pitiful on Thompson's home turf. See: "Richard Thompson" by Will Harris, AV Club website, February 8, 2012.

feminist, as she uncovered the sociological agendas determin-
ing the timid silence of oppressed groups.

Armstrong is well-accustomed to people telling her that they
can't sing. Thousands of the participants in her workshops have
arrived paralyzed by what she calls "shoulds"—"inhibitions,
anxieties, embarrassments and the desire for approval. Too often,
these are imposed on us by the competitive and judgmental ways
in which music and singing is taught in our culture."* One way
she gets around this is to have her participants exercising the
rest of their bodies. The group moves purposefully as though
walking in the fields, and Armstrong draws them into call-
and-response hollers, into which she gradually "sneaks" more
sustained sung sounds until, whaddaya know, the group is following melody lines. In other words, she allows them to believe
they're not being required to sing, just make rough noises, and
then she teases those rough noises into music.

"I have never criticized anyone's voice," Armstrong tells me
when we discuss singing, politics and feminism at length.† "I
think it a mean and unhelpful thing to do. For a lot of people,
especially women, the effect of judgment and criticism from parents, teachers, choir leaders, can be devastating. [They think:]
'If my voice is horrid, and it comes from inside me, then *I* must
be horrid.'"

If it's true—as many anthropologists surmise—that the earliest examples of human singing were lullabies sung to infants,
it's especially sad that women in our competitive, performance-
oriented culture are so often ashamed of the musical noises they
make. It would be a wicked irony indeed if the people who felt
disqualified from breaking into song were those who invented
song in the first place.

---

* "NVN President—Frankie Armstrong," Natural Voice Network website, 2021.

† My thanks to Frankie Armstrong for our correspondence from 2018 to 2020.
More of it will be quoted, I hope, in a future book addressing all the topics
that didn't fit into *Listen*.

'The word 'safe' is still central to my teaching," Armstrong
ys. "And, paradoxically, once people feel safe and able to trust,
hey're much more able to take risks and challenge themselves."

o   o   o

Things get tricky for me here. Criticizing people's voices is one
of the main things that a music critic is supposed to do. Granted,
I've never been formally employed as a music critic, and even
when I reviewed books for *The Guardian* it was understood between me and my editors that I would steer clear of anything I
was likely to disparage. Telling any creative person they're rubbish is not a role I relish.

On the other hand, I'm not a social worker or a therapist. I've
devoted my life to the appreciation of art, and part of that devotion has taken the form of evaluating—is this thing magnificent, excellent, good, mediocre, bog-standard or terrible? I may
not be the sort of pundit who feels the need to award albums
scores out of ten or to concoct lists of artists ranked from best to
worst, nor do I waste time pondering whether Miles Davis was
more or less "significant" than Wagner. But I can't help noticing the difference between one sound and another, and I can't
help having preferences.

To my ear (that is, to my brain, or more specifically my complex philosophy of aesthetics, arrived at through my idiosyn-
cratic response to enculturation), the Japanese folk singer Kan
Mikami is an interesting singer, whereas Ian Gillan, lead vocalist of Deep Purple, is an uninteresting one. This judgment
is impossible to defend in objective terms. Mikami and Gillan
both exaggerate shamelessly, presenting a sort of caricature of
passion—macho and clownish at the same time. Mikami sounds
"authentic" to me, while Gillan sounds "fake," but I'm aware
that I'm not Japanese and ill-equipped to gauge such nuances
in a foreign tongue.

Ian Gillan has continued to sing with Deep Purple into his

seventies. His voice is not what it was when he was in his twenties. No one's is. Hearing him attempt melodies he composed when he had a much wider range than he does now makes me feel embarrassed on his behalf. Old age has nonnegotiable physical consequences. I wouldn't wish to watch a former Olympic runner hobble along a racetrack at ninety.

The operatic soprano Joan Sutherland retired from public performance in her early sixties. In a radio interview five years before her death, she was urged to reconsider. "For goodness' sake, dear, I'm seventy-eight," Dame Joan retorted. "I don't want to get up and sing with what I might have called a voice now [...] You don't only just use your *voice*, you use support from the lungs and diaphragm, and everything gets old [...] I mean, the body gradually disintegrates whether you like it or not, and I was not having the response with my organs, liver, lungs, heart, et cetera [...] It was time to stop."*

o   o   o

Is it ever time to stop? Frankie Armstrong might argue that it's never too late to start. Professor Grenville Hancox, who you met in an earlier chapter, would certainly reject the notion that anyone grows "too old" or too disintegrated to sing. What we're uncovering here is our culture's lack of agreement about what singing is *for*.

Joan Sutherland dwelled in the kingdom of classical music, an environment infested with nitpickery and disapproval. Even in her prime, she had to defend her reputation against accusations of "mushy" diction and "flaccid" rhythm.† The critic whose harsh adjectives I've just quoted identifies himself as one of Sutherland's admirers, ultimately deciding that her merits outweigh

---

*   "La Stupenda: Dame Joan Sutherland," interviewed by Monica Attard, *Sunday Profile*, ABC Radio, March 27, 2005.

†   "Sutherland: A Separate Greatness" by an uncredited writer, probably William Bender, *Time* magazine, November 22, 1971.

her demerits. Comparing her point-by-point with another top-rated soprano, Beverly Sills, he describes them both as being "on the coloratura high wire," a phrase that evokes the unforgiving standards of their circus, where the listeners are constantly waiting for the singer to fall.

Standards in rock music are a lot more lax. The forensic analysis with which classical critics assess whether a soprano has failed to hit the high F in the crucial eighth line in the fourth aria is not brought to bear upon a Deep Purple concert at Moscow's Megasport Arena. Indeed, while a few attendees may complain that Ian Gillan's voice is "shot," many others will insist that he's fucking awesome and as good as he ever was. There is, in vintage rock, a solidarity between the aging performers and the aging fans—a communal gratitude that, despite hair loss, expanding midriffs and cancer surgeries, the band is still able to get on a stage and the fans are still able to turn up to see them. Death does not quite have dominion *yet*, as long as Ian Gillan can have a crack at the old faves one more time (even if he does dodge the high notes). In a strange kind of way, this is exactly the "safe" space that Frankie Armstrong fosters.*

The safety (or otherwise) of the space Frankie Armstrong works in becomes a thornier question when we listen to Frankie singing today, as opposed to fifty years ago. When I play my old LP of *Lovely On The Water*, a voice issues forth from 1972 and

---

* I think the reasons why rock fans are more forgiving when it comes to dodgy singing go beyond social demographics. Classical music, by its very nature, worships a repertoire that predates and outlives any of the performers who might tackle it. The work of art in question is Donizetti's *Lucia di Lammermoor* or Mozart's *Così Fan Tutte*, and everyone understands that an international army of sopranos du jour will sing it until they perish in the battle against their own waning lungs, only to be replaced by fresh new singers. By contrast, the repertoire of Deep Purple is considered to be uniquely theirs and thus there's pressure on the members to keep on trucking. So strong is the link between popular songs and their original singers that people would rather go to see an original Motown group whose elderly members can barely sing anymore than hear those same songs sung much better by young "imposters" "falsely" trading under the group name.

it is lovely indeed. Free of artifice or ornament, it nevertheless ticks the boxes of accuracy that most singing teachers would want ticked. In the decades since, Armstrong has encouraged throngs of people to find their own voices without shame or self-denigration, and she herself has grown old. The pipes that once led vulnerable, ordinary humans from a position of weakness to a newfound strength have themselves weakened and made Armstrong vulnerable. In short, she has joined the ranks of those she once helped.

o   o   o

Is the wear and tear in a singer's voice something to be celebrated or regretted? The answer is different for different singers. Smoking cigarettes is an insanely stupid idea and causes all sorts of health horrors like cancer, emphysema and chronic obstructive pulmonary disease. Nevertheless, most listeners agree that Marianne Faithfull's singing voice became more interesting after a sustained regime of self-abuse, and she herself might not wish to trade her famously ravaged instrument for the pastel purity she had as a teen.

Faithfull, by necessity or desire, has become an icon of self-reinvention, training her audience to expect, or at least accept, drastic shrinkages of her vocal range. If she lives long enough to make another album (her most recent, *She Walks In Beauty*, was spoken-word recitations of Byron poems), she could probably sing it entirely on one or two notes and still be greeted with jubilant reviews. That acclaim would be partly because she has learned to wring the maximum effect from whatever actions can still be performed with her battered equipment, and partly because her fans feel such affection for this woman who has survived COVID, pneumonia, breast cancer, broken bones, hepatitis, homelessness, heroin addiction, alcoholism, anorexia, tuberculosis and The Rolling Stones.

By contrast, Whitney Houston is an iconic nonsurvivor, a tragic failure to self-reinvent. Her alcohol and drug abuse changed the capacities and range of her voice, sure, but not as much as those same abuses changed Marianne Faithfull's. Journalists and horrified members of the public who described Houston as a shadow of her former self, a travesty, a wreck, and so on, were ignoring the fact that by the vocal standards of you or me, or Marianne Faithfull or Johnny Cash, she still possessed an instrument of formidable caliber. It's just that she couldn't conceive of using it in any other way than the way she'd used it to win her superstardom. Hemmed in by her management, by the rigid preconceptions of her public, and by her own lack of imagination, she felt compelled to sing "I Will Always Love You" and bungle it. In stiletto heels, desperately weary, drunk and dosed with cocaine, she tottered forth on the circus tightrope.

o o o

It's not always old age, illness or drug abuse that ruins a voice. Sometimes, it's forcing it to make noises it's not happy to make, over and over, because there's a job to be done. We all know what it's like to push ourselves too hard, straining muscles, promising ourselves that when the task is finished we'll take it easy. Sometimes we misjudge what we can get away with.

In 1984, Jethro Tull toured in support of their then-current album *Under Wraps*. Its short, synth-driven songs, much influenced by a younger generation of popsters like Thomas Dolby and The Buggles, alienated many of Jethro Tull's older fans. Yet the group's leader, Ian Anderson, was determined to move with the times and was also very proud of his vocals on the record, which "were as good as they would ever be, extending my usually limited range and power like never before."[*] This was true, but the challenge of singing the material night after night inflicted serious harm on Anderson's already strained larynx. His efforts to win audiences over to what remains a relatively unloved album

---

[*] Ian Anderson, liner notes for reissue of *Under Wraps*.

left him with permanent scars, and nowadays he employs a wing-
man called Ryan O'Donnell to sing the bits he can't manage.

o   o   o

Session singer Linda Peters, who later found fame as Linda
Thompson, has one of the lonesomest voices in the world, ideally suited to her former husband's exquisite exercises in melancholy like "Withered And Died" and "Down Where The
Drunkards Roll." After their rancorous breakup, the elegant
anguish that had always tinged her vocal tone seemed to seep
into the basal ganglia of her brain and she succumbed to a
mysterious condition called spasmodic dysphonia. The larynx
goes into spasm, either rendering the person nearly mute or
afflicting their vowels with an uncontrollable sigh. The condition is said to be incurable and lifelong. Thompson retired
from singing, and opened an antique jewelry shop.

Since her nadir in the 1980s, Linda has sung again—spasmod-
ically, so to speak. Injections of Botox directly into her throat
helped, as well as encouragement from her loving family. As
with so many brain dysfunctions, it's difficult to tell whether
emotions are making a piece of physical hardware go wrong,
or whether the misbehavior of the hardware is what creates the
fear and distress.

Shirley Collins is another eminent folk singer who lost her
voice after a marital split. Whether the problem was spasmodic
dysphonia or something less pathological, she ceased to be a
happy songbird in 1978 when her husband Ashley Hutchings
left her for another woman. "My voice got damaged, my ego
got damaged, and my heart and everything and I stopped being
able to sing properly."* Performing in a National Theatre production alongside Hutchings and his new girlfriend, Collins did

---

* Shirley Collins interviewed by Johan Kugelberg, Perfect Sound Forever
website, February 2005.

her best to be a trooper. "Some nights I could sing. Sometimes I would try to sing and my throat would just close up, seize up. And sadly, the more I tried to sing, the worse it got."[*]

Eventually, Collins's brand of folk was deemed outmoded and irrelevant, as Anglo culture moved into the era of Sheena Easton, Simple Minds and Bros. Shirley slipped out of the music industry and took jobs at Oxfam, the British Library and in an unemployment center. At the age of seventy-one, retired in a small cottage in East Sussex, she was coaxed to sing one ditty on *Black Ships Ate The Sky*, an album by the avant-garde group Current 93. The group's leader, David Tibet, a passionate and persistent encourager of lost and neglected talents, somehow managed to persuade her to sing two songs at a Current 93 concert in London's Union Chapel in February 2014.

"I wasn't very good,"[†] she says, and although her admirers showered her with love and validation, she was right: she wasn't very good. She sounded like a very nervous seventy-eight-year-old who hadn't sung for decades. But from this tentative seedling, a fresh phase of her illustrious career grew. A couple of years later, she issued her first album since the late 1970s, *Lodestar*, to great acclaim, and in 2020 came an even better one, *Heart's Ease*. The voice was not lost after all. It had only been mislaid.

o o o

I have no doubt that there is such a thing, medically speaking, as dysphonia. I also know that the vocal cords can become inflamed, develop nodes, grow estranged from the lungs and venous system that once supported them. But I can't help noting the role played by sexual politics in the stories of singers who lost

---

[*]   Interview with Shirley Collins in the documentary film *The Ballad Of Shirley Collins*, directed by Rob Curry and Tim Plester (Fire Films, 2017).

[†]   "'I want to challenge the toxic side of Englishness': Folk legend Shirley Collins on making a comeback at the age of 82" by Shaun Curran, *The Independent*, November 23, 2017.

their voice. While there may exist men who never sang again after their wives or girlfriends left them, I don't know of any. In the patriarchy, it seems that women have often had trouble "finding" their voices in the first place, and then run the risk of being literally "silenced" when they're abandoned or abused by husbands or boyfriends.

o   o   o

One voice whose psychological ups and downs have been mercilessly documented is that of Beverley Martyn. When she was still a schoolgirl, she was chosen to front a folk group, The Levee Breakers. On "Babe I'm Leaving You," issued by Parlophone in 1965, Beverley Kutner unleashed a confident vocal that sounded more like a mature American wayfarer than a teen from Coventry. Within a couple of years, she was working with the top session players in Britain—Jimmy Page, John Paul Jones, Nicky Hopkins, John Renbourn. Everyone thought she had a bright future. Bert Jansch taught her to play guitar; Paul Simon flew her to New York to meet his illustrious friends. While her recordings as the mononymous "Beverley" were less self-assured than her Levee Breakers debut—she was somewhat bewildered at being groomed by star-makers ("As soon as my breasts began to develop it was as if I lost all of my power," she later recalled)*— she appeared at the Monterey Pop festival alongside The Byrds, The Jimi Hendrix Experience, The Who, Janis Joplin and Otis Redding.

But there was a dark irony in the words of "Babe I'm Leaving You." The bold self-protection she celebrated in the song would prove absent from her emotional arsenal in real life. "Friends told me that you had no heart," she'd sung. "You took mine and it broke apart." In 1969, she fell in love with exactly that

---

*   Beverley Martyn, *Sweet Honesty: The Beverley Martyn Story* (Grosvenor House Publishing, 2011).

man, John Martyn, a baby-faced charmer who would terrorize her and destroy her self-confidence.

In the first flush of love, John and Beverley Martyn were a duo. *Stormbringer!* and *The Road To Ruin* featured several songs each by Beverley. Fewer, though, than there might've been. On "Here I Am," Beverley paid tribute to her man and his supposedly guiding hand. It was left off the original issue of *The Road To Ruin*, perhaps because of Beverley's unconvincing vocal and the band's desultory performance, or perhaps because somebody in authority judged that John's songs were more worthy. So, "Here I Am" became a case of There I Wasn't.

When the babies came, Beverley was confined in a remote house in Hastings looking after them, while John expanded his reputation with constant touring. Monstrous drug and alcohol abuse amplified his insecurity and jealousy into violence and paranoia. "You'll never get away from me," Beverley recalls him saying. "I will hunt you down and kill you and whoever you are with." Finally, after years of beatings, she took refuge in the local police station, where she was told that she could be prosecuted for deserting her children.*

We cannot know if Beverley Martyn could have developed a talent comparable to John's. He was a supremely gifted guitar player, certainly, and his voice, merely adequate on early efforts like *London Conversation*, evolved into a unique woodwind instrument. What's undeniable is that John's ambitions were supported by the male-dominated music industry and that Beverley lived on benefits, careerless, as a survivor of sustained abuse and the mother of a troubled son.

By the time John Martyn died, his voice had been reduced to a bronchitic croak by chronic alcoholism, smoking and obe-

---

★   "Beverley Martyn: 'I'm still here and I know who I am now'" by Graeme Thomson, *The Guardian*, April 17, 2014.

sity, yet there were still fans who worshipped him as a sort of bad boy icon, and he was awarded an OBE.*

By contrast, when Beverley Martyn attempted a comeback in her late sixties, after many post–*Road To Ruin* years when "nobody wanted to know," her voice was compromised not by bad habits but by nerves and battered self-esteem. On *The Phoenix And The Turtle*, released to kind reviews in 2014, Martyn misses more notes than she hits, sometimes singing a dozen or more words in a row before she chances upon one that's in tune. On YouTube, a visitor checks out an upload and opines: "Beverly never really had it in her to be a singer." Another visitor takes the trouble to write an extended put-down so brutal and derisive that I can't bring myself to quote it here.†

What happened to the gutsy teenager whose talent shone in The Levee Breakers? For answer, we can access another piece of footage available on YouTube—Martyn's contribution to the Bert Jansch Tribute Concert at Royal Festival Hall in December 2013. She walks onstage, framed by a luminous back-projection of the cover photo of Bert Jansch's *It Don't Bother Me*, which features her nubile young self relaxing on a futon in the background. The band builds expectation with a swampy voodoo rhythm, Beverley acknowledges the audience with a smile and a nod, then unleashes an imperious, perfect rendition of "When The Levee Breaks." For a few minutes, the Royal Festival Hall is her court and she is its queen.

The version of "Levee Breaks" released on *The Phoenix And*

---

* I saw him in the mid-1990s, when he'd already lost his looks but hadn't yet lost his right leg. He'd been dropped by his record company, had released no original material for some years, and was hardly the most fashionable artiste in the marketplace. Yet he bestrode the stage with careless self-confidence, taking his fans' adoration for granted. It's difficult for me to imagine a female singer in the same position—unfashionable, with no new repertoire or product, her beauty faded—claiming the limelight with such cocky entitlement.

† "Reckless Jane; Beverley Martyn & Nick Drake," uploaded to YouTube by Marc J. Pavey on April 17, 2014. The negative comments have since been removed by the channel's owner.

The Turtle the following year is tame, stilted, racked by self-consciousness. Something has gone wrong again, not in Beverley's throat necessarily, but in the region of the soul where the voice takes its sustenance or is denied it.

As I write these words, Beverley Martyn's "official website" has faltered and fallen, and its domain name is up for grabs. "Don't let this space go to waste," says the automated advert. "Make beverleymartyn.com work hard for you."

∘ ∘ ∘

There are many ways of having a voice. I may not be able to sing, and I may arouse a twinge of pity in my friends when I try. But you are reading these words of mine, published in a book that's just one of a stack of books I've been allowed to publish. Each of those books was an opportunity for fate to close a door on me. Instead, I've been invited in. Sometimes there's applause as I take my seat, before I've even opened my mouth.

At any literary festival, writers of my socioeconomic background are a rarity. Things are slowly changing now, but in the years when I was presenting my novels and hanging out backstage with my fellow scribes, it seemed to me that just about everyone, regardless of their color, had been educated at elite schools. They certainly had parents who provided more than the eleven dusty books my parents owned.

It's easy for me to play the working-class card, to tell stories of the time I pushed my junk-shop piano up the steep hill to my hovel, of the cockroaches and rotting floors in the shoebox flats where I wrote *The Crimson Petal*, of the nice middle-class lady who took me on as a cleaner and then immediately sent me a letter canceling the agreement, because she'd found that employing servants who were "too close to me in intelligence" led to problems.

But these are misleading anecdotes. Poverty and disenfran-chisement were, for me, adventures. Sure, I've been a fringe-dweller, but the fringes were mine to explore on my own terms. I thought my thoughts and took it for granted that I had the right to think them. I was a young white heterosexual male who wanted to devote my life to art. Hell, yeah! I'd wear charity shop clothes and shoplift food and paddle around on the polluted river in my plastic dinghy and write my stories until the world was ready to read them.

Nothing and nobody stomped on that fantasy. I wasn't beaten into line and I wasn't ordered to keep my goddamn mouth shut. I've never been raped or shamed, and no one has ever judged my worth according to my physical attractiveness, let alone the color of my skin. I didn't get thrown into jail and I didn't get pregnant and I didn't have to beg police to save me from an abusive husband. Indeed, when I was vulnerable and depressed and crazy, a devoted wife cared for me and fed me and reassured me that she would love me no matter what.

I always had a voice, and I still do. Here I am, singing, and you're listening.

TENDER EXOTICS

Over the last hundred years, the British Empire has lost most of its overseas territories and currently seems fated to shrink down to Little England. The USA, which looked for a while as if it might impose its brand of democracy on the entire world, is now in trouble deep, tearing itself apart.

But in one respect, the Anglo superpowers remain superpowerful and omnipresent: in music. Music produced in Anglo countries continues to dominate the globe, often crowding out indigenous sounds on local airwaves and claiming disproportionate attention in foreign-language media.

It wasn't always so. As late as 1914, England was dismissed as *"das Land ohne Musik"*—the land without music—by the German polymath Oscar Adolf Hermann Schmitz.* You'd think no nation would take such a slur lying down, but plenty of culture lovers in Britain did. For centuries, Germany and Italy had been racking up the geniuses and the sensations—Bach, Beethoven, Mozart, Verdi, Handel, Brahms, Puccini and so forth. What did Britain have to offer? Learmont Drysdale? Lindsay Sloper?

It seemed that the English were importers rather than producers, sunk by their innate lack of talent.† Uncouth peasants

---

*　Oscar A. H. Schmitz, *Das Land Ohne Musik: Englische Gesellschaftsprobleme* (Georg Müller, Munich, 1914). Assuming you're fluent in German and French (you *are*, aren't you?), you can read more about Schmitz on the German or French versions of Wikipedia—the Anglo version doesn't consider him worth remembering.

†　Here I paraphrase material from Amy Dunagin's essay for the catalog of *The*

barking their folk ballads and clueless philistines yowling along with their parlor pianos might disagree with those imperious snipes from Abroad, but the true connoisseurs hung their heads in humility.

That humility went back a long way. In 1675, the composer Matthew Locke acknowledged Italy as "the great academy of the world,"* while Henry Purcell felt that the key to achieving anything was "learning Italian, which is the best master," although England's fruits were still doomed to be inferior, "being farther from the sun."† The eminent eighteenth-century theater and opera producer Owen Swiny agreed that the precious foreign flower of music "languished, like tender exotics, when removed into our colder region."‡

Likewise, the greatness of German music put Anglo efforts to shame. Bach was a veritable Leonardo da Vinci of composition, while Beethoven was the archetype of a genius. Thank goodness Handel relocated from Hamburg to England or we'd have no *Messiah* to sing.§ And what about all those luminaries

---

Land Without Music: Satirizing Song in Eighteenth-Century England, an exhibition of prints she curated at the Lewis Walpole Library, Yale University, May–September 2017.

* Matthew Locke, preface to *The English Opera, or, The Vocal Musick in Psyche* (London, 1675).

† Henry Purcell, *The Vocal and Instrumental Musick of The Prophetess, or, The History of Dioclesian* (London, 1691).

‡ Owen Swiny, program note to *Camilla: An Opera, as it is perform'd at the Theatre Royal in Drury-Lane* (London, 1707).

§ My classical-loving friend Jo Falla felt that I'm overstating the German contempt for English music. Focusing on musicians themselves rather than on critics, he asked: "Why did so many European composers and musicians come to England? Because they knew they'd find a large, appreciative and enthusiastic audience willing to shell out and listen to foreigners… The English commissioned—yup, paid for—a lot of German music when cash was distinctly unforthcoming at home in Germany. The London Philharmonic Society commissioned Beethoven's 9th, and had previously sent him a cheque when he was hard up."

This doesn't disprove the notion of an Anglo inferiority complex, of course. It suggests that the British had an easy solution to their "land without music"

in other parts of Europe? Rachmaninov, Ravel, Tchaikovsky, Chopin, Liszt, Debussy, Bizet... The list of titans to put English dabblers in the shade went on and on.

Meanwhile in America, Canada and Australia, patriotic bravado gave way all too easily to cultural cringe. How could there be such a thing as "classic" music in these shallow-rooted, upstart colonies? While slaves and Aborigines sang their "artless" songs somewhere outside, ignored, the slave owners and well-educated white folks sat in their drawing rooms and worshipped the glories of antiquity.

American musicians, if they showed any promise, typically traveled to Europe—often to Germany—to study; then, with any luck, brought the gold dust home. Australian musicians were not considered truly credible by Australians until they'd had some success in Europe, despite the fact that Europe was ten thousand miles away and pointedly uninterested in anything from the antipodes.

Let's face it: culturally speaking, all roads led to Rome (and Vienna and Berlin and Paris and so on).

o o o

Blues, jazz and rock 'n' roll changed all that. Something alchemical happened when dispossessed brown people had to regrow their old musics in new countries. The transplanted hybrids were not "tender exotics." They proliferated joyously, and proved to be hardier than most other plants.

What's more, these innovations were a hit with white listeners. The general public wanted to dance to the new sounds, imitate them, idolize them. Socially and politically, people of color were still disempowered, but culturally, they'd conquered their former oppressors.

By the middle of the twentieth century, scandalized guard-

---

problem—import German music to make up for the local shortfall.

ians of good taste were burning and smashing records tainted with "primitive" and "degenerate" influences. It was too late. These sober gatekeepers, who'd once been the arbiters of western civilization, were now beleaguered blimps, irrelevant to the mainstream conversation. Soon The Beatles would be singing Chuck Berry's "Roll Over Beethoven," and the masses—not just in England and America, but internationally—would signal that, yes, it was indeed high time for Beethoven to roll over.

In the decades since, reggae, metal, rap and digitally tooled pop have fortified and expanded the new empire. Classical music is still being played in concert halls, of course, but pop is what the world runs on now. And that pop is overwhelmingly Anglo.

o o o

Wherever I've traveled, the songs that emanate from hidden speakers in public spaces, restaurants, cafés, hotels, taxis and people's homes sing to me in English. In my hometown, there's no way I would ever hear German or Czech or Norwegian being sung at me from a sound system in a shopping mall or an eatery; that would be bizarre. But the reverse is normal.

I've heard Otis Redding's "Dock Of The Bay," The Hollies' "Bus Stop" and Tina Turner's "The Best" many times over in places as far-flung as Budapest, Dubai and Gothenburg. When I was in Romania in 1990, my host was patiently carving the body of an electric guitar from a block of wood so that he could play Dire Straits songs. When I was in Ukraine with Médecins Sans Frontières, the photographer chatted with the locals about the Cheeky Girls' hit "Cheeky Song (Touch My Bum)" and they were familiar with it. When I was in Poland, I was lucky to survive a high-speed dash through the Carpathian Mountains during which our driver insisted on playing his favorite group, Johnny Hates Jazz.* When driving around concrete housing

---

*   Actually, he identified the artistes as "Johnny Hates The Jazz." Poles and

estates in my old hometown of Den Haag, I was serenaded by Bruce Springsteen's "Streets Of Philadelphia."

I would probably need to go to North Korea to be wholly certain of hearing no Anglo pop music, and even then I'd probably hear it being played illicitly on some smuggled recording proudly possessed by whoever brought me there.

Because here's the thing: not only is English dominant, but it's cool. It speaks—or is perceived to speak—of cosmopolitanism, of universality, of freedom from parochialism of one's own town or village. Every hipster I ever met in a foreign country fastidiously avoided any radio station whose policy (usually dictated by the government) was to play local fare. They gravitated to the stations airing the latest sounds from Detroit, New York, Seattle, Manchester, Athens (Athens, Georgia, that is). Young people who could barely hold a conversation in English could sing along with hundreds of songs filled with the slang of Anglo indie, punk, hip-hop and heavy metal. They walked around with their allegiance stamped on their T-shirts.

Of course, the dominance of English goes way beyond the music industry. English is the language of turbocapitalism generally. It's the language of fast-food chains, Hollywood, gadgets and gaming. If I go to a foreign country and imploringly mention the word "apple" to a local, chances are they won't give me an *Apfel* or a *mela* or a *maçã*, *yabloko* or *seb*, but will prepare to help me with my iPhone or MacBook.

Music, however, is the cultural weather with which this Anglo hegemony is blown across the world. It's no longer an import or an export; it's just *there*.

This is not to say that Anglo music has rendered the music of other countries extinct. Far from it. Local culture survives. It's just that we—the Anglos—don't respect it. Foreigners eagerly learn to speak the imperialists' language, but the imperialists remain stubbornly monolingual.

Czechs love English, but their relationship with the definite article is troubled.

In short, all the foreigners know The Beatles, Bob Dylan and Bob Marley. But we don't know *their* heroes. Why should we? No music of theirs could possibly be as important as ours. If any of those foreign guys are good enough to merit our attention, they'll surely learn English so they can sing to us direct. Penetrating the Anglo marketplace (by becoming quasi-Anglo) is a sign that they've "made it."

o   o   o

In the chapter that follows, I will look at a few "foreign" pop artists who never "made it." Artists who, in all likelihood, you've never listened to—perhaps never even heard of.

They are not niche artists whose work is appreciated by a coterie of poseurs. They are megastars, whose records have sold in the millions. They are known and loved (or hated) by everyone in their home country, and in other European countries round about. In receptive soil, they flourish. In our supposedly green and pleasant land, they die. Tender exotics.

Ascoltare. Słuchać. Ecoutez. Luister. Listen.

THE KIND OF THINGS THAT
HEGEMONY JUST CAN'T BUY

Cierpliwość, proszę. Patience, s'il vous plait. Geduld, alstublieft. Pazienza, per favore. This chapter will, eventually, be about Czesław Niemen, Alain Bashung, Herman van Veen and Franco Battiato.

When I was growing up, those names meant nothing. Not to me, not to anyone I knew. There's a very good chance they mean nothing to you, either. The reasons for that have little to do with your taste. They have to do with a word you'll seldom see outside essays about radical politics: hegemony.

○ ○ ○

I'm writing this book in Microsoft Word, a word-processing program invented in the USA. One of its features is that it puts a squiggly red line under any word that Microsoft thinks might be a typing error.

Microsoft's database of what it considers real words is impressive. It has no problem with "tergiversation" or "supercalifragilisticexpialidocious," for example. And it's a wizard at recognizing names. There are no red squiggles under "Sinéad O'Connor," "Frank Sinatra," "Morrissey," "Jay-Z," "Eminem" or even "Beatles" (surely that's not how you spell "beetles"?).

There are, however, squiggly red lines under "Czesław," "Bashung," "Veen" and "Battiato." A programmer at an American tech corporation is suggesting I might like to double-check those names, in case I made a mistake.

o   o   o

I grew up in Australia. Australia was and is part of the Anglo world empire, whose epicenters are North America and Great Britain. We Anglos decide what's "universal." Foreigners gabbling in non-English languages are, by definition, not universal. They are a fringe concern.

So, during my childhood, the media never offered me anything sung in other tongues. How many words of Italian were there in Dean Martin's "That's Amore"? About seven, I think, if you count "pizza." There were ten words of French in The Beatles' "Michelle." Three words of Spanish in "Una Paloma Blanca" by George Baker Selection (whose singer Johannes Bouwens changed his name to George Baker because a Dutch name wouldn't cut it in the "international" market).

Somehow, "Guantanamera" and "La Bamba" managed to sneak through—God knows how. "Je T'aime (Moi Non Plus)" was mostly sex noises and Brits bought it because it was naughty, then ignored everything else Serge Gainsbourg ever wrote. In Australia, "Je T'Aime" (sung entirely in English) was a hit for the mononymous Abigail, a soap opera star who would occasionally give me a split-second glimpse of her bare breasts when my parents were out for the evening.

On that same TV, my parents would watch documentaries about leopards, or British comedies like *The Benny Hill Show* and *Mind Your Language*, which poked fun at crudely stereotyped foreigners struggling to learn English.

Oh, and Nana Mouskouri. They liked Nana. They especially enjoyed it when she sang the odd song in Greek, backed up by The Athenians, who wore quaint national dress.

Mouskouri was for middle-aged squares, though. And, in any case, she was only permitted on our TVs because she spoke English. World-class entertainment had no truck with subtitles.

o   o   o

Once a year, there was the Eurovision Song Contest. The USA ignored this, because most Americans have only the haziest notion of where and what Europe is, but the Brits loved it, as it provided an opportunity to mock foreigners for not being like Brits. Those Germans are so kitsch! So...*German*! And those Italians! So narcissistic! So preposterous!

What underpinned this contempt was the conviction that everything important in modern music had been invented by Anglos. Blues, jazz, rock 'n' roll, soul, rap, Dylan, The Beatles, Bowie—we had it all. What did Germany have? Oompah-oompah and "Autobahn." What did France have? A few glamorous chanteuses in the easy-listening field, admirable more for their cheekbones and lustrous hair than for the songs they sang. What did Italy have? Umberto Tozzi? Don't make us laugh.

o   o   o

I first started questioning this Anglocentrism when I was in my midteens. That was when the older brother of a German-born schoolmate lent me his reel-to-reel recorder and a stack of self-compiled tapes from *das alte Land*. I discovered krautrock—a cornucopia of great music. Who knew that the country I'd previously associated with James Last had wrought this sonic miracle?

Even so, a lot of krautrock was purely instrumental, or else sung in English. The best-known of the groups, Kraftwerk, routinely issued their albums in two languages—their own, and the one that would get them into the rock history books.

In the twenty-first century, our gatekeepers have lightened up a little: krautrock has become a modest fixture on Spotify playlists. So many influential Anglo musicians from David Bowie onward have raved about this wonderful "genre"* that the general

---

*   Not a genre at all, just a cover-all (and initially disrespectful) term for any modern music made by Germans, from the most raucous rock to the most

public (and, more importantly, the entertainment conglomerates who supply our marketplaces) have made room for a few items. Three or four, out of the hundreds of artists known to Germans.

I used to have regular music chats with an expatriate Düsseldorfian called Axel. I was trying to reconcile him to krautrock, particularly to bands who sang in his own language. I myself had a soft spot for Grobschnitt, and could recite, in my ropey accent, some of their madcap skits. Axel had seen them play live when he was a teen, and enjoyed them, but got the impression that enjoying them wasn't cool. What he really wanted to talk about was jazz, or else AC/DC, Deep Purple, Rush and Cold Chisel.

o o o

In the late seventies, I developed a taste for Italian progressive rock. A horror movie called *Deep Red*, starring David Hemmings, made a big impression on me and I learned that it was actually a dubbed version of Dario Argento's *Profondo Rosso*. I bought the soundtrack LP, on a label I'd never heard of before, Cinevox. The words *"colonna sonora"* sounded so much more exotic than "soundtrack." The group didn't sing, and had given themselves an English name, Goblin, but still, there they were: five *ragazzi*, responsible for the *idee*, the *arrangiamenti*, and the *esecuzione*.

o o o

In Italy, as in other European countries, Anglo albums have always been ubiquitously available. It would be madness to deny *il popolo* their Pink Floyd or Tina Turner. But Melbourne boasted only one tiny shop where Italian rock albums could be found.

---

ethereal electronica. Imagine how the Brits would feel if German journalists spoke of a "genre" called limeyrock, or how Americans would feel if everything they'd produced, from Jimi Hendrix to Tina Turner, was referred to as yankrock.

Almost nobody bought them. "Does Italy even *have* rock bands?" a music buff once asked me. "What about that yodeling one— Focus? Are they Italian? Oh no, they're Dutch, aren't they?"

The shop went bust.

o   o   o

A few Italian groups tried hard to solve the conundrum of how to make us listen. Le Orme got their 1973 LP *Felona E Sorona* translated into English by one of their Anglo idols, Peter Hammill of Van der Graaf Generator. All they had to do was re-record the vocals. This they duly did, and *Felona And Sorona* sank like *una pietra*.

More successful were PFM (Premiata Forneria Marconi), who got signed up to Emerson Lake & Palmer's vanity label, re-recorded their material in English, and were rewarded with a placing of number 180 on the American charts. They toured the USA exhaustively, supporting such wildly *non simpatico* artists as ZZ Top, Peter Frampton and The Beach Boys. Being "international" meant singing in somebody else's language to stadiums full of Californians or Texans impatient to see somebody else.

I did try out the English-language versions of Le Orme and PFM albums, but could tell within seconds that these Venetian and Milanese youths, normally so exuberant, weren't happy. They'd lost heart.* Imagine Frank Sinatra being told he had to sing in Serbo-Croat, or The Supremes accepting that they would only make headway if they were willing to sing "Je Kunt De Liefde Niet Haasten."

So, I began buying the originals. What on earth were these people singing? I hadn't a clue, but it was a happy exploration. Hundreds of Italian prog bands rose and fell during the 1970s, often producing just one eccentric LP before vanishing. If you

---

*   An unfortunate thing to lose, given that heart was what set Italian prog apart
from its solemn Anglo equivalent.

blindfold me and play me virtually any Italian prog album from that era, I would recognize it within seconds of the opening salvo, but would be hard-pressed to name any of the songs. *Non parlo Italiano*, you see.

This linguistic disadvantage, which stops me speaking authoritatively about bands whose names I often can't even pronounce, may be one of the reasons why Anglo folks who profess to love all kinds of music so seldom bother to investigate outside the Anglo sphere. We don't want our ignorance to be noticed by others; we'd be embarrassed to stumble on names and titles, and to have to confess total ignorance of what the music is "about."

But just think: this is the same hurdle that faces the Hungarian who's curious about Bowie, or the Greek who likes the sound of Public Enemy. And their response? They learn a bit of English—enough, at least, to enthuse about what they've found. They may not have the comprehensive access that an Anglo person is blessed with, but they figure that *something* is better than nothing.

Our Anglo empire, by contrast, is not big on that sort of humility.

o o o

By the 1980s, I thought I had a pretty decent sense of what was worthwhile in Italian rock music. I felt I'd covered the most important bases and was now picking through the peripheral obscurities. There couldn't be anything terribly significant left that I hadn't clocked, surely? In the wake of punk, my love of prog was growing less forgiving, more picky. My favorites were the Milanese outfit Area, who were not as florid as the other Italian proggers—harder-edged, violently experimental. I evangelized on their behalf to anyone who would listen.

One name still escaped my notice, though—Franco Battiato. He wasn't really a prog artist, nor was he punk or "post-punk." And the albums he made in the mid to late 1970s, when I was enthusiastically exploring the Italian scene, were so austerely avant-garde that even if I'd been exposed to them, which I never was, I probably would have balked.

Later on, when I was heavily into Einstürzende Neubauten and other abrasive fare, Battiato had drifted back into pop music, making albums that might have struck me as New Age if I'd heard them—which I didn't. No one in my tribe—including music journalists who prided themselves on their omnivorous tastes and encyclopedic knowledge—had detected him on their radar.

o   o   o

1984 was the year when Franco Battiato had his moment of greatest international visibility, as he and Carla Bissi (professionally known as Alice) performed "I Treni di Tozeur" for the Eurovision Song Contest. I wasn't aware of this, either. By 1984, I was working as a nurse in Sydney. I didn't own a TV and had lost all interest in pop music. On the rare occasions when I went to a concert, it was the sort of event where heroin-addicted waifs walloped amplified violins with sticks and tossed raw meat into the audience.

What would I have made of "I Treni di Tozeur," if I'd encountered it then? I might have been put off by the mechanized plod of 1980s drumming, the hollow tinkle of 1980s keyboards. But I hope I would have been intrigued by the quality of the composition. "I Treni di Tozeur," like many of Battiato's "pop" songs, is not constructed the way a normal pop song is constructed, with a simple repeated verse and chorus and maybe a middle eight. It's more like a piece of classical music. It goes on an unpredictable journey, and, if you're up for the adventure, you can come along.

Nowadays, "I Treni di Tozeur" fills me with joy each time I hear it. Its lyrical depth and elegant composition are typical of Battiato, but rare in pop music and very rare indeed in the world of Eurovision. It was a hit in Italy, and if it had been played on Anglo radio it might have seduced millions of Australians, Brits, Canadians, New Zealanders, Americans. But of course it wasn't played. It was in Italian—and it had a bit of German in it as well. Double disqualification!

o   o   o

Let's leave Battiato disqualified for a while. Fast-forward to the early 1990s. I had access to a television again, and regularly watched *Rage*, an all-night music program that had a policy of airing videos that wouldn't be aired anywhere else.

If you've spent any time investigating unusual music on You-Tube, you will almost certainly have seen videos with the telltale *Rage* ID stamp at one corner. Quite a lot of our videographic music history comes not from the BBC or MTV, but from this Sydney-based resource, now the longest-running music video channel in the world. For its first twenty years, it was programmed by two visionary female producers,[*] and the dead-of-night slot meant that there was little censorship and no obligation to stick within the safe parameters of daytime shows.

One mischievous viewer tested out his theory that "even a dog could get a video on *Rage*" by strapping a camera to a pal's dog and posting the woozily psychedelic results (accompanied by some electronic noodling) to the program, whereupon, very early one morning, Forrest the terrier was given his media debut between N-Trance and Roots Manuva.[†]

The open-mindedness that benefited the dog was likewise extended to Alain Bashung, a French superstar who nobody in the Anglo world deigned to notice. Recipient of multiple

---

[*]   Stephanie Lewis and Narelle Gee.

[†]   "Why Rage is the greatest music TV show of all time," Mixdown website, February 14, 2022.

awards,* he'd issued eight bestselling albums by that point, and distinguished himself as an actor. I caught the video of "Madame Rêve" at two in the morning,† just before going to bed.

My first impressions were tainted by the dominant-culture superiority that all of us in the English-speaking world are encouraged to feel. Bashung is seated on a stool and the first thing we see is his foot, shod in a Cuban-heeled boot. *Beatles homage!* I thought, without pondering why flamenco footwear developed by Spaniards and Cubans should be identified as "Beatle boots." Bashung wore a spangly jacket that reminded me of Bryan Ferry in the very early days of Roxy Music. His face, sultry and cupid-lipped, seemed to me like a handsomer, more pensive Sid Vicious. It was actually the face of a Breton-Algerian Parisian.

Bashung's mimed performance of "Madame Rêve," all murmur and doom-laden melancholy, is intercut with footage of him fondling, kissing and fucking (or perhaps dry-humping?) a remarkably submissive woman. He lays his hand on her ass when she sits down next to him at a public bar. At another juncture, she kneels at his feet to tie his shoelace.‡

The clip was more sexual than Anglo clips I was used to— not in the amount of flesh bared (the woman never removed her clothes) but in the *vérité* eroticism of the participants, so different to the saucy playacting of Duran Duran or Prince. It was, I thought, very French.

Clichéd preconceptions aside, "Madame Rêve" seeped into my consciousness. Its dreamy string arrangement haunted me. Bashung's sepulchral croon made me want more of it.

Thirty years on, I know that the video's erotic sequences

---

*   In addition to his music industry awards for artistic excellence and million-plus sales, Bashung was, in the year of his death, given an Ordre National de la Légion d'Honneur, the highest honor that the French government can bestow.

†   Probably. I've not kept diligent records of the exact times I watched music videos thirty years ago.

‡   What happened to his Beatle boots, eh?

come from the film *Rien Que Des Mensonges*, directed by Paule Muret (a woman) and starring Bashung and Fanny Ardant (a César-winner who has worked with Truffaut, Resnais, Volker Schlöndorff, Costa-Gavras, Agnès Varda, etc.).

And, thirty years on, I'm playing *À Perte de Vue*, a twenty-seven-disc set of Bashung's entire oeuvre, and loving it. I had to get it sent over from France, it weighs *une tonne*, and I paid more for it than I've ever paid for a musical item. *Je ne le regrette pas*. Bashung was a richly talented artist, restlessly versatile, reliably exciting in concert.

A while ago, one of my correspondents, Martyn Barker, the drummer for Shriekback, wrote to me: "So glad you've discovered Alain's work and especially *L'Imprudence*. I worked on his last 3 albums, *Fantaisie Militaire*, *L'Imprudence* and *Bleu Pétrole*, the first of which was voted the best album in French music history over the last 50 years. All 3 albums collected Grammys!

"As a drummer and musician, working on his music was a revelation. I had all the words converted into English but really enjoyed playing the songs following the French lyrics and phrases. They're beautifully written and so different to English in meaning and expression.

"This gave me an opportunity to approach things in a different way. I learnt so much as a player on how to really get inside the songs written in a different language. The fact that there were no choruses and all the songs were stories. You went on a journey with them.

"Alain gave me a free rein on all the work, to allow my personality to bond with the songs. *L'Imprudence* had 2 or 3 [co-] writers and arrangers, one being Ludovic Bource who wrote the music to *The Artist* that won an Oscar. We all became very close.

"Recently, I performed a concert of Alain's music with a complete orchestra in Lille to celebrate his music (he passed away 10 years ago). It was indeed a very special evening.

"I can go on and on, and feel very lucky."*

Reader, did anyone inform you in 2009 that Alain Bashung had died? Do you recall any retrospective features on his work in the newspapers and magazines you read, or on your TVs? Indeed, had you ever heard of him before now?

Days after Bashung died, Aaron Richter, an American music critic who has worked for *Esquire*, *The New York Times*, *Billboard* and *GQ*, published the article "LISTENING TOO LATE: Pondering the Death of Alain Bashung." He wrote: "Alain Bashung died on Sunday, March 14. The next day, I listened to the French singer's music for the first time. I found a copy of *Bleu Pétrole*, released just this past year and considered Bashung's late masterpiece, and heard a voice—familiar and bold, sorrowful and dramatic, broken yet defiant. [...] The record charted No.1 in France but didn't earn a single vote on the *Village Voice*'s annual Pazz & Jop critics poll—shameful neglect for such remarkable songwriting [...] His death felt strangely emotional for me..."

Richter goes on to meditate upon the deaths of Elliott Smith, Kurt Cobain, Arthur Lee and The Notorious B.I.G.—artists whose work he'd been aware of before they expired. He gestures toward feeling guilty in his "responsibility" as a journalist; he is sad at the thought of Bashung releasing all this great stuff for decades, alive at the same time as *he* was alive, and that he "missed out." He inquires: "Can tardy ears overcome the stigma of sweeping inadequacy?" And concludes by urging everyone to check out *Bleu Pétrole*.†

I'm not here to urge anyone to check out *Bleu Pétrole*. I'm here to ask why Alain Bashung was ignored by the Anglo media for so long, and why I had to discover him, quite randomly, at two

---

*   Martyn Barker, email correspondence with me, December 2019.

†   "LISTENING TOO LATE: Pondering the Death of Alain Bashung" by Aaron Richter, *Self-Titled* iPad magazine, March 2009.

in the morning on an Australian video show with a reputation for playing any weird shit including Forrest the dog.

Who's in charge here? And what's their game?

o   o   o

Herman van Veen has been making records since 1968. His discography is vast, not only in his native Dutch but also in German. He made one in English once but it didn't work out.

Everyone in the Netherlands knows van Veen. Some hipsters—the sort who venerate The Velvet Underground or The Pixies—regard him as a boring old fart. He hasn't been trendy since the seventies, although now that he's pushing eighty, most people acknowledge him as a national treasure, much like Leonard Cohen was regarded in his old age even by those listeners who were never keen on his music. As it happens, van Veen has recorded fine versions of several Cohen songs, "Een Ochtend Vol Van Liefde" ("Hey, That's No Way To Say Goodbye"), "De Vluchteling" ("The Partisan") and "Suzanne." "Liefde Van Later," his version of Jacques Brel's "La Chanson des Vieux Amants," is the loveliest version of that song I know.*

There's a genre of music that's always thrived in the Netherlands and Belgium that barely exists in English—songs that combine serious, grown-up subject matter with cabaret-style, middle-of-the-road music. Beguilingly breezy or apparently schmaltzy tunes that tackle topics like cancer, the regrets of old age, marriages scarred by resentments, the humiliations of illness and decrepitude, the agony of grief. All the hard questions, tackled in a nice sit-down venue by conservatively dressed entertainers.

Van Veen is a notable exponent. Ramses Shaffy (knighted by the Dutch government in 2002 after an illustrious career

---

*   If Anglo pop stars weren't so reluctant to sing about old age, every famous vocalist you could think of would've had a crack at this song. Instead, the only famous Anglo singer who attempted it was Judy Collins. In French.

and most likely wholly unknown to you) is another. The big daddy of them all is Jacques Brel. You'll almost certainly know Jacques Brel. Not to the extent of owning any of his records, mind, but you'll be familiar with some of his songs, translated into English, sung by people like Marc Almond, Scott Walker and Shirley Bassey. I struggle to think of Anglo songwriters in this genre. The Beautiful South, perhaps. Jake Thackray?* Randy Newman? The Divine Comedy? It's really not something we do.

This is reflected in how much of a damn we give about Herman van Veen. His English-language Wikipedia entry, at the time that I write this book, is a mere 116 words long, only three of which allude to his achievements as a chansonnier for adults. The other 113 digress to his creation of the cartoon character Alfred J. Kwak (the cartoon was aired in the USA, thus qualifying it for significance to our empire). A separate Wiki entry for "Alfred J. Kwak" runs to more than four thousand words.

This in itself is revealing. Imagine an entry for Paul McCartney that mentions in a brisk few sentences that he wrote songs both solo and in a group called The Beatles, then spends four thousand words describing *Rupert and the Frog Song*.

The disrespect is breathtaking.

∘ ∘ ∘

Here's some disrespect of my own. Even though I'm Dutch by birth, I've lived in English-speaking countries most of my life and I love the language. I've written novels in it, and like to think that its potentials are almost limitless. Occasionally I read about the things other languages can do that English can't, and

---

*   Thackray was, in any case, deeply in debt to the French chansonnier Georges Brassens, whose work he discovered while living in France for a spell. Brassens's name meant zilch in the Anglo marketplace and the only gig he ever played in Britain was organized by Thackray—at the Sherman Theatre in Cardiff. See: "Cult heroes: Jake Thackray was the great chansonnier who happened to be English" by Jeremy Allen, *The Guardian*, September 15, 2015.

I'm not convinced. For example, the complex system of honor-
ifics (*keigo*) in Japanese, denoting the social nuances of rank and
status, seems to me a burden rather than an asset.

I have a particular prejudice against inflected languages—
languages in which the spelling of every damn word changes
depending on whether you're talking *to* or *about* someone, and
whether that person is male or female or neuter, doing or being
done to, and so on. Anglo-Saxon was an inflected language many
hundreds of years ago and grew out of it. Good thing, too. What's
the point of adding suffixes to all the words (including people's
names) depending on whether the case is nominative, genitive,
dative, accusative, locative, vocative or ablative? Madness.

Deep down, I know that inflected languages neatly avoid the
ambiguities and syntactical traps that can make English treacher-
ous. The meaning is always clear. I can see that this could be a
good thing. But I'm so used to how English works that I allow
myself to fancy that it's superior to the others. That's linguistic
bias, pure and simple.

Maybe the vehemence of my disapproval of inflected languages has a personal grudge behind it. My late wife Eva (Ewa,
Ewca, Ewunia, etc.) spoke fluent Polish and I've been to Poland
many times; I got married there, in the town hall of Gdansk. I
even tried learning some Polish.

"It's a pig of a language," I grumbled after a while. "Why inflict this crap on innocent schoolchildren?"

o o o

The name "Czesław" is pronounced, roughly, "cheshwuv," and
"Niemen" is "nyemen." Czesław Niemen* is one of the tower-
ing figures in progressive music. A household name in Poland
due to some of his 1960s pop hits, like "Dziwny Jest Ten Świat"

---

*   Christened Wydrzycki, another of those perverse consonant clusterfucks that
    Polish apparently delights in.

("Strange Is This World"), he seemed destined at first to be a histrionic cabaret act, a Slavic version of yowling western fist-clenchers like Johnny Ray, Chris Farlowe or Tom Jones.

But something strange happened toward the end of the decade as Niemen's facial hair grew and his apparel defied Communist convention. He transmogrified into a charismatic creature, not just outwardly but in his art. His vocals ascended to a strato-spheric level occupied by few others—Diamanda Galás, Tim and Jeff Buckley, Nusrat Fateh Ali Khan, those sorts of ulula-tors. His improvisations on the organ and synthesizer—soulful, mysterious, audacious—propelled him into an international elite of progressive keyboard players. Or would've done, if anyone in the Anglo world had been listening.

To be fair, Communism made it difficult for music to leave the country. Niemen would've been a sensation at Glastonbury or Woodstock. He was respected and welcomed in France and Italy, but travel was bureaucratically problematic and the au-thorities were always looking for pretexts for banning or even imprisoning artists. Maybe Niemen should've accepted Blood, Sweat & Tears' invitation to be their singer and defected to the west. But he stayed in Warsaw and died there in 2004.

Also, his output was literally fragile. Eastern Bloc LPs were pressed on low-quality vinyl and packaged in sleeves that were much flimsier than British or (especially) American ones. Find-ing copies that have survived the decades without being trashed is almost impossible. And by the time the CD era came around, the Polish public was chasing pop and rap. Niemen will have to wait a little longer before history does right by him.

In the meantime, western record companies release multi-disc box sets of every minor sixties/seventies Anglo artist who can be exhumed for the nostalgia market, speciously making the "neglected genius" argument for all sorts of also-rans with a tenth of Niemen's talent.

o   o   o

Niemen's records, rumpled and crackly though they were, have been favorites of mine since my first visit to Poland in 1990. By contrast, I didn't discover Franco Battiato until I visited Italy in the mid-2000s, in the wake of the success of *The Crimson Petal and the White*.

By then, Battiato's career, although far from over, was as full and accomplished as that of any major figure in modern music. Anglo rock critics kept making lists of the 100 best *this* and the 50 greatest *that*, and regarded it as their duty to check out obscure stuff by upcoming artists—as long as it wasn't by foreigners who didn't even have the courtesy to sing in English. Franco had tried singing in English a few times, but he wasn't very good at it. Face it, he was never going to reinvent himself as "Frank Batt" and appear on the David Letterman show.

As my own literary career took off, Battiato was still producing significant and enduring works in a number of styles, including opera, electronica and heavy rock. His old albums had been reissued on CD and I bought a pile of them on one of my expeditions to Italy, carrying them back to Scotland in my suitcase. Thus began a love that deepened over time, and reached its high point when Battiato composed a piece especially for Eva. It was called "I Have A Message For You." I played it at her funeral.

Battiato died in 2021, at the age of seventy-six. He'd done it all. He'd been a fountain of creativity, offering us enough material for a lifetime of listening. The only question is: Who is "us"?

o   o   o

Now that Battiato is gone from the world, it's possible that Anglo hipsters will discover him at last. Who knows? A famous Anglo rock star may "curate" a CD of his most charming compositions, with liner notes in English, whereupon, slowly, stiffly, with bad grace, our marketplace may make a little space for it. Journalists in London and New York may even write articles about how Battiato was shamefully overlooked "back in the day." Not by *them*, of course. By someone else.

o   o   o

Listen: next time you're idly rummaging through the release hype of forthcoming reissues of forgotten Anglo artists who were arguably *almost* as good as Buffalo Springfield or Funkadelic or Genesis or Linda Ronstadt, stop. What are you doing? Why are you investigating something that some journalist or record company tells you is surprisingly not-too-bad-at-all and reasonably sure to appeal to people who like that sort of thing, broadly speaking, if they're in the mood?

Why not explore the oeuvre of some giant figures who flourished in countries you're not familiar with, and who sing in languages you don't understand?

Why not be the foreigner, for a change?

AMBIENT 1:
MUSIC FOR PRIVATE BANKING

I'm at Heathrow Airport, Terminal 5, in a "lounge." That's what they call the private waiting areas for the higher class of people, shut off from the crowded public thoroughfares where the hoi polloi sit. I have a laminated plastic card that grants me admission to this oasis. The walls of the lounge are flimsy but they're padded with insulation material and might as well be solid stone. It's a different world in here.

Snug enclosures of any kind are scarce in an airport. There's the toilets and the lounges—and then there's the vast cattle yard of the rest of the place, where all the shops and restaurants and seating areas and walkways merge into each other, so that the activities of shopping/eating/wearily hanging about/hurrying to Gate B24 get blurred into one restless herd meander.

This cattle-yard design seriously messes with your ears. The acoustics lack the spacious nonresonance of the great outdoors, yet they also lack the timbres of properly defined buildings. A log cabin and a cathedral respond to your words and footsteps very differently, but they both let your body know where it fits in the space. You've come inside from the outside, and it's obvious which is which.

By contrast, airport terminals don't enclose you, only expose you. Your hominid equivalent of a bat's sonar cannot reach the extremities to bounce back to you; the impulses travel into cluttered expanses, falter and get lost. You're surrounded by sound, yet everything you hear is either too quiet to catch, or too loud to ignore, and your animal instincts tell you you haven't found the center, but are being held back at some periphery. Only the toilets and the private lounges feel like chambers where you could hear yourself breathe and make a nest if you had to.

The access card for this lounge was sent to me, unrequested, by my bank. It was a fringe benefit for letting them overcharge me shamelessly for "private banking," a service I signed up for in the wake of my wife's death, when I was having trouble with scary brown envelopes and forgotten access codes. I needed a real person I could email for help whenever I was sent forms I didn't understand, and in return I got permission to be slightly elite at Heathrow.

It must be said that my fringe benefit is, in itself, somewhat fringe. Heathrow has many private lounges but only a couple of them accept my particular card. The British class system is never content with just one simple insider/outsider dynamic. It prefers a hierarchy of competing eligibilities that render you just that wee bit more, or less, privileged than the next person. In each airport, I've learned to find the lounges where the smartly uni-formed staff will not shake their heads at my silvery-gray little rectangle that says RETREAT REFRESH RELAX.

Private banking offers me other travel-related perks as well, which I don't comprehend and will never claim because they would require me to fill in forms and/or learn how to use vari-ous tech-y processes—exactly the challenges I needed the pri-vate banking to spare me from. But the challenge of keeping a small plastic card in my wallet so that, at an airport, I can sit down in a comfortable armchair in a quiet kennel and eat freshly cooked food—yes, my brain can manage that.

So, here I am, lounging in my lounge at Terminal 5, check-ing emails and eating samosas. At regular intervals, handmaid-ens bring out more rosemary potatoes and sautéed mushrooms. Small children lie curled up in their seats, sleeping, while their parents draw breath for the next leg of their journey to Bangkok, Amman, Madrid. I have ages to wait until my flight to Krakow.

The samosas and the emails fill in a bit of it, but I spend most of it listening to the music that's being piped through high-quality speakers into this privileged space.

o   o   o

Music in airports has a long backstory, with many ups and downs. Its most illustrious "up" arguably came in 1978, when Brian Eno issued *Ambient 1: Music For Airports*, whose back cover included an influential essay titled "Ambient Music." Eno argued that background music need not be irritating and lightweight, but could "induce calm and a space to think."[*] Many years later, he explained the genesis of the album. He'd been waiting for a flight at Cologne Airport, "a very beautiful building [...] The light was beautiful, everything was beautiful, except they were playing awful music."[†]

What he particularly disliked about the stuff piped through the terminals was its breezy cheerfulness, which he ascribed to the airport managers' desire to reassure passengers that they weren't going to die in a plane crash. What Eno wanted to provide instead was "music that said 'Well, if you die, it doesn't really matter' [...] a different feeling that you were sort of suspended in the universe and your life or death wasn't so important. So, rather than trivialize the thing, I wanted to take it seriously."

Eno, an atheist, shows wonderful disregard here for why humanity invented religion in the first place. The great majority of humans do not wish to be "suspended in the universe," meditating on their cosmic insignificance. And, if they are nervous flyers, they really, really don't want to die in a plane crash.

---

[*]   Brian Eno, liner note for *Ambient 1: Music For Airports* (EG Records, 1978).

[†]   Brian Eno, interviewed by Martin Large, June 5, 1999, for a TV program produced by the Nederlandse Omroep Stichting (Netherlands Broadcasting Foundation), uploaded in part to YouTube as "Brian Eno – Music For Airports Interview" by nathanidiothend on October 29, 2007.

When Eno's music was first installed at New York's LaGuardia Airport in 1980, the airline and terminal workers were not pleased. "It sounds like funeral music," one remarked.* The album was trialed for nine days at Greater Pittsburgh International Airport and many travelers reportedly complained that it made them uneasy and asked for the usual background music to be restored.† Irritated employees at Berlin's Tegel Airport registered their protest against the piece in 1984.‡

Academic musicologists can analyze exactly why Eno's *Music For Airports* gave some sensitive souls the willies and made the LaGuardia terminal worker think of funerals. In an essay for Cambridge University Press, a professor observes that while the overall composition of the track "2/1" "mainly tends toward F Aeolian due to the bass f notes, the occasional appearance of the d♭ implies a major subtonic triad or seventh chord (VI or VI7) before proceeding back to an implied tonic (eg, 0:48; 1:20). This i–VI Aeolian pendulum…is often associated with ominousness, resignation, or death in much European and American music (for instance, an Aeolian pendulum famously starts Chopin's 'Marche Funèbre')."§

Of course, there are people who like those Aeolian pendulums very much. I'm one of them. *Music For Airports* is, to my ears, a lovely record. The person who uploaded the above-mentioned interview with Eno to YouTube is likewise a fan: he was serenaded by it at Christchurch Airport in New Zealand and thinks "it works just fine." Another admirer is Jimmy Stamp, an architect who writes for the Smithsonian. Stamp prefers to schedule

---

★   "Brian Eno" by Gregory Miller, *Omni*, November 1980.

†   Joseph Lanza, *Elevator Music: A Surreal History of Muzak, Easy-Listening, and Other Moodsong* (Picador, 1995).

‡   "Review: Brian Eno: Tegel Airport, Institute Unzeit, Berlin" by Ursula Frohne, *Flash Art*, May 1984.

§   "Unsettling Brian Eno's Music For Airports" by Victor Szabo, in *Twentieth-Century Music*, Vol. 14, Issue 2, June 2017.

his air travel at times of night when airports seem empty, and thus readily identifies with Eno's fond vision of an "ideal airport" where you're virtually alone and "you're just seeing planes take off through the smoked windows."*

But this talk of an "ideal airport" takes us back to class, to tribe, to demographics. Ideal for whom? For the hip globe-trotting architect who writes for the Smithsonian, no doubt. Not for the proletarian family from Barnsley who are going on holiday to Mallorca. The tired parents have promised their kids lots of fun in the sun and do not want to sit in a ghostly becalmed terminal listening to Brian Eno's subtonic triads while the occasional Swissair flight to Zurich takes off into the gloom. They want lots of people around, they want all the shops to be open and, if there's going to be any music, they want it to cheer them on in their big adventure.

o   o   o

The unrestricted public part of Heathrow no longer has piped music; nor does Gatwick. I'm not sure why. Maybe too many customers complained. Maybe the airports noticed that the customers who wanted music were listening to it on private earbuds connected to their smartphones. Maybe the costs of reimbursing Sony and UMG for broadcasts of their product were considered prohibitive. Whatever: the sections of the airport where the people without laminated cards congregate are no longer serviced with tunes.

But my lounge is. And very dignified music it is, too. Tasteful. It's punctuated every now and then by one of the handmaidens clanking a metal lid to deposit more samosas, but mostly it plays with little sonic competition, as my fellow lounge-dwellers are absorbed in their phones and our insulated bunker admits only a muted susurrus from the terminal beyond.

---

* "Music for Airports Soothes the Savage Passenger" by Jimmy Stamp, *Smithsonian* magazine, June 7, 2012.

What I'm hearing is pointedly unlike Eno's *Music For Airports*. It's solo acoustic guitar, similar in style and sonority to the works of William Ackerman or Michael Hedges on the Windham Hill label—high-quality wallpaper for people who don't want their muzak tarnished with cheesy synths or New Age tintinnabulations. Good honest acoustic études played by earnest men with earnest faces. I fantasize that this particular man is called Brad,* and I picture him wearing an unbuttoned workman's shirt over a Jack Daniels T-shirt, blue jeans so pale they're almost gray, chunky boots that look old and a bit beat-up but are actually quite new and very expensive.

Outside this little sanctuary, the less privileged mill about in their musicless cattle yard. Would they enjoy Brad's tasteful fingerpicking if they had a chance to hear it? Maybe they would.

But if the airport had decided that there must be music out *there* among the masses, there probably wouldn't be any in *here*, among the private banking beneficiaries. In that case, a judgment would probably have been made that travelers of my caliber don't want or need music while they're waiting for their flight to Krakow.

That's how class works. Its soundtrack can be switched on or off, as required.

---

*   Why do I assume he's a man? Because I'm not aware of this field having any women working in it. The purveyors of solemn acoustic guitar background ambience are a highly particular tribe. Females have their own domains. There are plenty of New Age damsels who wear Guinevere gowns and make a fortune with albums called, for example, *Whispers Of Serenity*. And then there are the cowgirls who do their pickin' and strummin' in a work shirt, but want to play for real people who hoot and cheer, not for a narcoleptic waiting lounge at Heathrow's Terminal 5.

LET'S HEAR IT ONE
MORE TIME FOR LUDWIG!

I've always wanted to love classical music. I've tried very hard to. I've failed.

During the mid to late 1980s, when the pop and rock in the mainstream media was particularly rotten,* I decided to educate myself about the jewels of antiquity. If only I could learn to appreciate Chopin, Tchaikovsky, Mozart and all the rest, then Spandau Ballet, Rick Astley and Poison might fade from my consciousness like bygone bouts of indigestion. With more than a hundred Haydn symphonies to investigate, would I really have spare time to be aghast at A Flock of Seagulls?

In those days, I was living in Melbourne, which was served by two classical radio stations—ABC-FM (the Oz equivalent of BBC Radio 3) and 2MBS-FM, a subscriber-funded enterprise that was staffed by high-minded enthusiasts, some of them elderly, some of them younger, all of them articulate, knowledgeable, and passionate. Evangelists, you might say, for the anti-pop cause. I listened for hours every day, month in, month out, for years. I taped dozens of hours of the broadcasts so that I could listen to them over again. I learned a lot.

But I did not learn to love classical music.

---

* I could write a self-indulgent book-length diatribe about how deplorable the 1980s were, but one example of my prejudices will suffice. To me, Jan Hammer was a serious jazz musician whose groundbreaking improvisations were integral to The Mahavishnu Orchestra. In the 1980s, I glanced up to find that he'd metamorphosed into a showbiz dude clunking out the lame-brained theme to *Miami Vice* on a keytar while wearing hideous Versace suits with the sleeves rolled up.

o   o   o

In the mid-1990s, after my emigration to Scotland, I had another go. Several more years of listening. More assiduous study. Many Oxbridge-educated announcers telling me that so-and-so in 1758 found favor with the Duke of Westphalia and was thus able to move from Linz to Leipzig. More mounds of cassettes. In my compendious database, which had hitherto consisted almost entirely of music made after I was born, I conscientiously typed entries like "J.S. BACH transcribed by HEITOR VILLA-LOBOS—Preludes and Fugue from the '48' (Pleeth Cello Octet)—Tape 499." It was as if I was striving to complete an Open University degree without a diploma to show for it.

Inevitably, in all that time, among all those hundreds of compositions and performances, I did find a few things I liked. They tended to be either very ancient (Gothic plainchant, medieval dances, a rendition of Pergolesi's *Stabat Mater* by the Lithuanian Chamber Orchestra augmented with a choir of eerily pagan-sounding girls) or quite recent (Ligeti's piano studies, John Adams, Martha Argerich's 1960 performance of Prokofiev's Toccata). The period of classical music that didn't do much for me was the bit between the early seventeenth century and the late nineteenth, i.e. the bit that's proper Classical in the commonly understood meaning of the term. The bit that's supposed to encompass all the greatest sonic achievements of western culture.

o   o   o

It would be an exaggeration to say I didn't care for any of it. There's a mono recording of Beethoven's Eighth and Ninth symphonies that thrills me. I like a blast of Handel's *Messiah* when I'm in the mood. Bach's *St Matthew Passion* is undeniably fab.* Albrechtsberger's Concerto in E major for Jew's harp al-

---

*   Although two and three-quarter hours of it may be too much of a good thing. But then, maybe two and three-quarter hours of *any* sort of music is too

ways makes me smile. (That tiny metal contraption going *bjoing, bjoing, bjoing* all over a po-faced chamber orchestra—bonkers!)

But, if I'm honest, if I had to choose between all the classical music I've ever enjoyed and the first forty seconds of Coil's "Are You Shivering" or Blind Willie Johnson's "Dark Was The Night, Cold Was The Ground," there'd be no contest.

o   o   o

One way I could have responded to my indifference to two hundred and fifty years of masterpiece-making was to hang my head and apologize, like an embarrassed lover who can't get aroused. "It's not you, it's me."

However, when we don't fancy things that other people adore, there is another policy that's much more tempting: criticism.

I took the critical route. I found fault with classical music. I analyzed why it was undeserving of my love.

o   o   o

This wasn't just sour grapes. Endearing as it may be to its admirers, the genre has some less than admirable qualities.

o   o   o

Its aura of God-given sovereignty is problem number one. Did I really just read an eminent musicologist calling Bach the "supreme arbiter and lawgiver of music"?* Supreme arbiter? Lawgiver? What fusty papal court have we blundered into here? The

---

much. I've grown up in a pluralistic world. When global capitalism collapses and we all have to make do with what's available in our own little village in Sussex or Senegal or wherever, we'll have to adjust to a limited menu. Until then, I do prefer variety.

* Nicolas Slonimsky, entry for Bach in *Baker's Biographical Dictionary of Musicians* (Schirmer Books, 1940). To be fair to Slonimsky, he was actually a great supporter of contemporary composers, a pal of Frank Zappa, and the dedicatee of John Adams's *Slonimsky's Earbox*.

language that the champions of classical music use to describe and celebrate the music they favor is often larded with smug elitism, imperialist arrogance, special pleading, fogeyish nostalgia, even white supremacism. Some sort of Supreme Being has anointed this music as the finest and noblest of all possible musics—certainly the most worthy of preservation and state funding.

Some would argue (and I wish *I* could) that music is merely notes and textures produced by dedicated players whose sole concern is to produce those notes and textures; music cannot, in itself, be snobbish, entitled or elitist. As an aesthete, I would much prefer to view classical music through this perfectly transparent lens. But the reality is that music comes with sociological strings attached, and, when I walk into the foyer of a classical concert hall and mingle with the patrons, those strings are very conspicuous. They are more like a cobweb.

Every genre of music has its snobs, but jazz snobs or blues snobs seem to actually quite enjoy the niche status of their taste, and make no grand claims about the role that jazz or blues plays in the larger scheme of civilization. Whereas classical snobs perceive nonclassical music as an epidemic of crassness that threatens to destroy all that is noble in society. The barbarians are at the gates; only the stalwart defenders of high culture hold out against them, bravely wielding their Mozart shields and Donizetti spears.

Harsh rhetoric, I know. Also, it unfairly ignores the phenomenon—once unheard of, now increasingly common—of the young cellist or oboist who enjoys a bit of heavy metal or reggae in their off-duty hours.

I think part of the reason for the harshness of my response is that one of the first snobs I encountered as a child (after the odious Zachary Smith in the sci-fi series *Lost in Space*) was Hans Keller. He was a Viennese violinist who came to prominence in Britain as a critic and broadcaster. I must've been about thirteen when I saw an archival (1967) clip of him interviewing Pink Floyd.

Keller, dressed in a dark suit and tie, preposterously sour-faced and radiating superiority, announces that he doesn't want to prejudice the listeners before they hear the group. Then, without pausing for breath: "but four quick points I want to make before you hear them." Those points include that they're boring and much too loud. "Perhaps I am a *little* bit too much of a musician to appreciate them."

Syd Barrett and Roger Waters, dressed in their psychedelic finery, politely defend their music as best they can. Disdain drips from Keller's heavy Austrian accent as he repeatedly pokes his guests to admit that their intolerable racket is an act of aggression toward audiences. In conclusion, he turns to the camera and addresses us, the viewers: "Well, there it is. I think you can pass your verdict as well as I can. My verdict is that it is a little bit of a regression to childhood."[*]

As a thirteen-year-old Dutch-Australian boy whose pocket money didn't stretch far, I didn't know much about Pink Floyd. But I knew I disliked Hans Keller and the haughty elitism he stood for. Call it formative aversion therapy if you will.

o   o   o

As I grew older, I would occasionally hear a representative of High Culture holding forth on what should be done to ensure that High Culture was not swamped by Low Culture. The philistine majority and adherents of "pop" music, i.e. plebs like me, might gravitate toward worthless trash, but it was vital that governments should subsidize classical music so that, if any enlightened souls should develop an appreciation for it in the future, it would still exist. I was given the impression that classical music was endangered, on a par with the giant panda or certain species of albatross.

---

[*]   Hans Keller, interview with Roger Waters and Syd Barrett, *Look of the Week*, BBC television, May 14, 1967.

o   o   o

My schools were not the sort of schools that fostered classical music and my parents were not the sort of people who went to concert halls. I was in my early twenties when I finally sat down among formally dressed citizens to watch real classical music being performed by bona fide professionals. It was Puccini's *Madama Butterfly*.* I detested everything about it. It was self-important and stiff and cheesy and silly and false, like a primary school pantomime without the charm of children and mishaps. The lady sitting next to me, with the annoying dangly earrings, wept.

Then I was invited to a very special event—"a rare privilege," I think the phrase was—by a friend's mother who played violin (or was it viola?) in a prestigious ensemble, maybe the Melbourne Symphony Orchestra. What I do remember was that no less a personage than Krzysztof Penderecki was "at the baton," conducting his own works.

When I told my friend's mother afterward that I'd been left cold by the music, she confessed that she didn't enjoy it either. It was her job to master its formidable technical challenges and not let her colleagues and the esteemed conductor down. She used a term that classical players often use to describe "modern classical" music that's nothing like Bach or Beethoven and requires the orchestra to make unpleasant noises—"squeaky gate music."

My friend's mother seemed regretful that I hadn't had the opportunity to see her playing Mozart or Schubert or whatever—the sort of stuff that soothed her troubled soul. The sort of stuff that bored me rigid.

---

* At the Royal Opera House in Covent Garden, June 15, 1981, conducted (Google tells me) by Lamberto Gardelli. The seats were so steeply raked that I wondered whether anyone had ever leaned down to pick up a dropped brochure, toppled forward and broken their neck at the bottom far below. This, sadly, was my sole excitement all evening.

The illustrious violinist Jascha Heifetz once said (half in jest, one hopes): "I occasionally play works by contemporary composers and for two reasons. First to discourage the composer from writing any more and secondly to remind myself how much I appreciate Beethoven."* Arrogance worthy of Hans Keller himself.

In recent years, the PR departments of orchestras, concert halls, record companies and teaching institutions have become self-conscious about the image of classical music—that of a clique of privileged white people of a certain age attending heavily subsidized performances by privileged white players, of a tired repertoire of pieces written by white men, most of them dead. They've striven to address this image problem, with mixed success. The patrons buying the tickets are still mostly pale-skinned, gray-haired and well-heeled. They are a distinctive tribe, and when members die off they tend to be replaced by remarkably similar specimens.

But there has been some evolution in the workforce onstage. Nowadays, Asians are a common sight in classical orchestras. A few brown people are popping up. Women have come a long way since the days when ladies were forced to play the cello sideways, to avoid the unseemly sight of a female with an instrument between her legs. In the 1970s, the Berlin Philharmonic consisted of more than sixty men and not one person sans penis; it wasn't until 1982 that the first female was hired.†

Today, twenty-four of the one hundred and twenty-five Berlin Philharmonic members are women. (No dark people, though.) The London Symphony Orchestra has a more impressive chromosomal mix: twenty-seven of the eighty-five are women. (Still no dark people, however.) The Bournemouth Symphony Orchestra is fifty-fifty, gender-wise, and, although

---

★   This much-reproduced quote originally appeared in *Life* magazine, most likely the June 1952 issue.

†   "Schlag ins Konto," *Der Spiegel*, January 9, 1983.

there are no dark people, I see the group has vacancies for "Principal Tuba," "Principal Trumpet" and "Sub-Principal Clarinet," which could be some Mahler-loving Caribbean clarinetist's golden opportunity.

Seriously, I believe that many classical ensembles and conservatoires today are no longer hotbeds of racism; I believe they would be only too delighted to include black trombonists and violinists and so on (if only to demonstrate their progressive credentials). But classical music is, by its nature, elitist and focused on frightfully particular, conformist skills. To play Beethoven well, you need to be not only bloody good, but bloody good in an extremely specific way that has been developed over centuries by white practitioners. How many black pianists are going to be interested in spending fifteen, twenty years learning how to play approximately like Daniel Barenboim or Artur Schnabel?

Historically, the racism in classical music was cruel and disgraceful. We will never know how many musicians of color spent years practicing their pianos and violins and flutes for hours a day, pluckily defying the naysayers, determined to win a seat in the orchestra or to be spotlit onstage playing Mozart or Ravel, only to be told to try elsewhere. But even when active racism is removed or eroded, racial barriers remain.

Nina Simone is an illuminating case in point. She actually wanted to be a classical pianist. To be precise: she *was* one. A piano prodigy, she specialized in Bach. A couple of benefactors who recognized her potential paid for her to attend an integrated school, whereupon she won a scholarship to study at Juilliard for a year. She used her time there to prepare for the entrance exam to the Curtis Institute, a prestigious conservatory—the only one that would waive the fees she couldn't afford. She pinned all her hopes on getting in, performed well—and was denied admission.* Simone always insisted that she was a victim of racism. Her illustrious career in pop had arisen, it seemed, because the door to classical music was shut in her face.

This is the Simone story that's retold over and over, but the truth is more complicated, and damning in a different way. The judges who rejected Nina (then a teenage girl called Eunice Waymon) were looking for applicants who could play in a particular style to a particular standard of dexterity. Competition was fierce—sixty-nine other applicants (white kids, presumably) were rejected along with Eunice. Contrary to Simone's later claims about her thwarted ambition to be the first black pianist accepted by Curtis, the institute had been taking in black students for decades.

"Believe me, it had nothing to do with her skin color," a Curtis piano tutor told a French documentary team. "Our attitude is completely to take the best." It may therefore be that on that day in 1951, Miss Waymon was good but simply not good enough.†

To my mind, the problem with the conservatory was not that they had a bad attitude to black people, but that classical music itself is inflexibly determined by racial parameters. Anyone who has heard Simone play knows that she was a phenomenal musician. What were the judges looking for that Nina didn't possess? Might it have been that difficult-to-define thing: a white person's sensibility, a white person's finger-touch?

This goes to the heart of one of my problems with classical music. Unlike the other musics I love, which adjust and metamorphose according to the individuals playing them, classical

---

*   "Nina Simone (1922–2003)" by Mariana Brandman, National Women's History Museum website, March 2022. Incidentally, the conservatory granted Simone an honorary degree fifty-three years after they'd rejected her. She died of cancer two days later.

†   See: "Curtis Institute and the case of Nina Simone" by Peter Dobrin, *Philadelphia Inquirer*, August 14, 2015.

music punishes deviation from an established norm. You must play it the way it "should" be played or you fail the exam.

∘ ∘ ∘

Another problem I have with classical music as a genre is its worship of the past. Yes, I know there are people who love music of all vintages, grooving to Verdi one evening and Al Green the next. I've met some. One of them is my girlfriend. But there is also a tribe that considers itself persecuted by contemporary civilization, and seeks sanctuary from the ugliness of Now.

I already struggle with the pop nostalgists who moan that nobody knows how to write songs anymore, none of the rubbish today can hold a candle to The Kinks or Carole King or Queen or those other "classic" rock artists, those giants of yesteryear who had "class." (Are you spotting a linguistic theme, here?) But the composers of the classical period can be roped in to an even more extreme form of nostalgia: the notion that everything went downhill a century or more before any of us were born. The Great Composers are not just greater than anybody alive today, they also offer listeners with elevated tastes a refuge from the modern world and all its crassness.

Yet Bach, Mozart, Beethoven, Verdi and all the other composers who are nowadays categorized as "heritage" did not conceive of themselves as guardians of old-fashioned values, nor did they see themselves as estranged from the marketplace. In their own era, they were innovators, entrepreneurs, celebrities. Hustlers, even. They kept up with the latest trends, the latest gadgets. They were anxious not to become yesterday's thing.

∘ ∘ ∘

Classical music, by its nature, is yesterday's thing. "Contemporary classical music"—that oxymoronic term that covers new compositions in the field—accounts for only the tiniest percentage of the viable repertoire. A very typical concert program will start with a new piece that the audience tolerates and instantly forgets, a little-known older piece that the audience thinks is surprisingly OK for a change, finally followed by the familiar fixture they've all been waiting for. The vast majority of freshly composed works by living composers are performed one, two, perhaps three times before vanishing into oblivion. Ancient and well-established is what the listeners want and what they'll pay money for.

The average classical musician must therefore dedicate themselves to being exponents of the distant past.* They practice until they get every note perfect, reassuring themselves that they're doing a better job than the thousands of competing violinists or pianists or conductors who misunderstand or ignore the composer's tempo instructions or the precise meaning of terms like *poco forte* or *sehr mäßigend*.

o   o   o

Hans Keller looked every inch the sort of critic who might sit in the audience at a concert with the score in his lap, checking for inexcusable liberties and errors. (I'm not joking. Critics actually used to do this.) But although his sour visage is branded on my memory, I only ever saw him on a TV screen. Two in-person encounters I've had with classical musicians—one in the 1990s, one in the early 2000s—have done much more to prejudice me against the whole shebang.[†]

---

[*]   The most zealous of them even reject violins and keyboards that postdate Bach's or Beethoven's era, substituting more "authentic" period instruments that, to be honest, sound tinny and harsh. Most listeners hate it, but the zealots feel the public should be hearing what audiences in 1750 heard, not some newfangled (i.e. nineteenth-century) refinement.

[†]   I write this shortly after having coffee with my pal John Woolrich, who writes mainly for string ensembles. He is one of many open-minded classical musicians I've met in recent years, so it seems unfair to focus on the two unfortunate encounters I relate in this chapter. But that's the nature of prejudice, I guess.

At a dinner organized by an Italian arts festival, I was seated next to an eminent piano virtuoso. He ticked every box in the cliché department. He was dressed in the most formal of suits, as if he'd just officiated at a funeral or endured an impromptu photo shoot with heads of state. He moved stiffly, straitjacketed into his own importance. He might've been any age between forty-five and seventy; he had the air of never having been young, not even as a baby. The only smile he had was one of courtesy.

We talked briefly about music and I confessed I was very much into the modern stuff. He assumed, without inquiring, that I must mean Schoenberg or Webern. I struggled to convey that I meant more…erm…contemporary things, like electronica. "Ah, Stockhausen," he nodded sagely.

It dawned on me, as we bent over our plates of food in that dimly lit, ornate Milan restaurant, that history, in his view, had ended quite some while ago.

My other alarming experience was with a representative of the younger generation. Hitchhiking from Inverness to London, I was given a lift by an intense, handsome, thirtyish man who turned out to be an Icelandic concert pianist.

Iceland, as anyone from Iceland will tell you, is a small place. As I chatted with my benefactor, it emerged that he'd gone to school in Reykjavik with Björk. He wasn't impressed with her, however. She was a mere pop musician. Her keyboard skills were rudimentary. Her compositions were childish compared to the glories of Baroque counterpoint. She was, he supposed, quite talented at what she did, but what she did could hardly be taken seriously.

We drove for hours. He was looking for a ferry terminal to take him across the channel, and the turnoff was elusive, and he was reluctant to stop and ask directions. He explained to me at some length what the life of a dedicated classical musician entails. You have to practice many hours a day, he said, just to

---

We look for the evidence that confirms the negative outlook we already have; we turn individuals we barely know into anecdotes.

"keep on top of" the repertoire. The number of pieces you attempt must be restricted, since it's better to play a narrow range superbly than a wide range adequately. It was a shame, he mused, how many pianists spread themselves too thin.

He saw himself very much as a denizen of the modern world. He'd set up his own record company back in Iceland and it was going places, winning awards. "All my recordings are DDD," he assured me, and seemed quietly pleased when I had to ask what that meant. It meant that his performances were captured on digital recording equipment, then mastered on digital mastering consoles, then released on digital media. Not one byte of sound quality lost. With my prattle of vinyl LPs, I may have come across as the old-fashioned one.

He happened to have with him a couple of CDs of his renditions of Bach and Mozart, and he gave these to me, partly out of generosity, partly in the hope that I might see the error of my anticlassical ways.

"And do you compose music yourself?" I asked at last.

"Oh no," he replied. "I don't have the time. Besides, after the genius of Beethoven and Brahms, what is there to add?"[*]

It's bad manners to argue too much with someone who's given you a lift. So I didn't protest that there was something terribly wrong with his attitude. But I thought it was appalling and I still do.

In historical terms, for a competent musician not to make music of their own is a bizarre aberration. Most of the great musicians of past ages were composers too. Their fame arose from their originality. Baroque masterworks that we accept "as written" were really only riffs for hot young violinists and keyboardists to improvise on. When the likes of Beethoven and Mozart

---

[*] The quote is accurate but I've decided not to identify the Icelandic pianist who so kindly drove me so far toward my destination. Ignorant as I am, I have no idea whether he's well respected within the world of Bach and Mozart renderers. I listened to his CDs dutifully, twice, and then kept them in my house for a spell, until one day they weren't there anymore.

gave concerts, it was all new material, much of which they'd only just finished, or made up on the spot. Clara Schumann and Franz Liszt loved to jam (sadly not with each other). I'd argue that Beethoven had much more in common with Joe Zawinul or Alice Coltrane than with Rudolf Serkin or Vladimir Ashkenazy. He would have struggled to comprehend what the hell my Icelander was playing at.

o   o   o

If you read the biographies of renowned violinists and pianists, you will often discover that, as youngsters, they harbored ambitions to be composers. Those ambitions almost invariably melt away. The enthusiasm that carries rock, pop and rap musicians through those early years when they're naive, second-rate or even awful, until they find their own voice and achieve their potential, seems not to be available to musicians in the classical arena. Something makes the dream die.

Typical is Alfred Brendel, lauded for his "scrupulous attention to the pillars of the classical repertoire, and to Mozart, Beethoven and Schubert in particular."[*] As a teen, he wrote some stuff of his own, but gave up composing shortly after his debut concert. Instead, he dedicated himself to doing "justice" to the giants of the past, to whom he has a sacred responsibility. His aging fingers eventually obliged him to drop the more strenuous pieces from his repertoire, but he expressed the hope that despite having played his ever-diminishing set countless times, it was still fresh. What this freshness was supposed to consist of was mysterious, however—he disapproved of creative mavericks like Glenn Gould, who try to be "original at the expense of the composer."

---

[*]   "Keeper of the flame" by Nicholas Wroe, *The Guardian*, October 5, 2002. In subsequent years, Brendel grew too old to do the necessary fingering for Beethoven and Schubert, but continued to evangelize on their behalf at lectures and masterclasses.

Conversations I've had with classical musicians in my own friendship circle have uncovered this same attitude to creativity over and over again. These people sincerely love their instruments. They love the compositions that they so faithfully render. It's plain to see that they're in a lifelong romantic relationship with music. But the relationship is unequal. Music requires a lot of them, demands unstinting devotion, punishes them if they take their eye off the ball, and leaves them very little space to be themselves. They can never dare to ask music to do what *they* want.

During the latter years of writing *Listen*, I corresponded with Judith van Driel, a member of the Dudok Quartet. She'd originally contacted me because she thought I might like to write something about Brahms. She was crestfallen when I confessed that Brahms meant nothing to me, and I was embarrassed, but we got over it and went on to have many sincere conversations about music and why it does for some people what it doesn't do for others.

Judith's take on her own compositional creativity is much the same as I got from my Icelandic pianist. She regards herself as a "translator," she doubts that she could possibly add anything worthwhile to the greatness of the past, and of course she and her fellow Dudoks are very busy practicing. Coming from her, the rationalization seems more valid. She lacks the arrogance of my Icelander; she doesn't bad-mouth pop music; she doesn't have the air of someone who's waging a war against evolution.

In any case, she said, "the main reason why I still like to play 'old' music, is simply because it touches me. When I hear a great piece by Bach, or Brahms, or Shostakovich, I just want to share it. And then it is our task as performers to find a personal and up-to-date interpretation which connects the music with our audience. Every live performance is a new version of the piece, and a new experience for us as musicians and for the listener. I guess this is the same for artists who write and perform their own music, because usually they play their pieces hundreds of times. And audiences like to hear pieces time after time, because every time you hear it, it makes more sense, you find new layers and elements, and the recognition also adds an extra emotional layer in your brain."[*]

That last point is an especially good one. When people go to a concert, they do like to hear things they've heard before, whether it's Brahms's String Quartet No. 1 in C minor, or Elton John's "Your Song." (A bad example, perhaps. Elton famously detests the pressure to perform "Your Song," and has been trying unsuccessfully to retire it from his set list since at least 1978.) There are plenty of rock artists who declare that they never get tired of performing their hits (or never get tired of the audience applauding them, which may not be quite the same thing). They claim that each performance is different (even if it demonstrably isn't) and that the meaning, for both the performer and the listener, changes with the passing years (undoubtedly true).

Here, I stumble on another reason why classical music and I are not a good fit. When I go to concerts, unlike most humans, I don't actually want to hear stuff I'm already familiar with. Most of the concerts I've gone to (after a couple of formative disappointments in the late 1970s, where everyone around me seemed to be in transports of nostalgic joy and I was bored) have involved a high ratio of improvisation and risk.

o   o   o

In an earlier incarnation of *Listen*, written when my estrangement from classical music still had the fresh sting of a newly failed romance, I skewered the whole enterprise of classical performance with a lance of polemic.

All those prestigious orchestras (I said)—all the Berlin Philharmonics and Dresden Staatskapelles conducted by Herbert von Ego, all the piano virtuosos hunched over their grands,

---

*   Judith van Driel, email correspondence with me, March 2022.

all the solemn cellists looking to the rafters for divine inspiration, all the sopranos braving the high Cs, all the percussionists in the back row waiting for their designated moment to tinkle the triangle—are nothing more than tribute bands. They are The Bootleg Beatles, ABBAsolutely, Think Floyd, Pink Fraud, The Counterfeit Stones, The Strolling Clones. The fact that you have to pay a fortune to see them in a grand symphony hall rather than in a pub in Maidstone for a tenner does not alter the fact that they're tribute bands. They offer you a simulacrum of an experience you might've had if you'd been around ages ago when this music was fresh.

Sure, they do their best to get everything right. They invest in the vintage gear, they labor at the harmonies, they obsess over every detail. But despite all the effort, they can't help being—in some melancholy, trainspottery, tacky way—*wrong*.

The Bootleg Beethovens. The Shortlizst. The One & Only Albinoni. Vivaldi from Aldi. I Can't Believe It's Not Mozart. You see?

o   o   o

Put-downs can be beguiling. Once you've perceived a symphony orchestra as a tribute band, you can't unperceive it. For those who feel as alienated from classical music as I do, and who are perhaps looking for reasons to justify that alienation, the slavish recycling of centuries-old compositions will seem a self-evidently retrogressive enterprise. The balloon of classical music, inflated with the hot air of snobbery and self-importance, is popped.

o   o   o

But this is supercilious and unfair.

All genres of music have their problems and faults. All can be skewered by a critic who just isn't into them.

Also, I'm using my skills as an author to bolster an argument that's very far from objective. I've combed through this chapter countless times, sharpening a phrase here, softening a blow there, nuancing where I suspect an exasperated classical-loving reader will demand nuance, fudging positions that are indefensible, going in for the kill when I feel I'm on firm ground.*

A good polemic cuts through distracting verbiage to reveal a provocative truth underneath—but in so doing, it cuts through lots of other stuff as well, including other kinds of truth. Classical music, even in its narrowest sense, encompasses thousands of hours of music that continues to give enormous pleasure to a great many people. I am not smarter or deeper or worthier than all those humans. They possess something I lack. They can listen to a piece of Vivaldi or Mendelssohn—a piece I will rudely dismiss as vacuous or saccharine after giving it a mere thirty seconds of my attention—and perceive depths of beauty in it that only grow profounder with the years. In treating Scarlatti or Bizet with impatience and cold intolerance, I poison a potential friendship—I don't give them a chance to love me back.

Also, what gives me the right to argue that today's classical musicians should be making music of their own? Not everyone has the talent to be a good composer. There are many practitioners of jazz, pop, rap and rock who write their own material because that's what's expected in those worlds, but who would've spared us much boredom if only they'd humbly accepted that they were better suited to playing other people's stuff. I can imagine a classical-loving polemicist arguing persuasively that pop or rock or electronic music is infested with clueless plodders who have nothing new or worthwhile to offer.

---

*   I can't resist reproducing here a marginal note that Louisa Young wrote on my manuscript: "It seems a little ungracious not to acknowledge the huge amount that classical music has contributed to jazz, songwriting, rock, country etc, whether or not it allowed those musics to contribute to it. All these membranes are semipermeable, even though things don't pass through equally both ways, or at the same time, or same speed, or with the same effect. Music is soup, not a filing system."

Moreover, performing old compositions that one considers beautiful has been a fundamental part of music-making throughout history and always will be. "Sumer Is Icumen In," the song with which my novel *The Courage Consort* ends, was composed in the thirteenth century. The hymn "Let All Mortal Flesh Keep Silence" is medieval too, and ultimately leads us back to fourth-century Greece. Some tunes are just too strong to die.

Also, my demands for originality are not consistent. Like most humans, I am forgiving of weaknesses in things I like, and unforgiving of weaknesses in things I don't. A few years ago, I got very excited by a new band from Germany, a trio of "krautrock guerrillas" called Camera. They played impromptu gigs in subway stations, underpasses, shopping centers, public toilets and so on. I would watch them on YouTube and feel quite jealous of the lucky Germans being treated to their performances.

The music Camera played, however, was an homage to the pioneering krautrock pieces by Neu!, recorded in the early 1970s. Camera had not a single original idea. I'd heard it all before. I just happen to like hearing that sort of thing. A drummer starts a metronomic beat, a bassist locks into it with a throbbing drone, a vaporous shimmer of FX-laden guitar beams down from the ether, and I'm in a transport of joy. A very similar transport, no doubt, to the joy felt by a classical buff when thirty string players in an orchestra simultaneously bow their violins and cellos and violas and double basses, connecting once again with the celestial imperative that is Beethoven.

Let's hear it one more time for Ludwig!

o   o   o

I will leave the last word of this chapter to Jacqueline Shave, director and first violinist of the Britten Sinfonia. I interviewed her at her home, the morning after she'd given her final performance as leader of that august ensemble.

If I were to cherry-pick quotes from our conversation, and use Jackie as an instrument in my little symphony of disapproval, she could serve as further "proof" of my anticlassical argument. She has spent much of her life playing other people's music ("you can become a slave, really…") and has yet to make her mark as a composer. "When I was fifty, I thought, I need to stop this… I'm gonna be dead before I know it, and actually, who *am* I? What is my own musical voice?"[*]

But Jackie is no cliché of the conservatoire-bred virtuoso. She's no snob; she's delightfully open-minded, curious, thoughtful. We first bonded at her sister's housewarming party, sharing our mutual enthusiasm for Bowie's *David Live*. I wasn't even aware then that she'd played on records by Massive Attack, Seal, Goldie, Mory Kanté, Nick Cave, Spiritualized, Peter Gabriel and Goldfrapp, among many others.

Moreover, her path to classical music was wayward and instinctive. "I had a really bad violin teacher till I was eighteen. Terrible. He'd never heard of Brahms, didn't know who Brahms was. He wanted me to play his own little tunes. He was very small and used to eat dandelion leaves. It was an extremely unusual introduction to playing the violin, almost by mistake. I wanted to do French, really. And then I ended up going to college and I didn't have a clue why I was there, and so I literally used to ride round the Circle Line reading books rather than going to class. I bunked off, basically, and then gave up and left, and went into selling double glazing and all sorts of other things. And then a friend[†] said 'Come play the Schubert quintet,' and I said 'I don't really play anymore,' but I went to play it and I thought *This is amazing*. Weird, isn't it?"

---

[*]   Jacqueline Shave, interview with me, May 2022.

[†]   Paul Cassidy, pianist and longtime collaborator with the Brodsky Quartet.

I tell Jackie my theory about classical ensembles being "tribute bands," and my impression that the scene is full of stuffed shirts.

"We all know that it is," she replies. "But it isn't *only* that. There is, for me, a real light and truth. Let's talk about Beethoven, the late string quartets, because for some reason that does speak to my soul. Rather than feeling like a tribute band, it almost feels like a séance to me. I mean, Beethoven couldn't have played a string quartet, so it's not as if he was able to make it exist; he didn't do it. You're enabling his concept to come to life. So I always think of it more as a séance—tuning into that man and his humanity. There are no words, for me, that could possibly describe the opening of Opus 131 [String Quartet No. 14 in C♯ minor]. It just has me pinned to…" Whereupon words fail her.

As we discuss my immunity to classical music, she muses that the spirits awaiting their summoning are dependent on very specific performances, devoid of ego. "It's a rare thing. Most live performances I go to, I have to leave. There are artists—unfortunately in the minority—who are vessels for the music to come through. I did have it with Barenboim playing Beethoven in the Festival Hall, and it was like Beethoven was sitting next to me. I remember when we performed the Beethoven cycle on the Isle of Harris, Gavyn [Wright, Jackie's husband, original violinist for Penguin Café Orchestra and superstar arranger] said 'You can't possibly expect people to understand this if they're not educated in the language.' And yet people came and found themselves in tears; they didn't know why. If you can find a way for the frequency to come through, something can happen."

CODA

While I was transcribing this interview, something happened. I went to YouTube and chose, at random, a performance of

Beethoven's String Quartet No. 14 in C♯ minor, Opus 131. It was by the Danish String Quartet. I have no idea if they would meet Jackie Shave's criteria as rare egoless vessels. I have no idea if they followed Beethoven's score with absolute faithfulness. But the beginning of the piece—the bit that Jackie says pins her to…to what?…the universe? some ideal of the sublime?—touched me.

Was this Beethoven séancing through? Or was I moved by the way these devotedly focused Scandinavians weren't distracted—as I was—by the coughing, snuffling, chair-scraping and other noises coming from the audience? How much of my joy was caused by the sight of the four young men moving their upper bodies like birds in flight, a seated murmuration of graceful arms and torsos?

The music's hold on me weakened as it approached the twenty-minute mark. This goes against the findings of the classical musicologist Leonard Meyer, who argued in his 1956 book *Emotion and Meaning in Music* that Beethoven's deliberate avoidance of a restatement of the tonic E major chord throughout this piece makes us increasingly desperate to hear it. "He wants to preserve an element of uncertainty in his music, making our brains beg for the one chord he refuses to give us. Beethoven saves that chord for the end." The suspense, claims Meyer, is what makes us feel about the piece the way we do.[*]

Was I waiting for that E major chord? If so, did I get fed up waiting?

In my conversation with Jackie Shave, I raised the possibility that my musical illiteracy—my inability to read a score—is one of the things that holds me back. She wasn't having it.

"I listen to the opening of the *St John Passion*, which for me is just a huge stirring of humanity, it's just overwhelming, I don't

---

[*]   Summarized by Jonah Lehrer in "The Neuroscience Of Music," *Wired*, January 19, 2011.

know what it is. And then someone will say, 'It's gone to a Nea-politan sixth* here, and then he does such-and-such...' I don't understand that, I don't have that knowledge."

On YouTube, I check out a couple of other string quartets doing Opus 131. The Takács Quartet, who I suppose must be more famous than the Danes because their name rings a bell, don't transport me. I admire their skill, but am unmoved. I try the Alban Berg Quartett. They've sold more than a million copies of their version of the Opus 131, apparently, and have the singular honor of having Helene Berg's blessing to name themselves after her dead husband. I start listening to their play-ing, but am soon distracted by the shots of the audience, which seems to consist entirely of mature gentlemen in suits and ties. The Albans (if I may be so bold as to call them that) are dressed very stiffly too. The viola player looks alarmingly like a Re-publican senator.

Have I merely exhausted my limited ability to focus many times over on the same Beethoven piece? To test this, I go back to the Danes and let them start again from the beginning. They still do something to me. But what? Maybe it's enough that it's something.

As for Jackie Shave, I'm glad that after performing all those séances for Beethoven and other dead geniuses, she feels ready to do her own thing. The concluding segment at her valedic-tory Britten Sinfonia gig at the Barbican was a joyous suite of self-composed pieces with tabla player Kuljit Bhamra and guitarist John Parricelli. She credits her meeting with Bhamra, and her fervent desire to play with him, for the leap in her de-velopment. "I always did have a little person somewhere inside me saying 'You can do that.' But there was never enough time, until I made the time. Jumping off a cliff and finding your own

---

* A major chord built on the lowered second scale degree, which Wikipedia helpfully informs is known, in Schenkerian analysis, as a Phrygian II.

language, not having to be bound by that [classical] language...
I'm still very much in my infancy, the early days of letting go of
the dots. But now that I've left the Britten Sinfonia, the doors
have opened, and I can feel something coming. I'm not sure
what it is, but it's exciting."

Something happening; something coming. I suppose that
means that neither of us can say we've failed yet, because the
music each of us has yet to find is patient while we make the
journey.

WHERE I GOT MY PARKA

I was fashionable once, by accident, for five minutes.

The year was 2000. Oasis were huge, poised at the edge of that downward slope where the trendy kids had already gone off them but the older mainstream demographic had belatedly decided that they were the coolest thing ever. Within a few years, Oasis albums would be discarded by the truckload, but in 2000 the Gallagher gang seemed to be kings of the universe.

I wasn't doing too badly either, fame-wise. My debut novel had just been published and got excellent reviews. There was a buzz, at the time, around Scottish fiction, a far-north New Wave to shake up the complacency of the oh-so-English literati. *Under the Skin* was already gaining cult status.

To help publicize the book, I traveled down to London to do a photo shoot for a magazine. I wore my usual clothes: second-hand gear bought in charity shops. I was forty but looked a lot younger. My hair was the same length it had been since 1977: BritPop length, some might say. The shoot was in a gritty alleyway where I could appear appropriately noir.

The photographer was in his late twenties, very much in thrall to monthly style bibles like *Dazed & Confused*, a perfect candidate to worship Oasis just before they fell out of fashion. He was immensely impressed with my coat, which was similar to the ones Liam Gallagher ponced about in.

"Where did you get your parka?" he said, pale with envy.

I explained that in Tain, a small town in the Highlands near my home, there was a charity shop—Barnardo's, Salvation Army, Cats Protection League, I couldn't remember which—where coats of this sort were often donated. I'd paid maybe £7 for this one.

This was not the answer he wanted to hear. He wanted me to tell him about a boutique or a men's outfitters in London where he could buy a parka just like mine. He thought I was a member of a tribal elite, looking fabulous in my trendy jacket, a man who could go to an exclusive party and hang out with cool writers and musicians and filmmakers and supermodels. I was wearing the garment that signaled those things to him.

o o o

My parka is not fashionable now. It is just a parka, and BritPop won't come again.

The lesson, though, is that when people talk about culture, they are often not talking about culture in any artistic or philosophical sense, but about parkas. Or T-shirts, or trousers, or hairstyles, or accessories. Indeed, music is the accessory, and the clothes and grooming are the main thing.

o o o

Humans sorely need to be members of a tribe. Taste in music is part of that. But taste—one's liking for this or that, one's opinion about the coolness or crapness of things—is invisible. You can discuss it with your peer group, or sometimes with strangers if you're gathered together in a special space where discussing music is on the agenda. But passersby—onlookers—the world in general—can't look inside your mind and divine whether your allegiance is to Oasis or heavy metal or techno. For that, they need external visual clues.

Your garments and footwear, and how much of your hair you remove, and how you treat the hair that's left, are crucial in this signaling. You groom to inform other people what gang you're in.

Being in a gang locates you in a sweet spot between branded and bespoke. Unlike dogs or mice or bees, who aren't bothered by the fact that they're indistinguishable from others of their breed, we yearn to be unique. Part of a clan, sure, but also an individual. Our submergence in the tribe reassures us we are not alone. Our individuality reassures us we are not dispensable.

In our need for individuality, we fixate on the things that make us me-and-not-you; we fret and obsess over them. When we were children, our parents chose our clothes and our haircuts for us. Many of us look back on this state of affairs with keen embarrassment. Oh, the humiliation of someone else deciding how we'll look! (Instead of us deciding for ourselves whose appearance we will copy.) We feel pity for inmates of institutions who have no choice but to wear the clothes and haircuts the institution provides for them; that lack of agency seems emblematic of these poor souls' imprisonment.

And yet, true individuality in dress is rare—arguably nonexistent. Almost all of us will end up wearing a "uniform" of some sort, but we want to pick it ourselves. Which to choose? The range of styles is bewildering. The obvious solution is to pick a look that's been picked by other people who seem to share our values and aspirations.

Our gang may be a literal gang, in the sense that we hang around with them, doing stuff together. Or it may be a conceptual gang, in the sense that strangers we'll never meet, in other towns and other countries, wear very similar clothes and haircuts to ours, because this is the uniform of individuality they've decided best expresses how they wish to appear to onlookers. The Goth or the hippie or the gangsta is at pains to make clear that they're unlike their next-door neighbor, but feels solidarity with Goths and hippies and gangstas in far-off places.

Most people choose an identity quite early on and cling to

it for dear life. Whatever may happen to our bodies and faces as we grow older, our sartorial and stylistic identity markers stay much the same. The lipstick, the beard, the clean shave, the Nike trainers or the cowboy boots, the fluffy fringe or the close-razored skull, the tattoos, the tight shirt buttoned up to the throat or the loose shirt unbuttoned to the navel, the T-shirts and fleeces emblazoned with the names and heraldry of our chosen artists, our chosen attitudes—these keep our hold on our selfhood secure.

o   o   o

I watch an interview from the archives of BBC television. Prog rock keyboardist Rick Wakeman, punk rocker Joe Strummer of The Clash, enfant terrible music journalist Nick Kent, and *Melody Maker* editor Ray Coleman are sitting in adjacent chairs, disagreeing about stuff.*

Who are these people, really? Strummer is the son of a diplomat, and thus upper-middle-class. Kent, son of an Abbey Road sound engineer, grew up in suburban Llandaff, and is solidly middle-class. Wakeman's parents worked in the building and removals trades, which I'm told makes him working-class. Coleman, a former *Leicester Evening Mail* tea boy, is a bona fide prole.

By 1978, when this interview was filmed, each participant has chosen an identity, largely expressed through clothing and hairstyle. Nick Kent, barely awake and shrouded in cigarette smoke, wears black leather trousers and a black shirt unbuttoned halfway down his chest. The spiky lapels are turned up toward his artfully tousled hair, to signal that this shirt has said "fuck you" to any possibility of accommodating a tie. Ray Coleman, by contrast, wears a smart suit, a neatly buttoned-up white shirt, and—to signal his connection with the colorful world of pop—a bright orange tie. Rick Wakeman wears a suit too, but is long-

---

*   *Don't Quote Me*, BBC 2, May 20, 1978.

haired and bearded, as befits his "old hippie" status, although, as a matter of fact, he's only a couple of years older than Kent and Strummer. Strummer wears a Teddy Boy jacket, a loud yellow shirt and lots of product in his hair to make it stick up. He speaks with a Cockney accent that he clearly did not pick up in his boyhood in Ankara or at boarding school in Surrey.

It hardly matters what these famous personages are saying in this interview. We could turn the sound off, and just watch four self-conscious humans displaying the plumage of their chosen outward form, striving to make sure you can tell at a glance what creature they wish to be.

o   o   o

In 2016, Oasis released a high-definition remaster of their 1997 video for "D'You Know What I Mean?" to publicize a deluxe reissue of their chart-conquering album *Be Here Now*. This caused excitement on YouTube, among fortyish blokes who Were There Then.

"ive always wanted a parka since this video came out"

"Pretty Green that's were I bought mine."

"I own both. Because of Liam."

"Liam's parka is biblical."

"Get a Northface their the best"

"haha my husband always begs me for money for new Liam sunglasses. those are his favorites, Dolce&Gabbana."

"Listening this song walking on the streets with my earphones, green jacket and sunglasses. I'm feeling powerfull."

o   o   o

Do any of these Oasis lovers have anything to say about music? Well, one fan tries to sum up the band's superiority to the pop stars of today:

"Oasis, No Lesbian Haircuts, No Hipster Fashion, No Muscles

and Abs, Nothing False, Just Music."* The hint of homophobia is consistent with the band's laddish stance, but what's interesting here is the assertion that Oasis—poseurs par excellence—were somehow bravely authentic, solely interested in music, and outside of fashion.

o o o

What might a person who is genuinely "outside of fashion" look like? I can imagine a profoundly eccentric girl in Idaho who wears her grandfather's overcoat because it reminds her of her grandfather, and bright pink socks because they happen to be the warmest she's found, and her own hand-knitted yellow sweater because she's crazy about yellow, and an old floral dress because she likes flowers. I've never met this girl, but I'm willing to believe she exists.

All the trendsetters I know of, however, have been intensely conscious of past and present trends, and have thought hard about their tribal affiliations and the precise message they wish to give to the watching world. They put a lot of energy into looking carelessly casual.

o o o

Popular music is full of self-styled mavericks—insecure spirits with a gift for arrogant bluff. Dexys Midnight Runners were a perfect example. "We didn't want to become part of anyone else's movement," frontman Kevin Rowland declared early on. "We'd rather be our own movement."† Nevertheless, when asked decades later what his favorite "look" had been, he had fond memories of the band's formation in 1978.

---

*   "Oasis – D'You Know What I Mean? (Official HD Remastered Video)," uploaded by Oasis on August 18, 2016.

†   *Punk Diary: The Ultimate Trainspotter's Guide to Underground Rock 1970–1982* by George Gimarc (Backbeat, 2005).

"Jeff Blythe had an asymmetric haircut, a Phil Oakey, jodh-purs and sunglasses; Jim and Steve were Mods as a nod to the '60s; I had my hair like Stevie Wonder on *Talking Book* on the top, like a veil criss-cross across my face and wild at the back; Kevin Archer had his hair cropped with long strands and wore great big satin pantaloons and a short jacket. We knew that the fashion thing was going to be massive…"*

Throughout the early 1980s, Rowland's gang revamped their aesthetic several times. For their smash hit "Come On Eileen," the band (all from Birmingham) were given fake Irish-sounding names and dressed as raggle-taggle gypsies. Then they switched to the Ivy League look, of sober suits and ties, a style for the ages.

"Abraham Lincoln was shot wearing a Brooks Brothers suit," Rowland told short-lived music/style magazine *The Hit*. "They're men's clothes, they're not teenage fashion or any shit like that…"†

What inspired this Damascene conversion? At first, Rowland claimed it was a book about Martin Luther King, but years later he gave a different account: "I was walking down Madison Avenue wearing dungarees, a beret with a feather and a big over-coat. We saw this Brooks Brothers shop and some of the clothes reminded me of my skinhead days. It looked really clean com-pared to what I was wearing. I bought a pair of wing-tipped shoes, then we started going back every day. We were asking the staff how to wear things, how we should have our hair."‡

o   o   o

Punk, which fancied itself as the ultimate in nonconformity, quickly developed a set of sartorial and coiffureal rules. Seldom in the history of anarchy can there have been so many people

---

*   *Mojo*, October 2003.

†   *The Hit*, September 21, 1985.

‡   *Mojo*, May 2002.

declaring they wouldn't let anyone tell them what to do or wear, while being so dependent on leaders to tell them.

In the late 1970s, a girl from Dorking wrote in to one of the British music weeklies asking, "Where can one buy punk clothes and what do they cost?" The editors invited Vivienne Westwood, co-owner of the Seditionaries boutique in Chelsea, to supply the answer.

"It need cost nothing," said Westwood, helplessly displaying the impeccable grammar of a former schoolteacher from Derbyshire. She invited the youngster to come to Seditionaries and copy the ideas, or, if she couldn't afford the train fare, to add rips and safety pins to her school uniform. "Sorry, but in our shop the cheapest item is an anarchy handkerchief costing £2."*

£2 for an anarchy handkerchief? Vivienne Westwood's prices were always quite steep. In 1977, for a mere £2.65 including postage, the wannabe punk who didn't fancy wearing torn clothing (too drafty!) could purchase, from a mail-order company in Berkshire, T-shirts featuring "authentic-looking chains, razor blades and rips printed on high-quality cotton."†

Just in case the girl from Dorking had indulgent parents, Westwood mentioned that "punk jackets are grease-impregnated, three-button double-breasted, leather-trimmed, waterproof and warm with a quilted lining. They cost £35. (Seditionaries hates the traditional zip leather jacket which we find too trendy and quite MOR.)" That would have been news to regular custom-

---

*   Letter to *Melody Maker* or *Sounds*. Sadly I noted down no exact details when I cut it out.

†   Adverts for clothing in *Melody Maker*. I cut out lots of these over the years, starting with an advert for denim jackets and Afghan coats (*de rigueur* for all British hippies) in October 1974. The first thing that leaps out at you is how much postage prices have gone up since the midseventies. Getting your denim bomber jacket sent to you by Royal Mail cost a mere 25p. The dead-sheep weight of a full-length Afghan coat would've set you back £1.50.

     As for Vivienne Westwood's anarchy handkerchief, my copy editor consulted an inflation calculator that informed us that the £2 price tag would be £14.50 today.

ers Sid Vicious, Steve Jones and Paul Cook, all of whom wore the traditional zip-up kind.

"To dress like a punk is the first step to becoming an anarchist," Westwood concluded. "When you know you're an anarchist then you're a punk."

Did the girl from Dorking have the faintest idea what anarchism was? Did Westwood? It doesn't matter. What this is about is finding one's tribe—not via the arduous process of reading Proudhon and Bakunin, but by buying an anarchy handkerchief. Today, aspiring punks can buy anarchy bandannas on Amazon, eBay, Etsy, and zazzle.com.

o   o   o

In 2013, one of the internet's longest-established bloggers, Robert Lee aka The Naked Listener, began an essay thus:

"SHOES are the thing that really sets off one generation from the rest of the other rodents. Nothing says 'alternative' or 'subculture' more than a pair of brothel creepers. They make quite a statement [...] A wearable idiom meant to be seen. A meaning that's hidden and obvious at the same time [...] 'Grunge' look works too—carefully crafted messy hair, leather bits, tight bottoms, slack tops. The most-favored styling today is leopard print with or without black trim—but be warned, creeper aficionados generally consider leopard print 'camp.' Be a rebel, but stick to the rules too."[*]

o   o   o

"It's in the way your pants hang or the way your cap tilts. It's about identity," says Sasha Jenkins, director of *Fresh Dressed*, a documentary about hip-hop style.[†] Whereas rich white rock

---

[*]   "Why brothel creepers are rad'der than you think" by Robert Lee, *The Naked Listener* blog, October 23, 2013.

[†]   "So fresh and so clean: a brief history of fashion and hip-hop" by Lauren

stars often dress like hobos, the stars of rap use pristine new gear and designer labels to signal their escape from poverty. At the extreme is Kanye West, who displays his wealth with garments by Givenchy and Louis Vuitton, thus reminding onlookers that his tribe is now the elite of the superrich. The majority of hip-hop artists and hip-hop fans, however, continue to wear apparel that references sports or crime. Hoodies allude to the need to hide your face while you're spraying graffiti or selling drugs; sportswear suggests that you're trying to escape the poverty of the ghetto through your physical prowess at basketball or boxing.

Of course, the vast majority of hip-hop fans and hip-hop artists don't roam the streets with spray cans or drug swags, nor do they play serious sports. They simply want to look as if they might. They want fellow tribe members to nod in recognition, and they want the members of other tribes to back off. They want the world to understand that they are a law unto themselves, and at the same time they worry that their shoelaces aren't fat enough, or that their jacket errs on the wrong side of the dividing line between retro and old-fashioned.

o o o

I could tell similar stories about all the different music genres. Music as a soundtrack to the serious business of choosing clothes and hairstyles. All the gangs, all the subspecies, waiting for a naturalist like David Attenborough to point them out in the wild, his hushed voice murmuring, "And *here* we have…"

The Mods with their rules about the permissible number of buttons on their jackets and the number of permissible holes in their shoes. The 1980s second-wave punks in their mohawks and leathers. The Goths in their pancake makeup, black lace and vampire mantles. The R&B devotees with their elaborate fade cuts and bling. The Teddy Boys and their girls (wrinkly

---

Cochrane, *The Guardian*, October 27, 2015.

and arthritic now). The rude boys and ravers and rhinestone cowboys and New Romantics. All the clonely people. Where do they all belong?

o   o   o

You may object that the "fellow-travelers" are not the core of a music scene. The core is people who love the music for its own sake, who accept certain sartorial norms as the price they have to pay in order to enjoy the sounds they truly, deeply love.

I'm inclined to believe there is no such core. The "fellow-travelers" are the majority. The masses constitute the mass. It's the passionate music lovers who are the exceptions.

o   o   o

Imagine if nobody had a clue what music you like. Imagine if your favorite sounds were locked away in your home, enclosed in your head, unguessable by anyone out there.

Imagine not caring about that.

Imagine cutting your hair very short, if it's long, or letting it grow long, if it's short. Imagine no longer dyeing it, if you dye it, or imagine dyeing it, if you don't. Imagine realizing that your particular shape of nose or cheekbones or your sticky-out ears or your dark skin doesn't go well with the hairstyles and clothing that are associated with the music you enjoy.

Imagine trying on a T-shirt that advertises a music group or a cultural artifact you have no connection with—Guns N' Roses, Andrew Lloyd Webber's *Cats*, The Black Eyed Peas, whatever—and discovering that the colors and the patterns are absolutely perfect for your shape and bone structure and coloring. It suits you so well, it could've been designed just for you. Imagine wearing that T-shirt and looking good in it.

Imagine not minding that other people—passersby, random strangers who will never have the slightest personal significance to you—may think you like heavy rock or cheesy musicals or whatever the thing is that you're not into.

Imagine other people feeling no compulsion to jump to such conclusions, but simply admiring, when they see you in your Aerosmith or Grateful Dead T-shirt, how the wings of the logo help to define your bosom, or how the yellow on the design makes your skin seem to glow.

Imagine wearing a charity shop parka because it's warm and keeps the rain off, even though Oasis are *so* uncool now.

Imagine all the people, all the billions of people, not worrying about what all the billions of others think. D'you know what I mean?

OVERCOME WITH
ALL THE EXCITEMENT

Every superstar is a nobody before they're a superstar.

This may seem an obvious thing to point out, but it's one of those truths that people assume they understand but may not understand at all.

We're encouraged, when we think of the not-yet-idolized idol (David Jones-not-yet-Bowie, Nonnie Ciccone-not-yet-Madonna, Mark Feld-not-yet-Bolan), to imagine them as a god or goddess in disguise, moving among the herd of mere humans, the blinding radiance of their stardom hidden inside cheap garments. It was only a matter of time before that radiance would be unveiled…

Whereas, in truth, the guys and gals who will one day be worshipped are no more godlike than you or me or anybody. Pop idols are not born with a mysterious hysteria-inspiring gene, latent until the superpower bursts forth, scattering bits of chrysalis everywhere.

Nor is hysteria, in the pop sense, something that one individual can feel for another. Mass hysteria is what the term implies—a mass response, a psychological phenomenon of crowds. Fans get frantic only when other fans fan them. Astrophysically, the star is not a star at all: they are a moon, and a moon contains no light; it waits for rays from a giant ball of fire.

Rudolph Valentino, who would one day have thousands of women fainting at his funeral and whose death caused heartbroken devotees to commit suicide, was once a young man in urgent need of a job. He would've *loved* to be charismatic. He did his best, with the intrinsic qualities he possessed, to charm as many people as he possibly could. He batted his eyelashes, he hinted at how very special he could be if you only gave him a chance. No one considered him worth employing in his native Italy, so he relocated to America, where he ended up homeless after getting fired from odd jobs like gardening and clearing restaurant tables.

Frank Sinatra, who would one day have more than a thousand fan clubs catering for hordes of teenage girls high on Sinatra-mania, and who would be so adored that the chambermaids at the hotels he stayed at were bribed to let worshippers touch the sheets on which he'd lain, was an acne-ridden little punk with sticky-out ears. It would have suited him to dazzle all and sundry with his charisma during the years when he was hard up. But until the time was ripe for him to be marketed to the bobby-soxers, he had to settle for delivering newspapers and singing for cigarettes.

David Bowie, a Bromley lad with good cheekbones and bad teeth, commenced his attempts to become famous in 1962. He released flop single after flop single, chased every fad and fashion, and depended heavily on his manager Kenneth Pitt, who tried every conceivable trick to get David noticed. There can be few superstars whose prefame years are documented with such a copious number of photo shoots, promotional films and media interviews—all secured by Pitt, all to little or no avail. By 1969, Bowie's most notable breakthrough was winning a statuette at the Carosello Internazionale del Disco in Pistoia, Italy, just days after coming second to a Spanish child star at another song festival in Malta.

In spring 1969, when Bowie played a lunchtime gig at Ealing Art College, one of the students there was very helpful, offering to carry David's gear and shove tables together to make some sort of stage. That student was Fred Bulsara, who would soon drop out of his studies to flog "bits of tat, the odd cricket blazer" and other secondhand clothes at a stall in Kensington Market.*

Even when Fred had rechristened himself Freddie Mercury and Queen had become moderately popular in Britain, a head-lining gig at the Sunbury festival in Australia failed to impress the locals and the band were regaled with drunken shouts of "go back to Pommyland, ya pooftahs!"† In the oft-retold mythology of Queen, the storytellers always insist that Freddie was born to be a star, but in Sunbury, a rural town forty miles outside Melbourne, thousands of thrill-hungry festivalgoers saw nothing special in this yammering little poseur with his protruding teeth. In the dominant cultural narrative that determined the crowd's response, Fred signified a lot less than the Australian band they were impatient to see, Madder Lake.

o   o   o

I am not saying that these artists lacked charm—if we define "charm" as a knack for impressing individual strangers as likable. If we define it more literally as the ability to cast a magical charm, to enchant, to captivate, to enrapture, and any of those other words that imply spellbound onlookers who helplessly do the charmer's bidding, then Rudolph, Frank, David and Fred demonstrably had no such power. At least, not until the public, by mass consent, was ready to thrust that power upon them.

o   o   o

The Beatles have done much to muddy our understanding of pop music hysteria. Their conquest of the world made us inclined to think that hysteria could be caused by Art rather than

---

*   Mark Blake, "The Secret History Of Rock's Greatest Frontman," *Mojo*, January 2011.

†   "Sunbury 1974" by Duncan Kimball, MILESAGO: Australasian Music & Popular Culture 1964–1975 website.

by the communal needs of a multitude. Truth is, it was sheer coincidence that the four Beatles included two exceptionally talented composers and a third who blossomed when given the opportunity. Their talent was a wonderful gift to the history of western culture, but surplus to the requirements of their flock.

The true nature of Beatlemania was easier to perceive in the early 1960s, when it was in full momentum. The avalanche of Beatle lunch boxes, Beatle wigs, Beatle board games, Beatle bubble bath, Beatle candy, Beatle talcum powder, Beatle hairbrushes and Beatle breath (captured in cans and sold on the streets of New York, allegedly) is just a memory now, like bygone wars and storms and floods. The debris has long settled into antiquarian recesses or simply vanished. What we're left with is the art, and this tempts us to suppose that the hordes of screaming girls who stampeded American stadiums throughout 1965 were driven crazy by great songs like "A Hard Day's Night" and "Help!" (or even, for that matter, lousy songs like "I'm Happy Just To Dance With You").

The songs, however, were mere triggers. The group only needed to walk onstage for the kids to start shrieking, whereupon they shrieked and wept and swooned until the concert was over. Where did they learn to shriek and weep and swoon? From each other. They were a murmuration of flapping emotions, and their synchronized swoops were awesome to behold.

The hysteria around the Beatles was no different, biologically and psychologically, from the hysteria around Frank Sinatra or Johnny Ray or Elvis Presley or Fabian. Granted, Beatlemania was on a larger scale, but the media and the entertainment industry ecosystem weren't yet equipped for that scale in the 1950s, whereas by the 1960s conditions were ideal.

Don't get me wrong: I love The Beatles. We're fortunate that Beatlemania sprang up around them rather than some less talented group who might've been chosen if The Beatles hadn't existed. A foursome of handsome but dull lads called The Ear-wigs or The Scotties or The Yummies would not have ended up composing "Penny Lane" or "A Day In The Life." But when a large number of hormonal children are primed to get hysterical about something, they do not require genius. They will happily opt for Earwigstasy or Yummiemania.

This ought to be obvious to us, but we don't want it to be true. The world went mad for The Beatles, and The Beatles had artistic merit, therefore it must've been artistic merit that made the world go mad. And this notion, in turn, makes us complain when "unworthy" acts like the Bay City Rollers or New Kids on the Block or Ateez inspire mass hysteria. We look disapprovingly at the tearful teens as they declare their eternal devotion and offer their newly ripened uteruses for seeding, because ohfergodsake we expect any half-rational person to choose idols who are smarter and more talented.

We might just as well deplore the low aesthetic standards of birds who choose to nest in ugly plastic roof gutters rather than in beautiful trees.

o o o

Hysteria has always been with us. We've enlarged the scale of it in the last sixty years or so, because megacapitalism makes phenomena global and viral that would otherwise have been localized and self-limiting. If we make the appropriate adjustments for the evolution of mass communication and the role of the media in promoting celebrity, Beatlemania was probably the most spectacular outbreak of pop hysteria the world has seen.

That said, each new teen sensation tends to be hyped as the most seismic ever. The newly graduated policeman or reporter who stands in the street and feels fear at the advance of a numberless crowd of frenzied youngsters will naturally be convinced that this must be a phenomenon bigger and crazier and wilder than any in the past.

Beatlemania was followed by Monkeemania, T-Rextasy, Bowiemania, Rollermania, Cassidymania, Osmondmania.

"Being in the Osmonds was like being in a war zone," recalled Merrill Osmond as a snowy-haired sexagenarian. "Fans ruined limousines by jumping on top of them and smashed windows as we tried to leave places. When we played arenas, we couldn't hear anything because of the screaming […] Once, in Manchester, we played a two-hour concert and by the end had only managed two songs because the show was stopped 10 times. By the end of the evening, every chair in the place was destroyed. It was crazy but amazing."[*]

o   o   o

We can, of course, bring all the vocabulary of music criticism to bear on The Osmonds, Marc Bolan, Take That, the Jonas Brothers, Oneus and so on. There's a world of difference, artistically, between David Bowie's "Life On Mars" and the Bay City Rollers' "Shang-A-Lang." Not all famous people are equally talented. Marc Bolan's killer couplet from "Children Of The Revolution"—"I drive a Rolls-Royce/'Cause it's good for my voice"—gives literary connoisseurs more pleasure than One Direction's unintentionally grotesque "I might never be the hands you put your heart in."

Then again, an apologist for The Osmonds might point out that The Beatles were lousy dancers whereas The Osmonds were wonderfully twinkle-toed. John Lennon wouldn't have lasted five seconds with Ginger Rogers.

All that sort of debate is interesting to journalists and culture vultures, but it takes place in a realm far removed from the hypothalamus, the adrenal gland, the limbic system, the ovaries.

A few years ago, I visited a car boot sale, and one of the trestle

---

[*]   "The Osmonds: How we made Crazy Horses," interview with Dave Simpson, *The Guardian*, January 23, 2017.

tables displayed a mound of boy-band dolls whose plastic faces stared up at me with sightless painted eyes. I understood then, in a way I'd never understood before, how irrelevant any judgment I might make of the musical merits of One Direction or the Spice Girls was, how utterly beside the point.

o   o   o

Hysteria for pop idols is largely a teenage girl thing, but this doesn't mean that mad, overwhelming enthusiasms are exclusively female or even exclusively teenage. Mob frenzy can infect entire communities. Groupthink does not confine itself within gender or age boundaries.

In early 2021, the Capitol building in Washington was stormed by a horde of would-be revolutionaries—middle-aged moms, bearded pensioners, ex-soldiers, shopkeepers, regular folks—who were high on the adrenaline of saving America from a conspiracy of Satanic pedophile cannibals. In the resulting riot, in which several people were killed, one Alabama man—less physically robust, clearly, than the teens who were able to scream at the tops of their lungs for the duration of a Beatles concert—dropped dead of a heart attack, overcome with all the excitement.

o   o   o

America's remarkable upsurge of hysteria after the 2020 election may yet lead to civil war, but in the shorter term it has led to intense academic study of delusional humans and what makes them tick.

All the studies point to the same conclusion: delusional humans don't analyze the merits of a belief and then feel feelings about it. They feel feelings and then look around for a belief that allows them to express those feelings. Like hormonally driven fans of the latest pop star, they're sure that nothing could be more self-evidently important than their passion, while, on another level, they have not the faintest idea what the hell they're doing.

Say what you like about the irrationality of the kids who shrieked and sobbed and fainted at Beatles shows, but puppy-eyed Paul was a lot cuter than Donald Trump.

o   o   o

There's archival footage of Donny Osmond singing the sugary ballad "Why" on a French TV show called *Midi Premiére*, in early 1973. Riotous hysteria for The Osmonds was enveloping Britain and America at the time, but France is another country. We see Donny wandering among a seated studio audience of fresh-faced girls. He too is fresh-faced—fifteen, at the height of his prettiness, on the cusp of manhood. His hair is glossy, his teeth are luminous and his skin is without flaw.

"I love you," he sings, gazing soulfully into each *jeune fille*'s eyes.

He sidles up to one girl's shoulder. He kisses another on the cheek. They smile faintly and indulgently, utter not a sound, barely blink, watch him calmly as he passes by.*

"What was wrong with these girls??" an Anglo Osmonds fan furiously types in the YouTube comments section. "They sedated or something??"

But of course they are not sedated. They would probably scream with excitement if one of France's teenybop megastars walked into the studio. Instead, they have this foreign visitor. They think he's sweet. A sweet American Mormon boy. But why would you suddenly start screaming or fainting, right there in front of all your peers, just because some foreign kid is making eyes at you? Nothing of the sort has been agreed.

o   o   o

When a girl sits among a crowd of thousands and calls out the name of her idol, or holds up a banner saying "DAVID I LOVE

---

*   "Donny & Osmond Brothers -Why (1973)," uploaded to YouTube by Mr Mige on May 21, 2016.

YOU," she derives enormous excitement from the idea that he might hear her voice in among all the others, or that he might see her message. I've read many interviews with fans who are convinced that their idol made eye contact with them across the auditorium. The idea that he might have recognized their individual existence, even for a moment, gives them immense joy and consolation.

Yet the unattainability, and the like-minded community from which that unattainability is experienced, are an essential part of the deal. You share the yearning and you share the sweet sadness of unrequited love.

If what you really, truly wanted was to be recognized and valued by a pop musician, to have them turn their attention to you and only you, this would not be so difficult to organize. All you have to do is support a pop musician who is not already loved by countless others. It's a numbers game. A celebrity who receives a hundred letters a day is not going to reply to yours. An aspiring contender who receives only one quite probably will.

In September 1967, when David Bowie had recently released his flop debut LP, very few people in Britain were interested in him. Imagine his surprise, then, when a fan letter arrived all the way from New Mexico, from fourteen-year-old Sandra Dodd. David sat down in his manager's office and typed out a long and chatty reply, ruminating on reviews, his aspirations as an actor, the color-cast of the American edition of the LP ("they've printed the picture a little yellow. I'm really not that blond"), his hopes of one day getting to America, his liking for American films and the poetry of Robert Frost, and so on. "My birthday is January 8th and I guess I'm 5'10"... Thankyou for being so kind as to write to me and do please write again and let me know some more about yourself." This response, along with some fresh publicity photos, was duly sent to Sandra by international post, free of charge.*

---

* "Remembering David Bowie's charming personal letter sent to his first

This is a level of personalized attention that's completely different from the microsecond of imagined eye contact a fan might get from the superstar as they survey the crowd at a giant arena. It can be yours for the cost of a stamp, or even for free, if you email an encouraging message to the website of some obscure artiste whose efforts you and a few dozen others admire.

The catch, though, is that no one around you will break into screams and orgasmic convulsions when the artiste thanks you for being so kind. Sandra Dodd's peers would have given her no validation for corresponding with this foreign nonentity.

He might as well be Rodolfo Guglielmi.

He might as well be Fred Bulsara.

He might as well be you or me.

American fan, 1967," on Far Out website, January 24, 2021.

THE AWFUL TASTE OF
YOUR INFERIORS

Some people…how can we put this? Some people just have shitty taste.

They can't help it. It's the way they're made. They think they appreciate fine things. They're wrong. Oh God, how wrong they are. Words fail us sometimes, when we contemplate how wrong they are. I mean, how could anyone with properly functioning discernment admire Dan Brown? Stephenie Meyer? That painting of puppies in a basket, or the glow-in-the-dark tiger? Liberace? Celine Dion? Andrew Lloyd Webber? Susan Boyle? The songs of Billy Joel as played on the panpipes? Wet Wet Wet? Richard Clayderman?

Before us stands a person who waxes lyrical about the incomparable artistry, the sublime genius, the consummate skill of artists who suck. All the words we use to describe the magnificent things we like (including "magnificent," "consummate," "sublime," etc.) are used by them too, to describe the rankest garbage. How can we explain this?

It must be an intelligence problem. The ability not to be taken in by exploitative baloney comes with a superior class of brain to what these poor suckers have been born with.

It's not a matter of education. A lot of these people were educated alongside us, attending the same schools, provided with the same opportunities, targeted by the same cultural recommendations…and it evidently didn't do any good. We can tell that these are not folks who might grow to prefer Lyle Lovett to Shakin' Stevens, or John Adams to Andrew Lloyd Webber, if only they were exposed to the better options. These are folks who like crap because crap is all they're capable of liking. They're just cheerfully, proudly dumb.

∘   ∘   ∘

Can we say such things?

Dividing human beings into superior and inferior is, admittedly, out of fashion. We did a lot of it for a very long spell. (By "we," I mean people with the educational privilege and leisure to read treatises on art and culture.) God or Nature had decided, it seemed, that some folk just weren't cut out to be literate or well-fed or clean, and those creatures settled into the dregs of society, a smelly if sometimes useful class of subhumans.

Prejudice against "inferiors," however, is nowadays discredited as indefensible. After centuries of slavery, genocide and misogynistic oppression, equality is considered not just a noble idea whose time is overdue, but humankind's only hope of redemption.

If only it weren't for the fact that some people are keen on Daniel O'Donnell, Cliff Richard, Limp Bizkit…

On the face of it, prejudice against people with crap taste is unlike the toxic prejudices that cause so much misery in the world—racism, sexism, xenophobia, homophobia. Those prejudices refuse to look at the individual; they don't care what a person is like inside. Whereas prejudice against the taste-impaired is *all about* the individual. Is it even technically a prejudice at all? We don't *pre*judge; we wait until the person starts talking about their tastes, and once they're rhapsodizing about Barry Manilow or Nickelback instead of something good, we have the evidence we need to disrespect them.

∘   ∘   ∘

Many of you may have been discomfited by the harsh tone of the judgments above. You may have winced.

But many more of you will have felt free to make such judgments yourselves—if only within the safe confines of your own friendship circle. Expressing contempt for people's taste in music is one of the few prejudices educated folk feel they can get away with. In the 2020s, you'd need to hang around in very close-knit buddy cliques to make casually racist or sexist remarks without someone in the group objecting that actually, no, this is not OK. But to disrespect people who like "self-evidently" bad music is a harmless giggle, or even a principled stance for high standards.*

o   o   o

"Self-evident": now there's an interesting term. We hold these truths to be self-evident, that all men are created equal. And that all men (and women) who value what we consider schlock are our inferiors. Oh, we wouldn't harm them or put them in concentration camps or anything like that, but, hey, let's be honest, they *are* on a lower evolutionary rung than us.

Maybe we're so convinced of the dimness of these people that we can't imagine them being hurt by our contempt. Maybe we think they're like the guy with the comb-over, who thinks that his pathetic strands of hair, plastered across his bald skull with a spray of glue, impress onlookers as a reasonable coverage, and that the people who snicker as he passes by can't possibly be snickering at him. Maybe the people stupid enough to like Chris de Burgh are too dumb to understand that there could be anything wrong with them.†

---

*   Typical example: In 2000, *Guardian* journalist Tom Cox noted that 1980s superstar Phil Collins had gone out of fashion in the 1990s. "What turned us against Collins?" he mused, apparently speaking for Culture as a whole. After a trawl through Collins's unforgivable sins (his love life, his hair, his wealth), Cox writes: "Or was it simply that you can only treat your audience like moronic, sentimental peasants for so long before they cotton on, even if they are moronic, sentimental peasants?" See: "This man must be stopped" by Tom Cox, *The Guardian*, March 30, 2000.

†   I think most fans of "lowbrow" art are perfectly well aware when the thing

Is someone who likes Shostakovich really smarter than someone who likes Shakin' Stevens, though? Politicians, entrepreneurs and scientists appear on the BBC's *Desert Island Discs* and choose terrible music because they've spent their lives studying their particular fields rather than exploring modal jazz. Is a person who enthuses about Celine Dion* really struggling with an intellectual handicap that an Annette Peacock fan is free of?

o   o   o

Back in the 1950s, Liberace sued *The Daily Mirror* because its gossip columnist Cassandra had called him "this deadly, winking, sniggering, snuggling, chromium-plated, scent-impregnated, luminous, quivering, giggling, fruit-flavoured, mincing, ice-covered heap of mother love [...] the biggest sentimental vomit of all time [...a] slag-heap of lilac-covered hokum."† Liberace was well-accustomed to nastiness but perceived this as a threat to his

---

they like is despised by sophisticated critics. Type "Dan Brown" into Google and you'll find lots of his fans writing in to Quora, Reddit and other forums, earnestly asking questions like "Why do people hate Dan Brown?" and "Why do people make fun of Dan Brown's writing?" and "What's wrong with Dan Brown's novels?" They're caught between two irreconcilable truths—the fact that Dan Brown is surely a genius, because they've enjoyed his work so much, and the fact that many people regard it as self-evident that Dan Brown is a laughably bad writer. How can an author who's so good be bad? It doesn't make sense.

*   As a companion piece to this chapter, I recommend Carl Wilson's *Let's Talk About Love: A Journey to the End of Taste* (Bloomsbury, 2007)—ostensibly an anthropological investigation of Celine Dion. It's thought-provoking and fun. But Wilson can't quite bring himself to do justice to the book's title. His anxieties about his own taste, and his fear of losing his hipster cred, constantly get in the way. He concludes with a kind of defensive doublethink, simultaneously advising that we go easy on our schlock-loving neighbors (and the guilty schlock-lover hidden deep within ourselves) while also signaling that Celine Dion's intrinsic awfulness can't corrupt people as clever as us.

†   "Yearn-Strength Five" by "Cassandra" (William Connor), *The Daily Mirror*, September 26, 1956. The libel trial didn't come up until three years later. Liberace denied his gayness all his life, even when homosexuality became legal, even as he was dying of AIDS.

brand, his popularity with his target demographic. He couldn't afford to lose the love of the straight women who thought he was the bee's knees.

From our twenty-first-century viewpoint, it seems absurd that Liberace could sue someone for suggesting that he was gay, and even more absurd that he could win. But homosexuality was a crime then, and people convicted of it went to jail. What's an ultracamp pianist to do when reviewer after reviewer drops heavy hints? *The Guardian*'s Bernard Lewis, reviewing Liberace's gig at the Royal Festival Hall on October 1, 1956, wrote: "I was in the presence of a man who did not care how silly, how awful he looked and sounded, provided only that the adolescent girls, the middle-aged matrons, and the sprinkling of very queer-looking men rolled up, paid at the doors, and yelled the place down."[*]

Such reviews had no effect on how Liberace looked and sounded, nor on ticket sales, but they did result in some unwanted additional attendees: disgruntled macho-men holding placards saying "Send the Fairy back to the States"[†] and "Queer go home."[‡]

Unlike Oscar Wilde, whose strategy in his libel trial—to the extent that he *had* a strategy—was to declare his foppish brilliance and hope that the legal system was dazzled, Liberace indignantly denied being homosexual, and argued that his livelihood depended on his manly reputation. Also—and this is why he's so relevant to our chapter—he gallantly defended his fans and his beloved mother against Cassandra's viperous scorn. Who was Cassandra to say these people had bad taste? What right

---

[*]   Quoted in "Liberace Is Not a Fruit-Flavoured Mincing 'He, She and It'" by Jim Burroway, on [Emphasis Mine] website, March 30, 2018.

[†]   "Birk and Silman: Media, Finance and Philanthropy 1939–1968" by Nigel Watson, in *Nicholson Graham and Jones: The Story of a Law Firm in the City of London* (St Matthew's Press, 2009).

[‡]   "Housewives' Choice: Female Fans And Unmanly Men" by Richard Smith, in *The Popular Music Studies Reader* edited by Andy Bennett, Barry Shank and Jason Toynbee (Routledge, 2006).

did some hack from *The Daily Mirror* have to dismiss Liberace's music as silly and awful? Unlike Oscar Wilde, Liberace wasn't a sophisticated playwright; he was a huge international pop star who provided exactly the kind of art that the masses—including members of the jury—wanted.

Liberace's musical merits were not debated at the trial. The trial focused on whether or not *The Daily Mirror* had called the plaintiff a homosexual. In a way, though, the trial was also about the right of a performer to offer the sort of entertainment that sentimental middle-class suburban women liked, and not be humiliated for it. Cassandra's review was homophobic, to be sure, but it was also extremely snobbish.

We don't know what Cassandra considered good music or appropriate entertainment. Vaughan Williams, perhaps. One thing is certain: he didn't think that British housewives should be enjoying abbreviated versions of the classics played by a coquettish dandy, even if the housewives of Britain made very clear that this was exactly what they wanted.

Imagine Cassandra plunging his lexical dagger into a "good," "credible" artist like Nina Simone. Nina could be "this deadly, drunken, peevish, prickly, boorish, pompous, prattling, shambolic, self-inflating, increasingly fleshy, faux-Nubian, oversharing, overrated heap of melodrama." Invective is cheap, and if the reviewer is observant enough, they can make some of it hit home.

But who decides which artists are fair game and which should be shown deference?

o o o

Liberace's main way of dealing with the constant barrage of disdain for his music was to flaunt his success and wealth. "Crying all the way to the bank" was his customary quip when another bad review came in. For those who despised him, this was yet more proof of his shallow, exploitative nature. But Liberace's wealth came from his fans' support, and he knew it, and he thanked them for it. He wasn't as rich as Keith Richards or Eminem, but he was more gracious.

Chris de Burgh, by contrast, has not been content to let the insults roll off his back. He's proud and prickly. He doesn't want to be the schlockmonger who laughs all the way to the bank; he wants respect.

In 2009, a journalist for the *The Irish Times*, Peter Crawley, attended a Chris de Burgh show in Dublin's Gaiety Theatre. Safely home after the ordeal, Crawley wrote a wickedly reductive review. As a piece of craft, a composition of well-sprung sentences, it gives me pleasure. But am I admiring the journalism as a piece of craft alone? Is it even possible to admire language in the abstract? I doubt it. So what's giving me pleasure? Cruelty and condescension.

Crawley notes that de Burgh is short and unfashionably dressed, with thinning hair cut in an untrendy style. He irrelevantly alludes to a 1994 sex scandal that tarnished de Burgh's "squeaky-clean" reputation, makes fun of de Burgh's voice, derides his stage patter as fatuous, and reflects that "it's easy to snigger at de Burgh." Foremost among the sights that make Crawley fear that his toes "will never uncurl after this experience" is when de Burgh demonstrates his affection for his fans by running around the theater giving them hugs (or, as Crawley puts it, "invading boxes and draping himself over audience members").*

Stung, Chris de Burgh wrote a lengthy response, which *The Irish Times*, smelling the sweet blood of a public brawl, published in full.

"Were you much teased by your school chums in the schoolyard and called 'Creepy Crawley'?" de Burgh challenged, furthermore citing the opinion of an unnamed "much-loved and

---

* Peter Crawley, *The Irish Times*, September 3, 2009.

successful actress" that Crawley was a "loathsome little turd." There was lots more of this mudslinging, but what's important about de Burgh's letter is the way it highlights the fans whose tastes Crawley so imperiously trashed.

"How it must have galled you to hear the rapturous welcome I received at the start of the show," de Burgh wrote. "How you must have writhed at every standing ovation; how you must have cringed at every call of 'Chris, we love you'; how you must have felt isolated as the audience rose to their feet as one, singing, dancing and shouting out for more; how you must have growled to yourself as you left, surrounded by so many happy people [...] You really should look up the word 'entertainment' again, you might be surprised to see that it is all about people having a GOOD TIME!! Your churlish review is an insult to all those who enjoyed their night out..."*

De Burgh's bullish self-regard is much in evidence here. But so is the truth of his remarks. The shows were sellouts and there's no doubt that the fans who attended had the night of their lives. They were profoundly happy. Crawley, in identifying Chris de Burgh as a mawkish balladeer beneath the contempt of any listener with good taste, brands all those happy humans as inferior beings. Does he despise them, or merely feel pity? Forgive them, Lord, for they know not what they like?†

---

*   "Chris de Burgh Sees Red" [letter from Chris de Burgh], *The Irish Times*, September 11, 2009.

†   My friend Jo Falla, reading this chapter, sympathized with both sides in the de Burgh/*The Irish Times* dispute. Conceding that it was "supremely churlish" to deny a big audience their night of delight, he was nevertheless queasy about applying Bentham's principle of "felicific calculus." "If audience pleasure is the only measure, what are we to say of feeding Christians to the lions, or the Nuremberg rallies? We could say that all such entertainments (de Burgh included) answer a need in their audience—the need for Germans in the 1930s to regain some shred of national pride after decades of humiliation, for instance. But that won't excuse everything." On reflection, he concluded that "Some things really are in bad taste. Some entertainments we must be free to despise."

○ ○ ○

Before writing this chapter, I'd had very little exposure to the music of Chris de Burgh. I'd heard "Lady In Red" and "Don't Pay The Ferryman" on the radio but that was all. Nobody who's passed through my life ever wielded a Chris de Burgh item and said "Listen to this." He was little more than a name, a name I would flip past in record shop bins while looking for something else. For years, I got him muddled up with Chris Rea.*

Wikipedia tells me that before his commercial breakthrough, de Burgh made "cult" albums and supported Supertramp (themselves a critically respected cult band in the early 1970s). Seventies art rock is fairly well represented in my collection. This gives me reason to hope that, in investigating de Burgh's early years, I might discover something "up my street."

Spanish Train And Other Stories, his second album, was recorded in 1975, safely before the horrors of eighties production. Ah, there's Tony Reeves on bass, I see. He was in Colosseum, played with Sandy Denny and John Martyn. Ah, there's Barry de Souza, session drummer extraordinaire. He played on one the first albums I ever owned, Rick Wakeman's *Six Wives Of Henry VIII*, but also on LPs by Shawn Phillips, Lou Reed and Dana Gillespie. And ooh! Fancy that! There's Nick Drake's old friend Robert Kirby, arranging some of de Burgh's tracks for strings, brass, choir, recorders and ocarinas. Ocarinas!

Half an hour later, I find I have failed to bond with Chris de Burgh. His musicians are fine; it's him I don't care for. In fact, to put it with brutal honesty, his songs are textbook examples of how I would rather songs didn't function. Every decision de Burgh

---

* Who, unlike de Burgh, has earned critical respect in his old age. Notably after he got cancer and a large portion of his insides were removed, and he started playing the blues rather than the more commercial music he was making before. He also started swearing a lot. Is this what it would take for Chris de Burgh to be rehabilitated? Would he get invited to the Montreux Jazz Festival then, as Rea was in 2014?

makes, from microsecond to microsecond, about style and content and delivery, is exactly the move I wish he wouldn't have made. It's uncanny, how unerringly he denies me what I would like and gives me what I don't want.

o   o   o

This, of course, is the gulf between me and his fans. For them, the deal is the other way round. Every way that Chris wants to touch them is the way they want to be touched. Every dramatic tremor in his voice goes straight to their hearts—like an arrow, as he would no doubt put it.

Under the YouTube upload of "The Tower,"* dozens of people attest how this song makes them cry.

"Thankyou chris for absolutely everything that youve done for me," says Beth. "your music has helped me through every single tough time ive ever gone through."

"He sang this one in concert," relates otterpoet, "but forgot the words halfway through until 10000 voices joined him in unison."

"This is one of the songs I want played at my funeral," says Mojo Thieves. "I've loved it since I was a child. Album released in the year I was born. I thank my parents for introducing me to music of this storyteller."

"I remember writing the lyrics down, sentence by sentence, until I had the full song on paper," says Patricia. "Then I was able to learn it by singing it over and over, I was 11 years old and had undiagnosed autism and music was there for me, especially this mans beautiful songs, when the world was too much for me, this and all the very early songs would take me to a place where I felt safe. Thank you for helping me when I needed it. I still know every word of every song Chris de Burgh has written, I am 53 now and still love to leave the world outside and lose myself in his beautiful music xx"

---

*   "Chris de Burgh – The Tower," uploaded to YouTube by Steve Bennett on December 19, 2007.

Testimonials like this don't excuse de Burgh's boastfulness, but they explain it. If enough people tell Chris how much they love him and how much his art has done for them, his art is therefore lovable, important and therapeutic. It's a fact. A scientific fact, almost. The lone curmudgeon Peter Crawley, sent by *The Irish Times* to write nasty things about him, is like the flat-earther at a conference of astronomers.

Has the music I love ever done for me what Chris de Burgh's music has done for his fans? I don't believe so. I can't think of any jazz or psychedelic soul that has helped me through tough times or allowed me to "lose myself." For good or ill, I am constantly with myself, and when I go through tough times I tend to stop playing music altogether, because I'm spending all my energy dealing with the stresses. No doubt there are things that a Chris de Burgh fan could teach me that would improve my mental health, if only I had ears to listen. There is definitely courage and healing to be had when you're in a crowd of ten thousand voices singing in unison.

RCA's marketing department called one of their compilation albums, by a popular singer who had his detractors, *50,000,000 Elvis Fans Can't Be Wrong*. Nowadays, most sophisticated music fans—including prestigious scholars, critics and other cultural arbiters—consider Elvis a fine singer who was not only important as a historical phenomenon but an artist of considerable accomplishment. This was not the case in 1959, when RCA's marketing department first argued that any singer who was *that* popular had to be good.

How many fans has Chris de Burgh got? Apparently it doesn't matter. The historians have written the history and Chris de Burgh doesn't deserve to be in it.

Decades after the Elvis compilation, Bon Jovi upped the ante with the box set *100,000,000 Bon Jovi Fans Can't Be Wrong*. My cousin Tosca adores Bon Jovi. I like my cousin very much. I detest Bon Jovi.

o o o

What are we to do with these people who love what we cannot love? Would we be satisfied if we could somehow dissuade
them from their joy? Would we feel that some sort of aesthetic
justice had been served if we could only remove this happiness
and excitement from their lives, and direct them to the more
tasteful altar at which we worship?

And what *is* it about music anyway that so sorely tempts us
to adopt positions of superiority we wouldn't adopt in other
areas? I can't speak for what I would've been like if I'd lived in
the sixteenth century or even the nineteenth, but I know that
in the twenty-first century, where I am now, I can take my seat
next to a woman, or a person of color, and not think: *You are
inferior to me.*

What's art got that other prejudices haven't got?

THANK YOU FOR MAKING
MY OPINION COOL

We used to need other people to help us decide what music we fancied. Do we need anybody now?

Back in the day, all manner of experts were on hand to steer us away from the bad stuff toward the good. There were TV review programs like *Juke Box Jury* and *American Bandstand* in which panelists and celebrity guests reviewed the week's crop of singles. "It's got a good beat and you can dance to it; I'll give it an eight." Or, "Roy Ordison, is that his name? Terrible."*

But it was the professional record reviewers, writing in specialist music magazines, who were the real voice of authority. In that antediluvian era, millions of music devotees the world over read their favorite papers religiously—*Rolling Stone, Melody Maker, New Musical Express, Mondo Sonoro, Creem, Crawdaddy, Blues & Soul, JazzTimes, Juke, Džuboks* ("Jukebox" in Serbo-Croat), *Zillo* and hundreds more.

At first, the journalists merely attempted to describe what sort of thing the music was, and whether they felt it represented a worthwhile purchase for those consumers who liked that sort of thing. *NME*'s Derek Johnson pronounced *Beatles For Sale* to be "rip-roaring, infectious stuff, with the accent on beat throughout," and "worth every penny asked."†

---

* Waspishly patrician *Daily Express* columnist Nancy Spain, pouring scorn on "Blue Angel," *Juke Box Jury*, October 29, 1960. On the same show, a chain-smoking Carmen McRae opined that Connie Francis's arranger should be taken out and shot.

† Derek Johnson, review of *Beatles For Sale*, in *New Musical Express*, 1965.

As the years passed and pop music became more serious and self-consciously arty, the reviewers became more critical and self-important. They were no longer content to note if a record had a solid beat, or speculate that a fresh-faced combo was "sure to go far." Instead, they regarded themselves as aesthetic watchdogs and custodians of the counterculture.

In an article headlined "Lennon, You're A Pathetic, Ageing Revolutionary," Beatles connoisseur Tony Tyler expressed his disappointment with the trite lyrics on John Lennon's *Some Time In New York City.* "You've still got important things to say so *say* them," he scolded. "Don't alienate. Stimulate. You know, like you used to."*

◦   ◦   ◦

Reader, if you grew up in the twentieth century, you will have grown up with the notion of the record reviewer as a higher class of listener than you. For a start, they got their hands on the product before anybody else did. They'd heard it; you hadn't. And they'd been employed for their comprehensive knowledge, their penetrating insight, their contacts inside the music industry, their infallible bullshit detector, and other advantages that you, a mere fan, couldn't hope to equal.

How solidly founded was this prestige?

I've been reading music reviews for fifty years, and keeping them on file. As decades pass, certain pieces of audio art stick around, proving themselves to be works of enduring interest. Others are revealed to be figments of passing fads—opportunistic mediocrities that slip down the plughole of history once their moment is over. I would estimate that the percentage of occasions when professional reviewers have been "right" rather than "wrong"

---

*   Tony Tyler, "Lennon, You're A Pathetic, Ageing Revolutionary," *New Musical Express*, September 1972.

about the merits of the music upon which they pronounced judgment is about 50 percent.

It would be easy to compile a fat anthology of madly enthusiastic reviews of duff albums, or witheringly contemptuous reviews of masterpieces, dashed off in the heat of inebriation or careless ignorance by scribes who basked in their own anointed status. In the heyday of physical product, rock critics used to visit the offices of record companies and emerge with armfuls of albums, most of which they had no intention of listening to, or that they knew they would dismiss with a casual quip. Secondhand shops overflowed with "promotional only" copies of LPs and CDs that had been cashed in for dope money.

Does this mean that the whole business of music reviewing is one big confidence trick? I don't believe so. Many music journalists become music journalists because they love music and want to evangelize. They want you to see the light.

o o o

Charles Shaar Murray has been called "the rock critic's rock critic"* and there's a Penguin anthology of his writings called *Shots from the Hip*, an allusion to the days when the *NME* was advertising for "hip young gunslingers"† to join their staff. Posturing aside, Murray has loved rock music all his life. His love is sincere. Few people have loved an art form with greater commitment than Murray has loved rock.

In January 1977, he was high on the notion that punk might, in some ill-defined but energetic way, save the world. He was therefore not at all impressed with David Bowie's groundbreaking *Low* when it landed on his desk. "We're low enough already,

---

*   By Q magazine, apparently, according to his profile on the Rock's Back Pages website.

†   The phrase used by Charles Shaar Murray in a July 1976 advert inviting applicants for staff writer vacancies, quoted in *The History of the NME: High Times and Low Lives at the World's Most Famous Music Magazine* by Pat Long (Portico, 2012).

David," he lamented, damning the album as "an act of purest hatred and destructiveness...profoundly selfish and egotistical, encouraging each individual to lay on his ass and listen to his wounds fester rather than go out to help and be helped."*

o   o   o

What does a negative review by a sincere, music-loving journalist hope to achieve? What's the point of it?

One possible motivation is that the reviewer hopes that the bad review will alert the artist to the error of their ways and shock them into producing something better next time. Tony Tyler's severe dressing-down of John Lennon is an explicit example of this,† and Charles Shaar Murray clearly wanted David Bowie to pull himself out of the malaise that had spawned *Low*. Thus, the reviewer is like a medical practitioner or "tough love" counselor, whose timely intervention prevents the artist from becoming trapped in artistic ill health.

It seems a laudable idea, in theory. But in practice the reviewer is often mistaken. *Low*, in most people's (eventual) estimation, was a major achievement, one of the most distinctive, influential works of audio art of the twentieth century. In any case, even if *Low* had been a bad record (whatever that means), a bad record is not an illness. Bowie suffered much more harm from smoking three-quarters of a million cigarettes‡ than from making the feeble *Never Let Me Down*.

Making a bad record may not even be a mistake; it may be just an experiment, part of a lifetime of learning. Elvis Costello

---

*   Charles Shaar Murray, "Homage To Catatonia," *New Musical Express*, January 22, 1977.

†   Tyler's stern advice to John did not have the desired effect. Lennon's next album was even worse.

‡   He smoked sixty a day. He started in the early 1960s and stopped in 2003 or thereabouts—let's say 1965 and 2000 to be really conservative. That's 766,500 cigarettes.

expressed this view with great clarity when he rebuffed an interviewer who kept pushing him to agree he'd lifted his game after a run of poorly reviewed projects: "Look, you're not going to get me to admit I made a mistake. I'm not going to make a big confession and say I was the wayward prodigal son and now I have returned and I repent. 'Oh, he went off and grew a beard and made weird music but now he's back and he's sorry.' I'm not sorry. It's not like I've suddenly seen the light. This isn't Saint Paul, it's music."*

Another possible motivation for the negative review is to save *us*, the potential listeners, time and money. The reviewer has been short-changed, and wants to spare us that same disappointment. Thus, Charles Shaar Murray is providing the same service as his predecessor Derek Johnson, helping the public decide whether the new platter is "worth every penny" or not. But is he? Nothing in Murray's tirade suggests he is trying to save us thirty-eight minutes and/or £2.99.†

Perhaps, then, he is concerned for our spiritual well-being. *Low*, he says, "comes to us in a bad time and it doesn't help at all." We are vulnerable creatures, at risk of depression and despair. *Low* may push us over the edge.

o o o

Do reviewers lie awake at night fretting about what unhealthy music is doing to us? Of course not. The person the reviewer is most concerned about is not you but them.

"I probably brought too much personal baggage to that review," Charles Shaar Murray conceded many years later, of his Bowie philippic.‡ "Around the time the album arrived, I had

---

* "Crimes and Misdemeanours" by Adrian Deevoy, *Q* magazine, April 1994.

† The cost of *Low* in 1977. Quite a hefty sum, given that the average weekly wage for working-class men was £70 (£43.70 for females).

‡ Charles Shaar Murray, *Uncut*, April 2001.

just about managed to haul myself and my then-wife out of the pit of severe amphetamine addiction [...] The album seemed to glamourize everything we'd just fought against."*

In 1977, I regarded Murray's rant against *Low* as a useful piece of commentary, and I still do. Sure, it's overwritten, because Murray was upset and because he had an indulgent editor. But it articulates a certain view of what music should and shouldn't offer to the listener, and each of us is therefore challenged to decide whether we agree. At seventeen, I was asking myself all sorts of questions. Did I want music to "help" society? Did I feel that music that encouraged defeatism was somehow irresponsible? What responsibilities, if any, does an artist have to the listener? Can a piece of instrumental music even be said to be defeatist? And so on.

These are all interesting issues to ponder. But the main upshot from Murray's belated admission that he was in the throes of addiction when he wrote the review is that his response was helplessly personal. Throughout this book, we've seen that people's response to music is thoroughly subjective and interweaved with autobiographical experience. Expecting a reviewer to rise above this common human trait is therefore a big ask.

There were plenty of people, even in 1977, who felt that *Low* was a damn good album. But not necessarily because they understood what Bowie was trying to achieve, or because they could foresee how influential the album would become. *Low* simply gave them sounds and visions that fitted in with—or could be bent to fit in with—the mood they happened to be in when they heard it, the stuff that was going on in their life at the time.

This is normal. When offended readers complain about the wrongness of a critic, they're expressing their frustration at finding that another person's emotions work differently—that the other person is, annoyingly, a different person.

---

*   "Charles Shaar Murray on THAT *Low* review," DavidBowie.com, January 9, 2017.

o   o   o

Complaints about the cavalier subjectivity of music reviewers were rare before the advent of "gonzo journalism" in the USA and punk in the UK. After that, the impish scorn that the editors heaped upon loyal readers who disagreed with their journalists became a spectator sport in itself. Letters pages were the newsprint equivalent of a record shop in which the staff forced the hapless customers to prove themselves worthy of tribal cred.

Such bad behavior depends on power, however—the confidence that one is unassailably in control. As the digital age dawned, the readership of music papers and magazines declined sharply; by the early years of the new century, it was in free fall. Critics could no longer afford to sneer at their fan base. Moreover, the distinction between fans and critics was increasingly blurred. Internet blogs proliferated while print publications perished by the dozen. The hip young gunslingers were no longer young and no longer hip and suddenly everyone in town seemed to be slinging guns of their own.

o   o   o

In our twenty-first-century ecosystem, are professional record reviewers simply obsolete? Should they cease to exist, like the knife sharpeners, bobbin boys and lamplighters of previous ages? Pretty much all music is available for free now, twenty-four hours a day, to anyone with internet access. If you haven't got around to hearing David Bowie's *Low*, for example, the entire album will unveil itself for you on YouTube in 0.52 seconds.

If I tell you that Richard Dawson's "Jogging" gives me great joy, and you're curious whether it might give you great joy too, you can be listening to it before you finish reading this paragraph. If the first listen leaves you undecided, you can listen as many times as you like, for a few pence worth of electricity. You can even lay this book aside and watch Richard Dawson jogging all over Newcastle, in an ingenious video specially shot for the song.

Even so, there are reviews of Richard Dawson all over the media. Why? Well, the reviews function as publicity. They alert newcomers to the fact that "Jogging" and its parent album *2020* and indeed Richard Dawson exist. But, having got our attention, the journalist *could* simply say "Now go and listen."

Yet the journalists are not content with this. They don't want to be mere notifiers, like the sandwich-board men of old. They want you to read their review, and ponder it.

Is this because they want you to perceive Dawson through the lens of their own insights? Do they want you to hear in his work what *they* hear, rather than what *you* might hear if you came to it fresh, with no prejudices?

Or are they simply mindful that in today's digital bazaar, where tens of millions of options are being tossed at us from all directions, we may be paralyzed with indecision as to what to choose next?

And what about short attention spans? Reader, when I mentioned that "Jogging" gives me great joy, did you immediately go to YouTube or Bandcamp and listen to it? If you didn't, and if I hadn't mentioned it again now, how confident are you that by the time you finished this chapter, you would've remembered your intention (if you had any) to chase up Richard Dawson? By tomorrow, would the existence of a song called "Jogging" still be lodged in your brain?

o   o   o

Ben Beaumont-Thomas, in his review of Richard Dawson's *2020* for *The Guardian*, seems not much interested in the music; it's the lyrics he wants us to focus on—Dawson's "stories of a benighted Britain." He briefly sketches the plot/theme of each song. "Jogging" is about "the person who [...] finds solace in exercise as they fight anxiety." *2020* as a whole is "a reminder of the need for basic decency in a country that is forgetting it, voiced by the most brilliant and humane songwriter working here today."[*]

Ben obviously likes Dawson's stuff and wants you to like it too. He knows that this may not be enough to make you investigate it. Next to his article, there's a small photo of Ben. He's a friendly-looking middle-aged chap, bald and bearded and white. A lot of *Guardian* readers are likewise bald, bearded, friendly-looking middle-aged white chaps so, on that basis alone, they might trust that Ben's tastes have a good chance of overlapping with theirs. But Ben has another enticement up his sleeve. He appeals to his readers' political values (this is *The Guardian*, after all), and then makes an impressive Authoritative Judgment: Richard Dawson is "the most brilliant and humane songwriter working here today." With that statement, Beaumont-Thomas repositions himself from mere enthusiast to critic.

Is Richard Dawson the most brilliant and humane songwriter working in Britain today? He is certainly brilliant and he is certainly humane. But *the* most? I don't know. I haven't heard all the songwriters in Britain. Nobody has heard all the songwriters in Britain. Ben Beaumont-Thomas's status is founded on the implication that he has.

In Thomas Blake's review for *Folk Radio*, we are told a little more about "Jogging" as a piece of music. It is "a very strange pop song, full of bulldozer guitars, industrially synthesized vocals, strings that are simultaneously massive and subtle and a pounding beat (it's like the soundtrack to a montage scene in a Rocky film directed by Ken Loach), but a pop song nonetheless."

This gets a person who hasn't heard "Jogging" (is that still you, reader? If so, what's keeping you from listening?) a little closer to being able to imagine what it sounds like, although in truth the description would fit any number of disparate records

---

[*]   "Richard Dawson: 2020 review – Britain's best, most humane songwriter" by Ben Beaumont-Thomas, *The Guardian*, October 11, 2019.

by Depeche Mode, Einstürzende Neubauten or Rammstein—none of whom sound anything like Dawson. The Rocky-meets-Ken Loach allusion is really an allusion to the video, but Blake can't bring himself to say "It's got a great video—check it out!" That would be the sort of thing an ordinary person would urge you to do, not a proper reviewer.

"Jogging," he elaborates, is "representative of the optimism and anger of the album's lyrical trajectory—an anxiety-ridden narrator drags himself away from numbing, agoraphobic internet binges in an attempt to exercise his way back to a better state of mental health, while around him England slowly crumbles." Blake goes on to paraphrase what each vignette in the lyric of "Jogging" is about, concluding that in Dawson's Britain, "those unseen forces meant to keep the country in good shape are singularly failing."*

It's all valid commentary. I'm satisfied that Thomas Blake "gets" *2020*. But his insights are necessarily less poignant, thrilling, witty and memorable than "Jogging" itself. "Jogging" is an exhilarating artwork; a review is merely journalism. What is the place of a music review in an environment where we can engage directly with Dawson's own art as soon as we've made the decision to do so? How much gabbing does a reviewer need to do before they cross the line between persuading you to check out the artist (bravo!) and pointlessly prattling on and on about what you'll find when you do?

o o o

Anthony Fantano is one of the most influential reviewers of our era. His YouTube channel, on which he does nothing but review new music releases, has more than two and a half million sub-

---

* "Richard Dawson: 2020 (Album Review)" by Thomas Blake, *folk radio*, October 14, 2019.

scribers. That's probably ten times the number of people reached by *Melody Maker* or *NME* in their 1970s heyday.*

Fantano, who brands himself "the internet's busiest music nerd" and is nicknamed "Melon" because of his bald round head, is articulate and arrogantly declarative. In the tradition of the *Juke Box Jury* pundits of yesteryear, he assigns each undigested new record a score out of ten. He's keen on Richard Dawson, and awards *2020* "a light to decent 9" (only one notch below a "strong 9").

Fantano likes the "galloping groove" on "Jogging," but has nothing else to say about it other than this psychoanalytical insight: "While it seems like Dawson is singing from the standpoint of other people on this record much of the time, his descriptions of dealing with anxiety on this particular cut just seem too detailed to not come from a personal place."†

Thus, we come to yet another way in which reviewers may earn their status as superior listeners: their ability to tell average folks like us things about the artists' personal lives that we wouldn't otherwise have known.

How does Fantano know that "Jogging" is autobiographical? He just has a hunch. And it seems that legions of people in America and beyond trust his hunches. Indeed, they seem to admire Fantano every bit as much as they admire the artistes he reviews.

"I'd love to know what you think of his album [*Nothing Important*]," a subscriber writes in the comments—one of many Fantano fans who are curious to know what he thinks of other Dawson albums. "I've never listened to the title song without sobbing. Also would recommend him live[;] he has a lot of

---

*   "The Life and (Uncertain) Times of British Music Publications" by David Chiu, quoting former *Melody Maker* editor Chris Charlesworth, Medium.com, March 12, 2018.

†   "Richard Dawson – 2020 ALBUM REVIEW" by Anthony Fantano, theneedledrop YouTube channel, October 18, 2019.

funny digressions in between songs." Why does a person who is already familiar with Dawson's work, and who already has their own deep personal response to it, and who, unlike Fantano, has seen Dawson play live, need to know what Fantano thinks of Dawson's work?

The answer can be found in another comment: "Thank God I'm not alone in loving this album. Thank you, Melon[,] for making my opinion cool."

It's awfully lonely, it seems, for humans to like something that they can't see other humans liking.

o o o

As it happens, Fantano's conviction that "Jogging" must be autobiographical is wrong. The song's protagonist is fictitious and Dawson has stated that he actually hates jogging ("and joggers," he added when he introduced the song at a gig in Folkestone).

Dawson is a humble and refreshingly sincere person. He knows the world is awash with music and he's grateful for the attention he gets. But, like many artists whose work is subtle and multilayered, he also knows his fate somewhat depends on reviewers who may not understand him very well, recommending him to listeners who may not understand him very well either.

Never mind. In January 2022, when I attended Richard's gig in my seaside town, seventy-five miles from London and hundreds of miles from his home, the venue was full, even though his record sales are modest and he gets no radio play. Some of those people must've read reviews. And there they were, swaying happily in each other's arms, mouthing every word.

ACCORDING TO WHOM?

The most-used encyclopedia of all time is Wikipedia. Billions of people use it every day. It's more popular than Amazon or porn.

Anyone can write articles for Wikipedia—you included, if you wish. Detractors argue that this is Wikipedia's fatal flaw, but the site is surprisingly reliable overall. A person who knows nothing about ribonucleic acid or Charles Pierre Claret de Fleurieu is not going to write a Wikipedia article on the subject. Even the unscholarly dude who wrote the Wiki about the grindcore band Agoraphobic Nosebleed knows quite a lot about Agoraphobic Nosebleed.

Just as democracy has been said to be the least bad of all political systems, Wikipedia may be the least bad encyclopedia. I sympathize with the bibliophiles who champion Britannica, Chambers and other shelf-warping franchises of yesteryear, I really do. They want encyclopedias to be written by responsible scholars and checked over by Professor Britannicus himself before being published as weighty tomes with gold-embossed spines. They're appalled by the rise of clicky-Wiki, that online free-for-all to which any bozo can contribute.

The awkward thing is, traditional encyclopedias are of no use to me now. I still own lots of the music-related ones, and I like to see their spines on my shelves, but I never consult them anymore; they're all hopelessly out of date. I consult Wikipedia. Sure, it's rubbish sometimes. But it's up-to-date rubbish.

Another advantage of Wikipedia is that although rambling articles are sometimes flagged with stern administrative warnings that the text is too detailed and should be pruned, these warnings are usually ignored. Bad news for prose quality, but good news for the availability of data. Traditional encyclopedias' compilers agonized about which articles they'd have to trim or jettison in order to make room for something new. After all, purchasers only had so much shelf space, and there was a limit to how much they were willing to pay. Moreover, there were practical considerations, like how thick a book can be before its pages tear loose from the binding, and how much weight the reader's wrists can support.

By contrast, Wikipedia simply expands invisibly and unnoticed, like the universe itself.* Nothing needs to be discriminated against and every subject gets its due.

Or does it?

o   o   o

Wikipedia, like any previous attempt to record the sum of human knowledge, is a reflection of how much importance our culture assigns to things.

The Wiki for "Dog booties" is very short—a "stub," as the site labels it—and consists of little more than a small photo of a poodle in blue snow boots. By contrast, the entry for "World War II" is more than fourteen thousand words long, has 465 citations, and is linked to many thousands of other, more specific Wikipedia articles about World War II–related topics. Thus, we

---

*   The most recent—and reportedly final—edition of *Encyclopædia Britannica* that you can plonk down on your bookshelves was issued in 2012. It contained 40,000 articles. *Britannica* thereafter migrated online and currently operates on a subscription model—you pay monthly or yearly to fund the scholarly labor that keeps the site up to date. The number of articles now stands at 120,000, most of the new ones being quite short. Wikipedia, on the day that I type these words, has more than six million articles, with a couple of hundred thousand articles, some short, some long, being added every year. Or, to put it another way, an *Encyclopædia Britannica*'s worth of stuff every couple of months.

signal (to posterity, to ourselves) that World War II is worthier of discussion than dog booties.

In theory, it's conceivable that a cabal of dog fanatics might compile a tremendously long article about dog booties, and that all the people who felt themselves responsible for writing about World War II might lack the motivation to write much, discouraged by the enormity of the challenge or by the sadness of dwelling on sad things, or because they were distracted by Facebook or a family emergency.

In practice, the communal model of Wikipedia's editorship makes such an outcome impossible. The number of people who believe that World War II was important is too great, and the number of people who believe that dog booties are comparably important is too small.

∘   ∘   ∘

In any case, Wikipedia has "notability guidelines," aimed at making it a proper encyclopedia and preventing it from filling up with piffle.

Wannabe editors are cautioned that any person who's going to be the subject of a biographical article should be "worthy of notice," "remarkable," "significant, interesting, or unusual enough to deserve attention or to be recorded." If you're a worthy musician, you will be "known for originating a significant new concept, theory, or technique." You will be a person who "has made a widely recognized contribution that is part of the enduring historical record in his or her specific field."

Not all musicians are icons and trailblazers, but fear not. Other ways you may satisfy the notability guidelines are to have a record deal with a major label, to have a song "placed in rotation nationally by a major radio or music television network," to win a Grammy or some other high-profile award, or to be given "lead roles at major opera houses."

What if you're well-respected but not terribly well-known?

Again, fear not. You may have been the subject of multiple "nontrivial" newspaper articles. You may have released albums on "one of the more important indie labels (i.e., an independent label with a history of more than a few years)," and you may have "become one of the most prominent representatives of a notable style," or have "credit for writing or co-writing either lyrics or music for a notable composition," or have "composed a number of notable melodies, tunes or standards used in a notable music genre," or be "cited in reliable sources as being influential in style, technique, repertory or teaching for a particular music genre."

None of this is an exact science. The administrators of Wikipedia are relying on their wannabe editors (you, me, anybody) to come to a sensible agreement on what terms like "remarkable," "interesting," "unusual," "significant," "widely recognized," "important," "prominent," "influential" and indeed "notable" mean. A degree of trust is being invested in what Aristotle called the wisdom of the crowd.

There is, however, one big problem.

The wisdom of the crowd, to a worrying extent, is the wisdom of the *male* crowd. When we talk about Wikipedia, this male dominance is the elephant in the room. And the elephant has a big dick.

o o o

Listen: there's a band called Ratt. They're exponents of a genre called glam metal or hair metal. This genre, according to Wikipedia, is characterized by "very long backcombed hair, use of hair spray, use of makeup, gaudy clothing and accessories (chiefly consisting of tight denim or leather jeans, spandex, and headbands)." Its performers are "infamous for their debauched lifestyles of drugs, strippers and late-night parties." Mötley Crüe were the trailblazers here, taking the basic Rolling Stones template of plowing through each town's pretty young girls and customizing it to remove any trace of musical talent, sartorial style or rakish charm—cutting straight to the ruthless seizure of teen pussy, fresh gash, kneeling bitch, and all the heroin, cocaine, Jack Daniels and projectile vomit a poodle-haired man could want.

Does that qualify as "originating a significant new concept, theory, or technique"? Perhaps it does. Mötley Crüe got there first, but Ratt weren't far behind, so I suppose that makes them co-trailblazers, semi-seminal, or something.

What's beyond dispute, in the notability stakes, is that Ratt sold truckloads of albums to air-punching American adolescents. Hence, their Wikipedia article runs to almost four thousand words, with thousands more devoted to individual members and, of course, to each of their albums.

Here's another possible tick of distinction: Ratt featured a Playboy Playmate on the cover of *Invasion Of Your Privacy*. According to the author of Ratt's Wiki, "using a beautiful female model on an album cover later became a trend copied by many glam metal bands of the 1980s, including Great White and Slaughter."* The cover image on the band's debut EP shows rats running up and down the silk-stockinged legs of a woman in bright red stilettos; she's pictured from the knees down only, but the Wiki helpfully informs us that "the legs on the front cover belong to Tawny Kitaen, the then-girlfriend of guitarist Crosby."

o o o

On that note…let's talk about anti-feminism and feminism. Let's talk about women's music.

o o o

There's a modest Wikipedia article about women's music, or more specifically the 1970s sociopolitical movement that was called

---

*   Were Ratt really the first to "use" a beautiful female model on the covers of their albums? Surely Roxy Music…? Bert Kaempfert…? Nelson Riddle…? Oh, never mind—it's best not to examine this sort of claim too rigorously.

Women's Music. It's 1,904 words long, as opposed to the 12,143 devoted to Heavy Metal. Or, to make another comparison, a few hundred less than the 2,354-word article on Women's Professional Wrestling. Men like to listen to heavy metal and they like to watch women wrestling (though not as much as they like to watch men wrestling). They are not interested in women singing feminist songs, particularly from a lesbian perspective, which, inconveniently, constitutes a lot of what they would encounter in the women's music field.

When I first started working on this chapter, a few years ago, the Wiki on Women's Music was a mere fifteen hundred words and was flagged as problematic by Wikipedia's administrators because (they said) "its sources remain unclear." In fact, by the standards of Wikipedia overall, the citations and references were reasonably transparent and comprehensive, especially for such a short article. This is not to say that I'm opposed to the high editorial standards that Wikipedia's founders want Wikipedians to abide by. I'm all for accountability. If someone makes a groundless claim, they shouldn't be surprised if editorial watchdogs add "[*citation needed*]" or "[*according to whom?*]." I just can't help noticing that such cautions appear more in some articles than in others.

Today, the article on Women's Music is no longer hung with red flags. That's progress, I guess.

o   o   o

One of the founders of the women's music movement is Margie Adam. She has a brief Wikipedia page, too—410 words. That's about a tenth of the length of the Wiki on the 1970s porn star John Holmes.* Indeed, it's less than the 559 words devoted to

---

*   Not to be confused with John Holmes the Renaissance composer, who gets 65 words, compared with John the porn star's 3,218. Sometimes size does matter.

the size of Holmes's penis in a subsection of the Holmes entry headed "Penis size."

Actually, the penis gets more words even than that, because it rears up all over his Wiki. The second and third sentences, for example, read: "Holmes was best known for his exceptionally large penis, which was heavily promoted as the longest, thickest, hardest, and longest lasting in the adult film industry, with seminal volume second only to fellow adult actor Peter North's. However, no documented measurement of Holmes's actual penis length, girth, tumescence, sexual stamina, or ejaculate volume has ever been confirmed."

Wikipedia's watchdogs currently have no issue with Margie Adam's article. They were not always so satisfied. In the version of the Wiki that existed when I began work on this chapter, only the first sentence, stating Adam's year and place of birth, was allowed to pass unchallenged. The second sentence read thus: "Adam is recognized as one of the pioneers of the women's music movement. [*according to whom?*]"

According to whom, indeed.

o o o

Historically speaking, there was such a thing as the women's music movement, arising in tandem with the civil rights movement. It may not be much discussed in the mainstream media today but it existed and it was pretty damn big at the time.

Margie Adam was one of its innovators. She co-headlined the first National Women's Music Festival, held in Illinois in 1974. She started her own record label at a time when such a thing was almost unheard of. She toured with all-women production crews—again, almost unheard of. One of her songs was adopted as an anthem for the lesbian-feminist movement and is archived as such by the Smithsonian Institution. Although not a stadium act, she played concerts for many thousands of people and helped change the lives of countless women.

It is safe to argue, therefore, that the thrust behind that *"according to whom?"* went beyond academic rigor. Here's what it boiled down to: a woman wrote that Margie Adam was important, and a gatekeeper to public recognition, almost certainly a man, challenged that view.

o   o   o

The revisions to any Wikipedia article are available to inspect, simply by clicking on the "View history" tab near the top right corner. It transpires that on August 30, 2018 (at 3:47 p.m., to be precise), a fresh version of Margie Adam's Wiki was uploaded, which no longer contained the *"according to whom?"* challenge. Oh, good! you may say. The watchdogs backed off, shamed by their overaggressive treatment of a feminist heroine. Or maybe the person who wrote Margie Adam's article supplied the appropriate citations.

In fact, neither happened. In its current form, the Wiki on Margie Adam makes no claim about her importance. The original second sentence, about being recognized as one of the pioneers of the women's music movement, was simply deleted and replaced with one that begins "Her father was a newspaper publisher..."

o   o   o

Are we glimpsing a conspiracy here? A deliberate campaign by misogynist men to belittle a woman of considerable historical significance? I doubt it. The people who write, revise and correct Wikipedia articles are almost always pseudonymous and there's every possibility that the person who removed the claim about Margie Adam's importance was a woman. A woman who felt herself unequal to the task of finding the requested citations and logging them according to the obligatory electronic footnoting protocol. Or maybe a woman who misread a request for clarification as a rebuke, and lost heart.

There is no doubt that plentiful documentary support for Margie Adam's importance could be found, but it would largely be in magazines and newspapers produced by the women's movement during the 1970s and 1980s, and the woman who wrote Margie Adam's Wiki might not have access to that material, and in any case a lot of that material has fallen through the net of history, because history is largely compiled and archived by men.

o o o

Belligerent sexism exists, just as belligerent racism exists. But the more common and intractable manifestations of these isms are unaggressive, unaware of their own unfairness, woven into the fabric of normalcy, preserving the status quo while never having to think about who the status quo favors and who it doesn't.

Wikipedia is an encyclopedia invented by admirable idealists who wanted to make all human knowledge available to all humans, for free. It has no dark agenda. But it is edited by the general public, and the general public operate within a society, and our society is patriarchal.

Ninety percent of what you find in Wikipedia is contributed by males.* Mostly retired males, or else males in their midtwenties. What this means is that you get lots and lots of articles about the things that young males and retired males consider significant. It means an 8,206-word article about the lunkheaded rap metal band Limp Bizkit, punctiliously footnoted with 209 citations, some of them translated from Spanish, Hungarian and Italian. It means solemnly respectful Wikis for all the pulp sci-fi writers of the 1940s and 1950s, whose work originally appeared in magazines festooned with lurid paintings of lecherous robots kidnapping helpless women, and it means no Wikis for the contemporaneous

---

* Wikipedia article: "Wikipedia: Gender bias and editing on Wikipedia."

romance writers whose prose was no worse and whose readership no less avid. It means very detailed articles about high-altitude reconnaissance aircraft.

It means that whenever the question *"according to whom?"* might reasonably be posed, the immediate answer is "according to us"—us being the 90 percent of Wikipedians who have a penis.

○   ○   ○

Ratt are, it seems, worthy of note. Their albums shipped multi-platinum. Their clumsily written Wikipedia article is flagged as having "multiple issues" but notability is not one of them, and the main assumptions are left unchallenged. No gatekeeper wags a finger when "the Ratt sound" is said to be defined by "DeMartini and Crosby's impressive guitar solos." (*Impressive to whom?* one might ask.) Much of the article details sordid legal squabbles among various factions of this wretched combo about trademark infringements. The prose falls well below the standards of run-of-the-mill rock journalism, let alone what one might expect of an encyclopedia.

But none of that makes any difference. Ratt sold product to testosterone-fueled young men. The nostalgia of middle-aged guys who were once testosterone-fueled young men is one of the driving forces of cultural history. Heavy metal—even the stupidest, sleaziest heavy metal scraped from the bottom of the corporate crud barrel—is important. Whereas Margie Adam, with her groundbreaking career in female music-making, giving comfort and validation to a generation of lesbians who'd never been catered to before, is not important.

○   ○   ○

I've been playing Margie Adam's *Songwriter* while writing these words. Her smiling face has been reclining on my desk, as big as mine, gazing straight up into my eyes. She isn't smiling at me. She's smiling at her photographer Holly Hartman, forty-five years ago, and by implication she's smiling at "all the women who have supported me and helped me grow." The record is over and I slip it back into its paper sleeve.

Next up on my turntable is *Virgo Rising—The Once And Future Woman*, the sole album released on the Thunderbird label in 1973. It was one of the first albums produced, engineered and performed solely by women. It does not have a Wikipedia page. It was produced by Mollie Gregory, an award-winning film producer and screenwriter who went on to write many books including *Women Who Run the Show* and *Stuntwomen: The Untold Hollywood Story*. She doesn't have a Wikipedia page. The album was engineered by Joan Lowe, who also engineered Margie Adam's *Songwriter* and many other records. Lowe, a former electrical engineer at NASA, was already an experienced record producer by the time she sat at the controls of *Virgo Rising*. She must surely have been one of the first female engineers in the American recording industry. She died just a few years ago at the age of ninety-one. She has no Wikipedia page.

Virgo Rising—The Once And Future Woman is a various-artists affair that includes Janet Smith's "Freedom Ladies' March," Kit Miller's disarming rendition of "There Was A Young Woman Who Swallowed A Lie," and several contributions from the wonderful Malvina Reynolds, veteran of the civil rights movement and a prolific songwriter for children.

Reynolds's Wikipedia word count is 788. Compare this to the 2,279 devoted to porn star Jenna Haze, whose "notability" is founded on such achievements as an Adult Video News award for one of the sex scenes in *Evil Anal 2*, a "short appearance" in the role of Vagtastic Voyage Girl #2 in the teen comedy *Superbad*, and being ranked twentieth on a list of "The Top 100 Hottest Porn Stars (Right Now)" in 2011. Up against such attainments, how can composing "Little Boxes," "Morningtown Ride" and "What Have They Done To The Rain?" compete?

Seriously, Malvina Reynolds was an extraordinary woman and led an extraordinary life. Born in 1900, she grew up in a Communist household, but her career as a radical songwriter was sparked one night in 1932 when she was beaten up by the Ku Klux Klan for her solidarity with nine black boys who'd just been declared not guilty of the rape of two white women in Alabama.

I learned that part of Malvina's history not from her Wikipedia entry, which tells us virtually nothing about her, but from an extensive, commendably well-written article in the *Orange County Weekly.** Other pieces of the puzzle can be filled in with the aid of blogs written by Reynolds's daughter, Nancy Schimmel, herself a prolific writer of children's songs. (No Wiki.)

o   o   o

One of the things the patriarchy is awfully good at is convincing women that their unrecognized status is their own fault. It's not that the world is unfairly set up, it's that female achievements are simply lesser.

The letters of thanks ("You changed my life!") that a pioneering lesbian musician might receive from individual fans seem small-time and gossipy, compared to the highly public, solemnly prestigious honors the great men get.

Even a small gesture—like an anonymous Wikipedian putting a few sentences about you on the web—may seem like one sister doing another sister a favor. Special pleading.

o   o   o

But listen: Wikipedia has room to tabulate the endorsement deals associated with various styles of Reebok running shoe. It

---

*   "The Life and Times of Malvina Reynolds, Long Beach's Most Legendary (and Hated) Folk Singer" by D. Kelsen, *OC Weekly*, August 31, 2016.

has room for discontinued breakfast cereals like Mini Swirlz, Sprinkle Spangles and Kream Krunch. It has room for *Die Hard Trilogy 2: Viva Las Vegas*, a PlayStation game described even by gaming nerds as "terrible" and "awful." It has room for all the drugs that the various members of Mötley Crüe took. It has a *lot* of room for Ratt, and for John Holmes's penis, big as that might have been.

It therefore has room for a few more of the achievements of women.

o o o

Various theories are put forward as to why so little Wikipedia content is written and edited by females.

One theory is that women are too busy working and looking after children. I don't buy that. If most of the men who contribute to Wikipedia are retired or in their twenties, there are plenty of retired women too, and women in their twenties. In cyberspace, there are thousands of blogs founded and maintained by women, many of which celebrate precisely the phenomena that deserve to be better represented on Wikipedia. These women have the time and the articulacy to create content for a blog— even for an academically rigorous historical archive.

But something is stopping them from expending that sort of labor on the most widely consulted encyclopedia in the world.

When I contacted Nancy Schimmel, Malvina Reynolds's daughter, to ask her how she felt about the paltry Wikipedia coverage of Malvina's career, she replied: "While part of the problem with Wikipedia is that it's written/edited 84 per cent by men, it's also true that they want writers to refer to already-published sources, and probably less is published about women in music."*

---

* Nancy Schimmel, email to me, April 6, 2020. Compare her modest defeatism to the wildly unscholarly (and illiterate) Wikipedia entry for the French rapper Gogol Premier, which proclaims: "If it was the first, it is now the

Here we see the patriarchy suppressing women in complex, interleaved ways. First, as Schimmel surmises, information about women's music is less likely to be published in books. (Schimmel has long wanted to write, or oversee the writing of, a biography of Malvina Reynolds, a project that would surely have reached fruition by now if its subject had been a male musician with a comparably interesting life.)

Second, Wikipedia insists that its articles should be supported by citations from credible published sources—thus putting the onus on female contributors to find such sources for their unfairly neglected heroines, even though that neglect is partly manifested by the lack of publications they could cite.

Third, women may be stymied by the conscientiousness with which they play the game. The encyclopedia states what's required in order for an entry to be proper, so the women feel they should make sure their contributions are proper. Never mind that male contributors often disregard the rules with arrogant abandon.

One random example of that arrogant abandon (among thousands I could've chosen) is the 1,674-word Wikipedia article about an obscure, undistinguished Marvel Comics hero called Doorman. His abilities, we're told, are "Portal generation, Flight via skis, Intangibility, and Ability to bring souls to the afterlife." The fanboy who wrote this Wiki earnestly informs us, in the Fictional Character Biography section, that "little is known of Doorman's life before he responded to Mr. Immortal's advertisement for the hero team." Shortly after which point a scholarly-looking footnote leads us to a citation—which turns out to be a reference to the comic book *Great Lakes Avengers: Misassembled* #4. On inspection, *all* the references in the article are to the comic books our fanboy loves.

---

last of the Punks. And he is back with Kabaret Punk masterpiece anti-crisis thirteenth installment of his extensive discography."

"*According to whom?*" According to the imaginary superheroes themselves.

There are no warning flags above this wretched Wiki. It breaks or bends quite a few of Wikipedia's painstakingly devised rules, as well as being inaccessible to anyone who isn't a Marvel zombie, but in the seventeen years that Doorman the mutant's fictional biography has been hanging around in cyberspace, nobody has yet complained.

Is that because Wikipedia's administrators are superhero nerds, and therefore see no problem with semiliterate, inane material like this? No. Elsewhere on the site, you'll occasionally see them tackling the bloated articles written by fanboys, identifying dozens of problems clause by clause, and sternly advising the author(s) to clean up their act. But hundreds of new Wikis get uploaded each and every day, and the administrators can't comb through them all. In their optimistic idealism, they trust that the great majority of contributors to this grand repository of human knowledge will try their best to do the right thing.

What would happen if more women uploaded or expanded articles that didn't quite satisfy the highest standards of academic practice? Would they be disproportionately criticized and cautioned? Maybe. But the information would be up there, and that would be better, surely, than it remaining hidden?

Another theory about why so few women contribute to Wikipedia is that they have no appetite for the editorial skirmishing that can go on behind the scenes of a Wikipedia page. One guy makes a change; another guy deletes it; the first guy puts it back, and so on. I can see how such competition might suit Wikipedians with spare testosterone. But I'm not convinced that if someone were to expand Margie Adam's Wiki, or create a page for Joan Lowe, it would become a battleground.

A more credible reason, I suspect, is that women simply don't enjoy hanging out in environments that they sense are 90 percent male. If we regard Wikipedia as a workplace, it could be said to resemble the workplaces of fifty years ago, when women ventured into domains where few if any females had ever been spotted before. Maybe the prospect of being outnumbered ten to one is not relaxing to some potential Wikipedians.

Even so...intersectionality. There's a deservedly substantial Wiki article on Linda Tillery, the black homosexual drummer, singer, producer and arranger. Her ten-thousand-plus-word write-up, unlike Margie Adam's, evidently feels it can get away with claiming that "she is recognized as a pioneer in Women's music." Why?

In recent years, there has been a burgeoning of intellectual and cultural empowerment among African Americans. The imperative to redress historical inequities has become more urgent, surmounting the barriers of institutional racism, inertia, exhaustion, the serpent whisper of self-doubt. Racial minorities are only too familiar with the dynamics of "*according to whom?*"

o   o   o

The founders of Wikipedia know that their encyclopedia is unequal. They want more women on board. They've thrown money and ingenuity at achieving female participation of at least 25 percent, and they have failed.

There's a dedicated Wikipedia article about these failures, which runs to 4,355 words. It makes lots of valid points about microaggression, hacker elitism and "particular forms of socio-technical expertise and authority that constitute the knowledge or epistemological infrastructure of Wikipedia." Fine. I get it. It's complicated.

But on the other hand, there are vacuums of knowledge waiting to be filled. There are women who lived and died before the internet was invented who've still not received the recognition that's due to them. It's not my place to tell anyone how they should spend their time, nor do I feel that I'm the appropriate person to write or expand the encyclopedia entries on female musicians.

All I will say is that I hope that by the time *Listen* falls out of print, much of what I've said in this chapter will be obsolete, superseded, a relic of a bygone age. I would like readers to feel pity at all the trouble I took, all the time and energy I expended in writing so much about a problem that's no longer a problem. I want this chapter to be every bit as redundant as an old set of faux-leatherbound encyclopedias that have been consigned to a cardboard box in the garage or the attic, their pages fused together with damp and mold.

PLEASURE ABOUT HUMANS

In early 2019, my life was good. I had a nice warm home and a loving relationship and my health and enough money and a fine reputation and oodles of great music to listen to.

I saw plenty to complain about, however. The corrupt, inept government of Britain was pushing the country toward the fiasco of Brexit. Donald Trump was dragging America into a quagmire of criminality, bigotry, misogyny, xenophobia and deceit. Scarcely a day went by without the President of the USA saying or doing something that in saner times would have resulted in his downfall, but which only seemed to make him more brazen. Scarcely a day went by without a member of the British ruling class saying or doing something that in saner times would have required them to resign under a cloud of shame, yet these creeps and bunglers clung on to their positions, free to inflict fresh idiocy the following morning.

Unwisely, I kept up with it all. It goaded me toward despair.

Louisa and I took it in turns to help each other look on the bright side. We exchanged arty photographs, funny YouTube videos, inspirational music.

I think it might have been the weekend when Britain's lamentable prime minister and her entourage flew twenty-five hundred miles to a luxury Egyptian holiday resort for a hopeless bid to strike a "deal in the desert," and President Trump had declared a national emergency because Congress refused to give him billions of dollars to build a wall to keep the Mexicans out, that Louisa sent me an email titled "What gave me pleasure about humans today."

What gave Louisa pleasure was a YouTube clip of a classical pianist playing Bach for a blind elephant.

You can see it too: just type "Bach on Piano for Blind Elephant" into Google and away you go. The magic of the internet takes us to Kanchanaburi, Thailand. An old upright piano has been deposited in an expanse of scrubland, to parch gently under the sun. An amiable Englishman called Paul Barton introduces us to an elderly female elephant called Lam Duan, then sits at the piano stool and plays Bach's Prelude in C Major, a bit of the Goldberg Variations, and Schubert's "Ständchen."

Lam Duan, free to walk away, chooses to remain near the piano. She sways to and fro, responding to the rhythm. She appears to get into the groove.

Holy moly: she's dancing.*

o   o   o

At the time that Louisa and I watched this video, enchanted, more than two and a half million other people had watched it too. And 7,262 of them had posted comments under the upload—responses that ranged from the most gushing sentimentality to the most caustic cynicism.

"I really needed to see this today," says one visitor, expressing solidarity with me and Louisa and thousands of other weltschmerz-sufferers. "It brought me to tears as soon as the music started…to see someone care for an animal like this and take the time to brighten its life. I need to stop looking at the news and start finding hope through people like you."

---

*   "Bach on Piano for Blind Elephant," uploaded to YouTube by Paul Barton on
      June 30, 2018.

Many other visitors are likewise brought to tears, and no wonder: the clip features close-ups of Lam Duan's blind eyes, blink-
ing. There's something intrinsically dignified and sad about that
leathery gray-brown flesh. You fancy that Lam Duan would cry
too, if she could.

"poor elephant," laments Anna. "Looks like catterachs, I pray
for a miracle that she gets her eyesight back some day... I play
Chopin for my cats, (they love it to). Animals know good music
when they hear it."

"Thank you for being so kind to that elephant," says Seeing-
things. "You must be a rare and wonderful human."

"You are real kind and great person," affirms Kartik from India.

Sensing that Paul the pianist is getting some prime adulation
here, Leon butts in with a reminiscence of the time he serenaded
a wolf in a meadow with his Native American flute, an experience he sums up casually as "pretty cool."

Bhaleri gives Leon what he's after: "How brave of you to
continue playing with a wolf nearby."

But Der Otto rather punctures the mood: "Piss off with that
shitty fake Hogwarts story. Attention whore."

o   o   o

As for Lam Duan the dancing elephant, not everyone is convinced.

"Dancing?" sneers Jordi Sunset. "You are idiot."

"SHE JUST WANNA TAKE A DUMP," wisecracks Kjer
Errt. Scolded by other YouTube posters whose cheeks are wet
with tears, Errt swiftly escalates to: "FUCK ANIMALS," "ANI-
MALS SUCK ASS" and "AS IF I GIVE A FUCK ABOUT
WHAT U THINK."

Perusing the long column of chat, I note that there are no
mentions of Hitler, although a skirmish about God breaks out
halfway down. For every fifty people saying that their faith
in humanity has been restored, there's maybe one who feels

the need to interject such downers as "Meanwhile in Syria: Boooooom!!!!!" The orgy of elephant love provokes a vegetarian to suggest that humans stop eating animals, which triggers a heated debate about vegetarianism.

None of that troubles me. But in among the spats and buddy hugs, there are other comments that plant a seed of unease in my mind.

"I wonder what music sounds like to an animal anyway. We can only guess."

"Elephants' hearing range is about 14hz to 12,000hz. (Lower than humans). So maybe next time bring along a bass player too :)"

"Elephants sway when they're not getting enough stimulation, it's a behavioral tic that's not a part of their normal body language."

"Actually the swaying that she is doing indicates stress and anxiety…"

This is not what I want to hear. I want Lam Duan the dancing elephant to be having a lovely time with Bach, Schubert and the English eccentric. My good spirits depend on it. I can't feel consoled about Brexit and Trump if it turns out that the elephant is, in fact, stressed.

I find a comment from a guy who seems to know a thing or two about music. He observes that Lam Duan "sways more for consonant major harmonies, and would stop for minor or dissonant harmonies (like flatted 7ths), and would threaten to walk away over diminished harmonies."

I try to cling to this. A person who understands the difference between major and minor harmonies must know more than your average ill-informed YouTube poster, surely?

His odd use of "would" makes me wonder about his literacy, though. And the term "flatted 7ths" makes me frown. Shouldn't it be "flattened"? I google "flatted 7ths" and "flattened 7ths," get inconclusive results, try to reassure myself that "flatted" is probably an American variant that perfectly well-educated people—the sort of people who can be trusted to have a grasp of the musical capabilities of elephants—might use.

I'm aware that I've begun to sink into quicksand.

o o o

I leave the Bach clip and do some research into animals. The Born Free Foundation has bad news for me. Among the behaviors it characterizes as "stereotypic & abnormal" are "standing in one place swaying the head and shoulders—even the whole body— from side to side. Moving the head up and down, or weaving to and fro continuously. Seen in e.g. bears and elephants."*

I find some footage of bears in zoos. They're head-bobbing and swinging like disco dancers. It's agonizing. They are clearly miserable to the point of madness. I recall some of the long-term psychiatric patients I cared for when I was a nurse. Their rhythmic swaying was a way of silently screaming *no-way-out-no-way-out-no-way-out.*

Of course the comparison is not straightforward. At any concert of transcendental music—whether it be Pink Floyd at the UFO Club in 1967 or the congregation of a Southern Baptist church last Sunday—you'll witness humans swaying and rocking in much the same way as psychiatric patients afflicted by the akathisia that comes with dire mental illness. And what about sexual ecstasy? It uses the same facial expressions, writhings and vocalizations as unbearable pain. The only way of *really* knowing how the dancing elephant feels is to ask her.

Except we can't.

I tell myself that Lam Duan is in a sanctuary, free to do as she pleases. But several people remind me that elephants have exceptionally retentive memories and thus bear the psychological scars of their past mistreatment. The elephants at ElephantsWorld

---

*   "Stereotypic Behaviour," Born Free website, undated.

in Kanchanaburi were previously employed in the logging industry, or in sideshows, or as props for beggars. They've been beaten and chained and trained with sharp metal hooks. They have more weltschmerz than I do.

Several YouTubers authoritatively assert that Lam Duan is suffering from zoochosis, "a psychological condition of animals kept in circuses and zoos. Symptoms include pacing, circling, swaying, and self-injury caused by deprivation, loneliness, stress, desperation, and insanity." The word "zoochosis," however, does not appear in dictionaries, having been coined by actor and animal rights activist Bill Travers (star of the 1966 hit movie *Born Free*) and subsequently adopted by PETA and other pressure groups.

It's obvious—whether there's an "official" word for it or not—that captive monkeys gnawing the flesh of their own limbs are exhibiting anguish at their predicament. What's not so obvious is whether we can make the same judgment about Lam Duan. The pianist loves the elephant: that's clear. The elephant could walk away, but stays. The fact that swaying can be a sign of stress does not mean that *all* swaying is stress. Lam Duan could be a Bach fan yet.

And, if the purpose of the YouTube-sharing exercise, for me and Louisa, is to feel better about humans, we can surely take comfort from the fact that at ElephantsWorld once-abused elephants roam free, cared for in their weary old age by kindly volunteers?

Or are they? There are a great many of these elephant sanctuaries all over Asia and Africa. They're a growth industry for ethical and not-so-ethical tourists. The true nature of ElephantsWorld is murky. It posits itself as a charitable sanctuary but it is also (or solely, some argue) a business. Disillusioned former volunteers allege that the elephants are forced to spend much more time with humans than they'd wish, and that their mahouts—i.e. their handlers/riders/trainers—use goads and chains to ensure that the elephants stick around for the visitors.

One of ElephantsWorld's promotional videos swells with heroic orchestral music as a couple of English tourists wearing purple "Mahout Experience" T-shirts evangelize about how much it has meant to them to spend quality time with elephants. They can't see the absurdity of hand-washing animals who are perfectly capable of wading into a river. They can't see how insane it is to hand-feed fruits to those prehensile trunks that are so well-designed for foraging. Elephants need territory and other elephants; they don't need busloads of humans to stroke their ears, pat their hides and feed them bananas. Or play them Bach on the piano.*

But never mind that: pet cats don't *need* to lounge about on knitted blankets and be fed tidbits, but they enjoy the pampering. Maybe elephants enjoy the pampering too? I don't know. I honestly don't know.

○ ○ ○

Unnerved by my experience with Lam Duan, I begin to wonder what I actually know about animals and music. Here I am writing a book about how humans' relationship with music is not always what we like to think it is, and I find that I've been making wild assumptions about how nonhumans operate. How arrogant is that?

"Proof That Animals LOVE Music!!" is the promise made by another YouTube video. This one is a compilation of all sorts of different creatures.† A cockatoo kicks off the proceedings by dancing

---

* Although, arguably, the elephants do need the humans to feed them, since there are now so many elephants in Thailand that it would not be feasible to release them all into the wild. They're being bred specifically for Chinese and American tourists. See: "The Human Cost of Elephant Tourism" by Hilary Cadigan, *The Atlantic*, May 19, 2016.

† "Proof That Animals LOVE Music!! Video Digest," uploaded to YouTube on August 27, 2016. Interestingly, this video has since been removed. And

to a club stomper with what seems like great abandon. Another cockatoo—Snowball—stamps its feet emphatically to the Backstreet Boys' "Everybody," adding appropriate shrieks for good measure.* A guard dog bobs up and down to a disco track for a few seconds before wandering off. Another dog does some fancy footwork to a snatch of reggae. A violinist plays a classical piece to a pair of elephants. A luminous green parrot gyrates mesmerizingly to the Arabic music coming from its owner's cell phone.

The clip goes on and on. A tiny lapdog balances on its hind legs, apparently dancing to Turkish-sounding music. Tourists somewhere-or-other point and giggle as a trio of owls wiggle in front of a phone. A horse in a field plays a Casio keyboard with its lips.

A polar bear shimmies back and forth while a zoo visitor plays "Hotline Bling" by Drake through a phone. A very contented dog nods its head to The Geto Boys' "Damn It Feels Good To Be A Gangsta." A seal nods its head in perfect sync with "Boogie Wonderland" by Earth, Wind & Fire. A man squats on his kitchen floor, playing what to my untrained eye looks like a nyckelharpa, while his dog leaps around on its hind legs. A chimpanzee twirls in athletic John Travolta fashion to a burst of electronica. A penguin pogos to gabber, a subgenre of techno.

"Hahaha!" approves a YouTube watcher. "Dog bouncing to the beat! Thumbs up!"

I'm not so keen. The assemblage of music-loving animals is profoundly problematic.

Some of it is just plain fake: the pogoing penguin wasn't hear-

---

the videos that are currently available in its stead tend to be slickly staged, with soundtracks imposed on silent footage, digital trickery, and the usual YouTube stock-in-trade of cats and dogs being amusing.

* More rigorous scientific study reveals that Snowball only keeps the beat about 15 percent of the time, and that he's reluctant to dance when his owner isn't dancing too—a sure sign of imitative rather than musical behavior. See: *The Evolving Animal Orchestra: In Search of What Makes Us Musical* by Henkjan Honing (MIT Press, 2019).

ing any music as it frolicked near the ocean's edge—the *poom-poom-poom* soundtrack was added later.

Some of it is painfully sad, and makes you marvel at the ability of humans to witness obvious distress and misread it as pleasure. The polar bear ("so cute!" squeals Cassadanielle Picasso) is not interested in "Hotline Bling." He can't relate to Drake jealously wondering "if you bendin' over backwards for someone else." He probably can't even hear the song, as the gadget emitting it is several meters away from where he sways neurotically in his pitiful zoo enclosure, half-insane from boredom and claustrophobia. In the wild, his territory would be hundreds of thousands of times the size of this.

The elephants are puzzling. They're confined in some sort of compound, so you'd expect them to be more frustrated than their brethren at ElephantsWorld, who have a patch of Thailand to wander about in. Yet, as well as swaying, they're flapping their ears and waving their tails. Ear-flapping, according to those who know their pachyderms, is either an attempt to cool down in hot weather or an expression of excitement. Tail-wagging is universally agreed to be 100 percent good news. How this fits in with the alleged zoochosis, I've no idea. Might these elephants like the sonorities of the violin more than the Thai elephant likes the plinking of the piano?

As for the cockatoos and parrots, they look like they're totally into it. Doubting their sincerity feels like the ultimate in killjoy mistrust, a dreary denial of all that's spontaneous and gleeful on the face of this planet.

But then I remember: these birds are mimics. Parrots can say "how are you," "good morning" and so on, but they have no idea what the words mean; they utter the noises because they've learned that such utterances earn them food. I want to believe that the luminous green parrot in the video adores Arabic music. If he danced like that for me, I'd be sure to reward him! Which, of course, is exactly the problem.

The horse's lips make pleasant sounds on the Casio key-board. Pleasant to me, at least. Jazz noodling, interesting discords. Shades of King Crimson's *Thrakattak*. Mind you, we don't know what tasty substances may have been daubed on those piano keys. And there are other videos of this same horse—whose name is Sapphire—being fed treats as a reward, and not just nuzzling the keyboard but...erm...biting it.

The first dog in the "Proof That Animals LOVE Music!!" video is actually sick. A pathetic tremor, possibly Parkinson's or canine distemper. The dog doing the fancy footwork to the reggae track is, in truth, straining at the boundaries of its wire-mesh kennel. The dog leaping up and down near the nyckelharpa player looks suspiciously as if he's trying to snatch a treat that's being dangled by an accomplice just above the top of the video frame. The dog nodding his head to "Damn It Feels Good To Be A Gangsta" does indeed seem to be feeling damn good. But he's lying against the warm body of his master, and dogs feel happy in such circumstances.*

The twirling chimpanzee is in a cage, for fuck's sake. A small, wet cage.

o   o   o

But let's not despair yet: there's the sea lion. She's more than just a YouTube star. She's a bona fide celebrity in the field of animal

---

* In 2012, researchers from Colorado State University published a study analyzing the response of 117 kenneled dogs to classical music versus heavy metal. The dogs slept well to classical but found the heavy metal agitating. I do wonder about the volume that each was played at. My hunch is that a dog—whose ears are sensitive enough to hear a familiar car coming toward its house from hundreds of meters away—might be quite happy to have Iron Maiden burbling away gently in the background but might be reduced to anxious trembling by Haydn at high volume. See: "Behavioral effects of auditory stimulation on kenneled dogs" by Lori R. Kogan, Regina Schoenfeld-Tacher and Allen A. Simon, *Journal of Veterinary Behavior Clinical Applications and Research*, Vol. 7, Issue 5, September 2012.

musicology. Her name is Ronan and she bops her head to Earth, Wind & Fire and Lady Gaga. She keeps perfect time whether the records are sped up or slowed down. She's really tuned in. Ronan is officially "the first nonhuman mammal shown able to find and keep the beat with musical stimuli,"* which I guess means that the researchers are not convinced by the piano recitals at ElephantsWorld.

Whether Ronan gets any aesthetic thrill from "Boogie Wonderland" is another matter. Sea lions are natural show-offs and they love to win the approval of onlookers. In addition to her swimming and diving tricks, Ronan has hit upon another way to provoke admiration: nodding her head in synchronization with vibrations pulsing through her environment.

Still, credit where credit is due: she's keeping the beat.

o   o   o

Keeping a beat is an almost exclusively human skill. Indeed, calling it a skill wrongly implies we need to learn it; it's congenital. Newborn babies are ready to rock, in both senses of the word. Whereas other animals—even animals who share most of our genes—fail very simple tests like tapping along with a metronome.

"After a year of training," says Michael Blanding of Massachusetts's Tufts University, "the best rhesus monkeys can do is tap a few hundred milliseconds *after* each metronome click. In other words, they are only responding to the beat, not anticipating it."† Cognitive neuroscientist Aniruddh Patel explains that when we humans listen to music, we predict where the next

---

*   "A California Sea Lion (*Zalophus californianus*) Can Keep the Beat: Motor Entrainment to Rhythmic Auditory Stimuli in a Non Vocal Mimic" by Peter Cook, Andrew Rouse, Margaret Wilson, and Colleen Reichmuth, *Journal of Comparative Psychology*, April 1, 2013.

†   "We Got The Beat" by Michael Blanding, Tufts University website, May 19, 2014.

beat will be, and get pleasure either from our guesses being correct or from the rhythm teasingly wrong-footing us with unexpected syncopations. Apes just don't get that.

Or do they?

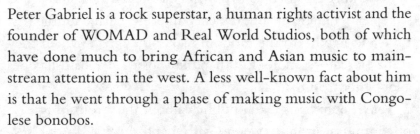

Peter Gabriel is a rock superstar, a human rights activist and the
founder of WOMAD and Real World Studios, both of which
have done much to bring African and Asian music to mainstream attention in the west. A less well-known fact about him
is that he went through a phase of making music with Congo-
lese bonobos.

Bonobos are the less common, more endangered of the two
sorts of chimpanzee. They are our closest relatives, genetically
speaking. To our nonchimpanzee eyes, they look much the same
as the common chimp, but they're very different. Common
chimps have evolved a brutally male-dominated society. Status
is everything; conflict rather than cooperation is the norm. The
alphas mate with whatever females they want and often kill the
babies. Bonobo society, by contrast, is matriarchal, sex is con-
sensual (there's a lot of erotic activity going on, all the time) and
no one kills the kids.[*]

Peter Gabriel's bonobo friend Panbanisha didn't grow up in
the Congo; she lived at the Georgia State University in Atlanta
and latterly the Great Ape Trust, a primatologist research facility
in Iowa. She understood English and could converse with the
aid of a lexigram keyboard. She also enjoyed music. (I write of
her in the past tense because, sadly, she died in 2012.)

There are two short films on YouTube of Panbanisha seated
at a keyboard, improvising with Gabriel and Tony Levin, a bass-

---

[*]   "In the Bonobo World, Female Camaraderie Prevails" by Natalie Angier,
   The New York Times, September 10, 2016.

playing *Homo sapiens* from Boston. They're excerpts from longer sessions, conducted on multiple occasions, which I've had the opportunity to hear highlights of. There is no fakery, no coercion, no Pavlovian bribery. Panbanisha wants to join in with her musician friends and, in a contentedly contemplative manner, makes noises that go nicely with the overall vibe.

I wouldn't go so far as to say she has special talent. But I've seen plenty of human children encountering a piano for the first time and I've heard the random racket they make when they realize it requires more skill than they possess. Panbanisha does a lot better than that.*

Tony Levin has spoken publicly about the astonishing ease of communication between Gabriel and the ape. In one session, Panbanisha dangled her hands over the keyboard, playing vague note clusters with the backs of her fingers. Recalls Levin: "Peter stopped and said, 'Panbanisha, I liked it better yesterday when you played it with only one finger of each hand.' And she stopped, and the rest of the day she played like this [Levin uncurls his hands and starts to play with one finger, judiciously sounding one note at a time, on the white keys only]. Soon after that, I was in a taxi, bass in a gig bag on my shoulders, and the guy picked me up to take me to the airport and he said, 'Isn't that the place with the monkeys? What are you doing with a

---

* "Peter Gabriel's 'Interspecies Internet,'" WBUR interview/podcast, July 9, 2013. Challenged by presenter Robin Young to prove that Panbanisha was doing more than just tickling the keys in ways that were coincidentally pleasing, Gabriel responds: "There's absolutely no [scientific] evidence. I just play [the tapes] to a lot of musicians, and [they recognize that] there were moments that were alive and there were moments of the interaction that were dead, and this is something that, as an improvising musician, you really get very familiar with. There's a point where she finds an octave. Now, she's not been exposed to a keyboard before, but she becomes fascinated in it, and repeats it. There's another point where she finds different harmonies to what I'm doing with the voice. These may be chance occurrences, but I think the more of them there are—and there were plenty of them—the less likely it is that they are chance."

guitar?' And it hit me then that it's gonna take a long time to process what just happened.'"*

How are we to process what happened in those interspecies jam sessions in Atlanta? The example of Panbanisha tempts us to be more open-minded, excited even, about the musicality of animals.

Sadly, it's downhill all the way after the bonobo.†

My next port of call is Lampang in Northern Thailand, where the Thai Elephant Orchestra is based. The word "orchestra" is a bit of a stretch. On specially designed hard-to-destroy gongs, bells, xylophones and drums, up to a dozen elephants play "conducted improvisations" in the gamelan mode.

This group didn't get together in the way The Beatles or The Rolling Stones did, with one pachyderm admiring the attitude, style or record collection of another. Instead, it was co-created by entrepreneur Richard Lair (described as an elephant conservationist) and the American neuroscientist David Sulzer, who has a parallel career in avant-garde music under the name David Soldier.

A concert or recording session begins with the animals being led by their mahouts to the array of gear. The subsequent clanging and banging tenuously resembles the music made by

---

*   "Fragile as a song (live !) by Tony Levin," uploaded to YouTube by JP Gauthier on July 25, 2013.

†   Had you been an eavesdropper in Namibia when a troop of baboons were played recordings of their own vocalizations through loudspeakers, you might imagine that the apes experienced some sort of aesthetic frisson—before learning that what intrigued them was that the recordings accidentally violated the strict rules of rank that determine which baboon gets to grunt first. See: *Baboon Metaphysics* by Dorothy L. Cheney and Robert M. Seyfarth (University of Chicago Press, 2007).

a human gamelan orchestra, except that humans don't need mahouts with bullhooks to direct their attention to the job. It's manifestly obvious that this is an exercise in ringmasterly control no different from elephants standing on pedestals, twirling hula hoops, or painting $450-a-pop pictures with brushes held in their trunks.

In our quest to find animals that make music spontaneously, without human assistance or pressure, we may be driven deep underwater. Or at least to the marijuana-speckled LP collections of elderly hippies.

Songs Of The Humpback Whale (1970) was a surprise bestseller in its day. The sounds are eerie as hell, more lonesome and strange than any amount of dark ambient electronica by bands calling themselves Lustmord, Aseptic Void and so on. They are the underwater moans and wails and clicks of *Megaptera novaeangliae*, a gigantic cetacean that's as different from us as a mammal can be. Despite the fact that we've shared the planet with them for millions of years, and almost exterminated them during an intensive spate of hunting, we still don't understand them very well. We know how to melt down their flesh for oil and fry their genitals, but the intricacies of their society remain a mystery.

The theory is that their vocalizations are meant to help them locate and attract sexual partners during the breeding season. The male whales seem to be sending advertisements through a hundred (or a thousand, or ten thousand, we really don't have a clue) miles of ocean. It's like some supernaturally potent musk aftershave that can be smelled in the next city.

Are these sounds music? There's nothing about the whales' vocalizations that's aesthetically much different from the lowing of cows, the hooting of owls or the moaning of hippopotamuses (an animal to which whales are closely related). It's the mathematically graphable patterns that have made researchers wonder if we're hearing a deep-sea oratorio.

o   o   o

Inevitably, some musicians have been keen to jam with the whales. My first exposure to whalesong was in the 1980s when I heard "And God Created Great Whales," a symphonic poem by the Armenian-American composer Alan Hovhaness. Excerpts from the deep-sea recordings issued on *Songs Of The Humpback Whale* were solemnly combined with violins, trombones, glockenspiels and so on.

Another snippet from *Songs Of The Humpback Whale* prefaced the opening track on Kate Bush's debut album, thus ensuring that the masturbatory fantasies of teenage males throughout Britain were accompanied by the mating calls of the randy cetacean.[*]

But these encounters were manufactured in the studio, and there'll always be people who want the "live" experience. Clarinetist David Rothenberg, a self-styled "interspecies musician" and long-term whale nut, tries to play along with the creatures as they swim unseen somewhere far beneath his boat.

"Most times when I drop my microphone and speaker underwater to play with the whales, I feel awfully lonely," he muses. "There I am, making a strange sound and sending it out un-

---

[*]   Doubt has been cast on the sexual purpose of whalesong. Scientists have found no evidence of female whales responding to, or even noticing, the noises made by their potential mates. Whale experts currently surmise that the singing "might serve the function of identification and association among males, so they can see who knows who, how they're involved and to what degree." The cetacean equivalent, perhaps, of Joy Division singing songs of romantic loneliness to a black-clad tribe of miserable young men, while all the frisky young women are livin' it up at a different gig. See: "The Secrets of the Deep" by Lara Cory, in Tobias Fischer and Lara Cory (eds), *Animal Music: Sound and Song in the Natural World* (Strange Attractor Press, 2015).

derwater, just hoping a whale might connect what he sings to what I'm playing. Often they just ignore me, but in the best of moments, and such a moment is just as rare as playing along with human musicians, some real contact may happen."[*] What Rothenberg means by "real contact" is presumably a moment when his clarinet and the vocalizations of the whales sound particularly nice together. Almost as if the whales were responding.

Rothenberg plays with other animals too. Birds and bugs, mostly. There's a particularly charming film of him playing his clarinet in a forest in New York's Hudson Valley, as a brood of cicadas in the treetops sing (i.e. rapidly clasp and unclasp their abdominal membranes) in a way that happens only once every seventeen years.[†]

"The more I do this, the more I expand my notion of what can count as music," reflects Rothenberg in a voice-over. "Sounds that previously sounded to me as noise, as annoyance, as just a kind of background nuisance, I start to hear as being beautiful, aesthetic, formed, organized, composed, and sort of necessary, as they've been for millions of years. And it's a privilege to hear such a sound, a rare privilege. And even more rare to find a way to join in."

In Hudson Valley, he plays his final note on the clarinet, looks up at the trees, and waves his hand like a conductor. *"Crescendo!"* he commands, then laughs self-deprecatingly. He's a university professor as well as a clarinetist; he must be aware, deep down, that the cicadas will do what they do regardless of whether he's there or not.

Or will they? Can I really speak authoritatively about animals' musical proclivities based on YouTube clips and maga-

---

[*]   "How to Make Music With a Whale" by David Rothenberg, *The New York Times*, October 5, 2014. One hopes that the clarinet squalls don't interrupt/confuse the messages that the whales are trying to send each other.

[†]   "David Rothenberg Jams with the Cicadas," uploaded to YouTube by PBS NewsHour on June 19, 2013.

zine articles archived on the internet? I decide it's time I bought some proper books and delved deeper into the science. I settle down with *Animal Music: Sound and Song in the Natural World*, and *The Evolving Animal Orchestra: In Search of What Makes Us Musical*. I feel righteously researcherly as I tackle these tomes, pencil in hand.

The Evolving Animal Orchestra turns out to be an elaborate tease. Henkjan Honing, Professor of Music Cognition at the University of Amsterdam, relates in exhaustive detail the experiments on rhesus macaques, chimpanzees and zebra finches he attends at various scientific institutes. He's convinced the animals have "beat perception," but the problem is how to devise a test that can withstand the animals' utter physiological and psychological resistance to being tested.

In the end, the procedures involve so much failure, painstaking training and Pavlovian reward that Honing's faith begins to look pitiful. The animals seem to be interested in almost any damn thing except music.

Animal Music: Sound and Song in the Natural World is a more rewarding but also more scatterbrained book. It includes, for example, an interview with an Amazonian shaman who, after ingesting a great deal of ayahuasca, shrank to minuscule size and had meaningful dialogue with an ant in a "tridimensional" language.*

For those of a more rational bent, *Animal Music* contains a number of interviews with sound recordists—wildlife professionals whose specialty is capturing the noises made by animals in their natural habitat.

---

*   "Music of the Plants, Music of the Animals" by Kate Carr, in Tobias Fischer and Lara Cory (eds), *Animal Music: Sound and Song in the Natural World* (Strange Attractor Press, 2015).

All of them struggle with the practical problem—which, to them, feels more like a *moral* problem—of how to edit down endless hours of sonic data to something that you or I could listen to. Editing falsifies, or at least imposes structure. The animals presumably have a reason for making a particular noise three thousand times an hour, or once every three hours, and the human editor distorts that reason by cutting and pasting.

Impeccably sensitive in their twenty-first-century ethos, the recordists are worried about cultural appropriation—the risk of offending a macaw or a wildebeest in the same way that a Muslim might take offense at how the meaning of a Koranic call to prayer is mangled by a westerner cutting it down to a more elegant shape.

"I do not change the animal sounds themselves," insists Jana Winderen, author of such albums as *Spring Bloom In The Marginal Ice Zone.* "I would not start to tune the animal sounds, for example. I feel it would be disrespectful to the animal to use them as instruments."[*]

No such scruple inhibited Graeme Revell, film composer and leader of the seminal Australian electronic group SPK, when he made his groundbreaking album *The Insect Musicians* in 1986. He was among the first artists to own a Fairlight CMI, a sophisticated sampler with which any sound can be manipulated by sculpting its waveform and playing it back on a conventional piano keyboard. Revell fed field recordings of Indonesian cicadas, tsetse flies, courting gnats, disturbed bees, deathwatch beetles and many more into his machine, then fiddled around with them until he achieved…something remarkably similar to the ambient synthesizer music he would've made without them.

To my ears, the noise made by David Rothenberg's cicadas in Hudson Valley sounds like cicadas doing a cicada thing that

---

[*]   "Excursion: Recording Technology," interviews edited by Tobias Fischer and Lara Cory, in *Animal Music: Sound and Song in the Natural World* (Strange Attractor Press, 2015).

has nothing to do with what humans call music, while Graeme Revell's "Balinese Twilights" or "Melancholia" sound like a human composer using crickets and hornets as decoration for his decidedly un-insectoid tunes.

In between those two extremes is a 1990s piece commonly known as "God's Chorus Of Crickets," by Native American composer Jim Wilson. Purportedly, this is a straightforward collage of crickets chirping at normal speed and the same recording slowed down drastically. The philosophical contention is that crickets live much shorter lives than us, so they have to communicate much faster, and it's only by slowing their sounds down "to match and mirror the length of the average lifespan of a human being"[*] that we can hear what's really going on.

The piece is awesomely beautiful. It is indeed a heavenly choir, or at least an alien one. The CD's liner notes state that it is "a simple diatonic 7-note scale chord progression and melody with a multi-layered structure" that can be "played continuously in the background to create a natural soothing atmosphere for peace, serenity, and healing direct from Mother Nature."

What's not clear is how much manipulation the crickets have undergone. Jim Wilson's account is vague. He mentions slowing down the recording "to various levels" and that, the more he worked on it, "this simple familiar sound began to morph into something very mystic and complex." Did he merely mean that the slower he played the crickets, the more their stridulations sounded like melodies? Or did he weave together a patchwork of sonorous cricket tones to create a melody of his own devising?

The answer lies in numerous attempts of skeptics to reproduce Wilson's experiment. All of them found that the crickets' chirping was infinitely repetitious, and that if you slowed it down, all

---

[*]   Quoted from an unidentified source, in "God's Chorus of Crickets" by David Mikkelson, Snopes.com, November 24, 2013.

you got was a monotone whose variations were solely textural rather than melodic.

No surprise there. It ought to be obvious to anyone who knows anything about insects and how they make their noises that they're as far removed from a celestial choir as a piece of Mozart is from a piece of mozzarella. One experimenter waggishly called his piece "Dawkins's Chorus of Crickets," alluding to the radical atheist Richard Dawkins.[*]

Still, some of the authentic cricket recordings are thrilling to my electronica-loving ears. Devoid of the rapturous melody that Wilson imposed on his version, the eerie tones of the insects reverberate mindlessly in the unnatural slowness of their time warp. I could listen to this stuff for hours, in the same way that I can enjoy the throbbing of a generator or the clackity-clackity rhythm of a train passing over the tracks. But the trains and the generators and the insects are not composing music.

Our final port of call is songbirds. Yes, proper singing birds, not those mendacious parrots and cockatoos who jump around pretending they're into the Backstreet Boys. Actual songbirds who wake us on a spring morning with delight at their melodious trilling.

David Rothenberg, unsurprisingly, is a songbird fan, and has played along with them on numerous occasions. He concedes that often they're not in the mood and remain silent while he serenades them. Gloomy weather dampens their appetite for performing. As well as other enigmatic factors. For a long time, he

---

[*]   "It's Just Not Crickets," Hummadruz blog, August 14, 2016. See also: "This is how slowed down crickets really sounds. Not so angelic after all…" uploaded to YouTube by Jack Vaudeville on November 24, 2013, and "God's Crickets Chorus: Real or Hoax?" Wafflesatnoon.com, December 8, 2014.

was plagued by the dispiriting conclusion that "birds just s[i]ng their own songs" and "they don't care about us."

But then one morning, when he was doing some *al fresco* clarinet improvisations, a white-crested laughing thrush started making sounds that fitted right in with the notes he was coming up with. "This bird was really interacting."[*]

Perhaps the most famous example of such an interaction happened in southeast England in the brief period of calm between World Wars I and II.

Beatrice Harrison was the foremost cellist of her day. She was Elgar's favorite soloist and the dedicatee of Delius's Cello Concerto. In spring 1923, she was practicing Rimsky-Korsakov's "Chant Hindou" in her garden in Foyle Riding, Surrey, when a nightingale began to sing along. The bird followed her notes "in third[s] and always perfectly in tune."[†]

Harrison persuaded Lord Reith, director of the BBC, to bring recording equipment to her garden in the hope of broadcasting the magic to the British public live, as it happened. On a warm May night in 1924, with microphones and engineers all around her, Beatrice played bits of Elgar and Dvořák and "Danny Boy," without any response from the nightingale. Then, fifteen minutes or so before the BBC was due to close for the night, the bird joined in.

The broadcast was a phenomenal success and, over the next decade, it became a sort of spring tradition, with BBC engineers returning to Beatrice's garden regularly until 1942, when the sound of military aircraft flying overhead was deemed to have spoiled the vibe. Bestselling 78rpm records were issued, of the nightingale(s) "accompanying" Harrison on various tunes. People bought them like they buy Ed Sheeran or Adele today.

---

[*]   "NJIT professor finds nothing cuckoo in serenading our feathered friends" by Ronni Reich, NJ.com, October 15, 2010.

[†]   "The Cellist and the Nightingale," *The Irish Times*, January 23, 1997.

I adore this story. It makes me happy. Not because I believe that the nightingales were jamming with Beatrice Harrison's cello. I believe they were vocalizing to mark their territory and to attract mates, just as whales and cicadas do, just as worms and snails would no doubt do if only they had any body parts to make noises with. Birds want to make more birds; they don't give a teensy white shit about Dvořák.*

Indeed, it has recently emerged that the nightingale in the historic duet with Beatrice Harrison wasn't a bird at all. It was actually the bird impressionist and virtuoso whistler Maude Gould aka "Madame Saberon." Ornithologist Tim Birkhead surmises that the BBC film crew tramping around the garden scared off the real nightingales. "It would [have been] a terrible admission, even later, to say that they'd wheeled in Madame Saberon. The temptation to not say anything must've been immense."

Birkhead is satisfied that in later broadcasts, when the crew trod more gently, the birds were real. But he also raises the likelihood that the nightingales sang in competition with human interference to their communication.†

So, with all these disproofs of birdy musicianship, why does the story make me so happy? For many reasons.

---

*   As well as not giving a shit about Dvořák, birds don't even give a shit about birdsong that isn't their own. Scientists have established that although birds teach their fledglings to make the noises they'll need for survival, they're immune to the calls of other species. "If a nestling male song sparrow and a nestling male swamp sparrow are raised side-by-side in a laboratory where they hear tape recordings of both species' songs, each bird will grow up to sing only the song of its own species." Not because of different vocal equipment—both sparrows are physically capable of singing the other species' songs—but because their evolution-honed brains tell them that the alien songs are irrelevant to them. See: *Baboon Metaphysics* by Dorothy L. Cheney and Robert M. Seyfarth (University of Chicago Press, 2007), referring to research in "Species differences in auditory responsiveness in early vocal learning" by P. Marler and S. Peters, in *The Comparative Psychology of Audition: Perceiving Complex Sounds* (Lawrence Erlbaum Associates, Inc., 1989).

†   "The cello and the nightingale: 1924 duet was faked, BBC admits" by Dalya Alberge, *The Guardian*, April 8, 2022.

I love that a classical cellist and the head of the BBC agreed that it would be a good thing for the people of Britain to hear a duet between cello and nightingale broadcast live from a garden at night.

I love the photos of Beatrice Harrison in her oldfangled Alma-Tadema gown and her forest-nymph headscarf and her formal shoes, playing her cello with her patient dog at her side.

I love the photo of the gardener in his cloth cap, advising the BBC engineers in their spiffy suits where best to position the microphones.

I love the idea that even as the Nazis were inflicting genocide on Europe, and even as large parts of London lay in ruins from Luftwaffe bombing, radio lovers were still tuning in to hear the nightingale sing in some posh eccentric's garden.

I find it poignant that Beatrice Harrison, who was once the most eminent cellist in Britain and had millions of fans, nowadays qualifies for inclusion on a website devoted to "Forgotten Cellists."

I cherish Beatrice's speaking voice. On one of the cassettes I taped off the radio during the 1980s, I have an interview with her in which she reminisces about the nightingale, talking with an accent that has long died out. I feel tenderly toward that dead accent, just as I feel tenderly toward the Caribbean-inflected English that many youngsters in modern Britain speak, which prompts old fogeys to complain that civilization is ending.

I love that Beatrice was born in 1892, well within the Victorian era, and lived till 1965, when The Byrds were preparing "Mr. Tambourine Man" for release.

I love that new generations of nightingales came to us all through that century and that they are coming still.

I love that no birds or humans were harmed in those innocent 1920s broadcasts.

I love the idea of a family gathering around a gramophone—kneeling in front of its big brass trumpet, the children shushed as Mom or Dad removes the shellac disc from its thick cardboard sleeve—all excited to hear this extraordinary new thing.

I love the sound of a cello, and I love the sound of a nightingale.

Getting back to the film clip that gave me and Louisa "pleasure about humans," I still get consolation from the idea of the classical pianist playing Bach for the elephant. Partly because my mind (or heart?) stubbornly resists the idea that the elephants are unhappy. I search for evidence that they're fine after all, like a religious devotee or political loyalist who obsessively searches for proof that the scandals swirling around their leader are mere slurs and rumors. Am I no better than the right-wing conspiracy theorist who insists that Donald Trump, America's best-ever president, was the innocent victim of fake news? Or the Michael Jackson fan who maintains that her hero never did anything but bring joy to an ungrateful world?

I flatter myself that I'm not quite that self-delusional. I find another YouTube clip, a strangely obscure and neglected one (i.e. a few hundred views as opposed to several million), in which Paul Barton plays boogie-woogie as a duo with an elephant.

The elephant's mahout stands nearby but has no bullhook in hand. The elephant is doing plenty of ear-flapping and tail-wagging: good signs. She whacks the piano's keys with the tip of her trunk, obliging Barton to improvise in the spaces left in between the bouncing proboscis. Occasionally, she nods her head, in perfect time with the music, not in a weary swaying manner but very much like a jazz fan having fun.

She's got to be having fun, hasn't she? It's inconceivable that she's not having fun. Or at least, I fervently prefer not to conceive it.*

---

*   "HOW MUSIC FOR ELEPHANTS BEGAN: PAUL BARTON INTER-
VIEW," uploaded to YouTube on November 22, 2017 (since removed).

o   o   o

Because, in the end, this is not about the animals. It's about us.

I am a sensitive human, vulnerable to despair as I survey the toxic forces that infest our planet—the omnipresent plague of despots, corporate thugs, misogynists, bigots, neo-Nazis, drug lords, sex traffickers, swindlers, goons and bullies. As an antidote to all that toxicity, I want to see kind, gentle people doing kind, gentle things. I'm fighting for a hopeful view of my species.

Let the eccentric pianist play. Give him a gerbil or a porcupine to play to if there's some problem with elephants. Whatever.

I feel under threat of extinction: have mercy.

IMPOSSIBLE TO HEAR
(ON ROLF HARRIS, R. KELLY
AND MORRISSEY)

Great art can be made by bad people. By which we really mean: stuff that gives us pleasure can be supplied by individuals we don't like.

Music, like any branch of endeavor, harbors its share of creeps, fanatics, bullies, rapists, leeches, narcissists and psychopaths. There are no laws to stop them having talent.

We may feel uneasy about giving encouragement or money to horrid individuals. We may make a resolution that we'll only support artists who are decent and kind. I was once invited, by hippie friends who've certainly increased the amount of decency and kindness in the world, to accompany them to a beautiful valley in Knockengorroch, Kirkcudbrightshire, where everyone was friendly and the children got their faces painted and there was organic food and real ale and impeccably multicultural music of a high standard. All good things.

But some of the music I've admired most in my life was made by egomaniacal, abrasive, "difficult" artists who would not have been at all compatible with the ethos at Knockengorroch. "Die, hippie scum!" they might've yelled, making the innocent children cry.

I love the music Miles Davis made. There's lots of Miles on my shelves. He was, however, a complicated man. I've just consulted a number of dictionaries and none of them define "complicated" as "capable of being very, very nasty," which is odd because we all know that this is what it means.

o   o   o

Boycotting a creative person because you don't approve of how they behave can be easy. Or it can be bloody difficult. It depends on the art form they're working in.

Literature is dead easy to shun. A book contains tens of thousands of words and you need to make a serious investment of time to read them. If you decide that Norman Mailer was a jerk, you can safely walk through any bookshop or library and remain wholly untainted by any of his work, even if the front covers are turned to face you and the blurbs say "SEMINAL." Someone could even send you one of his books as a present and it could sit gathering dust in your home without a word of it gaining access to your brain.

Film is quite ignorable too. A movie takes at least an hour and a half to watch and you need to choose to do so. If you're unlucky, a short trailer for a film by a director you disapprove of may be screened when you're waiting for your chosen film to start, but this is a rare and random hazard. Mostly, you're in control. For example, despite Quentin Tarantino's fame and ubiquity, I still haven't got round to watching any of his movies. I read a couple of interviews with him a long time ago and, without ever having met the man, did that thing we all sometimes do—took a personal dislike to a total stranger. Friends whose judgment I respect tell me that *Pulp Fiction* or *Kill Bill* are great films and that I would really enjoy them if I gave them a chance. I haven't given them a chance.

Painting and sculpture are trickier. You can decide that Dalí or Picasso were despicable shits or that Tamara de Lempicka was just a ghastly no-talent socialite, but there's always a risk that you will see a reproduction of one of their works and instinctively think: *Oh, I like that*. One glimpse, and bingo: this person you've been contemptuous of has given you a thrill. But you can turn the page, or avert your eyes, or click on something else, and the thrill is gone.

o   o   o

Music is the most dangerous of the self-forbidden pleasures, the most difficult to boycott. It affects us emotionally, spiritually and physically, barging into us without consulting our carefully constructed value system. A story or an argument or an image can be checked against the notions we claim to believe or stand for. A vibration in our ears can't.

The thing is, opinions are not as deeply rooted or robust as they're cracked up to be. We talk as if the way we feel about the American electoral system or Brexit or pandemics or transgender issues or censorship or racism or Ukraine was born into us, but the truth is that we're learning more about these things all the time, and adjusting our opinions as we receive fresh data and as we sense the attitudes of people around us changing. Our politically correct selves—and I use that term not in its usual pejorative sense, but as a recognition that we all want to be considered "right" rather than "wrong"—are updated daily.

The way we respond to music, however, is much more fundamental and less negotiable, determined by neural pathways that were created without words, neural pathways that may have been etched when we were so young we didn't *have* any words. Long before we understand what politics is, what racism is, what sexism is, we are already disposed to respond to sounds of a certain kind. Those sounds resonate with us, emotionally speaking, whether we want them to or not.*

---

* In this chapter, I'm generalizing about those of us who do have an emotional relationship with music. As we saw in the chapter "Who Doesn't Like Music?" this is by no means everyone. Obviously, a person who regards music as nothing more than an arbitrary succession of irritating sounds, or who values music solely for its social or practical usefulness, will have no difficulty rejecting music on moral grounds. Morals are as good an excuse as any for crossing music off the list.

o   o   o

Rolf Harris was one of the most beloved champions of light entertainment in Commonwealth history (and perhaps the most decorated—MBE, OBE, CBE, and Australian National Living Treasure, among many other honors). He did the Queen's portrait and was arguably Britain's most popular painter. He raised millions for charity. He presented nineteen series of *Animal Hospital*, thus winning the hearts of animal lovers young and old. He wowed the ravers at Glastonbury and played didgeridoo on albums by his dear friend Kate Bush. Even people who considered themselves too cool to like Rolf Harris had a soft spot for him.

In 2014, at the age of eighty-four, he was convicted on twelve charges of sexual assault.

The trial was confused, messy and skewed by media hysteria, but it exposed Harris as an entitled celebrity who, like many famous men in the 1970s and '80s, groped whichever unconsenting females he fancied. Just a few years earlier, the extravagantly loathsome Jimmy Savile, a prolific child rapist, molester and necrophile, had managed to die of old age without ever having been exposed, and there was a prevailing sense that the same mistake must not be made again. The demonization of Harris in the press resulted in millions of British people feeling that they'd loved music made by a monster almost as evil as Savile.

And not only had they loved that music once, a long time ago.

They loved it still.

o   o   o

"Two Little Boys" was a number 1 hit record in 1969. This fact alone would've been enough to make it resonate with a generation. People bond with the familiar. Six weeks at number 1 and countless repeat performances throughout Harris's five-decade career made that bond as strong as a blood tie.

"Two Little Boys" also happens to be a highly successful work of art. To my ears, it's the best British chart-topper of 1969, a year when pop's psychedelic flowering had withered and all the dandies seemed to have morphed into grubby heroin addicts.* Tellingly, The Beatles' two number 1 records that year, "Get Back" and "The Ballad Of John And Yoko," were both crudely inferior offerings, lazily composed, lazily played, wearily sung, arranged without finesse. "Two Little Boys," by contrast, is a little coup of panache.

Originally composed in 1902, it has the unashamed sentimentality of the late Victorian music hall. But the crank-up gramophone version, by the vaudevillian Billy Murray, fell short of the song's potential for stirring the emotions. Murray's performance was cheery, recorded before the Great War turned Europe into a mass grave.

In 1969, Rolf Harris and orchestral arranger Alan Braden overhauled the song's mood, rewrote some of the words, improved the melody and turned "Two Little Boys" into a perfect three-minute opera. Rolf was no opera singer, of course, but his vocal had the hammishly sincere commitment that children are drawn to in a storyteller.

The great majority of the shell-shocked Harris ex-fans who've left comments under YouTube uploads of "Two Little Boys" recall that they were six when they first heard it. Some had it sung to them by their parents. Six, it seems, is the ideal age for hav-

---

*   1969 really was a bad year for British pop. Many rock and progressive luminaries stopped bothering to issue singles, concentrating on albums instead, while future crazes like glam and funk were yet to arise. Desmond Dekker's "Israelites"—perhaps the most momentous record that year—wasn't British; it was a thoroughly Jamaican item, recorded and released there in 1968 before finally conquering the seat of empire in April 1969. Fleetwood Mac's "Albatross" and The Move's "Blackberry Way" were good records, more "grown-up" in their appeal than "Two Little Boys," but less audacious, less ambitious. Marmalade's version of The Beatles' frivolous "Ob-La-Di, Ob-La-Da" hit the top *twice*, interrupted by The Scaffold's clownishly arch "Lily The Pink."

ing one's tiny mind and heart blown open by pathos, the pity of war, the relief of unexpected rescue, the notion of poetic justice.

The kids who fell under the spell of "Two Little Boys" knew nothing about war, in the political or historical sense, but suddenly they knew how they *felt about* war, via music. They were also introduced, at a ridiculously tender age, to the concept of nostalgia. Those chords, ascending as if from the corpse-strewn battlefield, those bugle-like trumpets, those swells of brass emotion, the right-against-the-ear intimacy of Rolf's recitation: they all combined to make children imagine what it would be like to be a grown-up remembering being a child.

"Part of my cherished childhood is now defiled and soiled," laments one YouTube visitor.[*] Others reassure him that they feel his pain. It's obvious that they are all still deeply in love with "Two Little Boys," and feel spasms of pity and affection for those brave brothers on the battlefield, and for their innocent younger selves who didn't yet understand anything about anything, especially "indecent assault."

They cannot unlove those deeply embedded sounds.

o   o   o

For various reasons, including my ethnicity, date of birth, countries of residence, peer group and general cultural milieu, I was not trained to love the slick, glamorous hip-hop-lite that is often called "contemporary R&B." Its sounds are not deeply embedded in me. I first became aware of them in the 1990s, by which time I was a thirtysomething novelist living in the Scottish Highlands, squinting in bemusement at this foreign tribe of imperious hunks with their bling and their fine raiment and their forensically precise haircuts and their coded finger gestures and their half-naked handmaidens.

[*]   "Rolf Harris – Two Little Boys," uploaded to YouTube by TheVideoJukeBox3 on January 14, 2012.

Contemporary R&B is, however, one of the most popular genres in the western world, and Robert Sylvester Kelly was one of its megastars. There are many people, particularly in the USA, who only need to hear the first few seconds of R. Kelly's "Step In The Name Of Love" to be transported into a zone where they can feel safe and comfortable. "Follow me," the singer says, in his alter ego as the Pied Piper, and they follow.

Over a period of twenty-three years, the King of Pop-Soul (aka the King of R&B, the World's Greatest) sold 75 million records and won a clutch of Grammy Awards, but this was accompanied by a steadily worsening landslide of scandal. His brief marriage to a fifteen-year-old in 1994 was just the first warning sign of his appetite for underage girls. Dozens of women came out with horror stories of his predatory, abusive and controlling behavior, corroborated by incriminating films. Case after case was settled out of court, as Kelly threw fistfuls of his seemingly limitless fortune at the victims. Among the very few offenses of which he was officially found guilty were battery and failure to pay child support.

How did the world react, as a quarter of a century went by and Kelly was continually in the news, always indignantly protesting his innocence as the evidence mounted up toward his neck?

For most of that time, it was business as usual—awards, airplay, concerts, endorsements, high-profile collaborations. But in 2018, after one of Kelly's many arrests, the music streaming service Spotify temporarily stopped promoting his music, issuing the foggily self-contradictory statement: "We don't censor content because of an artist's or creator's behavior, but we want our editorial decisions—what we choose to program—to reflect our values."* His record label dropped him, perhaps no great sacrifice given that he'd produced no new music for some

---

*   "Spotify Pulls R. Kelly and XXXTentacion From Playlists, Stirring a Debate" by Joe Coscarelli, *The New York Times*, May 10, 2018.

years and his last effort had been the low-selling *12 Nights Of Christmas*. Still he toured on.

A social media campaign, #MuteRKelly, was instigated by black activists whose explicit aim was to make Kelly a pariah in the industry. The Twitter hashtag was devised by Kenyette Barnes—herself a sexual abuse survivor—and the action was provoked not just by R. Kelly's outrageous behavior but by the larger #MeToo movement. Even so, any observer sensitive to the dangers of vigilante justice, or who recalled the destruction of livelihoods in the McCarthy era or Stalin's Russia, might be perturbed by organizer Oronike Odeleye's declaration: "It's time for us to end this man's career."*

This is not to suggest that Odeleye's campaign against Kelly was wrong, or that it amounted to "the attempted lynching of a black man who has made extraordinary contributions to our culture,"† as claimed by Kelly's management, in a shockingly brazen attempt to weave the shame of two hundred and fifty years of American history into a protection of their client's brand. It's also worth noting that whereas the career-canceling authorities during the McCarthy era were "punching down," Barnes and Odeleye were "punching up."

In July 2019, Kelly was arrested on multiple charges of sexual abuse, kidnapping, human trafficking, child pornography, racketeering and obstruction of justice. As I began this chapter, he was still awaiting trial, because he was having trouble deciding on the optimal lineup for his legal team. To the last, he regarded himself as a powerful man who could swing things his way. As I revise this chapter a couple of years on, Kelly seems likely to

---

*   "#MuteRKelly campaign organizers take aim at the 'Pied Piper of R&B'" by Demetria Irwin, *The Grio*, January 24, 2018.

†   Statement by representative of R. Kelly's management, quoted in "R. Kelly Responds to Time's Up Campaign: Singer Is 'Target of Greedy, Conscious and Malicious Conspiracy'" by Jem Aswad, *Variety*, April 30, 2018.

remain in jail for decades as multiple court cases have ended in his conviction on all counts, and additional trials are under way.

Kelly's management are no longer arguing that their client is a victim of injustice. The tide has turned. But it hasn't been easy for that part of the black community reared on contemporary R&B and on the radiant myth of Kelly as a godlike black man standing proud in a racist world. Ardent fans who refused to believe the evidence sent hate mail to those who were working toward Kelly's prosecution. Identity was at stake—not just the intrinsic goodness of Robert Sylvester Kelly, but the intrinsic goodness of the fans who loved him and who, whatever happens, probably always will.

o   o   o

In the copious comments underneath a YouTube upload of "Forever," a woman called Penika reminisces: "This is song my husband proposed to me in front of my mom and daddy. I also used it in our wedding October 20, 2007. Rest on my beautiful husband Joe Clark Jr."* What do we see here? Love upon love upon loss upon grief upon love bigger than death. How could all of that be based on a lie?

Countless couples got married to "Forever," or renewed their wedding vows to it ten years later, believing that the sentiments sung for them by their role model would inspire them for a lifetime. Young black women daydreamed about finding a man as grand and sexy as R. Kelly; young black men daydreamed about living up to his example.

Just as the riff of Deep Purple's "Smoke On The Water" can make an old white guy from Munich or Milton Keynes instantly feel that all is right with the world and God is in His heaven, the programmed handclaps that usher in "Ignition (Remix)" can

---

*   "R Kelly Forever," uploaded to YouTube by fidelimages on June 20, 2013 (Penika's comment was added in 2018).

transport a generation of R&B lovers into a happy zone. That zone is not in the real world but in their brain, and while some of the paths to it now have roadblocks, others are still clear. It's the "Two Little Boys" conundrum all over again. They're all atremble. There's room on their horse for two. They're feelin' what he's feelin'.

Except that what R. Kelly was feelin' was not what they thought he was feelin'. And the limousine in the video will not take those slinky young girls to a fun party where they can feel naughtily empowered, but to a place of sordid entrapment.

o o o

The awareness that music, once we've loved it, cannot be un-loved, makes some people fiercely determined not to be charmed by artists they've taken a dislike to. Granted, it may be too late to protect yourself against something you heard when you were six, or even fourteen, but you're damned if you'll let someone new do it to you now.

But how can such preemptive self-protection work? Our neural pathways have already been laid for sounds of particular kinds. Voices and sonorities that remind us of the things we've loved in the past will tempt us to love them, too. We've been groomed by our sonic conditioning. One guitar chord is all it takes. One oboe note. One scrape of a fiddle. Four taps on the hi-hat before the drums go bam. And your heart goes boom. And then you find out that the musician who's made your heart go boom is your enemy.

o o o

Artistically speaking, the career of Steven Morrissey, former lead singer of The Smiths, has had its ups and downs. His debut solo album after the band's breakup promised great things, but by the mid-1990s his songs had become drab and plodding, reaching their nadir on *Maladjusted*.

Recent years have seen him taking more risks with style and instrumentation. His voice is in fine shape, as supple and expressive an instrument as it's ever been. His lyrics, once so fresh, are frequently convoluted and peevish, but, from a strictly musical point of view, he's in a good place.

In 2019, he released an album of cover versions called *California Son*, on which he illuminates unexpected facets of songs seldom if ever covered by other artists. As cover albums go, it's among the better ones I've heard, never less than interesting, full of subtle nuances.

Here is the opening sentence of the *Guardian* review of *California Son*: "A week after Morrissey appeared on a late-night talk show wearing a badge in support of an anti-Islam, far-right minor political party (not to mention the preceding decade of contentious proclamations), it is impossible to hear a number of the covers on *California Son* in anything but a chilling light."[*]

Accompanying Laura Snapes's review are photographs and links highlighting Morrissey's political views: "Badge of dishonor… Morrissey shows his support for For Britain on The Tonight Show"; "World's oldest record store bans Morrissey sales over far-right support (Read more)." The function of these links could be described as a kind of armor, protecting the review from any intimate contact with the despised creator of the music.

Over in Canada, Oliver Thompson's review in *Exclaim!* similarly kicks off with a litany of Morrissey's social sins, such as "a recent appeal to dog whistle politics on Jimmy Fallon, as well as many other indefensible comments." The ambiguity for which Morrissey was admired early in his career now "reeks of gro-

---

[*]   "Morrissey: California Son review—clumsy covers with a troll-like spirit" by Laura Snapes, *The Guardian*, May 24, 2019.

tesque hypocrisy" and Thompson concludes: "Do not listen to this album."[*]

Unlike the grieving Rolf Harris fans, or the R. Kelly fans who couldn't face the truth about their hero, these reviewers have no formative personal history with Morrissey. Laura Snapes wasn't even born when The Smiths broke up. She wants to nip any potential for a relationship in the bud. A suave, handsome voice is moving toward her, and it must be repelled before it takes any liberties.

I'm not suggesting that Laura Snapes or Oliver Thompson would've enjoyed *California Son* if they'd given it more of a chance. The album might not be to their taste even if its maker was a darling of the progressive left.

What I do feel confident to say is that the agenda of reviews like this is to make the music impossible to hear—to shut the reader's ears to it. The sounds emitted by Morrissey's vocal cords and by the instruments of his fellow musicians are distorted and muffled, buried under a barrage of disapproval. The reviewers are strenuously trying to hear as little as possible, and they hope that you, a potential sucker for Morrissey's tainted charms, will hear nothing at all.

o   o   o

Is it right to treat sounds this way?

Most albums, even the so-so ones, are labors of love. A great deal of time, effort, expertise and imagination are poured into them. Ideas are tried out, abandoned, upgraded.

The journey from scribbled ideas to final overdubs can be fascinating to read about. Getting to grips with The Beatles' thirteen albums, for example, would probably require a newcomer to read Ian MacDonald's *Revolution in the Head* (a book of about 115,000 words)—for a start. The reviews of *California Son*, focus-

---

[*]   "Morrissey: California Son" by Oliver Thompson, *Exclaim!*, May 21, 2019.

ing mostly on Morrissey's political views, are typically less than 300 words, with maybe 100 words discussing the music itself.

Listen: let's sit down with just one tiny aspect of one track.

The person playing synthesizer on Morrissey's version of Joni Mitchell's "Don't Interrupt The Sorrow" is Roger Joseph Manning Jr. He's had a substantial, eclectic career, collaborating with Jay-Z, Johnny Cash, Air, and Beck, as well as his own bands Jellyfish and The Moog Cookbook. On "Don't Interrupt The Sorrow," he conjures a sound that blurs the boundaries between a Fender Rhodes—that mainstay of the pioneering jazz-rock that made Joni Mitchell's ears light up in the late sixties—and the Moog—that mainstay of overblown prog rock, repurposed here in the subtlest of contexts. Two minutes into the recording, Manning executes a skirl that is uncannily similar to Mitchell's own Moog playing on "The Jungle Line" from her 1975 album *The Hissing Of Summer Lawns* (on which "Don't Interrupt The Sorrow" first appeared). The note lasts barely a second but its distinctiveness and impact are remarkable. I wouldn't be surprised if Manning meant it as an homage.

But you know what? No journalist is ever going to ask Roger Joseph Manning Jr. whether that Moog part was meant as an homage. No journalist will ask Morrissey about the arrangement of "Don't Interrupt The Sorrow" or indeed about any of the hundreds of decisions that were made in the arranging and playing of *California Son*. They will ask Morrissey what the hell he was thinking on May 13, 2019, when he wore a badge promoting a fringe political party on a late-night talk show.

o o o

Is this punishment just?

Maybe it is. Morrissey is a man as well as a musician. Melodious noises are not the only things he brings into the world. The social unrest whipped up by far-right groups causes harm and misery to citizens—more citizens, I imagine, than might be entertained by a rather good Morrissey CD. If a gentle, law-abiding Muslim is beaten up in the street by racist thugs, he will get no comfort from being told about Roger Manning's Moog work on "Don't Interrupt The Sorrow." And if I met Laura Snapes, she might righteously remind me that there are more important things to worry about than music.

Indeed there are.

But please, let's be honest about what we're doing when we take a stand against musicians on the basis of their moral short-comings or political allegiances. Let's not drag Art into the discussion and fool ourselves that we're using finely tuned aesthetics to torpedo our enemies' reputations. Let's not pretend we've listened to the work, analyzed and pondered it, examined what it's attempting to achieve and whether it's achieved it, and now, in our wisdom, we've come to the conclusion that it's bad.

No, we're glad that the music has not got its hooks in us, and we're determined to evade those hooks at any cost. We're opting out, we're backing off, we're slamming the door.

We're giving ourselves permission to cover our ears and loudly chant "La la la…"

LET'S RUMBLE

Henry Rollins doesn't look like the sort of guy you want to get into a fight with. Advancing age may have reduced his musculature to something less fearsome than the Incredible Hulk dimensions he once sported, but he is still a meaty dude with macho tattoos and a big mouth.* And the thing he feels most pugnacious about is the virtues of vinyl.

"There is no such thing as 'digital music,'" he scoffs. "There is no Led Zeppelin on a Led Zeppelin CD. There isn't a nanosecond of music on any music streaming service."

Music, for Rollins, only exists on vinyl LPs, vinyl singles, and…erm…cassettes, which admittedly aren't vinyl but might as well be because they're old-school and remind him of his formative years. Anything digital is the enemy.

Henry used to be a member of the hardcore American punk group Black Flag, but nowadays he's a member of a religion: the religion of vinyl worship. I'm not being flippant when I phrase it that way. Rollins's zealotry, which is replicated in many other like-minded souls throughout the world—almost certainly including someone you know, or maybe even *you*—ticks all the boxes of religious faith. He is a true believer.

★   Lest you think I'm being insulting or reductive here, one of Henry Rollins's many spoken-word albums is called *Big Ugly Mouth*. He has a sense of humor. Just not about vinyl.

o   o   o

During the twentieth century, in large factories in every developed nation, the music industry pressed millions and millions of circular plops of black plastic. Armies of workers at fast-moving assembly lines inserted the discs into cardboard sleeves and stockpiled them in warehouses. Yet a vinyl worshipper like Henry Rollins does not perceive these objects as mere units of mass production. To him, they were organisms with soul.

When computer technology came along and superseded vinyl, the worshippers were aghast: it was like those sci-fi nightmares where aliens infiltrate our Earth and sneakily replace humans with androids. Rollins shudders when he tells the story of how we were fooled by the lies of the CD manufacturers: "The truth is that the blood of the music was being squeezed out in the process, leaving the listener in an icy, tinny, music-free wasteland of digital information."

Asked what vinyl LPs provide that other formats don't, Rollins declares: "Full frequency. There is simply more on them."*

o   o   o

Reader, this is simply not the case. Vinyl LPs are not "full frequency" and there is not more "on" them.

While we're at it, communion bread and wine don't turn into the body and blood of Jesus Christ when a priest waves his hand at them. Holy water is no different from ordinary water except that it's often dirtier and more likely to make you sick. The universe was not created in six days and the earth is not flat.

It doesn't matter how many people believe these things: they remain false.

---

* "Every record I own is a must-have," interview with Henry Rollins by Jennifer Otter Bickerdike, in *Why Vinyl Matters: A Manifesto from Musicians and Fans* (ACC Publishing Group, 2017).

o   o   o

Scientists and audio engineers will heave a deep sigh to see me
bothering to write this chapter. For them, it's an argument that
was settled long ago, like the arguments over evolution, witch-
craft, the causes of plague and cholera, the natural superiority of
Aryans, etc. Why waste time and energy debunking stuff that's
already been debunked?

I bother because I'm a music lover and I regularly commune
with other music lovers. They are my family. And while there's
no one in that family who'll try to tell me that Aryans are superior, I will occasionally be told, by correspondents I respect and
am fond of, that vinyl is the most authentic and high-fidelity of
all the music formats. This troubles me.

o   o   o

Listen: here are the facts. The history of recorded music has been
a history of hideously compromised formats being replaced by
less hideously compromised formats.

Édouard-Léon Scott de Martinville's phonautograms, recorded
in 1860, are unlistenable. Literally. They were made only to be
looked at. A brass funnel caught vibrations and a needle scratched
white patterns on parchment coated with soot. Just recently, with
the aid of computer software, audio archaeologists converted the
phonautogram of Scott de Martinville singing "Au Clair De La
Lune" so that we could actually hear it. It sounds like an Alpine
shepherd humming to himself during a hurricane.

Welcome to the signal-to-noise ratio problem.

o   o   o

Thomas Edison's phonographs, invented in the late 1870s, were
hand-cranked metal cylinders wrapped in tin foil. They delivered such awful results that Alexander Graham Bell and his team

soon improved the concept by using wax cylinders instead. These were a big hit with the public even though the "background" noise was actually foreground noise and sounded like a squad of Cossacks attacking snowy ground with shovels, while the music was distressingly faint by comparison. Moreover, the "records" were not records in any permanent sense because they wore out after being played a few dozen times.

Next came the gramophone disc. This was a flat platter made from secretions of the larvae of lac bugs, native to the forests of India and Thailand. It boggles the mind how much of this insect's excreta must've collected in the forty-odd years when the 78rpm shellac disc reigned supreme. The needles that rode in the grooves were made of steel (good for a few plays only), thorns and chips of bamboo. The Cossack squad was less obtrusive; on a really well-engineered and well-manufactured shellac disc, their racket was no louder than the music, and the music could be amplified with the aid of a giant brass ear-trumpet.

Vinyl came next—not derived from bug juice anymore, but from petroleum and cheap chlorine.

Before we discuss vinyl in depth, however, we must note another momentous development in the history of recorded sound—the invention of magnetic tape.

The big drawback of etching music directly onto wax or hardened insect slime had been that it sounded worse each time you played it, then became unusable, and the music was gone forever. Whereas if you recorded sound onto tape, that tape could act as the "mother" for batch after batch of discs, allowing the worn-out ones to be replaced. Also, magnetic tape had a much better signal-to-noise ratio. There was hiss, but none of the extra impedimenta that came with wax cylinders and gramophones.

o   o   o

It's at this point in the story that the vinyl worshippers make their first major error of logic.

"Vinyl is what's called a lossless format," declares technology pundit Matthew Hughes in his article "4 Reasons Why Vinyl Is Better Than Digital." "Nothing has been lost when pressing a record. It sounds as good as the producer or band intended."*

This notion of vinyl somehow capturing the pure, unmediated intentions of the music's original creators is repeated endlessly by the faithful. They point out that digital reproduction requires the music to be disassembled and converted into soulless "zeroes and ones," resulting in a mathematical simulacrum of human activity. Whereas vinyl, supposedly, channels all that sonic flesh and blood straight into an organic vessel.

Bunkum.

First off, almost all music recorded since World War II was recorded with the aid of microphones. Microphones already disassemble the sounds we make and reassemble them as electric impulses. The "soullessness," if you want to call it that, starts right there.

Second, if we're talking about music that's not classical or ultratraditional folk, the recording will almost certainly involve electrified instruments. Here again, an "organic" action (e.g. a finger vibrating a string) is converted into electric impulses: what we hear is not the finger or the string, but a uniquely modulated electrical blend encompassing the wood and metal of the instrument, the amplifier it's plugged into, and any pedals or effects units the player might be using. And "capturing" those electric impulses is a challenge that can be tackled in an almost infinite variety of ways, depending on the vision of the artists, the know-how of the producers and engineers, the specifications of the equipment and so on.

You want truly "natural" music-making? Sing lullabies to your children or go to evensong at your local church.

---

* "4 Reasons Why Vinyl Is Better Than Digital," an April 2015 article by Matthew Hughes, quoted widely, e.g. in "Listening to Music: Vinyl Is Just Better," Medium.com, September 29, 2017.

Third, let's look at what a vinyl disc actually is and how it works. A vinyl disc is a pancake of plasticized polyvinyl chloride cooked up in a factory. The original tape (or digital file—most of today's vinyl LPs are actually mastered from digital files) emits its vibrations, and those vibrations are carved into a semimolten acetate with a cutting lathe. The resulting disc is then used to create a metal "negative" mold (a reverse of the disc with the carvings sticking out, like welts) which is, in turn, used to stamp thousands of shop-ready discs, until the mold wears out and a fresh one must be made.

Many vinyl records of music that was recorded in the 1950s and '60s, but reissued in the 1970s, '80s and '90s, were manufactured from molds that never "heard" the original tapes, because the original tapes had been thrown away or lost. Even when the tapes still existed, they were subject to decay because of the ferric oxide on them, which, if not stored properly, could turn them into musty ribbons of gunge.*

Anyway, let's be positive. Let's trust that the "stamper" used to create your disc was a good one and not defective or exhausted, and that it was derived from a healthy master tape rather than a sticky old mess hauled out of a rusted tin. At the end of the production line, you have your freshly manufactured LP or 45. A nice shiny splat of polyvinyl hot off the press.

When the disc has cooled, you can pick it up and peer at it, and you will see that each side contains a spiral groove. This groove contains thousands of microscopic bumps and troughs. At home, when you set the disc spinning at 33 or 45 revolutions per minute and allow a sharp object (typically a fragment of diamond, ruby or sapphire) to ride in that groove, the music's vibrations are reproduced, albeit very, very faintly.

This tinny, whispery signal (which you can hear in its "natural" state on those occasions when you try to play a record

---

* Attempts to rescue them involve a process that's reassuringly low-tech and "organic"—baking them in an oven.

having forgotten to switch the amplifier on) is then processed through many components of the equipment—the cartridge, the tone arm, the valves or circuitry in the amp, the speakers— emerging as a loud, vivid approximation of whatever was on the original recording.

But don't cheer too soon.

The needle that rides in the groove bashes and scrapes and judders against the contours of the landscape—that's what it's meant to do. Each time it makes that journey, there's wear and tear. Think of those Cossacks marching across a rocky field, hundreds of times over, in hobnailed boots. Eventually, the surface of the field changes.

When a vinyl disc is brand-new, the first play is the best you'll ever get. Almost inevitably, there will already be some unwanted pops, clicks and rustles, because molten polyvinyl chloride is prone to manufacturing defects—rogue bubbles, irregularities in the heating and cooling phases, or impurities in the vinyl itself. Each additional play will degrade the surface a little more.

For classical fans—the first tribe within the general public to get rid of their LPs and replace them with CDs—bidding good riddance to vinyl was a no-brainer. Classical music often includes interludes of silence or near-silence, in which vinyl's pops, crackles, clicks and rustles have ample opportunity to misbehave. A punk fan who plays his much-loved single of the Ramones' "Blitzkrieg Bop" may feel a frisson of satisfaction at the surface noise that reminds him that this copy of the record is his and his alone. A classical audiophile who wants to float away to a Debussy sonata probably won't feel the same joy when the vinyl goes *krok-krok fniffle fnerp*.

Even when brand-new, the vinyl LP will sound worse toward the end of each side than it sounds in the first few tracks near the outer rim. Back in the sixties and seventies, members of bands used to fight among themselves as to which songs would be placed at the beginnings of the sides and which would be pushed toward the spindle. The reason was basic physics: the speed at which the needle is dragged through its rut increases as the spiral gets smaller. So, in order for the needle not to be jolted out of the groove in those cramped spirals toward the end, the terrain needs to be less bumpy. Not so many low frequencies, not so many high ones. An increase in artificial compression, confining everything to the mid range. Which means the music has less oomph. If the artist was foolish enough to defy the engineers' cautions and insist on less compression, the stylus would skip.

Unavoidably, the ride itself makes noise, over and above the music. You're dragging a sharp object through a ditch and amplifying the results massively. It's a credit to the clever folk who design hi-fi systems that the rumble of "silence" in the non-eventful parts of a vinyl record is as muted as it is. But muted rumble is still rumble.

o   o   o

And here is where we encounter another of the vinyl worshippers' religious convictions. Matthew Hughes speaks for all his brethren when he extols vinyl's "warm, mahogany-rich sound."* "Warm" is the word that every devotee resorts to when trying to articulate why they love the medium so. "Rich," "lifelike," "full," "deep" and "depth" also feature frequently, but not as often as "warmth" and "warm"—contrasted with the supposed coldness and sterility of digital reproduction.

They're not imagining this "warmth." It's really there. Unlike the claims of vinyl's greater dynamic range, which can be easily disproved with graphs, the claims for vinyl's warmth, its mystical *presence*, cannot be discounted on scientific grounds.

The mistake the worshippers make, however, is to ascribe this warmth to the music the artists made—warmth that's been "lost" during the evil conversion into digital data. In fact, the

---

*   "4 Reasons Why Vinyl Is Better Than Digital," Matthew Hughes.

warmth is the added distortion that comes with the medium's limitations. It's the mechanical hum of the turntable as it turns. It's the rumble of the needle in the groove. It's the subtle swish of built-up dust and dirt. It's the way the highs and lows smoosh together in the mid range. Many people find those extra layers tremendously comforting—especially if they've grown up with them.

The phrase "mahogany-rich" in reference to sound is significant. Comparing mercurial sound waves to an inert material like mahogany is not, on the face of it, an obvious line of praise. But what the vinyl devotee has in mind is old-fashioned record players from a past era of decor. The cabinet that housed the phonograph and the radiogram might indeed be made of mahogany. It would certainly not be made of glass or black steel. In the devotee's mind, the organic luster of the wood has seeped into the plastic discs associated with that furniture.*

The wooden cabinet is a shrine, of course, in a way that a computer or phone can never be. (Although phones serve very well as rosary beads.) The record-playing furniture is a locus at which one must literally kneel. "Vinyl requires you to be where a record player is," explains Henry Rollins. "Time, place, ritual, etc. The area around the system is your temple—all are welcome. The system—the sermon [...] I can't explain to you how important this is to me."

Then there's the holy pilgrimage: "Sometimes, when I visit where I come from, I walk by houses and apartments where I would hang out with others and listen to records. Those places have a lot of meaning to me… I remember walking a long way through the snow to buy *Physical Graffiti*…"†

---

*   In a marginal note on my manuscript, Louisa suggests that a vinyl disc may evoke associations with horizontal slices of tree, complete with age rings.

†   "Every record I own is a must-have," interview with Henry Rollins by Jennifer Otter Bickerdike.

o   o   o

I don't intend this chapter to be a diatribe against vinyl, much less a diatribe against those who love vinyl. I'm very fond of my old records. As I get older and my eyesight deteriorates, I can no longer read the print in CD booklets, so I take refuge in the 12"x12" luxury of my LPs, perusing them like art books. Because that's what they are. Proper bits of publishing.

There's a turntable less than a meter from my elbow as I write these words. I play vinyl regularly. Sometimes it sounds fab and I reconnect with the pleasure of lifting the stylus with my finger and lowering it into the groove, the tactile knack of flipping the disc in my palms to play the other side. Sometimes it annoys the hell out of me, because the needle jumps, or the bass is feeble, or a scratch that I can barely see is causing ugly noises, or a sweaty thumbprint from thirty years ago has turned into a kind of superglue for motes of dirt. Sometimes, when I extract a disc from a stiff paper inner sleeve, I see that a crease in the paper has left a fresh mark on the surface of the vinyl, and I reflect on the sheer absurdity of a music storage medium that can be damaged just by brushing it against paper. Other times, I put on an LP, settle down with a sumptuous booklet of lyrics and pictures, and get pleasantly overwhelmed by the holistic overload of it all.

I'm not nostalgic, but I understand that most people are. I think it's sweet that the fourteen-year-old Henry Rollins walked a long way through snow to buy *Physical Graffiti* and I think it's sweet that he's proud of it. Many vinyl lovers have lifelong relationships with LPs that belonged to their dead parents, or that revolved on a turntable while they were losing their virginity, or whose covers have been wept upon or stared at in the hope that they might impart the meaning of life. I get that. Those relationships are poignant and good.

I also respect that some people enjoy the sound of vinyl more than they enjoy the sound of digital. Music happens in the brain, not in some abstract realm of graphs and meters. If the "warmth" of vinyl's groove rumble makes you deeply happy, you are more blessed than a CD nerd who is deeply dissatisfied by the kilohertz parameters of the 1995 German remaster compared to the 2003 Japan-only remaster that he can't get hold of but has read about in a hi-fi magazine.

Throughout the history of recorded music, listeners have used their highly adaptable brains to screen out distortion and compensate for poor fidelity. Our ears are clever. If bass is missing, we supply it. If the signal is feeble, we can make allowances. Love can surmount extraordinary barriers, and there's no doubt that people in the past fell passionately in love with sounds they heard on wax cylinders, platters of baked goo and transistor radios. Outrageously degraded approximations of Mozart or the Mississippi blues have given people sublime epiphanies. Even today, a person's life may be forever changed by a song they hear twittering out of their mobile phone. Each of us hears music uniquely, and each reproduction format behaves in ways that some find pleasing and others don't. God bless them all.

But keep in mind: the only medium that's "full frequency" is your head.

GIRL YOU KNOW IT'S TRUE

The music business has always been full of it. Pop stars miming to vocals sung by anonymous professionals. Pretty boys posing with guitars they didn't even know how to hold, let alone play. Sheepish drummers making approximate gestures in the video. The classic camera angle where the star who cannot play piano sits at a piano, hands obscured, or glimpsed for one brisk second only.

Everyone in the industry knew that such deceptions were par for the course. But the public mustn't know. Cred-wise, there was no greater shame than being The Monkees, who had openly admitted that they (*gasp!*) didn't play on their records.

As the production of pop became more and more technological, the challenge of keeping fakery a secret grew bigger. Fortunately, the public seemed determined to cling on to their innocence in the face of overwhelming evidence. The music they were buying transparently had little or no input from the poster children who posed for the *Smash Hits* photo shoots, yet the buyers seemed not to notice. Kylie Minogue, Frankie Goes To Hollywood, or Dead or Alive could enthuse to journalists about the music they'd made—music assembled in their absence by engineers.

The advent of MTV helped weaken people's grasp on reality. The channel broadcast music videos twenty-four hours a day, seven days a week, and almost everything was storyboarded and mimed. Viewers were taught to expect to see musicians exploring spooky castles, clowning around on yachts, flying through space, swordfighting in medieval battles, transforming into monsters. The artists got respect twice over—first for having recorded the music, unseen, in some earlier elsewhere, and then for their talent as video-makers.*

Within this jamboree of fabrication, the public's disapproval of anything "fabricated" remained staunch. Artists had a sacred duty to be authentic, to "keep it real." Let no one dare to betray the trust of the audience! Or else!

A spectacular "or else" moment arrived in 1990, when a scandal erupted. A scandal that, like many scandals, seized upon one totemic case from among thousands that had somehow been overlooked. A scandal that would prove fatal for one of the scapegoats.

∘ ∘ ∘

Fabrice Morvan was a French model and dancer of Guadeloupe extraction; Rob Pilatus was likewise a model and dancer, originally an abandoned GI baby adopted from an orphanage in Munich. They teamed up in a nightclub, where their dance moves and luscious physiques were noticed by German producer Frank Farian, mastermind behind the megaselling 1970s disco "group" Boney M.

Boney M had consisted of Farian himself and various employees, among them a nominal "singer" who had to mime Farian's vocals in public. Farian figured he could work the same commercial magic with these fresh new lads.

They were called Milli Vanilli, and (if we believe their subsequent version of events) they had fully expected to sing on their records only to be told that this service was not required. The

---

*   The Police, a trio of top-class instrumentalists who played every note of their 1983 hit "Synchronicity II," filmed the promo clip on a phantasmagorical sci-fi set of vertiginous scaffolds, buffeted by an artificial hurricane. Sting mimed his vocal while hanging, Tarzan-like, from a rope, pantomiming wild-eyed madness for all he was worth. All in a day's work for a modern musician.

debut single, "Girl You Know It's True," was already finished and Fabrice and Rob were recruited merely to caper around to it, mime the words, and look handsome. They spent their advance on clothes and hair extensions.

Milli Vanilli were a smash success. Three US number 1 hits, a platinum album (tellingly called *All Or Nothing*), and a Grammy Award for Best New Artist in 1990.[*] Multitudes screamed in delight whenever Fab and Rob wiggled their hips and shook their bogus locks. Glamorously brown, with no race affiliation except the race to the top, the boys spoke English with thick accents, but when they opened their mouths to sing, they sounded immaculately American—sounded, in fact, like Charles Shaw and Brad Howell, the real singers behind their miming.

The pretense came undone when, during a "live" performance in Connecticut in front of eighty thousand fans, the CD of "Girl You Know It's True" got stuck and the hapless pair were forced to flee offstage as the prerecorded vocal hiccuped "GirlyouknowitGirlyouknowitGirlyouknowitGirlyouknowit…" without mercy.

It was then that the shit that had been passing through cash registers began to hit the fan. Pushed into a corner by legal threats from one of the actual vocalists, Farian confessed that Morvan and Pilatus had not sung on any of the product.

The whole world rose up in righteous indignation. Under a hailstorm of hate, Fab and Rob gave press conferences in the hope of redeeming their irredeemable honor. "You get something," explained Rob, "but for that you make a pact with the devil."[†] Waving their Grammy for the cameras, they ceremoni-

---

[*]   Milli Vanilli and their Grammy Award were actually a pretty good match. The Grammys maintain an undeserved reputation as an artistic honor, while actually being an orgy of corporate schmoozing, where the major labels congratulate themselves on how much money they've made and how many managers are desperate to get their clients nominated.

[†]   "Rob Pilatus Death 1998 – The Truth About Milli Vanilli," uploaded to YouTube by MilliVanilliFanclub on March 22, 2014.

ally gave it back—but it had been rescinded anyway. The label dumped them and the album was deleted.

But the punishment of Milli Vanilli did not end there. A number of lawsuits were brought against the pariah duo and their erstwhile record company, for consumer fraud.* The plaintiffs (i.e. angry ex–Milli Vanilli fans) cited the "emotional distress" they experienced when they found out that their idols were lip-synching. Defrauded customers were entitled to claim refunds for the records they'd bought and the concerts they'd attended. Such was the thoroughness of redress that I'm surprised the fans weren't offered counseling for the terrible trauma of having been led to believe these dreamboats were the ones singing "Baby Don't Forget My Number" and "Girl I'm Gonna Miss You."

Rob Pilatus could certainly have benefited from some counseling. His life spiraled into alcoholism, suicide attempts, sexual assault, grievous bodily harm, and a stretch in prison. His adoptive family watched in despair as the gorgeous child they'd brought home from the orphanage disintegrated. He died of an overdose at thirty-two.

The message for musical fakers was clear. Don't do it. Or, if you must do it, don't get caught. The public will not forgive.†

---

*   Such lawsuits had occasionally been threatened before, with no traction. For example, ELO were a big concert draw in the 1970s but their studio perfectionism was not a good match for sports arena conditions. In 1979, a promoter tried to sue them for a gig at the Pontiac Silverdome, at which the backing tape failed and it became apparent that some of the vocals and keyboards were prefab. A spokesperson for the band protested: "Anyone who knows anything knows that a lot of groups use tapes as part of their show." By "anyone who knows anything" he probably meant industry insiders rather than the public. See: "Why ELO's *Out of the Blue* marked a turning point" by Nick DeRiso, *Ultimate Classic Rock*, October 19, 2017.

†   At the time, the almost universal judgment on Milli Vanilli's downfall was "Serves them right!" The only musician who spoke out in defense of Rob and Fab was Les McKeown, former lead singer of credibility-free teen sensations the Bay City Rollers, whose records often featured no Rollers besides Les. "As far as I'm concerned people shouldn't be suing Milli Vanilli," he opined. "They kept to their part of the bargain—they sold sex and looked good. Didn't Rembrandt sign pictures other people had painted?" Quoted in "The

o o o

Since the Milli Vanilli debacle, our civilization has been on a wonderful journey. Every aspect of our lives has been converted into digital data, to be manipulated and transformed. We have become accustomed to a steady supply of fresh miracles. Most of these miracles involve the conversion of sounds and images into computerized digits for ever-more-sophisticated transfigurations. As the science fiction writer Arthur C. Clarke said in the 1980s, "Any smoothly functioning technology will have the appearance of magic." We've been working on that smoothness very hard. The mission is to make magic routine.

We're on a voyage to the outer limits of the unreal.

A concert by a big-name artist nowadays is a multimedia spectacle, a synergy of illusions, much like a Disney/Marvel movie with its multimillion-dollar collaboration of producers, second unit directors, designers, technicians and stunt doubles. The audience is not coming to hear a singer sing or a musician play; the audience is coming to witness an amazing extravaganza.

When the fans of twenty-first-century divas attend a concert, they see a beautiful superstar bouncing around a stage in a variety of costumes while a horde of spangly accomplices help to generate the circus vibe. The diva moves her lips, Milli Vanilli–like, and what comes out of the PA speakers is prerecorded.

Is this a scandal? Not at all. The fans don't care. You can point out to them that Katy or Britney or Ariana is not really singing, or what I would consider singing, but that's like pointing out that Pepsi is not nutritious. Nutrition is not what people drink Pepsi for. Tens of thousands of Britney Spears fans have come to see Britney strut her stuff and Britney provides plentiful strutting.

To be fair, if Aretha Franklin had been required to perform the aerobic athletics that Spears executes at her concerts, she would be hopelessly out of breath within minutes, Édith Piaf

Award Sinners" by Caroline Sullivan, *The Guardian*, August 17, 1991.

would've fallen to her knees and sobbed, and Luciano Pavarotti would've dropped dead of a cardiac arrest. The attendees
at Britney Spears concerts don't want to hear the tuneless pant-
ing that's coming out of Britney's actual mouth any more than
they want to see substandard CGI in a superhero film. It would
be an insult to their ticket purchase.

◦   ◦   ◦

This understanding that the grand display is what people are
paying for, not the exhalations from some individual's windpipe,
has legitimized what used to be perceived as fraud. There's no
dividing line between flimsy starlets and award-winning artistes
anymore: deception is an equal-opportunity employer.

Beyoncé sang "The Star-Spangled Banner" at President
Obama's inauguration in 2013. Or rather, she didn't: she mimed
it. Beyoncé is a perfectly capable singer, operating at a level far
above Spears. Moreover, she was not required to dance or ca-
vort; she only had to stand still and radiate patriotic dignity. But
the presidential inauguration was a big deal, a national celebra-
tion, televised across the planet. If something had gone wrong,
the whole world would've heard the wrongness.

"I am a perfectionist," Beyoncé explained afterward, as she
prepared for her next big engagement, singing at the Super Bowl
football match in the Mercedes-Benz Superdome. "I practice
until my feet bleed, and I did not have time to rehearse with
the orchestra… Due to the weather, due to the delay, due to no
proper sound check, I did not feel comfortable taking a risk."
This discomfort, and her keenness to make President Obama
and the viewers "proud," justified her decision to "go with a
prerecorded track, which is very common in the music industry. And I am very proud of my performance."* The brass band

---

*   "Beyonce Sings National Anthem Live at Super Bowl Press Conference," *Rolling
Stone*, January 31, 2013.

who accompanied her likewise mimed to a tape. In other words, nothing was real about that historic anthem except the participants' shared conviction that fakery was OK.

As a sixtysomething who came to intellectual maturity in a bygone century, I can't help thinking that the whole point of being a musician is that you "feel comfortable taking a risk." Or at least that you rise above your discomfort and conquer your fears, to weave the charms on which your reputation rests. For thousands of years, singers have braved bad weather, delays and inadequate rehearsal, taken a deep breath and sung. Whatever Beyoncé is, she is not a singer in this old-fashioned sense.

Mariah Carey is another example of an artist who has the voice box of a classic singer and the soul of a twenty-first-century multimedia entrepreneur. Blessed with a five-octave range and widely known as "Songbird Supreme," Carey can produce melismatics that Britney Spears could only dream of. But in 2016, at a New Year's Eve concert in New York's Times Square, during a performance of "Emotions," the synchronization between the vocal coming out of the speakers and Carey's lip movements went seriously awry, and Carey abandoned the charade in obvious pique.

In the days that followed, there was a media kerfuffle. But it was not about the ethics of miming. It was about who was to blame for the lapse in quality control—Mariah Carey, or *New Year's Rockin' Eve* organizers Dick Clark Productions. Carey's manager claimed that her client had been given defective earbuds (in-ear monitors) that made it impossible for her to mime accurately, an act of organizational negligence that amounted to "sabotage." Dick Clark Productions retorted that such an accusation was "defamatory, outrageous and frankly absurd."

Eminent sound engineer Phil Palazzolo, a veteran of many large-scale events like the Grammy Awards, the National Basketball Association's All-Star Game and previous editions of New Year's Rockin' Eve, was asked for his thoughts.

"I was shocked," he said, "mainly because at these events, there's fail-safe upon fail-safe upon fail-safes... They don't leave things to chance... Everything has to go exactly to plan." In his interview for *Cosmopolitan*, Palazzolo analyzes the mishap in forensic detail, debating the role of runtime sheets, earbud mixes, reinforcement tracks, the role of the monitor engineer, foldback wedges and nondisclosure agreements.

One thing he does not question is whether it's right to step onto a concert stage and fake it. "I think it's very naïve of a lot of people to think that when you see someone open their mouth, they're really singing," he reflects. As far as this eminent engineer is concerned, that fond notion is as childish as the need to "believe in Santa Claus."*

∘   ∘   ∘

I'm sitting on a Tube train in London. Next to me sits a woman in her twenties. She is brunette and beautiful and has big hair and porn-star false eyelashes. She is possibly of Italian or Spanish extraction, although it's hard to tell with all the makeup. She holds her phone aloft and takes a photo of her own face. She examines the results, then takes another, and another, and another. Finally she has what she provisionally wants. She opens an app on her iPhone and starts working on the image. At the click of one of her manicured thumbnails, she makes her eyes slightly larger and brighter. She removes a blemish from her forehead. She smooths out the tiny wrinkles at the corners of her eyes. She enhances her cheekbones. She slims her nose, makes the nostril holes softer. She makes her chin more oval, decides this is a step too far, reinstates the original chin. She experiments with skin tone.

The whole process takes about fifty seconds; she has done

---

*   "Explaining Mariah Carey's Lip-Sync Fail: An Expert Weighs In," Phil Palazzolo interviewed by Peggy Truong, *Cosmopolitan*, January 4, 2017.

this many times before. She uploads the final result onto a so-cial media platform, to show all her virtual friends that she is on the train, traveling somewhere exciting, looking beautiful.

Mission accomplished, she inserts tiny earbuds into her ears and selects some music to transmit from her phone to her brain. Her gadget displays a picture of the singer—a woman much like her, except very tanned, or possibly African American or Caribbean, or possibly white-wanting-to-appear-black, with a luxurious wig and ivory lips.

I detect a wisp of the music as it pulses into the earbuds. It sounds expensive. I sit there for a while, osmotically absorbing the aural aroma of fake R&B manufactured by entrepreneurs, the genre that's been chosen by this woman as the soundtrack of her life. I feel very old, very obsolescent, and I feel a perverse impulse to berate this total stranger, to tell her she is a symptom of everything that's wrong with contemporary society, to make her feel ashamed of being a mote of algae in a vast sea of deceit.

Then I remind myself: shallow as this woman may be, she is not the right person to drive poor Rob Pilatus to his death. She wasn't born when Milli Vanilli were around, but if someone were to tell her the tragic story, she wouldn't be able to under-stand the crux of it. This Rob guy with the beautiful skin and luscious eyebrows…why was everybody so mean to him? He did nothing wrong! If he was alive and just as handsome today, she'd stream him into her gadget for sure, and click the "Like" button.

Maybe that means the world has become a more forgiving place. Which is a good thing, right?

THE DEAD GIVE UP
THEIR DOONICANS

About a third of a million old people die in England every year.* This is irrespective of wars or pandemics. It's just the way it is when you've had your body for seventy-five years or more. The thing wears out.

These hundreds of thousands of deaths can be a tragedy for relatives who are suddenly bereft of their beloved pa or gran. But they also pose a problem for the nation's charity shops. It seems there's a never-ending influx of LPs by Val Doonican, Shirley Bassey, Harry Secombe, Jim Reeves, James Galway, Moira Anderson, Richard Clayderman, Roger Whittaker, The Bachelors, et al.

I used to wonder if the Val Doonican LPs I was seeing everywhere were actually the same few copies, shunted unsold from shop to shop in a vast exchange conspiracy between Barnardo's, the Red Cross, Oxfam, the Salvation Army and so on. But I've visited many cities and towns over the decades, and in recent years I've learned a lot about how the charity sector works. And no, these scuffed donations do not all come, ultimately, from the home of Alf and Eunice Bryant in Dunfermline. They were bought brand-new in the 1960s, '70s and '80s by great multitudes of individuals who are dying in their droves and whose cluttered council houses continue to be cleared in anticipation of new inhabitants. Many of these records will have gathered an

---

* "Death in people aged 75 years and older in England in 2017," Gov.uk website, June 14, 2019.

additional layer of dust in the homes of the dead people's children, who remember that "Mom used to love this," before finally conceding that they don't have the space anymore.

As culture evolves and the consumers who were once the younger generation become, in their turn, old and frail and extinct, the contents of the bags of vinyl donated to charity shops evolves too. Phil Collins, Eric Clapton, Dire Straits and ABBA are some of the newer mainstays. Who knew Shakin' Stevens made so many records? The steady flow of Neil Diamond has swollen into a deluge, as the blue-rinsed ladies who still carried a flame for him cease to make appointments with the hairdresser.

But the bulk of the stock remains Doonican and Bassey and the rest of that middle-of-the-road, easy-listening stuff patronized by citizens who were already middle-aged during the heyday of vinyl. Here, and only here, is where you might find *Timeless Favourites*, *Golden Memories* and *Hymns To Follow The Sunset*, just three of the eight LPs that comprise the handsome Reader's Digest box set *Songs Of Joy*.

o o o

If you're a keen charity-shopper, you may not see these items on open display. Charity shops are run professionally these days, with regional managers and sales strategists issuing directives from central office. If the aim is to raise money for cancer research or maltreated cats or drought-afflicted Ethiopian farmers, it makes no sense for the shops to allot shelf space to items that nobody wants to buy.

The fiftysomething children of dead eighty-year-olds bring in their mom's Harry Secombe and Max Bygraves LPs, imagining that there must be someone out there who would enjoy them. Yes, there are many such individuals. But they are unfortunately buried in the ground and would cause much consternation if they were to walk into the shop.

Thus, as time passes, the mind-bogglingly compendious inventory of unsalable records lurks largely underground too. There's a sort of Doonican substratum in our retail environment, a melancholy limbo situated midway between the light of day and the landfill. Here, slightly crumpled box sets documenting the golden years of swing rub shoulders with mottled Music For Pleasure compilations of Mrs. Mills and Lulu.

o o o

Many charity shops circa 2023 actually have more vinyl on display than CDs. Not Shirley Bassey or Jim Reeves, but "classic" rock items by Whitesnake, Fleetwood Mac, Stevie Wonder, Kate Bush, Prince. The bottom has fallen out of the secondhand CD market, but the right vinyl gets a fresh lease on life. The demographic that spend a lot of time (and money) in charity shops are nostalgic about the music they liked when they were seventies/eighties youngsters, or else they're millennials on the lookout for cool retro. Another factor is that virtually any old CD can be procured for pennies from Amazon or eBay, whereas vinyl is bulky and thus incurs hefty postage costs if bought online. Much better to stash that vintage Wings album into your tote bag and support a good cause at the same time.

o o o

In the end, it's a numbers game. There are millions of discarded Shirley Bassey LPs still in circulation and perhaps only a couple of thousand living Britons who might want them. Whereas the number of David Bowie LPs in circulation and the number of people who think it would be cool to own one is more evenly matched.[*]

---

[*]   In the 1980s, *Lodger*, by far the weakest of Bowie's so-called Berlin Trilogy, used to turn up regularly in bargain bins, and in the 1990s you could pick up discarded copies of *Let's Dance* and *Tonight* for a few quid in pretty much any decent charity shop. Now those artifacts are becoming rarer and more prized, as Bowie continues to be meaningful to consumers who are still young and

According to this arithmetic, Freddie Mercury may be dead, but he's not as dead as Harry Secombe. Queen songs are still being played on mainstream radio, and Queen are still being written about in music magazines, and there are still plenty of friends and neighbors who remember seeing them at Wembley, which reassures the citizens of the nation that buying an old Queen record in a charity shop is the sort of thing that modern, vigorous, not-dead-yet people do.

o o o

The future? Hard to say. A lot depends on what happens to digital platforms. At the moment, almost all the music that anyone is in the mood to hear can be summoned up instantly on phones and other devices. That won't last forever. It may not even last for long. What will come in its place, I can't predict. How motivated will tomorrow's nostalgists be to hear Eminem or Taylor Swift again if the digisphere goes quiet? Will CDs by Alicia Keys and Oasis and Coldplay, which are currently tossed into waste bins, become expensive collector's items? It seems unlikely. But culture can move in mysterious ways.

One thing we shouldn't assume is that the music in the basements and back rooms of charity shops is unwanted because our parents and grandparents liked bad music whereas we don't. Bad taste, if there is such a thing, is eternal. That is, there will always be freshly made music catering for people who don't like music very much, who want something bland and inoffensive to tint the background, or who buy whatever their peer group is buying only to discard it when its moment of social relevance passes. Deservedly or undeservedly, 99 percent of the stuff that's "current" today will be obsolete and unloved fifty years from now. The zeitgeist just wears out.

---

healthy enough to shop for music.

o   o   o

How bad is Val Doonican? As "bad" as Bruno Mars or BTS or Jon Batiste, I guess. That is, like those up-to-the-minute luminaries of the twenty-first-century pop scene, Doonican was a run-of-the-mill entertainer servicing the ephemeral needs of customers wishing to be pleasantly distracted. To my ears, Doonican's version of "Wichita Lineman" is bad; that is, glaringly inferior to Glen Campbell's. But Glen, too, has been consigned to the musty basement next to Val. All too soon, Bruno Mars will twinkle out of mainstream consciousness and sink into the underworld alongside them.

In any case, Bruno will be seriously outclassed by some of the musicians down there. It was in a charity shop, for a pittance, that I picked up an LP by Les Paul and Mary Ford, pioneers of the electric guitar and multitrack technology, without whose visionary talents much of the music we listen to today could not exist. It was in a charity shop that I first discovered Johnny Cash, Bobbie Gentry, the Jacques Loussier Trio, The Andrews Sisters. There's lots of classical down there too: not just Gilbert and Sullivan or the Nutcracker Suite, but heavyweights like Beethoven and Wagner. These artists may have been thrown by pitiless market forces into the company of Liberace and Chas & Dave, but they have little in common. Imagine how you'd feel if you were Billie Holiday having to share a cell with Benny Hill.

I would not relish the responsibility of explaining to a Venusian—or even a Cambodian or Nigerian—why DJ Khaled is more important than Paul Robeson, or why Doja Cat is more worthy of respect than Nana Mouskouri.

o   o   o

Mouskouri is a particularly interesting example. Every bargain basement and charity shop junk pile is littered with her albums. Yet she had a strikingly fine voice, which she deployed with intelligence no matter what material she tackled. She could sing with admirable appreciation of nuance in four different languages—Greek, Italian, French and English—and had a credible bash at many more. She was physically beautiful but never pandered to the beauty industry, she had poise and grace, and she sailed through the male-chauvinist sixties and seventies without demeaning herself or being exploited. She was, as the Americans say, one classy lady.

And she sold more than 350 million records. Just chew on that figure for a moment. Three hundred and fifty million. Nana is the highest-selling female artist worldwide, ever.* That claim is often made for Madonna, who sold less, because the journalists and media folk who crunch such data automatically discount Mouskouri. Her face doesn't fit.

Conversing with music lovers about music is one of the main things I do. The talk sometimes drifts to female vocalists of the western pop scene. Who's in the pantheon? Names get bandied about. Aretha Franklin, Janis Joplin, Björk, Linda Thompson, Sandy Denny. Someone will carry a torch for Marianne Faithfull. Another will protest that we're forgetting Chrissie Hynde. A youngster might suggest Janelle Monáe. At no point will anybody mention Nana Mouskouri. The very idea is laughable. But why?

If, in such a conversation, I brought up Diamanda Galás (an American avant-garde vocalist who, coincidentally, has origins stretching back to Greece) I would have more chance of impressing my companions than if I brought up Nana Mouskouri. This despite the fact that Galás has sold comparatively few records, and makes a noise that many listeners would describe as ugly, and that even I, with my appetite for abrasive sounds, am not often in the mood for her terrifying screams. Yet she is Someone To Be Taken Seriously. If I derailed the cozy chat by enthusing about

---

*   "Nana Mouskouri: The Highest Selling Female Artist Worldwide," Greek Gateway website, undated.

"Wild Women With Steak-Knives" from Galás's *The Litanies Of Satan*, the unease would be mild compared to the embarrassment I would cause if I urged everyone to consider Nana Mouskouri.

This troubles me, not because I harbor some deep love for easy-listening fare sung by a Greek chanteuse. (I liked Nana well enough when I was growing up, but I own just one of her albums.) What troubles me is the invisibility—the deliberate erasure—of her 350 million records from any sophisticated overview of twentieth-century female vocalists.

It makes you wonder what else is being buried.

o   o   o

My father died in 1984, at fifty-nine, considerably younger than John Lydon or Iggy Pop are now. His musical taste had stenosed sometime in the early 1960s, before our family's emigration to Australia, so it reflected the enthusiasms of a working-class Dutchman in his mid to late thirties. He didn't own anything that dated from his teenage years or early twenties, maybe because he'd grown up in grim poverty, and then joined the army, and then been in a punishment camp for Nazi collaborators. The opportunity to be a connoisseur of phonographic art didn't come round, for him, till quite late.

Everything in my father's modest collection was charity shop material. The closest he came to cool was a budget Duke Ellington compilation.

My mother didn't care for music much. She preferred knitting, and the ticking of her cuckoo clocks in the stillness.

After my father's death, my mother had no use for his LPs so she passed them on to me. They hadn't been played in a long time; my dad had spent his declining years in silence broken only by the television, and by the ticking and cuckooing of the misaligned timepieces hanging in every room. Postimmigration, I suspect his records got more love from me than they got from him, and I can't say I truly loved them.

Apart from the aforementioned Duke Ellington, there was Lionel Hampton, Harry James, Louis Armstrong, Sidney Bechet, Benny Goodman. All well-respected jazz stars, key figures in jazz history, nothing for any hipster to be ashamed of, except that the albums my father possessed were on cheap reissue labels and thus not collectible.

Then there was the Dutch Swing College Band. It was only recently, when doing research for *Listen*, that I learned that this Netherlandish combo was originally formed as an act of underground resistance to the Nazi regime's ban on jazz. Was owning a couple of their LPs part of Henk Faber's attempted atonement for his fateful decision to join the German army?

Another of his LPs was *Mazzel* by Leo Fuld, a Dutch Jew who sang schmaltzy songs in Yiddish. Dad bought that only a few months before emigrating to the other side of the planet— more than ten thousand miles away from the country where he would always be under a cloud of shame. On the cover of *Mazzel*, a smiling Leo steps off the access stairs of an El Al jetliner, onto the welcoming ground of postwar Paris.

Another item I inherited, and swiftly donated to the Red Cross, was Jim Reeves's *Have I Told You Lately That I Love You?* I've lost count of the number of charity shops I've seen this in. I can only idly wonder what need Jim Reeves serviced in my father that wasn't serviced by jazz.

I can imagine more easily what swayed my dad to buy *Polynesia!: Native Songs And Dances From The South Seas*. The Pacific Island lady on the front cover is bare-breasted, with soft-focus but anatomically distinct nipples. I've no doubt that my father enjoyed the noises made by Charles Mauu ("an actual Tahitian chief," according to the liner notes) but I'm also aware that he suffered chronic sexual frustration.*

---

* Among the very few books in our family's petite bookcase was *The Joy of Sex*, which my dad had carefully sheathed in beige wallpaper so that visitors, and perhaps my mother and me, wouldn't be able to read the spine.

Polynesia was just one of the exotic foreign regions in my father's music stash. He was partial to Greek folk music, as exemplified by The Hellenes, who'd been "recorded live at an actual party." Another budget item was *The Heavenly Sound Of Negro Spirituals*, by Hugh E. Porter & His Gospel Singers, all the way from Harlem via the same company that brought us The Waikiki 12, and Juan Montez and His Flamenco Troupe. France was represented by Adamo's single "Vous Permettez, Monsieur?" and Italy by Nini Rosso's "Il Silenzio." Russia was a late arrival. The Ivan Rebroff LP *Starportrait* must've been bought in Australia, most likely in the early seventies. Both my parents liked Ivan's big furry Cossack hat and the way he sang "Ach, Natascha!" on the telly. They liked Nana Mouskouri too, but she was on every week so there was no need to actually buy an LP.

My dad harbored particular affection for Austrian and Swiss folk music, and, until his death, wore a Tyrolean hat made of green felt, with a discreet feather affixed to the band. His half-dozen Alpine LPs are all valueless today.

The one I've pulled out just now, *Alpenrose*, ticks all the boxes of kitsch. It's a mixture of oompah-oompah, yodel and waltz ditties by ensembles like Thomas Wendlinger und Seine Schrammeln and Das Alpengruß Trio. It starts with the cheerful clonking of cowbells (tick), the cover is a snapshot of a Swiss or Austrian mountain complete with babbling brook (tick), there's an Alpine rose entwined in the calligraphy (tick), my dad has signed the front with his surname in the top left corner (tick, although a Dymo label would've earned extra points), the spine is ragged with age and ineptly mended with piss-yellow sellotape (tick), and the back advertises LPs by other artistes (tick) on the same long-defunct label, such as Acker Bilk, Terry Lightfoot, Monty Sunshine, Bizet, and The Mena Minstrels (quintuple tick).

I play *Alpenrose*, expecting it to irritate me. Instead, the music is what it is—vivid, eccentric, geographically specific folk. The taste arbiters in our culture have judged that it is uncool, but it's the real thing from a distinct ethnic tribe, captured very soon after the end of World War II. Bandleader Wendlinger was born in 1909, when Bavaria was still a kingdom. I realize, as his ensemble yodels and wheezes at me, that this music is no less interesting, authentic and vibrant than Jamaican toasting, Tuvan throat-singing, Ghanaian highlife or any of the other folk musics that our culture has deigned to regard as artistically valid. Some authority somewhere has condemned it for reasons they'll never be called upon to justify.

o   o   o

The rest of my father's records were *schlager.*

Schlager was, and in certain households and hostelries still is, the pop music of working-class and lower-middle-class Germans. The term has been adopted in half a dozen other European languages and is recognized in many more. Whenever "common people" gather together, for street parties, birthday celebrations, funfairs and so on, in Albania, Austria, Belgium, Bosnia, Bulgaria, Croatia, Czechia, Estonia, Finland, France, Germany, Greece, Hungary, Italy, Lithuania, Netherlands, Poland, Romania, Russia, Serbia, Slovakia, Slovenia, Sweden, Switzerland, etc., there will be *schlager.*

It deserves a chapter all to itself and, in the housebrick-sized version of *Listen* that I was forced to abandon, it had one. In my madness, I translated *schlager* lyrics from Dutch and German into English, burrowing deeper and deeper into rabbit holes of intersocietal analysis. I noted that Morrissey is a huge *schlager* fan, and invited readers to verify the unmistakable links between his songcraft and such *schlager* classics as "Warum (...Nennt Man Dich Sunnyboy)" by Ruth Brandin & The Berlin Rundfunk-Tanzorchester. I meditated at some length upon what Gerard Cox's "1948," the Dutch reinvention of Gilbert O'Sullivan's "Alone Again (Naturally)," might tell us about the two nations' relationships with loss. That abandoned chapter alone could have kept me busy until 2043.

I can still understand why I was so tempted. There's a lot we can learn about the class (or caste) system from examining *schlager*. Not a single British person I talked to throughout the years of writing this book was familiar with the word. "What's that?" they would say, genuinely bemused. "It's the most popular music in Europe," I would reply. "Millions of people love it. Tens of millions. Not so long ago, maybe hundreds of millions." A momentary pause would ensue. "How do you spell it?"

Such is the ignorance of *schlager* in the English-speaking world that when Donna Summer used the word in an interview with *Mojo*, recalling her early days in Munich recording *schlager* with Giorgio Moroder, the journalist repeatedly spelled it "schlaga."* Evidently, we exist on a higher plane, too exalted to notice what the lower orders of other countries are making whoopee to.

o   o   o

One of the kings of *schlager* was Hans "James" Last, a Bremen-born bandleader and conductor whose specialty was arranging every conceivable style, from classical to calypso, to make it more "happy." So massive was his success that he even did what the Nazis failed to do—conquer Britain. Our charity shops are choked with James Last donations, like *Non Stop Dancing*, *Beach Party*, *Hammond A Gogo* and *Happy Summer Night*. My father's Last items included *Onder Moeders Paraplu* (*Under Mom's Umbrella*) and *James Last Op Klompen* (*James Last In Clogs*), whose cover featured (of course) a windmill and "Happy Hansi" posing in Dutch traditional costume.

Last sold millions of albums in the UK and performed at the Royal Albert Hall ninety times, more than anyone except Eric

---

*   "HELLO/GOODBYE," interview with Donna Summer by Alex Stimmel, *Mojo*, January 2004.

Clapton. But when the zeitgeist moves in for the kill, there's no escape. In 2017, no less an organ than the *Bournemouth Echo* reported that the British James Last Appreciation Society would, after forty-one glorious years, disband. There were only three hundred members left, and eighty of them gathered one last time at Bournemouth's Marsham Court Hotel.

"James Last sadly passed away in June 2015 at the age of 86," a member told the press. "Then, in August 2016, Peter Boosey, the founder of the appreciation society, passed away too. Norma Boosey took over the chairmanship of the group following the death of her husband. But she too died suddenly this July, just weeks after being diagnosed with bowel cancer. This was devastating for us all and has left us thinking this is the end of the road."*

o   o   o

Listen: here's how snobberies and prejudices get put in place and maintained. In the three paragraphs above, I used my rhetorical skills to cast a certain light on James Last and his fans. Supercilious quote marks around the word "happy." The crack about Nazi conquest. The "no less an organ than…" quip about the *Bournemouth Echo*. The smirking use of "glorious" for the forty-one years that the members of the James Last Appreciation Society followed their hero.

The effect of these verbal tweaks is to reinforce a sense of James Last fans as pathetic and tacky and provincial. I mean, for God's sake, they're apt to live in Bournemouth, which, let's face it, is not London or New York. (Where *is* Bournemouth anyway? How do you spell it?) And these James Last–loving people are so *old*! They get bowel cancer and "sadly pass away"! Whereas

---

*   "'It's the end of an era': James Last Appreciation Society to disband after 41 years" by Jade Grassby, *Bournemouth Echo*, October 16, 2017.

we are young (well…young*ish*…well, certainly not dead yet) and the artists we admire will live forever.

o o o

Dream on. A time will come when almost all the artists you love are regarded as the quaint, obsolescent fads of a bygone epoch. History cherry-picks. A Beethoven here, a Beatles there. Sometimes it doesn't even pick the best cherries, because life ain't fair.

But even when history gets it "right," there's just not enough shelf space for very much of what you value. Just an item or two, if you're lucky, from that collection of taste markers you've put so much energy into compiling. The rest will sink into whatever equivalent of a charity shop the future has in store.

And you? Where will you be?

THE TRACKS OF MY TEARS

I'm not much of a crier.

Maybe I was when I was a little kid; I don't remember. I don't remember my childhood at all. Other family members have filled me in, decades after the fact.

My mom and dad were both divorcees. They'd married their previous partners in the euphoria of the Liberation at the end of World War II. Those marriages produced offspring and ended very badly. My father disowned his daughter; she was never mentioned again. My mother hated the father of her first two children with obstinate intensity. When I was a toddler, she put my brother Tom in a "terhuis"—a sort of orphanage—because he was naughty. Tom wasn't even a teenager yet, so his naughtiness can't have been hormonal; it was probably just distress and insecurity. My dad—the new husband—liked Tom and was keen on having him in the family; my mother was against it. She tried having him home for brief spells a few times, but it didn't work out. He was the bad seed. The institution was the best place for him.

She'd disowned her daughter too, for committing the unforgivable sin of wanting to stay in touch with both parents. "It's him or me. Which is it going to be?" demanded my mother during a quarrel shortly after the divorce. The girl couldn't answer, started weeping. "I can see which one you've chosen," my mother said. "Pack your bags."

Me, I was never put into an institution or told to pack my bags. I can only presume I was no trouble. But then, by the time I was seven, my mother had inserted ten thousand miles between me and my siblings. I didn't meet my sister until she was almost seventy.

o o o

Why am I telling you these things, in a book about music? Because this chapter is about what makes some people cry and leaves other people unmoved. I know that there'll be readers who get moist-eyed a few sentences into this chapter, and by the end of the third paragraph will be wiping tears off their cheeks. Other readers will frown sympathetically but hope there isn't too much of this sort of thing before the book gets back on track. Others still will roll their eyes and think *For God's sake, if I'd wanted a misery memoir I would've bought one.* Or even *Aha! Caught you out! You weren't there when your mom had that conversation with your sister—how do you know what was said?*

o o o

We cry at different things, but we all cry sometimes. It's one of the things we do that other animals don't. ("Crocodile tears" have nothing to do with pretending to be sorry—the reptiles cry because they need to excrete excess salt.) Occasionally you see a police photograph of a psychopathic killer and you get the unnerving sense that there are people in the world who are utterly immune to anyone's pain including their own. Don't bet that they've never cried, though. They are not reptiles. Emotion may have been beaten out of them when they were small, but there's a good chance that the right song would bring it back.

Scientists disagree on what crying is for. Charles Darwin is often misquoted as having declared that emotional tears are "purposeless," but his actual views—aired in "Suffering and Weeping," a chapter of his cringe-inducingly obsolete tome *The Expression of the Emotions in Man and Animals*—are more speculative and bemused. Dig beneath the Victorian rhetoric and the anecdotes about cretins, idiots, hysterical women and African savages, and the exalted naturalist seems to be surmising that people cry because they think it will make them feel better and therefore it does.[*]

There's a persistent pseudoscientific argument that weeping rids the body of toxins, but no evidence supports this. More plausible is the theory that by showing vulnerability to our fellow humans, we defuse their aggression, stimulate their concern and involve them in a mutually supportive community that balances neediness and independence.[†]

One thing is for sure: emotional crying is different from mere hydration. The water that springs to our eyes when we slice onions or when debris irritates our eyeballs is just that—water. Our windscreen squirters are trying to wash our ocular apparatus clean. Whereas the tears we shed when we're overcome with emotion are enriched with prolactin (the same hormone that stimulates breast milk), adrenocorticotropic hormones, leucine-enkephalin (a mood-improving endorphin), mucus and oil. Our endocrine system goes to a lot of trouble to produce them. Unlike the eyeball-washing tears, they are highly visible and roll down quite slowly, thus giving our fellow humans a chance to notice and cut us some slack.[‡]

o   o   o

How much slack do I ask for? Not much, it seems. I don't cry when things go wrong in my life. I don't cry when people are horrid to me. I cried in the months following my wife's death, because it was so obvious to me that she ought to be alive and yet she was dead. It took a while, though. It's just as well I wasn't

[*]   "Special Expressions of Man: Suffering and Weeping," in *The Expression of the Emotions in Man and Animals* by Charles Darwin (John Murray, 1872).

[†]   "The Science of Crying" by Mandy Oaklander, *Time*, March 16, 2016.

[‡]   "How Crying Works" by Alia Hoyt, *How Stuff Works* website, 2008.

a member of a culture where one is expected to wail inconsolably at a funeral.

I don't cry when I see footage of innocent civilians cradling the bodies of their dead children in a war zone. I don't cry at famines or the aftermaths of natural disasters. Documentary evidence of starved donkeys or mistreated dogs makes me despair of our own species but doesn't make my eyes wet. The tragic case histories of Victoria Climbié and Baby P still haunt me but I never wept over them.

I can say with almost 100 percent certainty that any movie that a review advises me to watch "with a box of tissues handy" will leave me cold. Two hundred million dollars was spent on the most popular weepie ever marketed, *Titanic*, and the public spent more than a billion dollars to see it, and all I can think of is how very much money that is and how many organizations were worthier of receiving it than Rupert Murdoch's 20th Century Fox.

Nor is the world of literature a much more lachrymose proposition for me. I can't recall ever crying over a novel (although the odd one has momentarily choked me up). Many readers of *The Crimson Petal and the White* sob over the various bits of Victorian melodrama I crafted for that book, but the only fiction I've written that makes me cry myself is "Brave Again," a Narnia story that remains unpublished because C. S. Lewis's stepson threatened me with lawsuits if I should dare infringe his copyright.

Some people cry when they encounter something beautiful. I'm a big fan of beauty but not to the point of blubbering over it. Likewise, joy and sweetness are things I take in moderation. When youngsters get married or have their first baby I'm much too distracted by worries about how they'll handle the hardships ahead to shed tears of joy.

o   o   o

You get the picture. I'm not sentimental. But play me "A Proper Sort Of Gardener" as sung by June Tabor and I will weep. I will weep each and every time. At exactly the same moments in the song. It's Pavlovian.[*]

Thematically, I know what's doing it. The song has four verses. In the first verse, a child impulsively picks flowers from Mr. Harding's garden. The child's mother approaches Mr. Harding to apologize, but the gardener smiles and says, "She's just a little child/I knew that she'd be picking them for you." At this point, my tear ducts are already filling, but that's because I know what's coming. They didn't fill the first time I heard the song. On that occasion, emotion hit me like a tidal wave a few seconds later.

In the next verse, the child recalls being told a story about another garden—Eden—where a gardener's children play and explore. But when they take a fruit to taste, the gardener curses them and expels them from paradise. The singer tells us: "Even then I realized in my childish mind/That he wasn't a proper gardener of the Mr. Harding kind." By this stage, I am weeping freely. Even writing about it, now, for this book, making stylistic judgments about which bits to paraphrase and which bits to quote verbatim, my vision is blurred by tears. I wonder if a computer keyboard is at risk of an electrical short circuit if it's wept on.

In the third verse, Mr. Harding's garden is destroyed by urban development. The singer's parents grow old and frail, and eventually Mr. Harding "tends the grave where they both lie." The singer hopes that wherever they've gone, they'll find "a proper sort of garden." I appreciate that this may be the verse that pushes other listeners over the edge, depending on their personal history. Some people love gardens (I don't, particularly) and are unbearably saddened at the thought of a nice one being concreted over. They may associate gardens with childhood innocence,

---

[*] "June Tabor – A Proper Sort of Gardener," uploaded to YouTube by Elsa Cordeiro on November 21, 2013.

and therefore grieve about the end of that innocence.* Other people are terribly fond of their parents, and any lyrical reference to someone tending Mom's and Dad's graves will nudge the lacrimal glands.

My dad was a nice enough man, but I didn't cry when he died, nor have I cried for him since, despite my friends' insistence that it would "hit me eventually." And when my mother finally expired, severely demented at ninetysomething, I felt nothing but mild relief. I'd paid for her funeral many years before, at her request. She left me and Tom a few unwanted knickknacks in her will and donated all her money to the nursing home. Nobody who nursed her was even aware she had a daughter, and on her death certificate the space for "RELATIONSHIPS" was left blank.

In verse four, the singer reflects on her determination to show kindness in her own life. "Someday when I'm older, maybe I will find/That I've grown into a gardener of the Mr. Harding kind." Fresh tears come and I draw a long shuddering breath. My whole life's mission, right there.

No Freudian psychoanalyst is required to explain why this song affects me so deeply. My mother was a profoundly damaged person—damaged not only by a bad marriage but by sexual abuse in her early teens and by the Nazi Occupation in which she almost starved to death. It left her unable to forgive, unable to show kindness and forbearance to her own children. She was challenged to be a proper sort of gardener of the Mr. Harding kind, and she just couldn't.

Similarly, no expert diagnosis is needed to establish the reason I weep whenever I reread my Narnia story, "Brave Again." In that story, Susan, who was barred from Narnia as punishment

---

* In my correspondence with Maggie Holland, who wrote the song, I found out that this was the case for her. "In 'A Proper Sort Of Gardener' the loss of the garden/innocence etc is all bound up with my mother's death, only two years later" (email to me, July 10, 2020).

for a loss of faith during adolescence, is given a second chance, when she's a very old woman, to join her siblings in paradise. C. S. Lewis shut her out of Narnia to make a theological point, but in my story I give Aslan the power to demonstrate that he is a proper sort of gardener after all.

What's interesting, though, is that aside from my own "Brave Again," I can read any number of forgiveness tales and not weep. I may find them touching, but they don't have the Pavlovian effect on my tear ducts. If the C. S. Lewis estate's threats of legal action were ever lifted and I was free to publish my story, there's no way I could ever read the ending aloud in public. I wouldn't be able to get the words out for sobbing.

June Tabor, who sings the version of "A Proper Sort Of Gardener" that most reliably undoes me, is a vocalist of consummate skill and control. Some music buffs find her manner too austere, her facade too dignified. They argue that Kate Rusby has more charm and candor, or that nothing beats The Watersons for getting to the heart of things. Whatever merit these arguments have, it's a plain fact that Tabor is physically able to sing "A Proper Sort Of Gardener" without breaking down. In order to stimulate our tear ducts, she must keep her own tear ducts dry. How would I feel about a performance of the song that was less controlled, less continent, or simply less exquisite? Do I want truth or beauty?

o o o

I decide to investigate some other versions of "A Proper Sort Of Gardener," to establish how important specific *sound* is to my experience of the song. With a lyric so potent (potent for *me*, that is), does it even matter who delivers it?

My first port of call is the original version by the woman who wrote it, Maggie Holland.* The song first appears on her 1992

---

* Holland wrote the words. The tune was composed by guitarist Jon Moore.

album, *Down To The Bone*, a fitting title if ever there was one. In contrast to the lustrous, almost chapel-like acoustic of Tabor's performance, accompanied by richly chromatic accordion, Holland sings "A Proper Sort Of Gardener" in what sounds like an ordinary room, accompanied by her own functional but not flamboyant acoustic guitar picking. It's a lovely performance. I would call it moving, if I were a record reviewer reviewing *Down To The Bone*.

I'm not weeping, though. My eyes are a little moist, maybe, but I'm not weeping, even though here I am with the woman who picked those flowers, who knew that man, who lived that life.

When I contact Maggie Holland to discuss permissions for this book, she is gracious and unguarded. "I still get emotional when I sing it," she tells me. "The hardest performance I ever had to do was when a dear friend's family asked me to sing it at her funeral. Have actually had to do this twice—once about twenty years ago in West Flanders and once about five years ago in a village church in Nottinghamshire. Took a supreme effort not to break down myself."*

In the version on *Down To The Bone*, Holland skirts pretty close to breaking down in places. Her voice wavers on the word "child," wavers again on "kind" in verse three, and cracks altogether on "Mr. Harding" in verse two. These evidences of emotion don't spoil the song's loveliness for me, but nor do they nudge me closer to my own breakdown.

Hearing Maggie Holland sing, I speculate that I would probably like her if I met her, whereas I don't feel I'm seeing enough of the real June Tabor to have any instinct one way or the other about whether we'd get on. Yet she reduces me to a blubbering wreck.

I wonder if I'm misunderstanding the neurological science

---

*   Maggie Holland, email to me, July 8, 2020.

here. Perhaps it's not about the two voices, or the substitution of accordion for guitar, or the amount of reverb in the studio. Maybe it's just about neural pathways. I heard the June Tabor version first, and it etched a pathway through my cerebellum, establishing a network of emotion. Any version I hear later travels a different pathway and is barred from that network.

I would hate to think that this is true. I don't think it is true. In other areas of my musical appreciation I'm not a person who insists that the first version I heard of a song is the best. I let go of opinions if better-supported ones come along. I haven't a nostalgic bone in my body. I've sold off or given away most of the records I owned when I was young and I don't miss them; my favorite song of all time could come out next week.

o o o

So, how do other people fare with Maggie Holland's version as opposed to June Tabor's? The internet, as always, is ready with an answer. Seasoned journalist Colin Randall has retired from *The Telegraph* to blog about France, football and folk music. In a post titled "*A Proper Sort of Gardener*. Maggie Holland or June Tabor,"* he muses: "It is not a case of brutal honesty, just honesty, to suggest that June Tabor is technically a more accomplished singer than Maggie Holland. Normally, when confronted by a song Tabor and almost anyone else has sung, I will plump for her." For another few sentences, he extols the exquisiteness of Tabor, then says: "Why, therefore, do I prefer Maggie Holland's singing of 'A Proper Sort Of Gardener'?" The answer is authenticity. Voiced by Holland, "the song comes straight from the heart, from genuine childhood memory."

It's undeniably true that June Tabor never knew Mr. Harding,

★   "Cover Story: (22) *A Proper Sort of Gardener*. Maggie Holland or June Tabor" by Colin Randall, *Salut!* Live blog, September 28, 2017.

never saw his garden in Hampshire being bulldozed and taken over by the Bass Beer factory, and may never have nurtured any particular ambition to become a proper sort of gardener of the Mr. Harding kind. In performing the song, Tabor's keenest concern may be to make the most of those E flats. And yet, although the song demonstrably does not come straight from her heart, Tabor has the musical authority—an almost surgical skill—to find my heart and cut straight into it.

Holland is a good singer but would probably be the first to concede that her voice is not the phenomenal instrument June Tabor's is. Partly this is down to the pipes—the genetically unique cluster of muscles and tissues that Dolly Parton and Levi Stubbs and June Tabor were born with. But partly it's down to Tabor being a singer rather than a songwriter—in classical terms, an instrumentalist rather than a composer. Holland is a songwriter. She has written not only "A Proper Sort Of Gardener"—which alone would be enough to earn her distinction in music history—but also "A Place Called England" and "Perfumes Of Arabia." She creates things out of nothing. Tabor has never written a song in her life. Asked by *The Irish Times* if she ever would, she laughed and said no. "That's not what I'm any good at, and I only like things I'm good at. What I'm good at is finding other people's songs and giving them the attention that they deserve."[*]

The intrinsic timbre of Tabor's voice is no doubt one of the things that affect me on a visceral level—just as the sound of a cello pleases me more than the sound of a violin, and I'm much more easily thrilled by a Mellotron than by a Hammond organ. But Tabor also adds nuances to the narrative of "A Proper Sort Of Gardener" that none of the other singers I've heard performing it do (and I've heard more singers performing it than I discuss in this chapter). When she sings "He cursed them both

---

[*]   "June Tabor: 'Will I ever write a song? I would say the answer is no'" by Ian Maleney, *The Irish Times*, November 26, 2015.

and sent them on their way," she injects a spurt of venom into the word "cursed," and a cold obduracy that lingers to the end of the sentence. Did Maggie Holland consider attempting that same effect in her version of the song, and dismiss it as overly dramatic, or worry that she wouldn't be able to pull it off? When we corresponded, I was too bashful to ask. Maybe she'll tell me when she reads this book.

o   o   o

In the meantime, I listen to a bunch of other versions of "A Proper Sort Of Gardener," including one by Alan Rosevear, an elderly amateur local historian. He takes photographs of, and dutifully describes, tollhouses and other formerly significant buildings in his town, and gives lectures about life in Exeter before the railways. He is not shy about singing to those assembled. As Alan explains in his YouTube upload, Maggie Holland's song reminded him of a gardener he knew in his own childhood, Mr. Huskins. In singing the song a cappella in his own front room in Exeter, Rosevear is tempted to change the name "Harding" to "Huskins" but worries that this might be taking too much of a liberty. He's more accustomed to singing older songs whose composers are anonymous and long dead— "Foggy, Foggy Dew," "Scarborough Fair," that sort of thing.*

Rosevear's rendition is relaxed and amiable, a living embodiment of Frankie Armstrong's contention that folk song has become too much the province of an extravagantly gifted elite and should be returned to the ordinary folk it claims to represent. Alan's voice is certainly ordinary. It's no particular register—a sort of rough-hewn tenor, I guess—and he frequently hits notes that trained musicians would wince at as "wrong." His phrasing

---

* "A Proper Sort of Gardener – memorial to a nice man," uploaded to YouTube by Alan Rosevear on October 1, 2015.

is cavalier, rushing some of the most resonant bits of the lyric and lingering over other bits that don't need it.

The song has zero effect on me, beyond a faint sociological approval, a sense that it's A Good Thing for a friendly-looking old chap to enjoy the activity of singing. Whatever my cerebellum, endocrine system and tear ducts require in order to surge into action is not supplied by this combination of sounds. In theory, the words and their relevance to my own life are just the same, but in practice, Alan Rosevear's "A Proper Sort Of Gardener" might as well be "(How Much Is) That Doggie In The Window?" or "Knees Up Mother Brown."

Next stop is a young man calling himself wesmatron, who has his own YouTube channel. A competent acoustic and electric guitarist, he tries his hand at a broad range of stuff, from Pink Floyd and Jethro Tull to Tenacious D and The Stone Roses. Lest any passersby remark on the less-than-stellar nature of his performances, he heads them off with the following disclaimer: "The strict rule of the recording is 'One take… Mistakes stay in.' I like it that way. If you want perfection may I suggest the original recording?"

Despite this bravado, wesmatron is grateful whenever anyone drops by and bothers to leave an encouraging comment. "That's incredibly kind of you," he replies over and over. His version of "A Proper Sort Of Gardener," which I find endearing but not tear-provoking, impresses a few other people. One says he "got chills," another writes: "Absolutely beautiful. I have heard June Tabor's version and yours is equal to that," and a third says, "I like this version better than Maggie Holland's." To which wesmatron responds, "That is so kind, but come on buddy, her version is perfection. In truth, my mum had not long died when I recorded this so my voice breaks up at some of the more emotional bits. The line 'Mother faded faster than a flower' almost finished me off.'"*

---

*   "Jon Moore & Maggie Holland's 'A Proper Sort of Gardener' – Acoustic

wesmatron's delivery is indeed a bit wobbly but it's hard for me to tell (without the aid of wes's reminiscence about his mother) how much of that wobble is emotional and how much of it is wonky vocal technique. Knowing the dead mother backstory allows me to feel a little more touched, but then I fret about whether it's in bad taste, or bad faith, or bad something, to require supplemental anecdotal support in order to be affected by music. Isn't that like those people who would perceive van Gogh's *Starry Night* merely as a postcard-pretty picture but are persuaded to find it deeply moving by biographical info about the artist's pitiful mental state when he painted it? Shouldn't art's effect on us be direct and unmediated, like a ray of sunshine, a pungent smell, the injection of a drug? I listen to wesmatron again. I decide that at least two of his quavery moments are *definitely* convulsions of sentiment rather than poor breath control, and it brings me closer to the piece. Not close enough, though.

The final version I will discuss here is by Ken Hamer, singing at the Bridge Folk Club in Newcastle.[*] The stained glass window behind him makes it clear that the Bridge is, in fact, a late Victorian pub. Ken, a retired social worker, has been singing in folk clubs since the 1970s and his angel-voiced daughter (who tells me a little about him when I track her down) fronts her own semiprofessional band.

Hamer makes an unpromising impression at first, misnaming the song "Mr. Harding's Garden" and needlessly explaining that "it's really just about being nice to people." But once he begins to sing, he serves the song well. His voice is comfortably melodious and he adds an Irish-sounding lilt to some of the words.[†] It moves me, but in a different way from the Tabor. Verse two's

---

Cover," uploaded to YouTube by wesmatron on June 10, 2010.

[*] "Ken Hamer at The Bridge – A Proper Sort of Gardener," uploaded to YouTube by Bridge Folk Club Newcastle on May 8, 2017.

[†] Just a "northeast accent," according to Ken (email from Rachel Hamer to me, July 9, 2020).

line about how God wasn't a proper gardener, which in Tabor's rendition is a foolproof trigger for my tears, passes by without consequence. As the song progresses, I wonder whether it will run its course and I'll judge it to be merely sweet.

But the people listening in the pub are charmed by the song and want to sing along, hampered only by the fact that it doesn't have a chorus as such. They latch on to the only words that are repeated—"the Mr. Harding kind"—and each time the phrase comes round, more souls add their voices to it. My emotional engagement is cumulative, and by the end I have tears in my eyes. They got there by a different route and I'm not sure quite what did the trick—the shy participation of the audience, or Hamer's unfaltering delivery, or a sense that Ken Hamer is probably a nice man who has done his fair share of spreading love of the Mr. Harding kind. Maybe it's just the way he says "Thank you" a microsecond after finishing the song and walks off without basking in the applause. Whatever. The deed is done.

I can't prove it, but I also have a hunch that if I'd been there in that pub, and had never heard the song before, it would have had a bigger impact on me than it does when I view it on YouTube. Whereas the June Tabor recording will make me cry regardless of its mode of delivery. You could play it to me through a cheap mobile phone on a crowded escalator at St Pancras and I'd cry.

○ ○ ○

What other music has this sort of effect on me? Scientifically repeatable waterworks? Almost none. For a start, instrumental pieces, and songs sung in languages I don't understand, are disqualified. I've sat among people who were weeping freely at performances of Brahms and I've wondered how that can possibly work. Are they simply overwhelmed by the beauty of Brahms's composition, or by the tone of the violin? Do certain melodies somehow remind them of their first love or of their stillborn baby? Or were they just in the mood to cry and this visit to the concert hall gave them permission to let themselves go? It's a mystery to me.

There was a time in my life when I would get tearful to Donna Summer's version of Vangelis and Jon Anderson's "State Of Independence." Probably because I longed to have that same consoling sureness of why I was alive that Donna seemed to have. Nowadays, I merely love the record, dry-eyed, in the same way that I love any number of records.

Then there's Sandy Denny's "By The Time It Gets Dark," the version on the *Who Knows Where The Time Goes?* box set (not any of the other versions). I still get a bit emotional over it, depending on my mood, but it had its maximum potency in the 1990s when I was in the grip of depression.

"And maybe, by the evening we'll be laughing," sings Sandy, with that meltingly tender alto she had. "Just wait and see/All the changes there'll be/By the time it gets dark." I wept because I knew damn well that by the time it got dark there would be no changes—I would still be depressed. Sandy might just as well have been my long-suffering wife singing to me, doing her best to pull me out of the hole I was in.

And, because depression does what it must to preserve and justify itself, I wept not only because Sandy was being so kind, but because I was aware that she was counseling herself and was in a terrible state in 1974 when she recorded it and would later have her baby taken away for its own good and soon after that she would be dead. The song therefore was "proof" that, however much we might yearn to be laughing, we will never be laughing and the darkness will swallow us down into Hell.

I'm ashamed, really, of the way I used "By The Time It Gets Dark." I didn't let it be what it was. I used it the way some people use alcohol, getting drunk to give themselves permission to behave badly. Big surreptitious swigs of "By The Time It Gets Dark," until the desired state of misery is reached. But Sandy

Denny didn't write that song in order for me to wallow in self-pity, much less for people to pity her.

o   o   o

Decades ago, I'd get moist-eyed when Steve Harley sang about seeing the *Titanic* sail into Brighton in Cockney Rebel's splendidly bombastic showstopper "Tumbling Down." What I took those words to mean—what I evidently *wanted* them to mean—was that there is an alternate world, an alternate reality, where the doomed ship is not doomed but safely returns to harbor.* When my brother Tom speaks about our mother's rejection of him, and his wretched time in the institution, he shrugs and says *"Zo was 't nou eenmaal"* or *"'t was niet anders"* ("That's just the way it was"). If the *Titanic* can sail back into Brighton, however, nothing needs to be just the way it was.

Is that what the line means, though? "Tumbling Down" is a hodgepodge of sub-Dylan wannabe-Bowie imagery. The line about the *Titanic* sailing into Brighton is followed by "The Hemingway staccato, the tragic bravado can frighten." Do I have any idea what the hell that's supposed to mean? No, I don't. Maybe Harley is referring to the *Titanic*, or some fantasy version of the *Titanic*, picking up passengers in Brighton to transport them to their deaths far away. I can't be sure. And not being sure impedes the access to my tear ducts somehow.

o   o   o

A few Christian songs move me to tears, although I am not a believer. "Awake My Soul" by Hillsong Worship, with Brooke Ligertwood on vocals, is probably my favorite record of the last five years, and not just because it's a masterpiece in a genre

---

*   I appreciate that Steve Harley may not have wished to be restricted by the realities of shipbuilding, but Louisa points out that "there's no way the *Titanic* could have sailed into Brighton. Too big!"

that's held in contempt by critics, the mainstream media and quite possibly you. What undoes me is the poignancy of all those self-described "broken" millennials taking courage from the imminent coming of their Messiah. Handel's *Messiah* I find merely entertaining, but "Awake My Soul" can sweep me away on waves of pity.

Likewise, I well up while listening—and singing along—to Amy Grant's "Better Than A Hallelujah," because she's a formerly hard-line Christian who's learned to go easy on those who can't believe, and the burr of compassion in her voice gives me hope for humankind.

Then there's "Heaven (Fix Things)" by Jamie Grace.* I don't know if it qualifies, because in my mind the song is inseparable from the video in which she mimes to it. Grace is a prodigiously talented Christian singer-songwriter whose emotions are almost frighteningly close to the surface. (She has ADHD and Tourette's syndrome, among other issues.) She loves Jesus very much but she also loves her mom, who suffers from some sort of chronic and apparently incurable illness. "Heaven (Fix Things)" is Jamie Grace's earnest attempt to articulate how she feels about God's decision not to use His universe-shaping omnipotence to make her mom better.

In theory, I am a mere bystander without any emotional stake in this. I have no history of begging God to fix things. Jamie Grace and I probably have less in common than most pairs of humans picked at random. And yet I cry. Or at least get reliably moist-eyed.

To my eyes (so to speak), the video is among the most powerful music videos I've ever seen, from among the thousands I've watched in the last fifty years. Grace mimes faultlessly to her own prerecorded vocal, but there are a couple of points where she reconnects so strongly with the emotions that sparked the

---

*   "Jamie Grace – Heaven (Fix Things) (Official Lyric Video)," uploaded to YouTube by Jamie Grace on December 8, 2017.

song in the first place that she chokes up and cannot make the appropriate mouth-shapes. She's only a hair's breadth from dissolving into paroxysmal sobs. Her recorded voice sings on while she collects herself. It's these moments of mute distraughtness that undo me. Am I being affected by music, or by the sight of the naked distress of a vulnerable girl who hopes against hope that God will finally fix her sick mom? I can't tell.

For a moment in 2020, while revising this chapter, I think I might have the answer. I find a YouTube video of a girl calling herself Calimoon whose specialty is translating her favorite songs into ASL (American Sign Language). Watching her in action, while Jamie Grace's "Heaven (Fix Things)" plays,* forces me to focus on a different face, a different human altogether, thus breaking any neurological association I may have etched into my brain by watching Jamie Grace fight back the tears.

But what seemed to be a fair test turns out not to be. Calimoon, like Jamie Grace, is a youngster who clings to Jesus for solace in a world of suffering and racial prejudice. Her face and manner are equally mercurial, her emotions equally close to the surface. (Maybe she's doing that on purpose, in order to sign more effectively. She's no doubt intimately familiar with Grace's video and may be using it as a template for her own acting.)

Once again, I have moist eyes (albeit momentarily) and can't decide how much of that emotion is triggered by the music and how much of it is triggered by watching film footage of a human riding a roller coaster of hope and despair.

o   o   o

Friends tell me that any music that reconnects them to their early childhood makes them weep. There may be specific emotionally charged memories attached, or not. Just to be three years

---

* "Heaven (Fix things) by Jamie Grace ASL Cover," uploaded to YouTube by Calimoon on January 4, 2018.

old again, or six, or thirteen, is overwhelming enough. That person who was you, yet is gone. Conjured back into existence by Petula Clark, Vera Lynn, the old school song.

As I already confessed to you in the chapter called "Sorry For Your Lost," no music from my youth or childhood makes me weep. The earliest sentimental music I ever heard was probably "Il Silenzio" by trumpeter Nini Rosso, on a 45rpm single whose picture sleeve (two bottle-blonde Italian women in pink nightwear) I can still picture vividly. Sheer kitsch for those people who like kitsch.

Or perhaps it was Bach's "Jesu, Joy Of Man's Desiring" as performed by Dutch organist Feike Asma, another single in my parents' small collection. An interesting reminder of a historical era when a classical piece could be released on a single, with its center hole punched out, ready for jukeboxes. But is it anything more to me than "interesting"? No, it is not.

Given my family circumstances, you would think that Rolf Harris's "Two Little Boys," which I must've heard when I was around nine, would have done the business for me. Nope. Or how about Elton John's "Daniel," about missing the older brother, the brother who's feeling the pain of "scars that won't heal," which I must've heard when I was thirteen or so? Again, no. As a matter of fact, I disliked it. Middle-of-the-road mush, far inferior to "Elderberry Wine" on the same album, with its nifty horn riffs.

I was in my late thirties when I first heard "A Proper Sort Of Gardener." That's an awfully long time to wait for a good cry.

o o o

At my wife's funeral, I organized a number of pieces of music to be played. As the mourners took their seats in the chapel, they were greeted by the Dead Can Dance song that moved Eva most, "Sanvean (I Am Your Shadow)." After the introductory remarks, we had an unplugged version of "Six Months In A Leaky Boat," sung and played by Tim Finn and Eddie Rayner. In conclusion, there was a ridiculously beautiful piece composed specially for Eva by one of her favorite musicians, Franco Battiato, which lit up the chapel as the coffin rolled away through the curtain.

I didn't cry at any of it. Some people might say this was because I was numb with grief, or forcibly holding myself together. I don't think so. I was as emotionally present as I ever am. It's just that the neural pathways that lead to my tear ducts are not numerous, and none of the music played at my wife's funeral—lovely though it was—had forged any of those pathways. I suppose I could've played "A Proper Sort Of Gardener," because Eva helped me so much in my quest to become one. But I'm not sure she ever heard the song, and anyway, her funeral wasn't about me, it was about her.

o   o   o

Reading back over the last paragraph, I hesitate on the declaration that the Dead Can Dance song moved Eva above all others. Is this actually true? I don't think I ever saw her shed a prolactin-enriched tear over it.

But then, she wasn't much of a crier, either.

A THING THAT MERELY TAKES
UP SPACE AND GATHERS DUST

Among the birthday presents I've given Louisa is a 7″ vinyl EP called *Wildfowl Calling: Peter Scott Introduces The Virtuosos Of The Wild Chorus*, issued sixty years ago on His Master's Voice.

It is old, by young people's standards of what old is. But it is not a rare or expensive item; not the sort of thing that gets snapped up at auction by an anonymous millionaire with an Elvis or Beatles fetish. Peter Scott was an ornithologist and wildlife conservationist, and the record consists of him describing birds, and letting us hear the noises they make. It's hard to imagine many people—then or now—being motivated to listen very often to the quacking (in mono) of the Bar-Headed Goose, the Ruddy Shelduck, the Common Eider, the European Wigeon and so forth.

Indeed, I don't feel confident to guess how often Louisa has played this gift of mine. Once? Twice? Maybe not twice. It is a piece of Stuff, which briefly took up a seven-inch sliver of room in my flat and now takes up that same amount of room in her house.

The word "stuff" used to refer to clothing and furniture, and comes to us from the Old French verb *estoffer*, meaning to provide what is necessary, or equip. This in turn derives from the Old High German *stoffōn*, via the Proto-West Germanic *stoppōn*, meaning to fill, block or clog up. My own mother tongue, Dutch, has evolved slightly differently from English over the centuries. In Dutch, *stof* means (among other things) dust. So, when I hear people talking about how they don't know what to do with all their Stuff, I imagine them fighting a losing battle with dust.

And, in a way, they are.

o   o   o

Music used to be ephemeral, an event that could not be clung to. But ever since we figured out how to record and reproduce it, our industries have been working hard to convince us that music is a thing we must own. Our culture offers to equip us, to provide what is necessary. Music is a must.

o   o   o

Is music a must?

One might argue—with more emotion than scientific basis—that hearing Aretha Franklin sing is a must. But even if it were true that having heard Franklin somehow elevates every listener's life, hearing is not the same thing as owning. Many of us own music we seldom if ever listen to. And musicians are notorious for not owning copies of their own records. They're vague about what tracks appeared on what album, or even the titles they gave their efforts way back when. They have a life to live, and fresh music to make; they can't be bothered accumulating LPs and cassettes and CDs and Blu-rays and finding room for these objects in their homes. You might say they're like wildfowl who can't see the point of owning a 7″ EP called *Wildfowl Calling.*

So, what *is* the point of my gift?

o   o   o

There are many.

The EP is a physical token of my remembering (and celebrating) the day that my girlfriend was born. (Every day in the UK, thousands of such tokens, in the form of birthday cards, are handed over, even though most of them will be tossed in the bin a short while later and even though trees have been cut down to manufacture them.)

The picture sleeve of *Wildfowl Calling* includes a photo of Peter Scott, which helped rekindle Louisa's memories of him, because he was her uncle.

Moreover, this EP was issued in 1962, when Louisa was very young, so the slightly yellowed cardboard, the old-paper smell, the tired lamination, the old-school sketches of bird species, even the typeface, bring the long-ago back into the present while simultaneously recognizing how antiquated it is.

Moreover, any new addition to Louisa's vinyl collection perks up her belief that her relationship with that medium is not dead. We're living in the 2020s, when turntable ownership has dwindled to an eccentric niche. Louisa still plays vinyl, although she avails herself of YouTube and CDs too. Realistically, my gift of *Wildfowl Calling* cannot mean to her what the formative records of her early life meant. But she may benefit from the occasional fresh platter to help her classify her record player as A Thing I Still Use rather than A Thing That Merely Takes Up Space And Gathers Dust.

Entire areas of her past—all the personal, familial and social associations related to half a century of music—can thus be perceived as still viable rather than extinct.

◦   ◦   ◦

In my own collection is a 1970 LP by the progressive rock group Van der Graaf Generator called *The Least We Can Do Is Wave To Each Other*. I bought it in Australia when I was in my teens, and it's on the Philips label, rather than on the original British Charisma label.* It is rare but not hugely valuable—there's just one copy available for sale on Discogs in so-so condition for £26.50. By contrast, a Canadian issue would set you back £93.74.

My copy, however, has "added value." In November 2005,

---

*   I've just looked up this information on the internet; I've never been interested in the labels and serial numbers of my LPs.

I brought it along to the Crossing Border festival in Den Haag where Van der Graaf Generator—freshly reunited after twenty-seven years of hiatus—were on the bill. Backstage, I got each of the four members to scribble autographs under the photos of their youthful selves.

A few scrawls of blue ballpoint don't change the fact that I seldom play *The Least We Can Do Is Wave To Each Other*. But the cover serves to remind me of the hour or so that the band, my wife and I spent in the dressing room, waiting for the late-running Mercury Rev to finish their tedious set so that I could introduce Van der Graaf and the show could go on.

Emotionally, there was so much in play during that hour, and it went beyond the ebb and surge of the frustrated musicians' energy as the clock ticked toward midnight. I presumed the tension in the air was solely because of Mercury Rev's selfish hogging of the stage, but it transpires that Van der Graaf were on the edge of rupture anyway. "Focus, focus," murmured Peter Hammill as tempers frayed. This would prove to be David Jackson's final gig with the group before they parted rancorously, the end of a friendship that had lasted thirty-six years.

I probably don't need the LP, as an artifact, to remind me of that night. The experience is lodged in my brain. And there are photographs of the band in action, taken by me and by Eva. Yet the LP means something to me. It is special.

It is also one of thousands on my shelves, and my flat is too small for all the LPs I own.

I slide *The Least We Can Do Is Wave To Each Other* back into its alphabetical niche.

o   o   o

Could I do some weeding? There must be hundreds of albums I haven't played in years and will never play again. Would I really miss them if I plucked them out?

Immediately to the left of Van der Graaf on the shelf is a Canadian folk troubadour called Valdy, and immediately to the right is Vangelis.

The Valdy LP, *Landscapes*, has a laid-back, amiable Michael Nesmith vibe, and I keep it mainly because its cover is a life-size close-up of Valdy's face and he looks like a backwoods hobo and I just want to give him a bowl of soup and hug him for looking so unlike Michael Bublé.

I pull out *Heaven And Hell* by Vangelis, give it a spin for the first time in three decades. Crikey. It's wearisome bombast. Surely this is one LP I can donate to a charity shop without a second's hesitation? But I hesitate. Look at that kitsch cover artwork! Disembodied keyboard-playing hands, sculpted in ice, with little wings on. Classic 1975.

Hmm. Perhaps you are seeing a pattern. My relationship with my collection is not wholly rational, and often has nothing to do with musical merit.

One of my prize possessions is Дома Святых by Пед Зеппелин—that is, *Houses Of The Holy* by Led Zeppelin, issued illegally by a Russian bootleg label during the Soviet era when rock music was suppressed by the authorities. Some enterprising *poklonnik*, undeterred by lack of access to the original cover photography, hand-painted a naive watercolor copy of those naked nymphets clambering up the mountain, and printed that on the flaccid pulp that Russians were forced to use for their books and LP sleeves.

Why do I love this album so? I never play it. If I want Led Zeppelin's music, I can play it on CD. I suppose I just relish the historical poignancy of doomed political regimes. There's something so entertainingly sad about long-toppled governments who imagined they were building a utopia on the basis of banning the things people enjoy.

Speaking of which, in the interests of full disclosure, I've also got a painted Russian edition of Свети Ярче by Прокол Харум—and I don't even *like* Procol Harum.

On another shelf, there's *Odhams Quick German On Records*, a 1961 box set of two 7″ 33rpm singles plus a "handy pocket manual," all for thirty shillings. Thirty shillings seems a lot, but I got it for £1 and it was worth it for the cover art alone. A cartoon British couple—rendered in the unmistakable style of the period—sit in an open-air restaurant near a picturesque schloss, and the man is confidently ordering from the menu while a waiter in a green cap, green lederhosen and knee-length socks looks on.

Have I played more than thirty seconds of this item, ever? Again, I just like the poignancy of it. And the idea of it coming out a mere sixteen years after the end of World War II, an event as recent for those tourists as the launch of the iPhone is for us.

Odhams Quick German On Records, being a box, takes up a full inch of shelf space, and if I got rid of it, I would make room for half a dozen more singles. But I won't get rid of it. In fact, it reminds me that I quite fancy owning the Linguaphone record with which my father tried to learn English in the months leading up to our emigration from Holland to Australia. "This is my femmily: my wife, my son, my daughter and I. I am Mr. Black. My wife is Mrs. Black. I am Mrs. Black's husband. I am a man. My wife is a woman…" and so on. It's on YouTube, as so many vintage audio artifacts are, but my dad gazed at the physical Linguaphone record on the stereogram, willing it to make him fluent in a strange tongue, so I want to own the physical record too.

Maybe if I look on eBay…

o   o   o

I tell people I'm not a collector. Collectors are those nerdy guys who need to track down the rare export version of The Beatles' *Abbey Road* on the yellow-and-black Parlophone label, catalog number PPCS 7088. I don't care which edition of *Abbey Road* I've got. That makes me a music lover, pure and simple, right?

Well, as Oscar Wilde* said, the truth is rarely pure and never simple. It's true I can't be bothered with serial numbers. It's true I'm just as happy with a reissue as an original. It's true I get rid of stuff all the time, when I think it has become a mere possession rather than something I'm actively enjoying.

But of course I'm a collector—a collector of sounds and cultural phenomena. I bought my first copy of *Abbey Road* as a teen. In my twenties, I accumulated, on cassette tapes made from borrowed or broadcast bootlegs, the rehearsals and alternate takes and different mixes of all the album's songs. I can revisit the best of these on an unsanctioned CD called *The Alternate Abbey Road*, although my cassettes still exist, punctiliously cataloged and numbered in case I ever need to locate Take 2 of "Octopus's Garden."

In 2000 or thereabouts, I realized that my original vinyl copy of *Abbey Road* had been played too often with blunt needles, so I replaced it with a Russian pirate CD that contained both *Abbey Road* and the 1970 hodgepodge *Hey Jude*, which had (at that point) never been officially released on compact disc.

Another eBay purchase was the 2009 fortieth-anniversary reissue of *Abbey Road* on Apple, which I picked up because it was cheap and because it has a sixteen-page booklet that the original never had.

Oh, and one day when shopping at my local supermarket, I was bemused to see a brand-new re-pressing of the vinyl edition, courtesy of an Italian collectibles firm called DeAgostini, augmented with posters and booklets and leaflets advertising Beatles coffee mugs, T-shirts, backpacks and USB chargers. I bought that too, along with my groceries.

As I write these words, I'm well aware that a fiftieth-anniversary revamp of *Abbey Road* was released in 2019, featuring a new mix of the album plus a disc of sessions plus a

★   Coincidentally one of the people chosen to appear on the cover of *Sgt. Pepper's Lonely Hearts Club Band*.

Blu-ray. I don't own a Blu-ray player, and I already have most of the sessions on bootlegs, and I've generally been appalled by latter-day attempts to "correct" or "improve upon" the original mixes of Beatles albums, so I haven't bought this latest iteration. Yet. A day will no doubt come when I spot it going cheap somewhere.

o o o

Rationally, I know that my relationship with the music on *Abbey Road* reached its emotional and philosophical peak a long time ago. I will never top the awed delight I felt as a teenager, hearing the three-part harmonies on "Because" or the doom-laden coda of "I Want You (She's So Heavy)." Wise gurus and self-help books keep telling us that experiences rather than things are the key to happiness. Maybe I should cherish how I felt about *Abbey Road* when I was younger, and stop storing material versions of it in my overcrowded flat.

"Imagine no possessions, John," an old Liverpool buddy of John Lennon once remarked, when confronted with the ex-Beatle's multistory mansion filled with expensive acquisitions. To which John retorted: "It's only a bloody song."[*]

George Harrison, a convert to Hindu spirituality, sang of his estrangement from the material world: "Hope to get out of this place/By the Lord Sri Krishna's grace." This fervent wish for release from the trappings of life didn't hinder George from purchasing (among other properties) Friar Park, a palatial neo-Gothic estate in Henley-on-Thames, comprising (his widow was at pains to clarify) not the rumored one hundred and twenty rooms but only "maybe thirty."[†] Aerial photographs of the building suggest that thirty may be an overly modest guess.

---

[*]   *John Lennon: The Life* by Philip Norman (HarperCollins, 2008).

[†]   Interview with Olivia Harrison by Terry Gross, *Fresh Air*, NPR, March 18, 2004.

I'm not trying to shine a spotlight on hypocrisy here. "Imagine" is a problematic song to begin with, and John Lennon had every right to spend his legitimately earned money on whatever he fancied. George Harrison—another rich person who deserved his riches as much as any rich person ever deserved riches—rescued Friar Park from demolition, relished living there, and spent most of his time gardening, an activity that's hard to disapprove of.

o o o

The real issue here is not hypocrisy, but the eternal conundrum of material attachment. We value stuff. Stuff is meaningful to us. We need room (as much room as we can afford) to store all the stuff.

Jesus, in his Sermon on the Mount, cautions us to consider the lilies and the birds. The thing is, though, we are not lilies or birds. A devotee of transcendental meditation or yoga can sit on a rock and attempt to reduce herself to an organism as simple as a flower. But she can't. She has a complex consciousness that a flower doesn't have.

Flowers do not admire other flowers, let alone depictions of flowers in photos, paintings, sculptures, garments, poems and stories. We are hopelessly attracted and distracted by all the millions of things our overdeveloped brains tell us it would be cool to give a home to.

John and Yoko had ancient Egyptian artifacts in their mansion. Have you ever seen ancient Egyptian artifacts? They're great! I am very much in favor of ancient Egyptian artifacts. (If you have any that you aren't using, I'd happily take them off your hands.) The Ono-Lennons also owned paintings by Warhol, De Lempicka, Di Chirico... Not my taste, exactly, but I approve of paintings. I own a bunch of them by artists who aren't famous. If I had a neo-Gothic estate with thirty rooms (and thus a hundred and twenty walls to fill), I'd no doubt own a lot more.

What I own most of, however, is music. The thought of how many cardboard boxes it fills, and how arduous my collection was to pack, stack and unpack when I moved from Scotland to England, is one of the main things that would stop me moving house again.

o   o   o

In the early 2000s, Apple (the tech corporation, not The Beatles' record company) ran an advertising campaign in magazines likely to be read by music fans. Two adjacent pages showed the past and the future.

On the left was a color photo of somebody's den, with hundreds of LPs crammed into wooden shelves, hundreds more LPs and CDs lined up on the floor, an untidy pile of 7″ singles, a cabinet of self-compiled cassettes, and even a few eight-track cartridges.

On the right was a mostly blank white page with a monochrome iPod displayed in the center of it, and the tagline: "Every song you've ever owned. In your pocket."

The message was clear: music used to be mess; now it takes up no room at all. Your taste can be rendered clean, white, standardized, and your house or apartment can be made uncluttered and spacious.*

Just in case anyone seeing the advert might feel a pang of affection for the picture on the left, the designers of the advert scrupulously avoided displaying any familiar or attractive LP covers. As far as I can tell, squinting at the image through a magnifying glass, the music collection here is actually fake, an equivalent of those ice cream adverts that use mashed potato instead of ice

---

*   The ideal solution for people who don't actually like music—see the chapter "Who Doesn't Like Music?"

cream. For good measure, there are two kitsch ornaments, to suggest that the sort of people who live with music clutter are the same sort of people who have awful taste in knickknacks.* Buy an iPod and cure your uncoolness!

I pride myself on not being taken in by this digital puffery. Capitalism has hit upon yet another delusion to sell us. Smiling, gym-toned androids sitting in their streamlined, almost-empty apartments, communing with the infinite riches of the universe via their devices. No pesky corporeal objects, just insubstantial data, blossoming into vivid existence when we require it to, then winking back into nonexistence when we're done with it.

My disdain for that delusion makes me feel better whenever I contemplate the mounds of Stuff in my flat. I've been known to trip over CDs, scattering them all over the room. I spilled a cup of tea over a stack of vinyl last year. I still own some of the albums that got soaked in a flood in St Kilda in the 1980s, sprouting mildew when they dried. Not long ago, I rode backward in my office chair and its castors ran over a 7″ single ("Kinky Boots" by Honor Blackman and Patrick Macnee, if you must know), cracking the vinyl. It still plays, but there's a click, which probably doesn't do my stylus any good. I must replace that single one day.

"Why not just listen to whatever you're in the mood to hear on Spotify or YouTube?" a siren voice murmurs into my ear.

"Because the internet will vanish when western capitalism collapses," I hiss back.

This is true, but irrelevant. Western capitalism hasn't collapsed yet and may not do so in my lifetime. Also, if and when it does collapse, this event will involve catastrophic societal up-

---

*   A scan of the advert can be viewed on photobucket.com, tagged "ThenewiPod. png." Thirteen years after its launch, the iPod was obsolete, superseded by the music storage capacity of smartphones.

heaval and I'll have much more serious things to worry about than access to my favorite music.

o   o   o

This might be an appropriate juncture to mention that I'm sixty-three and that no male in the Faber family (as far back as anyone can trace) survived to be older than fifty-nine. We're not robust stock, it seems. Genetic mispresses.

That doesn't mean I'm about to drop dead. I have a few things in my favor. Unlike my father and grandfather and uncles, I'm not a chain-smoker, I wasn't stunted by the privations of World War II, and I actively take care of my health. But still…statistics. I'll be very lucky to have a couple of decades left in which to admire art, read books and listen to music, and I shouldn't be surprised to expire sooner rather than later.

I've done the math and acted accordingly. I've discarded several thousand books in recent years, and I don't pretend to myself that I'll read or reread the ones that are still on my shelves. I'll remain largely ignorant of the visual arts, apart from a few areas of specialism like comics and totalitarian propaganda. Mostly I'll concentrate on music, and even if I reach my eighties it's going to be touch and go.

o   o   o

When I die, somebody will have to come into my flat and deal with all the Stuff.

If you look back through history, you won't be able to help noticing that the success rate of dead people's stuff being looked after the way those dead people would've liked it to be looked after is…not great.

In rare cases, everything gets instantly preserved in a museum. More often a few bits and pieces get snaffled up by relatives and the rest ends up in secondhand stores or the dumpster.

My friend John, who manages the Oxfam bookshop in my town, is regularly overcome by pathos when he sorts through dusty boxes of donations. These are not only books, but photograph albums, personal diaries, letters and, yes, teetering piles of LPs and CDs, almost all of them deemed worthless by the collectors of such ephemera. "We've got someone's whole *life* here," he laments, shaking his head, even as he's already sorting the bulk of it into recycling sacks.

o   o   o

I like to think that my music collection is special. It contains very little of the mainstream material that millions of other people own. Much of what I've collected is scarce and obscure.

Which doesn't mean that anyone will jump up to claim it when I die. A typical example is *This Inheritance Must Be Refused*, an anthology of radical feminist music on the Hopscotch label from Dearborn, Michigan (the sole release on that label, as far as I know). It's a single-sided LP, with songs on one side and an agitprop illustration stamped on the other. It also contains a cool booklet of gender-political graphics and essays. Cool to me, that is. I wouldn't like to guess how many other people, especially in the aftermath of my death, would be excited by the thought of perusing the gender-political essays in *This Inheritance Must Be Refused*, while listening to mediocre punk songs by such artistes as Paxton Quiggly, Spitboy and Spork.

Having written these words, I wonder if even *I* am excited by that thought anymore. I consider retrieving the album from my shelves, giving it another listen. What are the chances that I'll love it? Slim, surely. If I get rid of it today, that will be one less item the people who sort through my possessions after I'm dead will have to decide what to do with.

It takes me a while to find. I don't file my "various artists" anthologies alphabetically by title. That would be nerdy, and I don't see myself as a nerd.

By the time I pull *This Inheritance Must Be Refused* into the light, I've made a vague resolution to file my "various artists" albums alphabetically after all.

The album starts well, with "Stupid Competitions" by The Ex, a prolific anarchist band from Amsterdam. I like The Ex. I'd forgotten they were on this. Drummer Katherina Bornefeld aka Katrin Ex is accompanying herself on percussion while she sings: "I won't wear high heels/For feet they are unhandy." Right away, I'm down a linguistic rabbit hole. Is the awkward syntax accidental or deliberate? The Dutch word for "clumsy" is *onhandig*. Is "unhandy" just Katrin putting her foot in it (so to speak) or is it clever wordplay?

I do a bit of research into The Ex, having thought very little about them since buying some of their records in the 1980s. They come across as decent humans and admirably adventurous in their choice of collaborators. On YouTube, I listen to *And The Weathermen Shrug Their Shoulders*, a sort of punk/world music/avant-garde album they made with cellist Tom Cora. To my surprise, it happens to contain a longer, rewritten version of "Stupid Competitions." Katrin has got rid of the "unhandy" bit, changed the perspective from first person to third, jazzed up the instrumentation. I find a secondhand copy of the album on eBay and buy it with the click of a mouse.

Meanwhile, I'm reading the booklet that comes with *This Inheritance Must Be Refused*. Lots of good stuff in there, if you're interested in the evolution of culture, which I am. "Fuck the idea of 'predetermined destiny.' We don't have to accept it," says a nonbinary person identified only as Rob. Way to go, Rob! "One by one the fairies come out to dance," proclaims the proudly effeminate anti-phallacy campaigner Andy Smith from Detroit. "Transgender tribe take me. Androgyny in butterfly wings." I check the date. 1994. Amazing. It could be 2023. And what a splendid cover collage by Freddie Baer! John Heartfield meets Gustave Doré. I wonder if there's a book of his work...

A couple of hours have passed, subtracted from what remains of my life span. I began by intending to get rid of a piece of Stuff, to reduce the burden of my material possessions (with or without Lord Sri Krishna's grace). I've ended up buying an additional piece of Stuff, which will arrive on my doorstep in the next few days, and I've made a mental note to keep my eye out for books by Freddie Baer, and I've realized that I was unfair to dismiss Spitboy as mediocre—they're very good really, for that sort of thing—and I've decided that I can't part with *This Inheritance Must Be Refused*.

Besides, the price sticker tells me I bought it in Recycled Records in Haight-Ashbury, San Francisco. That would've been in 2014, when I traveled to the USA to promote *The Book of Strange New Things*, deranged with grief. I was carrying Eva's red boots around with me, putting them down in various spots in the Haight that she might have found interesting, taking photographs of them.

Yes, it's all coming back to me now.

∘ ∘ ∘

Listen, don't worry about all your Stuff.

Be kind, try to treat your loved ones right, notice the moon sometimes, be grateful for the gift of incarnation.

You don't owe anyone a neatly ordered house, and you won't be aware of what happens to your Stuff after you're dead—which is probably just as well. Sure, if there's someone in particular you think would enjoy owning your Russian Led Zeppelin album, make a formal arrangement for them to get it. But keep in mind that they'll die too. Everyone dies. All the Stuff ends up scattered in the end. If you think your job is to make it last forever, passed from worthy recipient to worthy recipient, you are deluded and reality will crush your dreams underfoot.

In the meantime, you are not a flower or a bird: you are a human with an absurdly sophisticated brain, specially designed to take note of all the Stuff. You are a born appreciator. Live with it. Appreciate.

YOU'VE REACHED THE START

I've reached what people of a certain age call "a certain age"—the age where casually snapped photos of me are unflattering or even ghastly. Depeche Mode, Metallica, U2 and many other "classic" rock bands have reached that same point. They employ professional photographers whose special talent is to make walruses look like panthers. In all those publicity shots, the poses are eerily similar—the raised chins (to tighten their saggy jowls, double chins and wrinkled necks), the dark clothes (to slim their paunches), the cowboy/gangster/soldier stance, hard-set mouth and steely gaze (to signal that they're potent and slightly dangerous).

Truth is, they're old farts and so am I. So are you, perhaps. (Remember: to a teenager, anyone over thirty is old.) A temporal gulf separates us from youngsters who've just embarked on their musical journeys.

I watch Cat Burns, a talented twenty-two-year-old from South London, sing her brand-new song "People Pleaser," and she makes me happy. She's so sweet! To be honest, a lot of what I'm enjoying is that she's a baby animal, a restless pup who was born the day before yesterday, i.e. 2000. What she's singing about is issues I dealt with decades ago. I think: *Ah, what a helpful role model Cat Burns must be to girls her age. Bless her!* I'm not her peer or even her fan; I'm more like her retired schoolteacher.

I watch the grime artist AJ Tracey perform "Ladbroke Grove." I don't know much about grime; the last new dance music genre I seriously got to grips with, in the 1990s, was jungle. To AJ, jungle is ancient—literally prehistoric, since its history predates his birth. His mom was a jungle DJ. His mom! When my mom gave birth to me, Elvis Presley had just been discharged from the army, Stravinsky was still composing, and Connie Francis ruled the radio. For AJ Tracey, even grime "was a long time ago. Grime is not really lit any more. It's not what it used to be."*

AJ is an exponent of 2020s rap—monotonous, rapid-fire yet paradoxically phlegmatic, built up entirely from out-of-the-box beats and samples. The sole melodic flourish in "Ladbroke Grove" is a sped-up snippet of another rap vocalist I've never heard of, and the words are in a slang I don't understand.

Underneath the YouTube video, admirers line up to say that "Ladbroke Grove" is still a banger even though it came out so long ago, i.e. 2019. In the video, AJ looks healthy and cheerful; there are no guns, ostentatious wealth signifiers or submissive half-naked women. I note these things approvingly, as AJ's granny might. But what about the music? Is it groundbreaking, or just pretty good, or run-of-the-mill? I'm not equipped to judge. Ask me about something else, something from last century.

I drop in to a website I regularly visit, a website that promotes all kinds of new music. I browse today's arrivals. There's an album by the Afro-Brazilian percussionist Dendê Macêdo, another one by Jeremy Rose & The Earshift Orchestra, another by Norwegian pianist and electronic musician Anja Lauvdal, who apparently has "built up a formidable discography" since graduating from the Trondheim Conservatory of Music. There's the second album by Utah indie rockers The Backseat Lovers, a record called *peace places: kenyan memories* by Nairobi/Maryland/New York–based composer Nyokabi Kariũki, and the latest offering from an indie-folk guy who used to be in a band called Red River Dialect.

I've never heard of any of these people. The write-ups blithely assume I've been paying attention. I haven't been paying attention. For a moment I think I spot the familiar name of Björk but it's actually a 2022 release by a Danish artiste called Kasper

---

* "UK rap star AJ Tracey: 'I'm not all the way out of the streets'" by Tara Joshi, *The Guardian*, April 16, 2021.

Bjørke. And then there's *Caught In The Dilemma Of Being Made To Choose*, the eleventh release by avant-garde improvising trio Keiji Haino, Jim O'Rourke and Oren Ambarchi. Eleventh? I've got…erm…let me check…six of their albums, so I guess this means I'm missing five. How did that happen?

The internet is crowded with websites offering reviews, free listens, free or cheap downloads. Thousands of recordings are released each and every day, all yearning to be discovered. Millions upon millions of albums I've yet to hear.

When I was young, I was innocently unaware of how much music was out there. I had a lifetime ahead of me to sort through it all. Now, most of my lifetime is behind me, and I realize that the leisurely thoroughness with which, at fifteen, I investigated the oeuvre of Santana is not sustainable, and I'm going to have to let Nyokabi Kariũki and Anja Lauvdal go, even though they may be better than Santana or even the Best Thing Ever.

o o o

Reader, do you think you're "keeping up" with what's going on? Do you figure you've got most of the bases covered? If so, let me break this to you not-so-gently. Music is very, very big and you are very, very small.

If you're young, you arrived thousands of years late to the party. You will never "catch up." The past was there, and you missed it.

If you're middle-aged, you will soon reach a point where your brain can't process much more. Having once felt well-informed and connected, you will feel yourself growing increasingly ignorant and out of touch. More and more of the new music you wish to understand will be made by, and for, minds that don't work like yours. Music that speaks to formative experiences that didn't form you, music that riffs on cultural allusions that elude you, music that has no use for all the things you're an expert on. The future is here and you're not part of it.

○   ○   ○

This is not a cue to get depressed. It is not a defeat. It is liberation.

○   ○   ○

Just think: nobody can get to the bottom of music. Nobody knows more than the tiniest fraction of what there is to know. It can't be done.

If no human can possibly manage it, you don't have to feel you ought to. You're excused! Free to enjoy whatever strays into your life, in whatever random order you come across it. You will run out of time when you've barely begun. Relax. It's like that for everyone.

Don't let snobs and hipsters tell you you're uncool; in the time-lapse exposure of history, coolness forms and evaporates like dew. Don't disparage yourself as provincial, foreign or peripheral; there's no such place as the "center of things." Be aware that all sorts of forces are at work to determine what you should like or dislike, based on preconceptions of what a person of your class or gender or age or ethnicity will "naturally" prefer. Breaking out of those boxes is not easy, and you may find it more convenient to stay in, but please be mindful that the choice is yours.

There is no canon, no "Best 100 Albums Ever Made." You needn't own a single jazz record if you'd rather hear Renaissance lutes. Sure, people may think you're weird if you've never bothered with The Beatles or Beethoven or Marvin Gaye, but those artists get plenty of love from their fans, and you can give love to something else instead.

The important thing, as with *all* love, is that your feelings are sincere. Never pretend to love what you don't really love, and never allow anyone to induce you to ignore, belittle or mock what you're really fond of. Let your love be sound.

○   ○   ○

Thanks for listening.

ACKNOWLEDGMENTS

Listen was originally a much, much bigger book. Many musicians generously gave interviews for chapters that I had to cut out. It grieves me not to be able to give them the voice they deserve, and I hope that one day their thoughts can be heard elsewhere. As for *Listen* in its current form, I'm indebted to the team of music lovers who helped to carve it into shape—Francis Bickmore, Andrew Male, Lorraine McCann, Vicki Rutherford and Louisa Young.

SONG CREDITS

p. 52
"ABC" performed by The Jackson 5. Songwriters: Freddie Perren / Alphonso Mizell / Deke Richards / Berry Gordy. "ABC" lyrics © Jobete Music Co. Inc.

p. 63 (footnote)
"Reasons to Be Cheerful, Pt. 3" by Ian Dury. Songwriters: Charles Jeremy Jankel / David Stanley Payne / Ian Robins Dury / "Reasons to Be Cheerful, Pt. 3" lyrics © Peermusic Publishing, Warner Chappell Music, Inc.

p. 64
"The Message" by Grandmaster Flash and the Furious Five. Songwriters: Clifton Nathaniel Chase / Edward G. Fletcher / Melvin Glover / Sylvia Robinson. "The Message" lyrics © BMG Rights Management.

p. 65
"Expensive Shit" by Fela Kuti. Songwriter: Fela Anikulapo-Kuti. "Expensive Shit" lyrics © F.K.O. Music, EMI Music Publishing, France.

p. 87
"California Girls" by The Beach Boys. Songwriters: Brian Wilson / Mike Love. "California Girls" lyrics © Irving Music Inc., Sea of Tunes Publishing Co. Inc.

p. 91
"Wouldn't It Be Nice" by The Beach Boys. Songwriters: Brian Wilson / Michael Love / Tony Asher. "Wouldn't It Be Nice" (Stereo / Remastered 2012) lyrics © Sony/ATV Music Publishing LLC, Universal Music Publishing Group.

p. 96
"Ball of Confusion (That's What the World Is Today)" by The Temptations.

Songwriters: Barrett Strong / Norman Whitfield. "Ball of Confusion (That's What the World Is Today)" lyrics © Sony/ATV Music Publishing LLC.

p. 113
"MC's Act Like They Don't Know" by Lawrence "Kris" Parker, aka KRS-One. Songwriters: Lawrence Kris Parker / Christopher E. Martin. "MC's Act Like They Don't Know" lyrics © Universal Music-Z Tunes LLC, EMI April Music Inc., Gifted Pearl Music Inc.

p. 128
"Honey Pie" by The Beatles. Songwriters: John Lennon / Paul McCartney. "Honey Pie" lyrics © Songtrust Ave, Sony/ATV Music Publishing LLC, Warner Chappell Music, Inc.

p. 150
"This Is Me" by Benj Pasek and Justin Paul. Songwriters: Benj Pasek / Justin Paul. "This Is Me" lyrics © Kobalt Music Publishing Ltd., Sony/ATV Music Publishing LLC.

p. 155
"My Paddle's Keen and Bright" aka "Land of the Silver Birch" by Margaret Embers McGee.

p. 159
"True" by Spandau Ballet. Songwriter: Gary James Kemp. "True" lyrics © Warner Chappell Music, Inc.

p. 159
"(We're Gonna) Rock Around the Clock" by Bill Haley & His Comets. Songwriters: James Myers / Max Freedman. "(We're Gonna) Rock Around the Clock" lyrics © BMG Rights Management, Broadway Music Corporation.

p. 163
"Giving It All Away" by Leo Sayer. Songwriters: Leo Sayer / David Alexander Courtney. "Giving It All Away" lyrics © MCA Music Ltd., Universal/MCA Music Ltd., Silverbird Songs Ltd.

p. 180
"Overkill" by Motörhead. Songwriters: Edward Allan Clarke / Ian Kilmister / Philip John Taylor. "Overkill" lyrics © Kobalt Music Publishing Ltd., Sony/ATV Music Publishing LLC.

p. 180
"Everything Louder Than Everything Else" by Meat Loaf. Songwriter: Jim Steinman. "Everything Louder Than Everything Else" lyrics © Edward B. Marks Music Company.

p. 180
"Rock and Roll Ain't Noise Pollution" by AC/DC. Songwriters: Angus Young / Brian Johnson / Malcolm Young. "Rock and Roll Ain't Noise Pollution" lyrics © Sony/ATV Music Publishing LLC.

p. 187
"Tower of Song" by Leonard Cohen. Songwriter: Leonard Cohen. "Tower of Song" lyrics © Sony/ATV Music Publishing LLC.

p. 197
"Babe I'm Leaving You" by The Levee Breakers. Songwriter: Mac McGann.

p. 265
"Eleanor Rigby" by The Beatles. Lyrics slightly changed to "clonely people." Songwriters: John Lennon / Paul McCartney. "Eleanor Rigby" lyrics © Downtown Music Publishing, editionPlus Verlags GmbH, Songtrust Ave, Sony/ATV Music Publishing LLC, Universal Music Publishing Group.

p. 272
"Children of the Revolution" by T. Rex. Songwriter: Marc Bolan. "Children of the Revolution" lyrics © Spirit Music Group.

p. 272
"Perfect" by One Direction. Songwriters: Harry Edward Styles / Jacob Kasher / Jesse Samuel Shatkin / John Henry Ryan / Julian C. Bunetta / Louis William Tomlinson / Maureen Anne McDonald. "Perfect" lyrics © BMG Rights Management, Hipgnosis Songs Group, Kobalt Music Publishing Ltd., Peermusic Publishing, Sony/ATV Music Publishing LLC, Universal Music Publishing Group, Warner Chappell Music, Inc., Words & Music, A Div Of Big Deal Music LLC.

p. 326
"Hotline Bling" by Drake. Songwriters: Aubrey Graham / Timmy Thomas / Paul Jefferies. "Hotline Bling" lyrics © EMI Longitude Music, Peermusic Musikverlag Gmbh, Longitude Music (Sherlyn), Nyankingmusic, EMI Music Publishing Ltd., LW Music GMR.

p. 350
"Step in the Name of Love" lyrics © Universal Music Publishing Group.
Songwriter: Robert S. Kelly.

p. 402
"A Proper Sort of Gardener" by Maggie Holland and Jon Moore. Lyrics by
Maggie Holland. Used with permission.

p. 405
"By the Time It Gets Dark" by Sandy Denny. Words and music by Sandy
Denny. Jardine Music (NS). All rights administered by Intersong Music Ltd.

p. 409
"Daniel" by Elton John. Songwriters: Elton John / Bernie Taupin. "Daniel" lyrics © Dick James Music Ltd.

p. 418
"Living in the Material World" by George Harrison. Songwriter: George
Harrison. "Living in the Material World" lyrics © BMG Rights Manage-
ment.

p. 424
"Stupid Competitions" by The Ex. Songwriter: Katherina Bornefeld.

INDEX